Music in American Life

A list of books in the series appears
at the end of this book.

Go Cat Go!

Go Cat Go!

Rockabilly Music and Its Makers

Craig Morrison

University of Illinois Press
Urbana and Chicago

Publication of this book was partially funded by a grant from the National Academy of Recording Arts and Sciences, Inc.

This book is printed on acid-free paper.

Library of Congress Cataloging-in-Publication Data

Morrison, Craig, 1952-
    Go cat go! : rockabilly music and its makers / Craig Morrison.
        p.   cm. — (Music in American life)
    Discography: p.
    Includes bibliographical references and indexes.
    ISBN 0-252-02207-6 (cloth). — ISBN 0-252-06538-7 (pbk.)
    1. Rockabilly music—History and criticism. I. Title.
II. Series.
ML3535.M67   1996
781.66-dc20   95-41807
                                                            CIP
                                                            MN

Contents

Illustrations follow pages 72, 168, and 226

Preface

This work comes out of my interest in the roots of modern popular music, my desire as a musician to understand my own place within tradition, and my fascination with the development of music styles.

In learning about the vocabulary, history, and cultural context of rockabilly, I ingested it in large quantities, both recorded and live. I enjoyed it, analyzed it, transcribed it, read about it, danced to it, taught courses about it, and performed it. I talked to rockabilly musicians, promoters, collectors, researchers, and fans and visited the region where it originated. I hope that this book inspires readers to search out performers and recordings and to listen a little more deeply.

Rockabilly is a type of rock 'n' roll, an emotionally intense and rhythmic blend of country music (and other white traditions) and rhythm and blues (and other black traditions). White musicians from the midsouthern part of the United States were the first to perform it. Rockabilly is characterized by assertive and confident singing, moderately fast tempos, and small ensembles of three to six members using blues and blues-derived forms. Most pieces feature a single vocalist, although some contain harmony singing, usually just two voices, or background vocals. The songs often are original compositions, but reworkings of rhythm and blues (R&B), blues, country, gospel, pop, and folk songs exist. Slang, much of it originating in black culture, is often present. Some themes recur in the lyrics: fast living, cars, parties, unusual characters, male-female relationships, and teenage fashions and frustrations. Studio echo effects enhance most recordings.

Rockabilly crystallized into a recognizable style in 1954 with Elvis Presley's first release, on the Sun label of Memphis. Presley announced the arrival of rockabilly through his dynamic stage act, and the style spread into Arkansas, Mississippi, Texas, Louisiana, and neighboring states. Musicians inspired by Presley joined the movement, bringing their own backgrounds. In 1956 Presley reached millions through his TV appearances, achieving huge and international success. This begat a mountain of related records on major and independent labels. Within four years rockabilly had expanded stylistically to such an extent that it was absorbed into other styles, primarily country and mainstream rock 'n' roll. On its way, rockabilly became increasingly commercial and formulaic.

Besides Presley, other commercially successful rockabilly artists of the 1950s were Carl Perkins, Jerry Lee Lewis, Buddy Holly, Buddy Knox, Jack Scott, Ricky Nelson, Wanda Jackson, Eddie Cochran, and Gene Vincent. Other top acts, such as Bill Haley, Johnny Cash, the Everly Brothers, Brenda Lee, Chuck Berry, Little Richard, and Larry Williams, had elements of rockabilly in their music. Marty Robbins, George Jones, and Roy Orbison did rockabilly, but their real fame came with other styles.

Many artists less successful in the marketplace still merit an important place in rockabilly history. I will name a few: Mac Curtis, Sonny Fisher, Charlie Feathers, Sonny Burgess, Warren Smith, Ray Campi, Johnny Carroll, Janis Martin, the Collins Kids, Sleepy LaBeef, and the Rock 'n' Roll Trio. Several from this category found their biggest success during the style's revival, which began in the 1970s. Many performers who started in rockabilly but achieved limited success in that field found greater fame in country, gospel, pop, or rock. Persistence and changing styles gave eventual or further success to Wanda Jackson, Jerry Lee Lewis, Johnny Burnette, Charlie Rich, David Houston, and others.

By the early 1960s rockabilly had all but died, and almost all the musicians still active altered their approach to cope with evolutions in pop music. Between the rise of the teen idols in the late 1950s and the British Invasion, led by the Beatles in 1964, surf (and other instrumental) groups drew attention away from rockabilly. These later groups, however, did use the same kinds of instrumentation, blues tonalities, and energy. The tidal wave of British groups made it obvious that rockabilly held little promise of continuing to be a marketable commodity. Ironically, the Beatles were probably the most rockabilly inspired of these, recording several songs from that repertoire, especially ones by Carl Perkins. Although Gene Vincent's European

touring influenced musicians who became important in the rockabilly revival, few younger musicians emulated the original rockabillies. As rock immersed itself in new technology and diverse and exotic influences, it forgot part of its roots.

A phenomenal revival of the style occurred from the mid-1970s
to the mid-1980s. The activities of collectors eventually led to the
reissuing of records, younger bands playing the repertory and the
style, the renewal of careers of 1950s performers, and international
success for certain of the revivalists. After peaking in the early 1980s,
the revival continues, less intense and less obvious but more wide-
spread.

◆ ◆ ◆

For their interest and encouragement at the beginning of my research, I thank York University professors Bob Witmer, Bill Westcott,
and Stephen Blum. York's graduate program in music helped to cover expenses incurred during two trips to the southern United States
(1982 and 1983).

I thank the dozens of helpful and kind people I met in New Orleans, Memphis, and Nashville. Special thanks to Deborah Camp of
Memphis for her hospitality. For their openness and interest, I give
my sincere appreciation to the musicians whom I interviewed.

To David Evans of the University of Memphis, I am indebted for
encouragement to visit Tennessee, his support, and his perceptive
comments on the manuscript. Steve Tucker of New Orleans gener-
ously shared his ideas and writings on rockabilly, country boogie, the
Louisiana Hayride, and the southern mentality. Terry Gordon of Nashville graciously shared his ideas and his unpublished discography of
rockabilly; both were extremely helpful. Evans, Tucker, and Gordon
provided recordings and materials from their collections.

Montreal collectors who shared their resources are Jean-Pierre Cha-
pados, Bob Fuller, Clive Jackson, Edgar Bridwell, Serge Letosky, Yvon
Bonneville, and Jock MacKay. In addition, Sherm Sheldon of Victoria and Christoph Ebner of Germany were helpful. Several of them,
plus Linda Gross and Nelson Vipond, also proofread, clarifying language and facts.

Many people provided information through the mail: Derek
Glenister, Ronny Weiser, Gene Summers, Tommie Wix, Larry Donn,
Glen Glenn, Dave Travis, and others. Wayne Russell of Brandon,
Manitoba, provided information and photos from his archives.

Frances Rockhuizen kindly met with me in Amsterdam to shed
light on the record business and the European festival scene.

Special thanks to Marc Coulavin of Toronto, a deejay, researcher, and music enthusiast who provided encouragement, recordings, information, and images and proofread several different drafts of the manuscript.

Many thanks to Judith McCulloh, executive editor at the University of Illinois Press, for patience and encouragement. Dennis Lloyd, her assistant at the time, made several welcome suggestions. Bruce Bethell did some fine-tuning at the copyediting stage.

My brother Kevin expertly assisted at all levels of computer manipulations.

I dedicate this book to my family for their love and support.

Go Cat Go!

ONE

THE NAME GAME

"Look Out Mabel"

A friend wants to know what rockabilly is, so on goes the sound system: "Here, listen to this." If the song is a good example, the friend invariably will respond, "That sounds like Elvis," which will be basically true: a lot of rockabilly shows his imprint. Repeatedly you will read how a musician's direction changed after hearing or seeing Elvis Presley. With a little help, Presley showed a way out of the old and into the new. Now that we know the recipe, we can see that a few others in those days had a similar one, but after Elvis's emergence, who could avoid being aware of him? Consequently he became a part of their sound, too.

What is the recipe? Rockabilly can be identified by the appearance (or absence) of a number of elements. Defining it is kind of a parlor game, and devotees seem to advocate adding points for the following elements:

- obvious Presley influence
- performers with a country music background
- identifiable country *and* rhythm and blues (R&B) inflections
- blues structures
- use of echo effect
- strong rhythm and beat
- emotion and feeling
- a wild or extreme vocal style
- an energetic, blues-influenced electric guitar solo
- upright bass, especially if played in a slapped manner[1]

- moderate to fast tempo
- a date of 1954, 1955, or 1956
- southern origins

Points are often removed for the following items:

- obvious commercial intent
- condescendingly juvenile lyrics
- chorus groups, especially female
- harmony singing
- bland or uninvolved singing
- saxophone
- electric bass
- piano, unless it is Jerry Lee Lewis
- weak rhythm
- black performers
- slower tempos
- every year later than 1957 (until the revival)
- northern origins

The following elements score bonus points:

- the performer's perceived commitment to rockabilly (double if the performer is Charlie Feathers); this may be bolstered by hair, clothes, posture, or vintage instruments in accepted rockabilly fashion
- acoustic guitar and electric guitar with upright bass but no drums
- obscurity
- Sun label or Memphis origin
- the influence of Eddie Cochran, Gene Vincent, or the Rock 'n' Roll Trio (for revival performers)

The definition of the style is a very individual thing. People use their personal taste to weigh the factors when determining whether a song is rockabilly.

Billboard, the music trade magazine, printed an early appearance of the word *rockabilly* on June 23, 1956. While describing Ruckus Tyler's "Rock Town Rock" in "Reviews of New C&W Records," the reviewer wrote, "Tyler is still another rockabilly warbler with a good beat, tremulous tone and hackneyed material built around the word 'rock.'" The same page contains other reviews of songs now considered to be rockabilly, including two by Charlie Feathers: "Get with It" ("country blues with the deep bass beat and souped up vocal") and its flip side, "Tongue Tied Jill" ("Country blues. Charlie Feathers' style is not extreme, but carries a lot of true feeling"). For Autry Inman's "It Would Be a Doggone Lie," the review states, "Inman chants this country blues in a highly charged emotional style," and for its flip side, "Be Bop Baby," it says, "rock and roll type country material. Good example of the type." Other reviews from the same column use the phrases "chanting, shouting echo sound," "the Presley school," and "frantic, emotional rock and roll style currently popular." Under the heading "Talent Spotlight," the writer says that Ronnie Self "rocks the blues with plenty of feeling and expressive phrasing." Earlier in 1956, in the February 13 edition of *Billboard,* the country section reviewed Carl Perkins's "Gone Gone Gone" as "bounce blues in a flavorsome combination of country and R&B idioms." Of "Blue Suede Shoes" it said, "a lively reading on a gay rhythm ditty with strong R&B styled packing." Thus these (and other contemporary) reviews are consistent with the basic concepts still held to define rockabilly.

It is interesting, however, that the trade papers' reviewers for Presley's first record ("That's All Right" backed with "Blue Moon of Kentucky"), although perceiving crossover potential, did not find in it what we see now, the birth of a new style. According to one, "Presley is a potent new chanter who can rock over a tune for either the country or the r. & b. markets. On this new disk he comes thru with a solid performance on an r. & b.-type tune and then on the flip side does another fine job with a country ditty. A strong new talent."[2] One week later *Cashbox* described "That's All Right" as a "middle tempo bounce southern type blues. His feelingful vocal with a more than just a backer-upper bass and guitar support by Scotty and Bill looms like a potent piece of wax." For "Blue Moon of Kentucky" it said, "Presley sings a rhythmic country ditty with an interpretation that has that country feel all the way through."[3]

Another early use of the term was in the press release that went out on June 2, 1956, with Gene Vincent's first single, "Be-Bop-A-Lula," where he describes his music as "rockabilly." In the next couple of years the word became more used in lyrics, song titles, and even band names, such as that of Chuck Barr and the Rock-A-Billys, who recorded in 1958 for a label in Pennsylvania. The same year Curly Jim and the Billy Rocks recorded in Miami. Someone calling himself Billy Rocka recorded in 1957.

Rockabilly is accepted as a particular type of 1950s rock 'n' roll,[4] but its definition is still contentious. People in Memphis rarely used the term then. Malcolm Yelvington said, "when this first started it wasn't called rockabilly . . . it was called rock 'n' roll; it wasn't called rockabilly till years later."[5] Glenn Honeycutt told me that he did not hear the term until the 1970s.

One of the terms that had a limited use was *hillbilly bop,* and Buddy Holly used the term *western and bop* on the business card of his Buddy and Bob duo. The words *bop* and *bebop* show up in many lyrics and song titles, for instance Gene Vincent's "Be-Bop-A-Lula," "Bluejean Bop," "Dance to the Bop," and "Be Bop Boogie Boy"; Cordell Jackson's "Beboppers Christmas"; and Ricky Nelson's "Be-Bop Baby." That *bop* (or *bebop*) is the name of a seemingly unrelated jazz style that had started a decade before and was fading as rockabilly was picking up steam shows how much people groped for a name.

Actually, there are certain similarities between the two styles. Although rockabilly in no way stretched harmonic conventions as bop did, both use fast tempos and fill space with a lot of notes. Well-known songs may receive drastic rearrangement in both styles, and soloists make use of quotations from other tunes. Bop was a rebellious offspring of swing; rockabilly, of country. Musicians in both styles also took an outsider stance that included unusual clothes and hairstyles: the bop musicians' berets, horn-rimmed glasses, and goatees and the rockabillies' loud clothes (especially pink and black), sideburns, and greased hair.

The word *rockabilly* derives from the combination of the words *rock 'n' roll* and *hillbilly,* and the latter had unsavory backwoods connotations for many. Sam Phillips, the legendary owner and operator of the Sun record company, preferred the term *rock 'n' roll,* popularized by deejay and promoter Alan Freed. Of the word *rockabilly,* Phillips said, "I had nothing to do with it. I don't know why particularly I don't like it, but I never did. . . . Where [the term] rockabilly came, I think it was a slam at country music and at rock 'n' roll and I still don't like it . . . [the critics said] 'well, I'll insult the hillbillies.'"[6] Only one song recorded at Sun contains the word: "Rock-a-billy Gal," sung by Hayden Thompson and Roy Orbison at a Slim Rhodes session in April 1957. It was not issued at the time.[7]

Johnny Carroll, a Texan, and his mates called their music "country rhythm 'n' blues": *rockabilly* "was a term which, say, Faron Young or Hank Snow would use. It was a put-down. Later on I did a package show with Elvis and Hank Snow in Fort Worth and Waco and I can tell you Hank Snow hated Elvis with a passion."[8] In his autobiography, however, Snow expresses strong admiration for Elvis and speaks in glowing terms of their close friendship.[9] Nonetheless, we can see how Johnny Carroll perceived *rockabilly* to be a pejorative term used by disapproving, perhaps threatened country stars.

Johnny Burnette, a Memphis native recording in Nashville, used the word in different ways in the Rock 'n' Roll Trio's "Rock Billy Boogie" from 1956: as a noun ("do the rockabilly till the break of day"), a verb ("they're going to rockabilly a-wearin' their shoes"), and an adjective ("everybody knows her as a rockabilly queen"). The song title and band's name cover a lot of ground. Paul Burlison, guitarist with Burnette, stated, "We were calling ours some form of rock 'n' roll, we felt it was fitting in that category somewhere, but we didn't know what it was until somebody started calling it 'rockabilly.' I think the first time I heard anybody call it that was Alan Freed. He kept saying 'all you rockabilly guys'—this was 1956—and ever since then we started calling it 'rockabilly,' 'cause you can see we were trying to play rock music with a hillbilly flavor. It fit in pretty good so we just left it that way."[10]

"I think the actual term 'rockabilly,'" said Smoochy Smith in Memphis, "came from the Yankees, from the northern people. They had already figured out that the rock 'n' roll that was being played here was just country music speeded up."[11] According to Malcolm Yelvington, from the area north of Memphis, "practically all rockabilly is pretty fast, it has an up tempo. Back in the late forties, early fifties, when I was playing country, if we'd have had drums, it would have sounded more or less like rockabilly. It's just a hopped-up version of country."[12] Charlie Feathers grew up in Mississippi but settled in Memphis. He said, "we just took the speed of bluegrass, and we'd speed a blues tune up to bluegrass, copied the beat."[13] Carl Perkins, from Jackson, Tennessee, stated that rockabilly is "a country man's song with a black man's rhythm. . . . I just speeded up some of the slow blues licks."[14]

Jim Dickinson is a Memphis pianist, singer, and producer whose wide experiences in music include work in rockabilly, blues, and rock, recording at Sun, a solo album on Atlantic, session work with the Rolling Stones, and many years with Ry Cooder. He pointed out that rockabilly is also an attitude. The music that expresses that attitude is born of underlying tensions, musical, social, and racial. He distinguished those who had the attitude and the sound from those who had just the sound. Some musicians with the rockabilly attitude turned their back on it, such as Johnny Burnette, who became a teen idol, and a few musicians—here Dickinson named Marcus Van Story—were more legitimately rockabilly artists in later years than they were in the 1950s.[15]

Virtually all rockabilly performers also played and recorded non-rockabilly music. It is easy to find examples of the following styles: conventional country (Carl Perkins's "Sure to Fall" and Sonny Burgess's "Sweet Misery" [in waltz time]), crooning pop singing (Presley's Sun versions of Rogers and Hart's "Blue Moon" and Leon Payne's "I Love You Because"), and pop styles (the Rock 'n' Roll Trio's "Touch Me Baby" and their Latin-influenced "Lonesome Tears in My Eyes"). Therefore, not all music played by rockabillies—those who in Dickinson's terms have the attitude and the sound—is rockabilly. Conversely, not all players of rockabilly are rockabillies. It is the same in the blues: not everything played by a bluesman (or woman) is blues, and not every player of the blues earns the appellation.

In the 1950s the name or definition of the style was not an issue for the musicians; it was just music they enjoyed playing. It became more of an issue years later when they were approached by promoters, interviewers, and record companies about a style that was, for all of them, only one aspect of their repertory. Of course, the musicians in the 1950s were unaware of the ideals for which, by revival standards, they should have been striving.

Rockabilly has been widely discussed under that term only following its revival. It was neither defined nor consistently named in the 1950s. Since the 1970s, however, written definitions have been given in the notes to many albums and in publications. Even so, musicians have had to cope with labels from an ill-informed public and the music-marketing industry. Dave Alvin, of the Blasters, was uncomfortable with the rockabilly label: "in '56 it meant white country boys aping black country styles, and now it means white English guys aping white country guys aping black country styles."[16]

Performers who are considered to be rockabillies often find that their repertories will be accepted as such. On occasion a performer not accepted as a rockabilly—such as a pop artist or a black artist—will do a song that meets the formal criteria for rockabilly. It is hard to justify calling it anything else, yet the performer's reputation will make a straight call unlikely. Each and every song, by rights, should be considered separately, but is this possible?

An editorial in the autumn 1977 edition of *New Kommotion* (no. 17), a rock 'n' roll magazine from England, reported a fascinating experiment. A questionnaire asking whether the dozen records listed were considered to be rockabilly had received more than one hundred responses. Opinions varied greatly on the definition: of the dealers, deejays, collectors, and fans who replied, only two agreed completely. The songs were well chosen to cover a large part of the area that could be considered to be rockabilly, testing its borders with pop, R&B, and country. The following factors, I believe, influenced the respondents: the performer's reputation or race, the song's tempo, instrumentation, use of blues structure, recording date, label, or city of origin.

The songs are listed here in order of the percentage of respondents who named them as rockabilly. After each title I have noted some key considerations.

1. "Blue Suede Shoes," by Carl Perkins (95 percent): a Sun recording, made in Memphis by a famous rockabilly performer. Perkins's recording of his own composition was one of rockabilly's biggest chart successes, reaching the top five in the pop, country, and R&B charts (an unprecedented feat) in 1956. Historian Steve Tucker calls it the first successful original composition deliberately written in rockabilly style. (Presley's version ranks eleventh on this list.)

2. "Red Hot," by Billy (Lee) Riley (54 percent): a 1957 Sun recording from Memphis by an Arkansas artist readily identified with rockabilly. It was a regional hit.

3. "The Fool," by Sanford Clark (39 percent). Clark came from Oklahoma and recorded this moderately slow song in Phoenix, Arizona. With its insistent guitar riff and lots of echo, it hit top ten in the pop charts in 1956.

4. "Cast Iron Arm," by Peanuts Wilson (39 percent): a twelve-bar blues song with saxophone, by a member of Roy Orbison's Teen Kings, recorded in 1957 at Norman Petty's studio in Clovis, New Mexico. Reissued on an album entitled *Rare Rockabilly*.

5. "Whole Lotta Shakin' Goin' On," by Roy Hall (33 percent). At the time of its reissue on the *Rare Rockabilly* album, it was not widely known that Hall (under a pseudonym) coauthored the song. This version, recorded in Nashville in 1955, predates the smash hit by Jerry Lee Lewis, whose version ranks last on this list. Hall, a piano player from Virginia, had been a member of the *Grand Ole Opry* and had recorded previously in the country boogie style. There is no piano on this recording.

6. "That'll Be the Day," by Buddy Holly (33 percent). From Texas and influenced by early tours of Elvis Presley, Holly developed a unique style that, partly because of his pop success, makes him difficult for many people to classify. This song (Brunswick version) reached number one in the pop charts in 1957 and was the biggest of Holly's eleven hits.

7. "Look Out Mabel," by G. L. Crockett (31 percent): a song from 1957 by an obscure black singer on Chicago's Checker label. It appears on the *Chess Rockabillies* reissue.

8. "Blue Jean Bop," by Gene Vincent (28 percent). Vincent, recording for Capitol, had a commercial and polished sound.
This 1956 song was not one of his five pop chart hits.

9. "Slow Down Brother," by Ferlin Husky (26 percent): a low-key
boogie song recorded in 1956 by an established country singer, reissued on *Capitol Rockabilly Originals*.

10. "Rocking Chair on the Moon," by Bill Haley (18 percent): a
blues structure with slapped bass. An early (1952) recording
on the Essex label by this Philadelphia band.

11. "Blue Suede Shoes," by Elvis Presley (15 percent). Presley's RCA
recording of Perkins's hit was also a hit. The EP (extended play
45) reached number twenty in 1956.

12. "Whole Lotta Shakin' Goin' On," by Jerry Lee Lewis (13 percent). A worldwide hit in 1957, Lewis had roots in the country boogie piano tradition.

I consider all these songs except the ones by Ferlin Husky and Bill
Haley to be rockabilly. Husky's song is firmly in the country tradition, showing no influence from rockabilly or rock 'n' roll, although
"Bop Cat Bop" (under Husky's pseudonym Simon Crum) from the
same reissue album is rockabilly. Haley's song is western swing, but
his "Rock the Joint," another Essex recording, is even closer to rockabilly, although still somewhat emotionally and instrumentally cool
and detached. Among the ten songs that I consider to be rockabilly,
Peanuts Wilson's song exhibits the fewest stylistic elements.

J. M. Van Eaton, a Sun session drummer who played on the second and twelfth songs on the list, made the following comment after I had called them rockabilly:

> To me that's not rockabilly. Rockabilly had a lot of the slap bass
> in it and along about that same time people were changing over
> from upright bass to electric bass and that made a difference in
> the sound. All those Sun records seemed to be labeled "rocka-
> billy," which I guess for lack of a better term that's what they
> are. But I can see a very distinctive rhythmic difference between,
> say, an early Elvis Presley song with a lot of echo and slap bass
> on it which didn't even have a drum on it compared to those
> songs that came out . . . rock 'n' roll is what I called it. One kind
> evolved into the other.[17]

Three *New Kommotion* writers articulated their own opinions about
the list.[18] Influential in the revival, they shared information (as writers) and music (as compilers of anthologies) with an eager audience.

Tony "Superdisc" Martin thought that the only true rockabilly listed was by Perkins. He felt that record companies, after ignoring the pleas of record collectors, had recently done an about-face by using the word as a blatant commercial device. "The word rockabilly has certain magic qualities that will drive a small percentage of the record buying public . . . to purchase virtually anything [so named]." Soon "we might be faced with the prospect of Street 'n' Greasy Rockabilly (doo-wop) or Tex 'n' Mexabilly (the new Buddy Holly LP) or Rockin' Rhythm 'n' Billy (r&b)."

A *New Kommotion* writer known as Little Bo stated that rockabilly is "simple, uncluttered and very countrified . . . much of what is being released now as rockabilly is not but varies from country rock through to straight commercial rock and roll . . . which one generally sees on sales lists as 'White Rock And Roll.' . . . [making it] one step up from rockabilly." As rockabilly he named the songs by Perkins, Hall, Riley, and "possibly" Lewis; as white rock he named the songs by Presley, Wilson, and Holly. He classified Husky's song as country-styled rock, and he called Sanford Clark's entry "a cross between rock and rock ballad." Haley's song was "too early to be rock and roll and more influenced by country boogie while the Crockett I've heard described as 'negrobilly'!"

Rockabilly is primarily a white style, but is it exclusively so? This is the other side of the "can whites sing the blues" issue. Kris Kristofferson is supposed to have said, "if it sounds country, it is." The same holds true for rockabilly, according to the 31 percent who voted for Crockett's song. A few rockabilly anthologies contain songs by blacks. The *MGM Rockabilly Collection*, vol. 2, has a Hank Williams song interpreted by a black singer, but it is not rockabilly. Neither is Johnny Fuller's "All Night Long" on *Chess Rockabillies*, the album on which Crockett's song appears.

But black rockabilly exists, even if it is rare. Roy Brown recorded a couple of Burnette brothers compositions in 1958, and "Hip Shakin' Baby" in particular is black rockabilly. They are presented on *Imperial Rockabillies*, where Bill Millar's liner notes indicate that the songs were imposed on Brown. Horn players, usually a part of his sound, were absent as well on his 1957 covers of Buddy Knox's "Party Doll" and Jimmy Bowen's "I'm Sticking with You," which sold well in the R&B market. An additional black rockabilly example is "Down on the Farm," composed and sung by pianist Big Al Downing, who was born in 1935 in Texas and worked with the Poe Kats, a white band.

Brian Taylor, the third *New Kommotion* writer, did not think rockabilly could be precisely defined—"one man's rockabilly is another man's hillbilly or rock 'n' roll"—but named records widely accepted as rockabilly: Presley and Perkins on Sun and the first King recordings of Charlie Feathers and Mac Curtis. He suggested that the following questions are unanswerable: "'Is no Haley or [Ricky] Nelson material rockabilly?'—'Can one have fiddle or steel or harmonica on rockabilly?'—'If Johnny Carroll is rockabilly, why not Gene Vincent?'—'Are both or neither of Holly's cuts of "That'll Be the Day" rockabilly?'"

In noting that the word *rockabilly* originated as a catchphrase, like other terms for pop music genres, Taylor added, "Early references are often uncomfortable for us today," citing Guy Mitchell's "Rock-A-Billy," Buddy Knox's "Rockabilly Walk," and additional songs with the word in their titles. These songs, it is true, are not stylistically rockabilly. Knox's "Rockabilly Walk" is a bluesy guitar instrumental in a medium tempo, whereas Mitchell's "Rock-A-Billy" is happy pop music suitable for children.

The success of "Rock-A-Billy"—number ten on the pop charts in 1957—invites a closer look. Guy Mitchell, born in 1927, was a very successful singer from Detroit who sang pop versions of country songs, scoring number-one hits with "Singing the Blues" and "Heartaches by the Number." Many of his other songs now seem lightweight and corny. "Rock-A-Billy" is about rockabilly but is not rockabilly. In a very white vocal style, Mitchell suggests rockabilly by growling the very first syllable and pronouncing "it's cool" as "hit's cool." The singalong chorus consists of only two words, *rockabilly* and *rock,* chanted rhythmically and hypnotically. The colorful phrases paint a child's perspective of rockabilly: "the guitar man chased the old banjo." The lyrics use catchphrases—"blow my fuse," "crazy beat," "turn me loose," "go man go"—and use stereotypic images and expressions from the city perspective of country life—"mountain juice," "head for the hills," "do-si-do," "store-bought clothes," "lone prairie." With strummed banjo, piano, tambourine, and a female chorus (and no solo whatsoever), the music modulates up a semitone four times.

Terry Gordon, who worked for the Country Music Hall of Fame library in Nashville while compiling his discography of rockabilly, brought a historical perspective to the problem of definition. Of the songs in the survey, neither Crockett's nor Husky's appears in his discography (others by Husky are present). "When I started the discography I had a purist collector point of view. A song had to have a guitar break and no saxophones, no pianos, no choruses. That breaks down awfully quickly, because what you're doing in effect is defining the music as what I like: I like this record so it's rockabilly, I don't like this record so it's country-rock or one of these bizarre terms that collectors have created."[19] His definition changed after reading *Billboard* issues from the mid-1950s and realizing how that era's view of the phenomenon differed from the modern perspective. The music industry in the 1950s used the term *rockabilly* broadly; modern collectors tend to be very narrow in their definitions. Gordon modified his definition to incorporate pianos and even saxophones. "A lot of people say Jerry Lee Lewis is not rockabilly, he's country-rock, or just plain old rock 'n' roll. If you tried to explain that to someone in '58 they wouldn't have known what you were talking about. He was rockabilly, as pure as you could get . . . rock 'n' roll was an experimental music if there ever was one. There was so much mixing of influences in '55, '56, through '59, that if you start getting too precise, you're going to have to create forty different categories just to describe rock 'n' roll."[20]

It became apparent to Gordon that the term *rockabilly*

was just a convenience. Before then they called it "country and western rhythm & blues" and "country and western rock 'n' roll." . . . [These are] not easy to say, so somebody came up with "rockabilly." . . . It's rock 'n' roll performed by a country singer, or performed in a country style. And the most important thing about country rock 'n' roll versus rhythm & blues oriented rock 'n' roll, or pop oriented rock 'n' roll, is the string band. It's the guitar and the emphasis on strings instead of on horns. The idea that country music was string music is something that's been lost too, but it's just sort of taken for granted in *Billboard* that strings: that goes with country. Horns: that goes with rhythm & blues, and that orchestration is pop.[21]

A precise, universal, definition may be impossible and even undesirable. It is sufficient, I believe, to be aware of the opinions and differences and proceed onward. Most people who have a positive relation to rockabilly, whatever their involvement with it, will admit that their main motivation stems from a love of the music, and I have yet to meet a person who loves one narrowly defined style to the exclusion of all others.

Rockabilly, however it is defined, did not and does not exist in a vacuum. It is not as important to define it as to see it as a musical style in relationship to its precursors and neighbors, even if it is not always possible to determine exactly what one is observing. In any event, the mingling of elements is one of the delights of music. This mingling is readily observed in the words and performances of the musicians themselves; they are versatile and do not give narrow or rigid definitions to their music. They are aware of the broad distinctions—pop, country, R&B—but bring a personal stamp, great or small, to their art.

My own question was less "Is this rockabilly?" and more "How does this relate to the whole spectrum?" The answer to the second question is not a pat definition enabling one to account for various items. Too often there is a tendency when dealing with music (and other things) to feel a need to control the huge volume of data by relying on a definition to help sort it out: this I can cope with; this is beyond my interest or ability to cope. I prefer to make the definition fit the music rather than insist that the music fit the definition.

TWO

INGREDIENTS

"Come on Little Mama"

Musical genres have few distinct demarcations. Recognized styles like rockabilly are differentiated from related and coexisting styles through a broadly perceived agreement of performers and consumers. A few regional hits and explosive live shows by a handful of rockabillies were sufficient to start a trend. What these first popularizers did musically involved certain decisions about instrumentation, vocal styles, repertory, and so on. Their followers imitated, adapted, and evolved rockabilly into a diverse language. "Come on Little Mama," by Ray Harris, is a typical rockabilly song for its time. It was recorded in June 1956, the year of the rockabilly gold rush. The description of this song could serve for hundreds of other contemporary songs. Over electric guitar, acoustic guitar, acoustic bass, and drums, the lone vocalist, of fairly limited abilities, sings enthusiastically within a small range and in a raspy voice. He wrote the song with his guitar-playing friend; it's about "rockin'," and it uses a standard twelve-bar blues progression played nine times. The electric guitar solos through the third and sixth time. A stop time rhythm figure (accent on the first beat of a measure followed by empty space) is used in the first four bars in five of the seven verses. When this rhythm is used, it is followed by a refrain that begins in bar 5: "come on, come on, come on little baby, everybody rockin' tonight." The Sun Studio's tape echo, known as slap-back echo, provides a full sound to the small ensemble, which nonetheless plays in a rhythmically dense manner. Cymbals, if used, are inaudible. The overall sound is muddy, more so than many Sun recordings, but typical of dozens of other recordings from studios, living rooms, garages, and bars around the country. The song was released and subsequently reviewed by *Billboard,* but it was not a hit.

The presence of a particular instrument is not vital to rockabilly, as it is, say, to jug band music. Although specific combinations of instruments are favored, instrumentation is less central to rockabilly than it is to styles such as bluegrass or Dixieland.

The way that instruments are played and interact helps to define a style. In rockabilly the instruments provide a propulsive rhythm. Guitars—acoustic and electric, with the latter generally featured in a solo—are most commonly used. Also included are upright or electric bass, drums, and maybe piano or saxophone. The saxophone, almost invariably a tenor, started to appear in studio rockabilly in 1957, following a general trend in country music: after a simplification from the early 1950s until 1956, country instrumentation became more complex. Steel guitar and fiddle are also found, generally in working country bands that added rockabilly to their repertory. Other instruments occasionally heard in rockabilly include harmonica, mandolin, accordion, banjo, lap-style Dobro, trumpet, and various percussion instruments such as maracas and bongos. The use of less common instruments could arise merely from their availability or may indicate a conscious attempt at a more orchestral or artistic sound. Often, however, they were included solely for market appeal. When that motive dominates over artistry, the results can make for painful listening. As the decade advanced, obnoxious cuteness in instrumentation, vocal backups, and songwriting crept in more and more.

Variety in playing styles is more common than variety of instrumentation. Drums played with brushes are heard in Cliff Gleaves's "Love Is My Business," Jimmy Bowen's "I'm Sticking with You," and Gene Vincent's "Be-Bop-A-Lula." Most drummers generally use fills at the end of phrases, but once in a while a rhythmic pattern is set up on the drums and never varied. The greater use of tom-toms likely comes from the influence of Jerry Allison, one of Buddy Holly's Crickets, from his playing on "Peggy Sue," the Everly Brothers' "Till I Kissed You," and other songs. A rare use of the triangle is heard in "I'm a Hobo," by Danny Reeves. Less rare are songs using handclaps, as in Billy Lee Riley's "Red Hot" and "Pearly Lee" and Eddie Cochran's "Summertime Blues."

Rockabilly bands, which usually were small groups, often had all musicians playing at once. Soloists generally emerged from the texture for their featured moments and then returned to a more supportive role. The use of echo and the constant playing of the instruments produced a greater rhythmic density than was common in such previous musical forms as late-1940s western swing and hillbilly boogie. Although the bands were larger in these other styles, arrangements often called for staggered entries of instruments or their presence only for a solo. Careful arranging allowed for a great number of textural changes, often with harmonized fills by two instruments. Textural changes exist in rockabilly, but to a much lesser extent; instrumental passages by two instruments playing in harmony are almost unknown.

Each instrument has characteristic "moves" that may be utilized to get maximum sound and rhythmic effect. Guitars can be played with fast double and triple stops (two or three notes played at the same time); acoustic basses can be slapped for a percussive effect; pianos can be chorded in rhythmically dense ways or hit by palms, fists, or feet, as exemplified by Jerry Lee Lewis, who also uses the descending or ascending glissando to generate excitement. The voice also can be used to maximize rhythm through the addition of extraneous words and syllables, or even their judicious deletion. (Of course, the deletions may result from a casual approach to the lyrics or from a performer's incorrectly remembering a source version.)

Instrumental roles are often varied to create contrast in different sections; even in pieces with only one chord progression, the arrangements are conceived to exhibit, if not maximize, contrast. Sometimes the instruments play the same roles for the duration of a song, and contrast comes from rhythmic figures.

Rockabilly's first practitioners were young, mostly in their teens and early twenties, an age group affected by the postwar rise in urbanization and affluence of the working class. They were part of an emerging "consumption-oriented youth subculture centered around automobiles, fast food, movies, and especially, radio and recordings."[1] Concurrent was the development of the more durable, cheaply produced 45-rpm single. By the mid-1950s this format had taken over from the 78-rpm disc. The last U.S. pressing of a Presley song on 78-rpm disc was RCA's October 1958 release of "One Night" backed with "I Got Stung," far rarer than the 45-rpm version. This new teen culture had a lot to do with the sound of rockabilly. The desire for a dense rhythmic sound can be equated with the desire to make a lot of noise, with social rebelliousness and its expressions in arrogance, experimentation, and aggression.

Despite this rebelliousness, rockabilly is very much a cooperative style; the musicians work together to achieve an overall sound. This sound can take the form of almost complete integration, but more usually there are two or more levels of activity. The vocalist has the highest level of freedom and prominence, followed closely by the soloists. Usually there is one instrument, not required as part of the support, that has the freedom to improvise or fill, whether only in selected places (the solo) or throughout the piece. Almost all rockabilly songs contain at least one solo, whether by electric guitar, steel, sax, or piano. A soloist may take full advantage of his moment by showing off; alternatively, he may maintain a supporting role during the solo by playing very briefly or repeating his ensemble part. Occasionally a space is left for a solo, although none is played; the solo spot in "Don't Push," by Don Deal, is only rhythmic guitar strumming (perhaps no competent soloist was at the session). Solos often feel energetic and spontaneous, giving the impression of improvisation. No doubt many are improvised, at least in the sense of the instrumentalist freely drawing from a vocabulary of licks and connecting or expanding on them in different ways. Nevertheless, many solos are carefully worked out, as one ascertains by hearing alternate takes of the same song. In "My Babe," by Narvel Felts, the sax and the guitar not only play the riff together but also solo at the same time, although their interplay is obviously prearranged.

Rockabilly singing can be straightforward, simple, and unemotional, uncluttered by vocal devices. "Trouble Bound," by Billy Lee Riley, his first recording, exhibits all these traits. The characteristic vocal, however, is full of passionate emotion (real or simulated) and eccentricities: raspiness, exaggerated enunciation, added and deleted words and syllables, hiccuping, melisma, feathering[2] and falsetto, interjections, and melodic distortions. Steve Tucker described rockabilly singing as "extravagant, even histrionic, vocal acrobatics—grunting, groaning, moaning, mewling, whooping, whispering, stammering and stuttering."[3]

Many rockabillies did their first public singing in church. Elvis and Jerry Lee Lewis, among others, went to churches where members joyfully expressed themselves during services through singing and playing instruments, with more emotional abandon than was accepted anywhere outside church. "Holiness religion was . . . pervaded by dramatic and febrile instrumental and vocal styles and more than one student of rockabilly has noted the stylistic connection between the common Pentecostal practice of tongue-speaking and the seemingly uncontrollable vocal contortions of rockabilly artists."[4] No doubt the preachers' pulpit theatrics and zeal left their mark as well.[5]

The "sore-throat" rasp of many singers, especially liked by females trying to add a dose of assertiveness to their voice, gives a desired impression of strain. Slurring, the popping of syllables, and stuttering all distort the sound of the words. Carl Perkins's "You Can Do No Wrong" is a compendium of exaggerated enunciation. In his "Blue Suede Shoes" he sings "lay hoff-a them shoes." In "Beautiful Baby" Bobby Lord distorts the words to sound like "b-h-eautiful b-h-aby," with emphasis on the "h" sound. The word *well* is sung by more than one singer as "a-well-a-hell."

Many styles use interjections by the vocalist, especially preceding and during instrumental solos. Down-home bluesmen, playing solo, occasionally urge themselves on in the third person. Tommy McClennan says to himself, "take your time, play the blues right" in "Blues Trip Me This Morning" from 1942. Bob Wills made a trademark of calling out encouraging remarks and the names of his soloists. Rockabilly songs often contain interjections like those in Perkins's "Blue Suede Shoes"—"Aah, let's go cat!" and "rock!"—as a means of generating excitement. A scream makes a simple but effective interjection.

A sole vocalist is most common, although rockabilly also makes considerable use of harmony singing, band vocals, and chorus groups. The brother duet harmony singing tradition of country music is present in rockabilly and was boosted by the influence of the Everly Brothers. Female duets were less prevalent; one was the Miller Sisters (who were not actually sisters). Duet singing may occur throughout, as in "Bop Bop Baby" by Wade (Moore) and Dick (Penner), or alternate with solo singing, as in "Sweet Love on My Mind" by Jimmy (Lee Fautheree) and Johnny (Mathis).

Call-and-response band vocals are present in rockabilly as in previous styles: two or more band members, usually in unison, answer short phrases from the lead singer. Sonny Burgess's group, the Pacers, commonly featured band vocals, and this type of singing is heard on Billy Lee Riley's records, "Pearly Lee," for one. Earlier examples occur in jazz and in the refrains of many country boogie songs. Chorus groups sing nonsense syllables in the background—hard syllables when rhythm is desired or *oohs* and *aahs* when it is not—and answer or harmonize lines with the featured singer. "One of These Days," by Benny Barnes, shows a typical use of chorus vocals. Over a standard twelve-bar blues progression, the chorus voices sing a one-bar figure eight times: "da, da, da-da-da." In bars 9 and 10 they sing "aah," and in bars 11 and 12, while the instruments drop out, they sing "one of these days you're going to pay-y-yay" in harmony with Barnes.

Rockabilly's repertory derives from original material (composed by the performers or local musicians), professional songwriters, hits from other styles, and traditional sources. Some artists were prolific writers: Carl Perkins, Roy Orbison, Charlie Rich, and the Burnette brothers, to name a few. Most rockabillies used original material as a significant part of their repertory. On the many reissue anthologies of obscure artists with small recorded outputs, a high percentage of songs are original compositions, although some are thinly disguised rewrites of known songs. Some artists made almost exclusive use of other writers' material. Jerry Lee Lewis has only a handful of original compositions to his credit, and Elvis Presley, it seems, never wrote any songs at all (despite a few coauthor credits).

Certain writers actively solicited singers to record their songs. Wayne Walker, author of "Sweet Love on My Mind" and a great many more, did record as a singer but was primarily a songwriter, a rare one in tune with the attitudes of rockabilly. Songwriters' demo tapes are usually just singing with acoustic guitar accompaniment, intended only to teach or preserve a song. Roy Orbison's demo of "Claudette," later a hit for the Everlys, makes for interesting listening, and not just because he says "crap" at one point after hitting the wrong chord.

Recent hits made a sizable portion of the repertories of dance bands, which regularly recorded their versions from other fields, especially R&B. Artists with large followings could usually get sales even with a familiar song. Traditional songs were less often recorded.

Rockabilly vocalists convey emotion not only with the lyrics but also through their singing style. As Malcolm Yelvington said, "they're listening to your voice slappin' a lot of words together, and you can run 'em together, you can do most anything you want with it, long as you've got that hard-driving beat."[6] I have heard people who do not know English sing rock 'n' roll phonetically with no apparent understanding of the meaning, and I have known English-speaking singers to do the same when they could not catch the words. Arnold Shaw suggests that rock 'n' roll's lack of emphasis on interpreting the meaning of lyrics was a new aesthetic for teenagers. Of Buddy Holly's "Peggy Sue," he states, "Holly's admirers were unconcerned that his performance bore no relation to the woeful words of pleading. What counted was the agitation, tension, and energy of Holly's delivery. Here in a large sense was the dividing line between the eras of the Big Ballad and the Big Beat."[7]

Although rockabilly lyrics are generally simplistic and clichéd, some are clever, use striking images, describe a situation, or tell a story. Rockabilly lyrics rarely command attention and are almost never printed, even when compilations are accompanied by lengthy essays and booklets. It is now easy to download rockabilly lyrics from the Internet, however. Among the few original elements found in rockabilly lyrics are the underlying hedonism and the identification with the teenage lifestyle: dating, parties, and clothes. Not all song lyrics fit into these categories; "Grasshopper Rock," by Link Davis, is about grasshoppers.

Male-female topics form the bulk of rockabilly's lyric content. There is little of the fantasy devotional love of commercial pop, with its images of heaven, paradise, and love proved by superhuman feats; rockabilly songs are more realistic, although not without fantasy. Some songs merely describe a girl- or boyfriend. "Little Miss Linda," by Mac Curtis, repeats the title's words followed by "she's fine . . . she's mine . . . got crazy curves . . . shakes my nerves . . . flips me . . . trips me . . . rocks me . . . shocks me," and so on. Problems in communication are the basis of Curtis's "Say So": if you want something, he tells his girlfriend, just "say so." Responsibilities and commitments seldom rate a mention in rockabilly songs, other than the injunction to "be true." One song that actually discusses marriage is "Sign It on the Dotted Line," by Jack Earls. A wife tells her husband to "settle down and give the bottle to the baby, if you want me to baby you" in Charlie Feathers's "Bottle to the Baby."

Rockin' describes a way of life, or at least a time of life, that celebrates the moment, the dance, sensuality, sexuality, and freedom from care, money, and responsibility. The general attitude of many song lyrics could be expressed as "you can't take it with you, so use it while you're here," a line from "Bip a Little, Bop a Lot," by Joe Penny. The word *rock* is used frequently in lyrics and song titles—"All Night Rock," by Glenn Honeycutt, is just one of hundreds of examples.[8] *Rockin'* was not a new word or concept, but it generally replaced older terms, like *honky-tonkin'*, used similarly. Rockin' was also attributed to grandparents in many songs. The list includes "Grandaddy's Rockin'" ("in his rocking chair"), by Mac Curtis; "Grandpa's a Cat" ("he knows how to rock 'n' roll"), by Jimmy Murphy; "Grandma Rock and Roll," by Gene Sisco; Carson Robison's "Rockin' and Rollin' with Granmaw"; and Skeets McDonald's "You Oughta See Grandma Rock."

Danny Reeves's "I'm a Hobo" paints a picture of freedom without responsibility—"I'm a happy hobo, always on the go"—telling the story of someone who willingly gives up the role of a chauffeured hotel owner. Freddie Hart urges the opposite side of the economic coin in "Dig Boy Dig," where he is full of advice about upward mobility: if you want the easy life, to have money, women, and a limousine, to get ahead and "step out in the upper class," you've got to stretch your small change, pay attention to his advice, and watch out that you don't slip. These two views show the outer reaches of the rockabilly musicians' (and audiences') conflict between the desire for an unencumbered life of partying and the obstacles encountered. One of the restraints is simply needing parental permission, as in Gene Vincent's "Say Mama" ("can I go out tonight?") and Carl Perkins's "Pop, Let Me Have the Car."

Local heroes and their particular attributes are described in larger-than-life terms in "Wee Willie Brown" (who has no money, but all the girls love him), by Lou Graham; "Domino" (who is stylish, happy, and popular with women), by Roy Orbison; and "Bo-Bo Ska Diddle Daddle" (an unlikely named man popular as a dancing partner), by Wayne Walker. Singers rarely give details when singing of themselves, but George Hamilton IV, in his "If You Don't Know," sings:

> I finally wised up and I learnt all the tricks
> And now I'm the coolest cat in the sticks
> And I got more women than anybody else I know
> I drink hard liquor and I drive fast cars
> I like pretty gals and smoke filled bars
> I'm a traveling man and I'm always on the go

He enjoys this success because he is the local bootlegger.

Locations of particular teenage relevance—school, the drive-in, the soda shop—provide the backdrop for a central image, a person, or a situation. Less teenage and less frequently mentioned is the barroom, the setting of "Drinking Wine" (and "a little bourbon too") by Gene Simmons, although alcohol was commonly used by the musicians and their audience.

For urban and later fans, it can be a surprise to hear songs about farming and rural concerns and songs with animal imagery. In "Dear John" Warren Smith sings, "I sent your saddle home." Carl Perkins's "Movie Magg," his first recording, talks about plowing and horse riding. In "Mad at You" Mack Self sings, "my hens won't lay." There are also lyrics about technology and its vocabulary that now seem dated and quaint. Sonny James sings, "my baby's kisses are jet propelled" in "Uh Uh Mm." In "Eight Wheel" Edwin Bruce sings about the joys of being a train engineer.

Aside from exploring topics of songs, it is interesting to observe the use of vernacular, serious or humorous delivery, and the use of references. *Cat, cool, bop, stomp,* and other popular slang words occur in dozens of songs. *Cat* refers almost exclusively to a male; a female is sometimes called a *kitten*. A more specialized vernacular—terms for automobile parts—is present in Leon Smith's song about drag racing, "Little Forty Ford."

Many songs are like photographs or movies portraying a scene or situation or like windows into the singer's mental workings. In almost all cases this is done seriously and unself-consciously; that is, although neither singer nor audience can escape the simple fact that such information is being conveyed in a song, this fact is rarely noted. An exception is "Tennessee Toddy," by Marty Robbins: "I'll tell you more about it in the very next verse of my song."

Almost everything about rockabilly is intense, even the humor, which usually benefits from the contrast between droll or incongruous lyrics and serious delivery. Eddie Fontaine sings, "I love your eyes, I love your lips, they taste even better than potato chips" in "Cool It Baby." Clint Miller sings, "you tickle me from my head to my athlete's feet" in his version of "Bertha Lou." Danny Reeves gives a straight delivery of humorous lines in "I'm a Hobo": "Well I got me some beans and some turnip greens and a number seven shoe / When I get on down this railroad track I'm going to make me some hobo stew."

Although song lyrics rarely refer to geographical locations, apart from numerous mentions of Tennessee as the birthplace of the style, lyrics occasionally make reference to other songs and singers. Rock 'n' roll provided youth with its own cultural pantheon—the (real or perceived) personalities of the music makers and the characters they created in their songs: Charlie Brown (the Coasters), Maybellene and Johnny B. Goode (Chuck Berry), Dizzy Miss Lizzy and Short Fat Fanny (Larry Williams), and dozens more. As noted, some rockabilly songs also create characters, but others merely use names of artists, characters, and catchwords and phrases for their associative (and possible marketing) value. Presley's name is the most mentioned—an indication of his phenomenal popularity—although often just in passing. "If You Don't Know" by George Hamilton IV describes a person "shakin' all over like old Elvis Presley," although in this case, it is because of fear. Warren Smith sings, "like a pretty girl goes for Elvis, that's the way I go for you" in "I Like Your Kind of Love." "Hollywood Party," by Dick Busch, is basically an excuse to catalog song titles and artists. "Rockin' with My Baby," by Malcolm Yelvington,[9] lists numerous song titles in the verses. Yelvington mentions the Hank Williams wooden Indian character Kaw-Liga in "Yakety Yak."

Not all facets of the rockabilly sound were choices of the musicians. Rockabilly recorded in the 1950s did not preserve an uncontaminated oral tradition. Far from it: rockabilly was most definitely a product of commercial thinking. Record company personnel influenced all aspects of recording. Nevertheless, despite manipulations by industry figures, the best rockabilly is still able to exhibit sincerity, honesty, and the artistic expression of deep emotion. Oral tradition did play a part, however, especially in the learning of instrumental styles and repertory.

Records did not necessarily reflect performances. One way they could differ was through postrecording manipulation. Sam Phillips altered Carl Perkins's "Your True Love," presumably in an effort to make Perkins sound younger. The tape speed was increased, shortening the song by about seventeen seconds.[10] The alteration is quite audible; the singers sound young (a fact noted in the *Billboard* review) and unnatural. In the process the tempo increased and the pitch raised exactly one tone (from E to F-sharp).[11]

In the early 1950s Les Paul had pioneered the techniques of overdubbing in a series of recordings with his wife, Mary Ford. In rockabilly, overdubs were used primarily for background singing or solos. Norman Petty's multitracking of Buddy Holly's voice was an important aspect of Holly's sound and no doubt contributed to his commercial success.

One of the obvious ingredients in many rockabilly recordings is the use of echo. It was not a new idea. Illustrating the early use of echo in country music, Nick Tosches mentions Wilf Carter's "Sundown Blues" of 1935 and Eddy Arnold's "Cattle Call" of 1945.[12] Sparkle Moore's "Skull and Crossbones" uses echo selectively, increasing it dramatically at the very end while she is humming, giving the illusion of her walking away. In the 1953 Davis Sisters' country boogie song "Rock-A-Bye Boogie," the echo increases on each chorus almost to the point of feedback, and the guitar solo also has echo added.[13]

Some of the Decca recordings of Bill Haley and Buddy Holly took place in New York's Pythian Temple, a large space that gave a good natural echo. The quintessential rockabilly echo, however, is the enveloping one invented at the Sun studio. This famous technique, named *slap-back echo,* is produced at the recording stage using the tape heads on a reel-to-reel recorder. Sam Phillips described it thus: "Then I came up with this little slap-back: delayed tape. You record and you put your output of the machine—you have an erase, a record, and a playback head—so instead of putting my output on record I'd put it, I'd place it around—it sounds so simple that it's ridiculous to even mention the fact—and I would put it on playback and play it back on record just slightly delayed."[14] The sound recorded was thus a mix of the live music being played in the studio and a slightly delayed signal of the same thing sent back through the mixing board. The board was a six-channel mixer made for radio use and modified by Phillips for recording purposes. Five of the inputs were used for microphones, and the sixth served as the echo return. The echo was recorded on the master tape during the session, not added afterward. Since the delay was a function of the distance between the playback and record heads, the length of the delay was not variable. What made it seem to change on different songs was how much of the echo signal was returned for each of the microphones in the mix—meaning any channel, a voice or instrument, could have more or less of it—and how the echo affected the rhythms within each song. The musicians did not record with earphones and did not hear the echo until the playback, if indeed they were allowed to hear that.[15]

Sometimes the echo alters or obscures the sound of the instruments. In the unissued Sun version of "Pink Pedal Pushers" (1957), by Carl Perkins, the drums are affected: the bass drum is very strong, the snare drum is inaudible, and the rhythm of the cymbals is distorted.

The slap-back echo effect was attempted by other studios, but the sound was difficult for them to duplicate. Either they did not know how it was done, or the distance between the playback and record heads was too short or too long to produce the desired results, so the effect was approximated with conventional echo devices. The version of "Pink Pedal Pushers" that Perkins did for Columbia, less than a year after his Sun version, uses the conventional echo.

THREE

ORIGINS AND PREDECESSORS

"Move It on Over"

Increased media exposure helped to raise country music's popularity in the postwar years. Live radio barn dance shows remained popular,[1] and their televised counterparts shortly became available. Radio stations in Mexico, unlike those in the United States and Canada, had no limit on broadcast power, and country music programs from across the Texas border could be heard as clearly as local stations throughout much of the continent. One of these "border blaster" stations, XERF in Via Cuncio, Mexico, nine miles south of Del Rio, Texas, had 250,000 watts and was heard as far away as the Soviet Union.[2] Even the *Louisiana Hayride,* carried on a station with a 50,000 watt clear-channel signal—the maximum allowed in the United States—was heard from Yucatan to Canada.[3]

In the years before rockabilly, besides traditional hillbilly styles, the main types of country music were western swing, bluegrass, country boogie, and honky-tonk. Each was an important influence on rockabilly, as well as a repertory source. Many of the early rockabilly musicians had played in country bands, and some (including Buddy Holly and Eddie Cochran) started their recording careers in these styles.

Western swing is always associated with Bob Wills, who was born in Texas in 1905 and died there in 1975, and his band, the Texas Playboys, although Milton Brown, who died in 1936, is more accurately called the founder of the style.[4] Many people found careers and fame in western swing, and other important bandleaders in this style were Spade Cooley, Hank Penny, and Hank Thompson. Western swing emerged in the 1930s in the Southwest, especially Texas and Oklahoma, although the term was not used until the mid-1940s. This style was, in part, country music's reaction to early jazz and big-band swing, popularized by bandleaders Count Basie, Duke Ellington, Benny Goodman, and others.

Western swing evolved from the rural string band, incorporating repertory from and elements of jazz, blues, ragtime, fiddle tunes, Mexican music, and eastern European waltzes and polkas. Western swing retained the string band concept, using fiddles, guitars, bass, and steel guitar, and added piano and sometimes horns. The style was one of the early homes of the electric guitar, and it was also the first form of country music to incorporate drums, doing so in the mid-1930s.[5] Country music was slow to accept drums. They were not part of the tradition, and they interfered with the delicate blend produced by string band instruments, which could not compete in volume. During a 1943 appearance by Bob Wills and his band on the *Grand Ole Opry,* the drummer was concealed behind a curtain so that the audience would not be offended.

In western swing the name of the player was often called out at the beginning of his solo—sometimes with an encouragement ("ah, turn it on Johnny," or "take it away, Leon")—a solo being a display of musicianship to be acknowledged and appreciated and the band being a collection of fine players with individual identities. In rockabilly encouraging interjections serve to intensify excitement, to lift the feeling and boost the collective energy, not to single out an individual.

In the postwar years the few western swing bands that survived scaled down, largely for economic reasons, and guitars played some of the horn parts. This reliance on guitars, the use of drums, and an emphasis on dancing all had an influence on rockabilly, although songs from western swing are almost nonexistent in rockabilly, aside from those already taken from black sources, such as "Milkcow Blues" and "Matchbox."

Once rockabilly became established, veterans of western swing occasionally tried their hand at it, as did Cliff "Sleepy" Johnson, a veteran of the Light Crust Doughboys and Bob Wills's band, with his "Go 'Way Hound Dog" from 1957, and Bob Wills himself in 1956 with "So Let's Rock."

Although the term *bluegrass* was not used until around 1949, Bill Monroe and his Blue Grass Boys had been forging the style since the band formed in 1938. Born in 1911 in Kentucky (the "Blue Grass State"), Monroe is recognized as the father of bluegrass and its main figure, known for his high-pitched singing and intense mandolin playing. The style takes its name and sound from his band. Monroe was inspired by a fiddling uncle (immortalized in the song "Uncle Pen"), white gospel singing, and black bluesmen, particularly Arnold Schultz, a guitarist and fiddler whom Monroe accompanied at country dances around western Kentucky. The phenomenal influence of Bill Monroe and his Blue Grass Boys set the standard for bluegrass instrumentation—mandolin, fiddle, banjo, guitar, bass—and repertory: instrumental showpieces, gospel quartet singing, hard-driving blues, songs of sentimentality and morality from traditional sources, and a high percentage of original compositions. Bluegrass consciously avoided certain modernisms, not the least being electrified instruments. Many of the band's alumni, especially Lester Flatt and Earl Scruggs, were also very influential.

Bluegrass is a very serious music, tightly controlled and classical in a sense. When Monroe adds words to the beginning and ending of lines—"well," "oh," "lordy," "yeah," and so on—he is consistent in both choice of word and placement. That is, for Monroe, these words are part of the lyrics; for rockabillies they are free interjections.

Carl Perkins and Charlie Feathers strongly acknowledge the influence of bluegrass in rockabilly, and Presley did Monroe's "Blue Moon of Kentucky" and "Little Cabin on the Hill." Ronnie Self and Gene Vincent both covered Monroe's "Rocky Road Blues," although neither reveals any debt to bluegrass apart from the song's origins. Fast tempos, blues material, improvised solos, slapped bass, and acoustic guitar strumming are common to both styles, but their sound ideals are quite different. Not only is the blues component much smaller in bluegrass, but the concept of austere melodies sung in a nasal tone and high tenor range is quite foreign to rockabilly.

Country boogie was the country response to the boogie-woogie fad in jazz and popular music in the late 1930s and early 1940s. It is hillbilly music with a strong black flavor, the previous generation's rockabilly if you will, and most of the major country stars of the day tried it.

Boogie-woogie originated as a formulaic approach to solo blues piano performance and in its time was very stimulating and popular for dancing. Jimmy Yancey, from Chicago, was particularly influential among the many black pianists who developed the style. Its name derived from Clarence "Pinetop" Smith's 1928 piano solo entitled "Pine Top's Boogie Woogie." It is a restrictive style that achieves its excitement from the interplay of steady rhythmic patterns in the pianists' left hand with freer rhythms and notes in the right hand. Later the big bands got into the act: Count Basie recorded a version of

Smith's piece in 1936, and Cab Calloway followed suit in 1938. Tommy Dorsey's "Boogie Woogie," from 1938, was a strong seller for years.

The fad gathered momentum from the sensational performances of pianists Meade "Lux" Lewis and Albert Ammons, both from Chicago, and Pete Johnson with vocalist Big Joe Turner, both from Kansas City, at the ground-breaking From Spirituals to Swing concert presented by John Hammond in 1938 at New York's Carnegie Hall. By the early 1940s pop vocal groups like the Andrews Sisters had hits with songs like "Boogie-Woogie Bugle Boy."

The lyrics in country boogie songs make it seem as if boogie is a brand-new disease touching all aspects of life. An undefined force seems to have infected everyone and everything with dancing fits: longjohn underwear, barbershops, brands of bread, Indians, animals, bingo, mountain ranges, states, baby buggies, jump ropes, jukeboxes, blackberries, rivers, trains, pinball machines, elevators, milk buckets, paperboys, and on and on. Boogie, like the motion and dancing it celebrates, is something that just is; often sung about as inevitable, almost divine, it is right and cannot be wrong—it is "the best in town." Lyrics are delivered in a straightforward manner—no wasteful stretching out or toying with words or syllables—and rhyming is very important, even if it is only with nonsense sounds.

In country boogie the beat and the voices are relaxed, and drums are absent or brushed; the snare cracks occasionally for emphasis, not to provide a beat. The music is restrained and economical. Often there are lots of players all safely organized, unobtrusive and taking their turn. There is much ensemble playing, and the quality of the musicianship is generally high. Soloists show off their ability, not their aggressiveness, and the horn work is left over from swing and western swing. Melodies are often like riffs or arpeggiated bass lines, or they are drones and decorations of the tonic note.

The Delmore Brothers already had enjoyed a long career when they arrived at the forefront of country boogie with the hits "Hillbilly Boogie" (1945), "Freight Train Boogie" (1946), "Blues Stay Away from Me," and "Pan American Boogie" (both 1949), all on the King label of Cincinnati, Ohio. Born in Alabama, they were both inventive guitarists and sang in close, careful harmony. Influenced by blues, ragtime, and gospel, they had been members of the *Grand Ole Opry* from 1932 until 1938.

Several hit versions of "Hot Rod Race" in 1951 sparked a slew of sequels (up to "Hot Rod Race no. 5") and related titles. A remake of one of them, "Hot Rod Lincoln," by Commander Cody and his Lost Planet Airmen, made it to number nine on the pop charts in 1972.

In California Capitol had a string of country boogie songs. A particularly influential record was the 1946 piano boogie "House of Blue Lights," by Freddie Slack with vocals by Ella Mae Morse. Other prominent country boogie artists on Capitol were Cliffie Stone, head of the label's country music department, and one of the artists he signed, Tennessee Ernie Ford, who recorded a number of self-composed boogies such as "Shotgun Boogie," a country number one in 1950, and "Blackberry Boogie," a top-ten hit in 1952.

Red Foley was, in the late 1940s, one of the leading stars on the *Grand Ole Opry* and one of America's best-known country singers. His affection for and success with country boogie gave it added legitimacy. Between 1948 and 1954 he had twenty-six hits, many of them in this style, notably "Tennessee Saturday Night" and "Chattanooga Shoe Shine Boy."

Very influential for guitarists was Arthur Smith's instrumental "Guitar Boogie" (1945; charted in 1948). Records from the 1950s with guitarists soloing over the standard blues form are considered to be rockabilly by some, at least the compiler of White Label anthologies. *Rock-A-Billy Souvenir,* for instance, contains four instrumentals.

The term *honky-tonk* became current in country music through Al Dexter's "Honky Tonk Blues" from 1936, although it had been used in the Southwest since before the turn of the century. The music celebrates its working-class drinking and dancing origins. In 1941 Ernest Tubb recorded his now classic "Walking the Floor over You," helping to establish the honky-tonk style and Tubb as one of its foremost practitioners. Two years later Tubb joined the *Opry,* bringing electric guitars to the show, and Dexter's "Pistol Packin' Mama," later covered by Gene Vincent, was a number-one pop and country hit.

Honky-tonk's basic instrumentation is fiddle, steel guitar, acoustic rhythm guitar, electric lead guitar, and acoustic bass, often with the addition of piano. Vocalists cultivated their individual style and took pride in their abilities. Honky-tonk is earthy both in its brash and bluesy playing and in its lyrics, which deal with topics ranging from lighthearted frolic to failed romance to alcohol addiction. Aside from Hank Williams, most of the main figures in honky-tonk were born or raised in Texas: Dexter, Tubb, Ted Daffan ("Born to Lose"), Lefty Frizzell ("If You've Got the Money, I've Got the Time"), Floyd Tillman ("It Makes No Difference Now," "Slippin' Around"), Ray Price, who was taken under Hank Williams's wing ("Crazy Arms"), and Hank Thompson, also famous for his western swing ("The Wild Side of Life").

By the early 1950s country bands typically blended together western swing, country boogie, and honky-tonk. Take a leaner version of this blend, add youthful energy and additional doses of black influence, and voilà, it's rockabilly.

Some of the black influence on rockabilly came directly. Many older country musicians had early personal contact with black musicians. Black and white musical interaction was more common in the South than is generally acknowledged.[6] Many rockabillies have what Jim Dickinson calls a "yard-man story": a black man who worked for the family or in the neighborhood was persuaded to teach guitar or piano.

Some of the black influence on rockabilly came indirectly. Concurrent with country music's increased popularity was a rise in other minority and ethnic styles and their presentation on radio. With more black music programming, any interested listener could hear contemporary blues, R&B, and gospel. Although stations played black music for a black audience (often using white R&B deejays to avoid hiring black ones), they picked up white listeners also. Memphis radio station WDIA was the first in the United States to program black music full time (1948). White Memphis deejay Dewey Phillips was extremely popular, playing black music for a mixed audience six nights a week on WHBQ throughout most of the decade of the 1950s.

After the depression had diminished the careers of the legendary down-home bluesmen, who in turn had deposed the female stars of classic blues, the hokum style—small bands doing party music with double-entendre lyrics—had a period of vogue. Jug bands were popular, as were guitar and piano duets. Boogie-woogie piano became more prevalent. Although commercial field recordings were cut back, the Library of Congress, between 1933 and 1942, undertook extensive documentation of black folk music through field trips made by folklorists John A. Lomax and his son, Alan. These included the first recordings of Muddy Waters before his move to Chicago from Mississippi.

Bluebird, a budget label started by RCA Victor, dominated the blues market in the 1930s with a stable of Chicago regulars who backed each other and various vocalists, leading to a more homogenized sound. Stars such as Big Bill Broonzy, Lonnie Johnson, Memphis Minnie, and Tampa Red (all guitarist-vocalists) offered polished, urbane styles, whereas John Lee "Sonny Boy" Williamson, who was murdered in 1948, developed an influential harmonica-driven ensemble sound. Eastern seaboard singers were recorded mostly in New York, such as the popular fingerpicking guitarist Blind Boy Fuller from North Carolina, who was often accompanied by Sonny Terry on harmonica, both representatives of a regional style known as the Piedmont school.

Following World War II the popular black combos were the uptown jump blues bands fired by honking saxophonists and led by shouters such as Wynonie "Blues" Harris, Roy Brown, and Tiny Bradshaw; the entertaining mix of R&B and vaudeville of Louis Jordan and his Tympany Five, which featured clear diction, humor, and a solid beat that also appealed to whites; and smoother R&B groups emphasizing vocal arrangements. Concurrently, updated down-home blues, modernized by the electric guitar, made stars of John Lee Hooker and Lightnin' Hopkins. In Chicago Muddy Waters and his associates were developing an ensemble approach to the blues that incorporated a modern, amplified harmonica sound.

Judging by the songs picked up from various black styles, it was R&B that most affected the rockabillies. Rhythm and blues bands of the era typically consisted of piano, one or two guitars, bass, drums, and sax. The instruments, sometimes complemented by background vocalists, are arranged and rehearsed to the point of effortlessness. They contribute simple, repetitive parts that mesh, creating momentum and rhythmic interplay that calls attention to no individual sound while producing mellow, lilting, and often hypnotic textures. Singers appear to be emotionally engaged with their lyrics, sometimes intensely so, yet are still cool and relaxed. Vocalists and saxophonists may get wild but never out of control. Bands dressed in suits, even uniforms. The music feels somehow inevitable, and the lyrics often seem fatalistic.

Comparing several rockabilly versions of country and R&B songs with their sources clearly shows that fewer elements were altered going from country to rockabilly.[7] Regardless of source style, in rockabilly versions of older songs the singing commonly is more intense, flamboyant, and loose and makes use of a greater number of vocal effects. Many elements (form, lyrics, chord progressions, arrangements) are simplified. Tempos increase, and rhythm is more pronounced as subdivisions of the beat receive more emphasis. Texts are altered by deletions, additions, and shifts of meaning and emphasis. Often melodies are altered, and melodic variations occur from verse to verse, which is less common in previous styles.

Most nascent rockabillies were familiar with forceful black singing, from the impassioned blues of the delta and the shouting style of late 1940s jump blues to the melodramatic, emotional singing of gospel groups. Although it took on aspects of black singing style and blues tonality, rockabilly shied away from R&B's cultivated, trim, interlocking smoothness. Whereas rockabilly's instrumentation was sparser, a fuller sound was achieved by more percussive playing, which produced a denser overall texture.

Rockabilly brought its assertive and at times wild singing style and the desire for rhythmic impetus and density into a country music context. The elements, although intensified, were not new; only the context and combination were. Unmeasurable from comparisons of recordings is the strong influence black performers and performances had on the mental attitudes and stage presentations of rockabillies.

Blacks and whites have been influencing each other's music in America since slavery days. The predecessors of rockabilly are the country musicians who showed the effects of this in the years before Presley's debut. One of them is Aubrey "Moon" Mullican, a western swing player with a strong blues and R&B side who was born in 1909 in Texas and died there in 1967. A big influence on Jerry Lee Lewis, Mullican has been called the king of the hillbilly piano players. He was shown blues guitar by a black sharecropper on the family farm. In 1936 Mullican recorded—with Cliff Bruner's Texas Wanderers—a cover of bluesman Kokomo Arnold's version of "Milkcow Blues," a hit from two years before. One of Mullican's hits was "Pipeliner's Blues," an original recorded in 1940 with the Modern Mountaineers, another western swing band.

As a pianist Mullican could play straight, boogie, or blues, but he rarely strayed far from the four-square rhythm of western swing. As a singer he could be sentimental or humorous, but even on his blues he is generally controlled, cool, clean, and rather passionless. For a decade, starting in 1946, Mullican recorded for Cincinnati's King label, a place where black R&B and white country and rockabilly were recorded and the bands were not necessarily segregated. He cowrote tunes with Hank Ballard and with Hank Williams. "I'll Sail My Ship Alone" was a country number one in 1950 for Mullican, and that year he covered tunes by Roy Brown and Tiny Bradshaw.

Just as Mullican was not the only country musician covering R&B songs—Hank Penny covered the R&B hit "Open the Door, Richard" in 1947—R&B artists were covering country songs as well. Bull Moose Jackson and Wynonie Harris both covered Moon Mullican compositions, and Harris had an R&B hit with his version of Penny's "Blood Shot Eyes."

Another forefather of rockabilly was Hank Williams. Born in Alabama in 1923, Williams died there in 1953. He came out of the honky-tonk style to become the major figure and dominant influence in country music from the late 1940s until Presley shook the industry in 1956. The influence of Williams's simple style and sincerity shows in much rockabilly music—especially the side that is more "billy" than rock.

Williams was taught the basics of guitar, blues, and performance by a black blues and jazz street singer known as "Tee-Tot" (Rufe Payne), a familiar figure in the Alabama towns where Williams grew up. Payne likely was his source for "My Bucket's Got a Hole in It," a jazz standard by Clarence Williams using a chord progression and melody popular in New Orleans. Hank Williams's version contains his only recorded (acoustic) guitar solo, perhaps inspired by Payne. Williams acknowledged the influences of Roy Acuff and Ernest Tubb but was little influenced by Jimmie Rodgers or the Carter Family, the major country stars in his formative years. Williams stated that he was also a fan and composer of gospel songs, and he recorded a few songs with religious themes. His first recordings were made in Nashville in December 1946 and came out on the Sterling label. *Billboard* reviewed them as "backwoods gospel singing." While a member of the *Louisiana Hayride* he came into contact with Cajun music, later playing in Cajun communities.

"Move It on Over," his first disc for MGM and an original composition, scored a huge hit in 1947. It strongly points toward rockabilly with its twelve-bar blues form, walking bass, lightly accented backbeat, and rhythmic, confident, and expressive vocals humorously telling the dog to make room because the singer's woman has locked him out after a night of carousing. One of the jaunty breaks is a blues-tinged electric guitar solo by Zeke Turner that proved to be influential, as did the first four bars of the melody, later copied in "Rock around the Clock." As the Hank Williams style developed and matured, no other song of his came closer to presaging rockabilly. Certainly "Rootie Tootie" from 1948 is often mentioned in this regard, but it is cut from the same cloth as "Move It on Over": another blues in the same key (E), with the same call-and-response format in the refrain.

After a couple of years of appearing on the *Hayride*, Williams made his *Opry* debut in June 1949. His version of "Lovesick Blues," one of the few songs in his repertory that he did not compose, brought audience members to their feet at the start of the song and a brought a half-dozen encores after. He became an *Opry* regular, despite some alcohol-related absences. At his peak his charismatic performance style, personal warmth, genuine and memorable voice, and excellent backing band, the Drifting Cowboys, electrified audiences. His rhythmic, inoffensively suggestive movements contributed to the spell. His songwriting (aided at times by his publisher, Fred Rose) is still one of country music's highest peaks. (Although Williams wrote most of his repertory, documents show that, on occasion, he bought composition rights to songs from their writers.)

Many of Williams's best songs are intensely personal, especially the ones inspired by the joys and miseries of his relationship with his wife, Audrey. Twenty-one of his songs reached the top ten in the country charts from 1949 to 1953. His biggest hit, "Cold, Cold Heart," spent forty-six weeks on the charts in 1951 and was the top song of the year in its field. A pop version by Tony Bennett sold one million copies, establishing Williams as a pop songwriter. Other million-selling pop versions of his songs soon followed. These songs and others by him—"Your Cheating Heart," "Jambalaya," "I Saw the Light," "Kaw-Liga," "Hey, Good Lookin'," "I'm So Lonesome I Could Cry"— are extremely well known around the world through recordings by countless artists in a variety of styles.

Williams fought illness, drug abuse, and alcoholism and was moody and uncommunicative, although well loved and respected by his peers and fans. His premature death from alcohol-induced heart failure, in the back seat of his car on the way to a New Year's Day gig in 1953, made his legacy more poignant, despite the dramatic downturn in his life and career. He had been fired from the *Opry* less than six months before because of erratic behavior due to pills and booze, alienating audiences by being too drunk to perform or just not appearing at all.

Besides being performed by pop singers, Williams's songs were occasionally covered by rockabillies. "I Just Don't Like This Kind of Livin'" was sung by Laura Lee Perkins. "My Bucket's Got a Hole in It" was covered by Sonny Burgess in 1957 and a year later by Ricky Nelson (who got the idea after buying the Burgess version).[8] Jerry Lee Lewis has done a number of Williams's songs. Houston bluesman Jimmie Newsome did a strong rockabilly-tinged version of "Long Gone Lonesome Blues," complete with yodels.

Bill Haley is a predecessor whose style is a synthesis similar to that of rockabilly. Although his earliest recordings show him to have been a hillbilly and cowboy singer (a style that he returned to in a series of demo recordings made in 1959 and 1960, after his decline and his last records for Decca), the band in the Essex and Decca days was a modernized western swing band with big band and Dixieland elements.

Haley was born in Michigan in 1925 and died in Texas in 1981. He grew up in Delaware and in Chester, Pennsylvania, near Philadelphia, leaving home at age fifteen to tour with various bands as a yodeling hillbilly musician. He traveled widely from New Orleans to Chicago, returning to Chester in 1947, where he worked for six years at a radio station as the music director, also leading the house band, which was broadcast live twice a day.

In 1948 he and his band recorded on the Cowboy label as Bill Haley and the Four Aces of Western Swing. Over the next five years he recorded for various small labels, changing the band's name to the Saddlemen in 1949. The instrumentation of Haley's band in these years was acoustic guitar, steel guitar, bass, fiddle, mandolin, accordion, and piano. The band members wore cowboy hats, fancy cowboy shirts, and cowboy boots and played pop country music, a far cry from the ethnic and folk roots of country. It was a slick, tight, and very versatile unit, professional in concept and execution.

The first records and surviving demos contain covers of songs by Hank Williams, George Morgan, and Red Foley, and some have western images, namely, "My Palomino and I" and "Ten Gallon Stetson (with a Hole in the Crown)" ("where Dead-Eye Dalton tried to mow me down"). Some songs are comedy, some corny, some cute, and others more self-deprecating in their humor. There are sentimental songs, yodeling features, traditional songs, older pop songs, adaptations of nursery rhymes, songs with a moral, and emotional ballads. Haley sang sincerely with a smooth, well-controlled voice, very capably handling the melodic demands but, in keeping with the style of the times, without using any overt inflections or vocal devices except occasionally to sing with more hillbilly pronunciation, as in "Down Deep in My Heart."

His country radio show immediately followed an R&B show, and Haley, who especially liked Ruth Brown and Big Joe Turner, experimented by playing R&B songs with his band in live appearances, finding a positive response from the crowd although apparently angering promoters. Haley's first recorded cover of an R&B song was done in July 1951 at the suggestion of Dave Miller, owner of the local Holiday label. It was a version of Jackie Brenston's "Rocket 88," an R&B number-one hit now recognized as one of the most important specimens of early rock 'n' roll. It had been recorded, just months earlier than Haley's version, in Memphis at Sam Phillips's studio and leased to Chess in Chicago. Brenston played sax and sang in Ike Turner's Kings of Rhythm, and when the band recorded his composition, it was released as being by Jackie Brenston and his Delta Cats.

The flip side to Bill Haley's "Rocket 88," "Tearstains on My Heart," is unmistakably conventional country. This coupling shows the marketing problems present when rock 'n' roll was emerging; Sam Phillips also coupled R&B covers with country songs on Presley's five Sun singles. A single from November 1951, a male-female duet issued on Holiday as Bill and Loretta with the Saddlemen, features countrified covers of R&B hits on both sides: "Pretty Baby" from the Griffin Brothers and "I'm Crying" from Memphis Slim.

Recordings that Haley made in the spring of 1952 show an evolution in style. Still presented as Bill Haley and the Saddlemen, the band's first single on Essex (the label's new name) was "Rock the Joint," a cover, with toned-down lyrics, of a 1949 R&B hit by Jimmy Preston and his Prestonians on a Philadelphia label. For some, Haley's version of this song is bona fide rockabilly, perhaps even the birth of the style, but to my ears it is an energetic rendition of an R&B song by a small western swing band. Certainly "Rock the Joint" does point toward rockabilly. The flip side, however, is slow country—"Icy Heart," inspired by Hank Williams's "Cold, Cold Heart" from the previous year. The reaction to the A side, with sales of 75,000, was enough to persuade Haley to continue with uptempo tunes. He turned to jazz and pop sources, a practice he continued in later years, sometimes coming up with bizarre choices.

In 1953 the band name became Bill Haley and Haley's Comets, with drums added first and then a tenor sax, an instrument known but not common in western swing but common in R&B bands. The bass player used the slapping style. Later the role of the steel guitar was minimized.

"Crazy, Man, Crazy," Haley's fourth Essex single (April 1953), uses catch phrases picked up from school kids. It became the first white rock 'n' roll record to become a national pop hit, rising to number fifteen and getting covered by other artists. For the band, it brought a change in uniform from cowboy outfits to tartan tuxedos. The record's success led to Haley's signing with Decca in March 1954, where later that year "Shake Rattle and Roll," a cleaned-up version of Big Joe Turner's song, became Haley's first million seller. The movie *Blackboard Jungle* (1955) featured his "(We're Gonna) Rock around the Clock" (recorded the previous year), which went on to sell over twenty-five million copies, making it one of the best-selling rock records. Bill Haley was on top until late 1956, when Elvis, Little Richard, and those they inspired eclipsed him.

Haley's tour of England in February 1957 was the apex of his career. He arrived overseas greeted by thousands of fans, and his performances there provided the English with their first opportunity to hear real American rock 'n' roll. Expectations ran high, and Haley's slick professionalism and short sets were somewhat anticlimactic.

"Skinny Minnie" from 1958 was his last big hit and one of his best, with a Bo Diddley–style beat, but his other recordings tended to stick to formula and seemed square. Haley did not change with the times, maybe because he knew his limitations. The band remained popular in live appearances, however. Haley toured on and off for the rest of his life and was especially popular overseas and in Mexico. He made some bad decisions about managing his money, and he died confused and bitter in his home in Texas in 1981.

Bill Haley and his music are much maligned. The music sounds contrived because it is; Haley created one of the great personal styles of 1950s rock 'n' roll, refined it with his Decca producer, Milt Gabler (who previously had produced Louis Jordan), and stayed true to it, with rare exception, throughout his career. Haley and his band played a significant role in introducing hot guitar solos and a dance beat derived from R&B to pop radio. The weakest part of Haley's music is poor or inappropriate material, not the style. It is cool music with a hot beat, tight and controlled with arranged ensemble playing.

Haley projected the image of a cheerful, optimistic, uncomplicated, unerotic, almost quaint older person having good clean fun at a party. His music was, on the surface, rockabilly: a rhythmic mixing of country music with elements from black music. What, then, does rockabilly have that this music does not? In a word, rebellion. In addition, besides having a more personal and intense delivery, rockabilly has a more integrated mixture of black and white styles, the kind of intertwining that comes from direct contact within the community, more common to the South, and not just from paring down western swing and adding rhythms heard on R&B records. Of course, some rockabilly was made by people who had little or no personal contact with black musicians, but they were influenced by rockabillies who did.

Other country performers worked on ways to integrate the influence of R&B into their sound. Drummer and bandleader Billy Jack Wills was Bob Wills's brother and a veteran Texas Playboy. Born in Texas in 1926, he was the youngest of the family and was inspired by the black music of the 1940s and 1950s. An album of radio transcriptions recorded between 1952 and 1954 in Sacramento, California, presents a fabulously professional six-piece band, with three fine soloists and a forte for tight arrangements featuring ensemble playing. With three members doubling instruments, their sound palette contained drums, electric mandolin, fiddle, steel guitar, trumpet, bass, and guitar. Their versatility extended to their repertory, which covered country, conventional jazz, swing, western swing, cowboy classics, boogie, blues, and R&B. In their R&B covers—Ruth Brown's "Teardrops from My Eyes," Willie Mabon's "I Don't Know," and others—I find their synthesis of country and black traditions to be intellectual, too smooth a blend to become something new. Delightful music, it is just one of the styles covered by these versatile artists.

The air was becoming charged, but the lightning had not yet

struck. Or had it? Carl Perkins and Charlie Feathers are two artists who may have been playing what we would recognize as rockabilly before July 1954. Others claim to have been rockabilly before Presley, but it is a moot point, since we lack the recorded evidence. One record that does exist, although it is very rare, is suggested by some people (who likely have not heard it) as the missing link in the rockabilly-before-Presley issue: a single on Von by the future Rock 'n' Roll Trio, "You're Undecided" (a song they recorded again in 1956) and "Go along Mule," an old country song ("Go along mule, don't you roll them eyes, you can change a fool but a doggone mule is a mule until he dies"). According to Paul Burlison, the record features himself, Johnny and Dorsey Burnette, and Tommy Seely and was recorded in Booneville, Mississippi, in the fall of 1953 and released in 1954. The producer was Eddie Bond's father.[9] Both songs are fast, with "You're Undecided" in a pop country style and "Go along Mule" more hillbilly. Neither hints at rockabilly. Instrumentation is banjo (prominent), bass, and acoustic and electric guitar, plus fiddle on "Go along Mule."

Another Von single, future Sun rockabilly Hayden Thompson's first record, was recorded in April 1954 at a radio station in Hamilton, Alabama. Both sides are bluesy country showing the motion toward rockabilly. "I Feel the Blues Coming On," drummerless with fiddle and steel, moves into a fast tempo halfway through, the kind of fast blues that a bluegrass band might play. "Act Like You Love Me" is a blues that uses the following lines as a chorus: "Baby that's all right, that's all right with you [twice] / You treat me mean that's the way you do." It's an old blues couplet, but it is interesting that Elvis's "That's All Right" came about just three months later.

In hindsight it seems that rockabilly was inevitable: a generation of young southern musicians had similar backgrounds and influences, and the proliferation of small studios made more recording possibilities available. Of course, the inevitable could have happened in a different way, at a slightly different time, and with different individuals. Nonetheless, there is the sense that in Elvis history provided the right man at the right time. That the style was as powerful, as influential, and as artistic as it was is due to his great natural talent, the musicality of the supporting players, Scotty Moore and Bill Black, and the man who had the vision, patience, understanding, skill, and business acumen to bring it to fruition: Sam Phillips, owner, engineer, and producer of Sun records.

Sam Phillips is a powerful, charismatic man with a creative and inquisitive mind; a couple of his artists, Carl Perkins and Warren

Smith, labeled him a genius. He has tremendous insight, intuition, and conviction, and he thoroughly understood the technology with which he worked. Obviously his influence had a lot to do with the strength of the music he recorded. Phillips was always asking musicians, "Have you got something unique?"

In January 1950, with years of radio experience behind him, including live mixing of big bands for broadcast, Phillips opened the Memphis Recording Service (launching the Sun label in 1952) at the now world-famous address of 706 Union Street in Memphis. What he accomplished there helped to revolutionize American music and culture. Phillips had a nonracist attitude, unprejudiced ears, and a sense of justice that had led him earlier to dream about a career as a criminal defense lawyer. Besides recording weddings and funerals on location with portable equipment, Phillips was also enthusiastically recording music in his rented studio. Passion and potential profits coincided: Phillips, who was trying to get ahead in business, was well aware of the burgeoning blues and R&B market; because he liked the sound and spirit of the music he heard and felt a kinship with the artists, he was well placed to play a role in its development. Word soon got around, and musicians came to him to audition.

At the start Phillips worked primarily with black artists, with whom he had his first successes. Among them, almost all making their recording debuts at Phillips's studio, were Howlin' Wolf, Ike Turner, Jackie Brenston, B. B. King, Billy "the Kid" Emerson, Rosco Gordon, Rufus Thomas, Walter Horton, Bobby "Blue" Bland, Dr. Ross, James Cotton, Little Milton Campbell, Junior Parker, and Earl Hooker. In addition, veterans of the down-home blues era of the 1920s and 1930s were recorded, including Charlie Burse of the Memphis Jug Band, and Sleepy John Estes.

Phillips approached the recording process creatively. Warren Smith said, "Sometimes he'd put empty crates in the studio or he'd put something on the snare drums; he knew just how to get that sound, he had some kinky way of getting it. How he ever got people to cut in that studio I don't know, it was like a chicken coop."[10] Carl Perkins said, "He wanted his records to be different, and he tried anything. . . . He didn't tell us how to play. The only thing he did was relax you. He didn't have a red light that came on. He didn't have a time period. Sometimes we'd go into Sun at two o'clock in the afternoon and come out at ten the next morning."[11]

In discussing how much Phillips manipulated his musicians, Jim Dickinson said, "Psychodynamically, I don't think there's any end to it. Musically, I think he had other people do it. . . . He used the shock approach; I've had it used on me, I know what it does. You look into the black pool of madness in his eyes; the guy can definitely get things out of you that you don't necessarily think you can do."[12]

The white artists Phillips recorded before Presley played in a variety of country music styles. The Sun archives show no rockabilly prototypes (aside from Harmonica Frank) until 1954, although some of this music demonstrates Phillips's willingness to try things that were special or different. Phillips consciously avoided copying what was coming out of Nashville. Sun's first country release was by the decidedly old-timey Ripley Cotton Choppers. Slim Rhodes led a family band that enjoyed a very long career partly because of their versatility. Able to play boogies, western swing, and hillbilly, they later changed with the times and added rockabilly to their repertory.

Harmonica Frank Floyd is a fascinating character from Mississippi. A white street singer with some Indian blood and a background in vaudeville and medicine shows, his music is highly rhythmic and playfully dramatic. He started playing in 1922 at age fourteen, learning his harmonica style from a black musician in Arkansas. Floyd's unrestrained and charming folk music mixes prewar rural styles with his vital spirit and off-the-wall inventiveness. The black-and-white blend and committed delivery of his acoustic one-man band recordings point toward rockabilly. Greil Marcus has called his idiosyncratic style "a music of staggering weirdness, dimly anchored by the fatalism of the blues and powered by the pure delight of what was soon to be called rock 'n' roll."[13]

Some of the other white musicians that Phillips recorded include Howard Serratt, Earl Peterson, Gene Steele, Red Hadley, Sidney Gunter, and Doug Poindexter. Howard Serratt made charming and sincere country gospel music with total conviction and a wonderful command of his harmonica. Earl Peterson was part of the tradition of singing and yodeling cowboys, whereas Gene Steele got his inspiration from Jimmie Rodgers and had recorded in the 1930s himself. Red Hadley came out of the honky-tonk tradition. Sidney "Hardrock" Gunter was a country singer from Alabama who had been recording since the 1940s and scored a hit with "Birmingham Bounce" late in that decade. By the time of his Sun debut, he had added Bill Haley as an influence.

Doug Poindexter is remembered for his only recording session in 1954, which yielded exactly one record. That may not sound like much on which to base a reputation, but his record is important for two reasons: it was the last country music recorded at Sun before Elvis's first session, and it is the only place we can hear how Scotty

Moore and Bill Black (both members of Poindexter's band) sounded before their work with Presley. It is also a fine, quirky record in its own right.

Doug Poindexter had moved to Memphis from his native Arkansas by the early 1950s. He strummed guitar and sang with his band, the Starlite Wranglers, which contained not only Moore and Black but also another guitarist, a steel guitarist, and a fiddler, but no drummer, as was the norm for country bands of the time. They played around the area doing songs by Hank Williams, Red Foley, and the like at dances and on the radio for a few years before recording.

The session took place on May 25, 1954, and the record was issued six days later, with "Hillbilly" stamped in red on the label, for most of the previous Sun records had been blues. Scotty Moore cowrote both songs. "Now She Cares No More for Me," written with Bud Deckelman, is in the Hank Williams mold, and "My Kind of Carrying On," written with Poindexter, is a sprightly song about trying to get some lovin'. It surprises with its unusual melodic phrases in the chorus. Moore's deft guitar work in the intro, ending, solo, and in the rhythmic accompaniment propels the song with a youthful assurance.

I met Doug Poindexter, then an insurance salesman, in 1982 at his home in Memphis, but there was not that much to discuss. He said that it all "seems like a hundred years ago."[14] Six weeks after his session, Elvis, Scotty, and Bill recorded "That's All Right" and "Blue Moon of Kentucky" and put rockabilly on the map. Much has been written about that record, and speculation abounds as to how it occurred. Which of the four people involved, three musicians plus Sam Phillips, were responsible for creating this new hybrid style? I asked Poindexter whether Phillips had influenced the music at his recording session. He said emphatically that Phillips had in no way altered or asked them to change their sound. Also he felt that Moore and Black played in the same style with Elvis as they did with him. As to the difference between Presley's music and his own, Poindexter said that it was the black influence and that Elvis put everything he had into the song.

Because Elvis and "the Blue Moon Boys," as Scotty and Bill became known, had no stage show at the time of the release of their first record, Presley sat in with Poindexter and the boys at Starlite Wranglers gigs. Poindexter stated, "We were strictly a country band. Elvis worked hard at fitting in, but he sure didn't cause too many riots in them days. . . . Frankly, I thought the boy would starve to death."[15]

Poindexter himself was afraid that he would starve; within six months of his recording debut, he had completely retired from music after turning down an offer to play on the *Louisiana Hayride* at the same time as Elvis's first appearance there. In 1982 Poindexter attended a recording session organized by his old friend Paul Burlison as a tribute to the Burnette brothers. There Poindexter saw a lot of people for the first time in many years, but he declined to sing, thus turning down a musical career for a second time, or at least the chance to be a footnote in the rockabilly revival.

FOUR

THE RISE AND FALL OF
ROCKABILLY IN THE 1950S

"Whole Lotta Shakin' Goin' On"

Elvis Presley and his band toured extensively in the South and had a tremendous impact in 1954 and 1955, spreading the rockabilly approach. Other rockabilly artists with hits, strong local followings, or a lot of ambition also toured. Some of these shows now look very tantalizing, such as the package headlining Carl Perkins with Roy Orbison and his Teen Kings, Warren Smith, Johnny Cash and the Tennessee Two, and Eddie Bond and the Stompers.[1] As momentum grew, the territory expanded; a handful toured overseas in Australia, England, and even Japan.

Exciting stage shows increased record sales and influenced musicians. Stage theatrics were partly a product of the format of touring package shows. Each act was introduced by a master of ceremonies and given about fifteen minutes. Performers tried to outdo each other, pack as much energy into their time slot as possible, and keep it interesting for themselves. The most captivating performers—Presley, Jerry Lee Lewis, and Ronnie Self (known as Mr. Frantic) among them—took their appearance on stage as an opportunity to be released from the restraint of daily decorum. Possessed by rhythm and raw emotion, flailing their arms, legs, head, and hair, these unforgettable wildmen fed off the energy returned from amazed audiences entranced by the frenzied spectacle.

The new medium of television was able to communicate some of this excitement, bringing rock 'n' roll to millions, and rockabillies, usually the ones with big hits, appeared on national TV variety shows hosted by Dick Clark, Ed Sullivan, Ted Mack, Steve Allen, and the Dorsey brothers. Local TV shows also helped to spread the look and sound of rockabilly. Although the movies *Rebel without a Cause* and *The Wild One*—both influential on teenage attitudes—had conventional, big-band soundtracks, many movies wove their plots around rock 'n' roll themes and acts. Some musicians recall performing during intermissions at movie theaters or on the roof of the concession stand at drive-in movies.

Hundreds of artists responded to the infectiousness of rockabilly; not the least of its attractions was its financial potential. When Presley's success indicated that money could be made from rockabilly, companies, tours, and barn dance programs throughout the country sought a Presley type, and there were plenty from which to choose. In the case of female singers, this motive was boldly stated: Janis Martin, Alis Lesley, Jean Chapel, and no doubt others were all billed as "the female Elvis Presley" in promotional material.

Most places had their local Elvis. Pat Cupp, from Nashville, Arkansas, was one, and his few recordings from 1956 are held in high regard as prime authentic rockabilly. Picked out by a talent scout at the *Louisiana Hayride,* Cupp and his band, the Flying Saucers, paid tribute to Presley and Carl Perkins in "Baby Come Back" by mentioning song titles. One of them was Perkins's "Put Your Cat Clothes On"; because it was unreleased until the revival, Cupp must have heard it live.

Local dances where rockabilly was part of the repertory were held in such places as community halls. It is not difficult to imagine one of these dances. There might be Christmas lights strung across the back of the stage, tables and chairs around the perimeter of the room, food available for purchase, and maybe booze. Coats are scattered around the room, and some are even hanging up. The band is either bathed in white light or left in almost total darkness. Since the sound system is rudimentary and there are no stage monitors, on the more rocking tunes, the singer sings louder and closer to the microphone to hear himself, sending the audience a distorted vocal sound. The small guitar amp is also distorting. The drummer has a snare, a big bass drum, a ride cymbal, and a high hat and sits low, hitting stiff-armed. When the songs sag or push, he slows down or speeds up. While the band is busy tuning up (maybe it's "nicely out of tune" or worse), or someone is replacing a broken string, a drunk wanders up to yap in the mike. The band doesn't even look up. During the break a band member sells a few of the self-financed singles. The guitar, propped up against the amp, starts feeding back until one of the players returns to lower the volume on the instrument. The band plays country hits, a couple of original songs (including one about rockin' and a bluesy guitar instrumental), some well-known rockers learned from fellow musicians or from records, and probably a few old standards like "St. Louis Blues." There's a guy slapping the doghouse bass and a fiddle, steel, or banjo player who has been around awhile and has played a lot of country music. Each band member takes on a stance—expressionless or comic, very stiff or mobile—and a couple of them take a turn at singing. At center stage is a guitar-strumming, skinny, agitated, charismatic singer, spitting out syllables, screaming, shouting, and crooning. Although they have rehearsed, several songs sprout new endings in the confusion of two or three people giving cues. All try to follow the singer when he jumps to the bridge, and some entries are flubbed. In one song the singer introduces the musicians with a couple of funny comments. Each does a little solo after his name is called. The encore is a slow one.

Excepting hits by Presley, Perkins, and Jerry Lee Lewis, few rockabilly songs hit the national charts between 1956 and 1959, and most did not rise very high. Some hits were "Black Slacks," by Joe Bennett and the Sparkletones, a band of young teenagers from South Carolina; "Love Bug Crawl," by Jimmy Edwards from Missouri; "Nothin' Shakin'," by Eddie Fontaine; "Bertha Lou," by Clint Miller; "The Fool," notable for its slower tempo and higher chart position (no. 7 in 1956), by Sanford Clark, an Oklahoman living in Phoenix; "The Worryin' Kind," one of Tommy Sands's eleven hits and also in a slower tempo than most rockabilly songs; and Ronnie Self's "Bop-a-Lena," written by Mel Tillis and Webb Pierce. Besides being treated to the rockabilly that actually made the charts, record buyers heard some on the flip side of certain pop hit singles. Hit songs and acts were the models for a multitude of identifiably derivative soundalikes. Motives for copying could be admiration, desire for a winning formula to rub off, lack of creativity, or just habit from playing the hits at public shows.

Regional markets developed, often centered on record labels. Independent record companies, known as *indies,* have some advantages over major labels: they are closer to their markets and therefore possibly more able to perceive what may attract the record-buying audience. They are more likely to be in touch with and take a chance on untried musicians or ones with only local fame. A disadvantage for small independents is that their limited capital and connections hamper distribution and promotion.

Hundreds of little labels popped up in the 1950s, some created by the musicians to put out their own product, some run by entrepreneurs, and some owned by large firms that used them as a tax write-off, buying masters that they assumed would not be successful. A few companies offered a vanity pressing service. An unknown hopeful could tape himself in his garage or living room or at the local radio station and pay a company to press a few hundred copies on his own custom label sent in with the order or on the company's label. In Houston Starday used its subsidiary label Dixie for this purpose. Dixie released over 500 titles in a six-year period. The artist would then sell the record at gigs and probably give copies to radio stations and jukebox operators. With exposure came a bit of fame and better gigs, and maybe even a proper recording contract. It worked for a few. These records are extremely rare.

Mountains of rare rockabilly and related songs by both professional and amateur musicians became available in the 1980s on reissues, courtesy of collectors with a penchant for the obscure and a seemingly insatiable appetite for anything that could be considered or marketed as rockabilly. This music jokingly has been called "obscurabilly." This huge body of rare small-label recordings is worth its resurrection for historical reasons, and many gems have been unearthed. It provides a sense of how the music was experienced at the time in a way that listening only to the acknowledged masters does not. For modern sensibilities, however, many of these recordings provide a numbing listening experience. One may feel, on hearing a succession of average (or worse) performances, that the records deserved to remain in their former obscurity.

Hundreds of volumes have been produced between the Bison Bop (later called Buffalo Bop) label from Berlin and the White Label from Rotterdam, Holland. The jackets have photos and information about the artists, but in many cases little is known beyond the name, song title, and sometimes composer and publishing company. Using the information provided and sleuthing with the aid of Gordon's discography when such information was absent, I could in most cases determine a label's geographical location. Labels in forty different states, including Hawaii, as well as in Canada, attest to the spread of rockabilly in the 1950s. A little more light has been shed on a great number of obscure figures by Wayne Russell in his booklet *Footsoldiers and Kings* and in various magazine articles and by Jim Raper in his "The Great Unknowns" column in *Now Dig This* magazine. The column completed its alphabetical listings in 1994, after giving notes on about twenty artists every month for ten years.

One small label was Mar-Vel of Indiana, started by Harry Glenn in 1949 and run by him until 1966. He released over 140 singles, mostly country, rock, and rockabilly. The Mar-Vel sound is honest, the recordings are nicely balanced and professional sounding, the singers are usually good, and the musicianship is consistently strong. Bobby Sisco, later on Chess and with a voice similar to Carl Perkins, did great restrained rockabilly on Mar-Vel.

In Cincinnati, Ohio, a larger independent label was King, with a number of subsidiaries, notably Federal. Syd Nathan started the company in 1943, and it maintained high musical standards and thrived on diversity, recording extensively in country, rockabilly, R&B, and gospel, including some of the best-known names in these fields, James Brown for one. Among the better-known rockabillies who recorded there were Mac Curtis, Hank Mizell, and Charlie Feathers.

Memphis had many labels besides Sun, dozens by the late 1950s, many of them owned or run by musicians. Lester Bihari's Meteor label released rockabilly by Charlie Feathers, Malcolm Yelvington, Junior Thompson, and Jess Hooper. Another celestially named label was Moon, run by Cordell Jackson, who achieved recognition in the revival.[2] Marshall Ellis, a barber who had been a dance band musician in the 1940s, started his Erwin label in late 1954. This and his other labels—Clearmont and Stompertime (a partnership with Eddie Bond)—featured rockabilly from Bond, Jimmy Evans ("The Joint's Really Jumpin'"), Ray Scott ("Boppin' Wig Wam Willie"), Hoyt Johnson ("Eenie Meenie Minie Mo"), and female rocker Pat Ferguson ("Fool I Am").

Regional differences in record popularity are evident in sales and jukebox charts. One of these charts, C&W Territorial Best Sellers, was published in *Billboard* for various cities, such as Birmingham, Charlotte, Dallas–Fort Worth, Houston, Memphis, Nashville, New Orleans, Richmond, and St. Louis. *Cashbox* also published a similar chart. The June 1956 *Billboard* charts show the only Sun artists selling outside Memphis were Presley, Cash, and Perkins, whereas in Memphis these plus Warren Smith and Roy Orbison were listed.[3]

We can now recognize regional stars and markets, but the distinctions between regional and national success were not obvious to many listeners. Jim Dickinson, a little younger than the first rockabillies, said:

I didn't realize that the music that I was hearing on the radio and playing [learning] from there, that everybody in the country wasn't hearing it. I figured Billy Lee Riley was a hit artist. I figured Warren Smith was a hit artist. I didn't know they were a regional phenomenon. For *years* I didn't figure that out. And New Orleans music, which we were hearing a lot of on the radio, I didn't understand the regionality of that. I thought those were hit records too, until I got into the business and realized that these things were connoisseur records on any level other than for the people I'd grown up with.[4]

Since independent labels had limited promotional resources, musicians did a certain amount of the work. Malcolm Yelvington remembered driving with his band to radio stations in neighboring states, doing brief interviews, and getting their record played, sometimes followed by the thrill of having the deejay play their record a second time so that they could hear it on the air while driving to the next station.

When asked whether he sold records at his shows in the early days, Charlie Feathers replied, "No, we didn't have any records, just a few pictures. It was kind of odd back then, people didn't have cameras and things like they have nowadays, take a picture every time you turn around."[5] Autographs were also in demand. Feathers continued:

> I remember me, Elvis, and a guy named Jimmy Work—he had a tune called "Makin' Believe"; he was the first one that had that, and he had one way back yonder in the forties called "Tennessee Border," a pretty good tune. Me, him, and Elvis played a show. We wouldn't cross the [Mississippi] river on a bridge; we'd catch a ferry and go down the river to it: Helena, Arkansas. We played there in a school one night, and a lot of family people came, . . . kids and all. I never will forget it. A couple of girls there said, "sign an autograph on my leg here," and we did, me and Elvis both signed.[6]

Distribution and promotion took more than the sporadic efforts of musicians, however. In Sun's early days Sam Phillips drove thousands of miles delivering records to radio stations and jukebox operators throughout the South.[7] Sam's brother Jud was the national sales manager.

Barbara Barnes, hired as a secretary at Sun in 1957, recalled that they dealt with over forty independent record distributors, each of them promoting and selling in their territories. Other agreements were made for overseas distribution (handled by London Records), publishing (Hill and Range), and management (the William Morris Agency). For a record to become a hit, it needed big city airplay and promotion. All radio stations on the mailing list received the latest records and promo sheets, and the powerful deejays were called to check audience reaction to airplay. Promising records were advertised in *Billboard* and *Cashbox,* where they might get reviewed. Artists were booked on national or regional TV, made public appearances, and joined touring shows. Local distributors were sent lists of new records so that they could place their orders with one of the three plants that pressed Sun records (in Memphis, Philadelphia, and Los Angeles). Follow-up phone calls urged bigger orders and further promotional efforts. If a record became a hit in one of the targeted large midwestern markets, it was followed by a push on the East Coast, then the West Coast, and then across the nation.[8]

Most small labels had to concentrate their promotional efforts on proven acts. Plans could change rapidly. Sometimes old tracks were released without telling the artist, who might be on tour, unaware and unable to take advantage of it. If a record was hitting big, energy was poured into boosting it, and the proud performer might be rushed back in the studio to cut more tracks for an album, causing frustration for others hoping for more support for themselves. Many sought greener pastures when they felt in line for a big push and then realized that they were not in the inner circle.

Most artists were basically on their own, working only through booking agencies. Few had managers, and even fewer had good ones. The greatest success in rockabilly belonged to Presley; he deserved it through his talents, but he got it through his shrewd and enterprising manager, Col. Tom Parker.

Motivations to record rockabilly differed, from the frustrated country singer seizing an opportunity to go in the studio to the versatile session man able to fit into any prevailing genre, to those who embodied and expressed the particular stylistic synthesis of rockabilly. Their backgrounds covered all available styles. Their accomplishments ranged from the once-recorded to the prolific. Some were familiar with studios, and others with nightclubs or concert stages. Each person brought a different approach to rockabilly and contributed to its course.

There are sufficient sociological similarities to outline a general profile of the 1950s rockabilly (chapter 8 contains a sociological profile of female rockabillies). Rockabilly was really the music of a particular race, of a particular generation born in a particular locale, and its course is directly related to the personalities and transitions of its practitioners as they responded to the market, their audience, their peers, and their self-image.

Although the birthdates of those who did rockabilly range from before 1920 to past 1940, a typical male rockabilly, observed at his first recording session in 1956, could be described as having been born in the 1930s (especially 1932–35). He is not particularly well educated, from the lower middle class or the lower class (a class called "white trash," "white niggers," or "crackers" by more genteel southerners), possibly married or even married with children (as were Carl Perkins, Paul Burlison, and the Burnette brothers). He works in a trade—as a baker, electrician, welder, mechanic, auto bodyman—or at a job along the lines of mail carrier, driver, deejay, or salesperson. He has served in the armed forces. He has a country music background and at one time considered himself to be a hillbilly musician, but he is interested in black music and may have been taught by a black. He may or may not be skilled as a musician, but about his music he is passionate, sincere, dedicated, enthusiastic, self-confident, and eager to record. Personally he may be wild, shy, arrogant, self-effacing, assured, polite, eccentric, egocentric, rebellious, or a combination of these.

Affecting their personalities and music making were certain underlying tensions. Jim Dickinson identified six tensions faced by Memphis rockabillies. First were their racially ambiguous motives. Although inspired by music made by black artists, some rockabillies were uncomfortable associating themselves with black culture, sharing somewhat the general racial thinking of southern whites. At the same time, they had partially broken out of that thinking through their involvement with blacks and black music.[9] Dickinson said, "Imagine the way those guys must've felt about what they were doing in 1955 or '56 or even earlier . . . in terms of the reality of Southern life. . . . It was called immoral, and depending on what you believed, that's what it was."[10]

The second source of tension was the social defiance and nastiness of rockabillies, giving their music an angry, arrogant quality.

Third are the tensions stemming from their disenchantment with country music. In the early 1950s many young players raised in country traditions found more excitement in R&B or jazz.

Dickinson's fourth point of tension is the contempt with which many sidemen and session players performed the music. (Dickinson claims that this shame on the part of sidemen is an essential element in rockabilly, but although this attitude was present in many recording sessions, some were free of it.)

The guitarist is always some guy that's into playing jazz, and he thinks the music is shit. And the singer is a county purist

who thinks it's nigger music or something. That element *has*
to be there or it won't be real. . . . And it almost has to be an
insensitive producer. That commercialized element: it has to
come from outside because from inside you'd be able to hear
it. There's got to be some guy there . . . some jerk who's going
to rattle the change in his pocket and talk about something inappropriate to get it that edgy enough . . . [when] the old men,
and the country guys, and the jazz players who were coming
at it from all these different angles, playing this bastardized,
hybrid music, went off back into their weird places, it all became rock 'n' roll, a kind of one culture thing. But rockabilly
was not no one culture thing, 'cause there was always some guy
there who didn't like it. There was always some guy who
thought "we ought to be playing real country music," and there
was somebody else who wanted to get a drummer, and that was
the way it was. All that bitching . . . is part of it.[11]

Fifth is the style's unpopularity in certain quarters. Good citizens
found rockabilly to be hedonistic, cacophonous, loud, threatening,
corrupting, racially tainted, unpleasant, and abrasive. Anybody who
was seeking to please the public eventually was going to stop doing
rockabilly.

Sixth is the god versus devil music conflict. Music should express
the glory of God, it was argued; it should be morally uplifting or at
least proper. If not, it is sinful. In some live music venues dancing
was considered to be immoral and not allowed. For many rockabillies, religion exerted a powerful influence on their morality and
worldview. They had difficulty being true to their faith and to their
involvement with a music that was equated with the devil for its
worldliness. This conflict is clearly present in the famous conversation between Jerry Lee Lewis and Sam Phillips before the taping of
"Great Balls of Fire."[12] Dickinson confessed, "I'm vulnerable in that
department myself."[13]

The tensions inherent at the creation and in the early days of rockabilly ceased to play a large part for later singers distanced from them
by geography or age. The music's sting, brought about by social, racial, commercial, and musical conflicts among the musicians of a
particular region and era and between them and society and the recording industry, was lost as the music became commercialized and
musicians from different areas and backgrounds became involved.
According to Dickinson, "The typical pop musician has no racial
conflict to deal with."[14]

Rockabilly flourished for a few brief years. Even after the establishment of white rock, a newer substyle that owed a lot to Elvis's RCA recordings, rockabilly continued to exist alongside it while being influenced by it. Rockabilly then virtually disappeared because of various musical, sociological, and commercial factors.

The year 1960 is often considered to be the end of the original era, although rockabilly was produced, notably in Canada, at later dates. Terry Gordon pinpoints October 1959 because of a dramatic drop in the number of releases. A perfectly convenient choice, if history were cut-and-dried, would be December 31, 1959, the release day of Sonny Burgess's last single for Sun: "Sadie's Back in Town," an undiluted rockabilly sound.

Charlie Rich's "Lonely Weekends," also issued that day, soon became a national pop hit (no. 22). Although it features an all-star rhythm section of rockabilly veterans—Billy Lee Riley, Roland Janes, and J. M. Van Eaton—the singing, chord progression, modulation, and overall feeling are closer to gospel than to any other style. Van Eaton's drumming is the strongest link to rockabilly. Rich's voice is reminiscent of Presley's smooth style, not at all frantic. A large female choral group sings with very stiff rhythms (mixed distantly with a great deal of echo), the guitar's role is minimal, and the solo is by a baritone sax.

Carl Mann brought in new energy. Like Charlie Rich, Mann was a talented pianist and singer who had success as the new decade loomed. His specialty was to cover standards in his own style: he made the charts twice in 1959 with reworkings of Nat King Cole hits. The rockabilly part of his sound is heard to good advantage in "Baby I Don't Care." Mann was only twenty years old when he left Sun in 1962, and he played piano in Carl Perkins's band until going in the army in 1964. During the revival Mann was popular in Europe and did very convincing recordings, playing lead guitar as well as piano. While he and Rich enjoyed their first successes, however, most of the top Sun artists had moved to major labels.

Other things were changing for the little independent label. Shortly after the new decade began, Sun closed its studio on Union Avenue and relocated to larger quarters a few blocks away on Madison Avenue. Sam Phillips's interest in producing waned. One of the most vital elements in the company had been his uncanny ability to get the most out of any individual by getting performers to be unself-conscious, to feel out of the spotlight. Subsequent Sun producers used different approaches. Jack Clement, producer, arranger, performer, session man, and songwriter, stated, "I changed the direction somewhat, as I was a malcontent. I was trying to make more sophisticated music, less gutsy than Sam. Looking back he was right and I was wrong."[15] The Sun studio, no stranger to pop music, had changed with the times, and a great deal of music of little merit was released. Blatantly attempting market success at the expense of musical integrity is a good way never to see your record reissued in the future.

The marketplace increasingly rewarded a softer, less confrontational format, with bland, banal, or artificial subject matter. Buddy Holly, the Everly Brothers, Ricky Nelson, and a few others managed to infuse this lighter style with sincerity that transcended its commercialism. That the general audience found this style to be appealing and inoffensive may be related to the diminished influence of folk-based styles; many of the singers were nonsouthern whites raised on pop music, not on the roots of rock 'n' roll. Jim Dickinson, citing Holly and Eddie Cochran, felt that commercialism "did the music in prematurely." He was not in favor of "this concept of writing your own song that became so important. I still, to this day, believe it's important to interpret black music for it to be rock 'n' roll."[16] Sleepy LaBeef said, "I didn't ever see it change. The people were still digging it, and the musicians liked playing it, but the big companies figured it was a fad and took it away from the kids."[17] Although little recorded after 1960, rockabilly was still performed live into the middle of the decade.

Presley's TV appearances caused a popular sensation but also brought detractors and the censoring of Presley's "suggestive" movements, with one show filming him "from the waist up." Censorship was applied in radio, too: in 1957 numerous stations banned Jerry Lee Lewis' "Whole Lotta Shakin' Goin' On" as being too suggestive.[18]

Teen idols were beyond reproach. Most of them were manufactured by the record companies as clean, conventional, very white (i.e., safe) guys who sang cloying lyrics. They were the success stories of the late 1950s: Fabian ("Turn Me Loose"), Paul Anka ("Lonely Boy"), Bobby Rydell ("Wild One"), Bobby Darin ("Dream Lover"), and Frankie Avalon ("Venus").[19] Jerry Lee Lewis said, "All you could hear was Bobby Vee, Bobby Vinton, Bobby Rydell, Bobby Darin, Bobby This, Bobby, Bobby, Bobby. I got so damn tired of hearing Bobbys, they ran out of my ears, and here come these four cats called the Beatles, and that's the end of the Bobbys, thank God! That opened the door again."[20]

As the 1950s closed, many of rockabilly's innovative, popular, and charismatic figures were absent. Whatever the cause, their absence further diminished the music's energy, already on the wane on account of commercialization, lack of resources, and changes in musical tastes. Elvis Presley was in the army from 1958 to 1960, although his records continued to be released. His RCA recordings had steadily moved away from rockabilly, and his absence reduced his influence. He was expanding his repertory to include more pop tunes and began using session guitarists like Hank Garland, who played at the June 1958 session while Presley was on army leave. Scotty Moore worked on a per-job basis at this time. Buddy Holly died in a plane crash in early 1959. A year later Eddie Cochran died in a car crash in England. Cochran and Holly also had been moving away from rockabilly, expanding their roles in the music business and broadening their styles. Jerry Lee Lewis's career suffered a huge setback from the scandal in 1958 when the press learned that he had brought his thirteen-year-old bride, a second cousin, on tour in England. For years after that Lewis remained at Sun because no major label would touch him. Carl Perkins's career never regained its momentum after the fateful car accident of 1956. The Rock 'n' Roll Trio did not record after March 1957, although they continued to tour for some time before breaking up.

Black rock 'n' rollers were affected as well. For some, like Fats Domino, their records were simply less popular after a while. For others, their careers took unusual turns. Chuck Berry was charged in 1959 with a morals violation, and a lengthy trial and subsequent jail sentence disrupted his career (and seemed to sour his character). In October 1957, while on tour in Australia with Gene Vincent and Eddie Cochran, Little Richard gave up rock 'n' roll for the ministry.

By the turn of the decade the artists who had been working in rockabilly knew where they stood in terms of commercial success. As eager young hopefuls they had gravitated to the energetic new style; after a few years the style, and they themselves, no longer had a youthful freshness or carried the promise of success. They had been active at a professional or semiprofessional level for a number of years. They had toured, recorded, and written songs; they had been session men, producers, engineers, label owners, and so on. For most of them, they had been partially successful, but not wildly so. Most of them were then in their middle and late twenties and settling down. With a change of musical style in the air, they decided either to continue their involvement but modify their sound or role or to retire from the music business. A great number of them chose the latter; the excitement was gone. They made their living through their nonmusic trades. J. M. Van Eaton, younger than most, stated, "I was playing full-time between 1956 and 1961 and then I got married and quit. I still used to play little local shows and things like that but mostly I quit in 1961 or thereabouts."[21] Those who stayed in the music business had to find a viable niche for themselves.

FIVE

ELVIS PRESLEY

"Mystery Train"

ELVIS PRESLEY

Born January 8, 1935, Tupelo, Mississippi; died August 16, 1977, Memphis, Tennessee

Epitomizing the American rags-to-riches story, Elvis Presley was a mixture of flamboyance and shyness, rebellion and politeness, ego and modesty, lust and piety. His music affected almost every phase of rock 'n' roll, and his influence dominates the entire history of rock-abilly. He became a messiah-like figure to millions who still devotedly worship him through fan clubs, conventions, publications, iconic artwork, personal and public shrines, and collections of records, books, videos, and so on. The fans make pilgrimages to his birthplace in Mississippi and to Memphis, for the memorial services held on the anniversary of his death and for bus tours of his early homes, his high school, the old Sun studio, his statue, and especially his mansion, Graceland, which opened to the public in 1982 to capacity crowds of three thousand per day. It's easy to find, located on Elvis Presley Boulevard, just across from an Elvis-dominated shopping center where his image is for sale on almost every household object that can be carried and on some that cannot.

Elvis was an only child, doted on by his mother, Gladys. His father, Vernon, sold moonshine whiskey and avoided hard work if he could.[1] The family moved to Memphis, where they lived in project housing, and Elvis absorbed music from the streets, the radio, and the Pentecostal church, where he developed a love of white gospel quartet singing. As a teenager he sang in talent shows and hung around Beale Street, the main black commercial and entertainment district in the area, where he bought loud clothing. He wore his sandy brown hair (Charlie Feathers called him a "yellow head") in a duck-tail haircut, although he later dyed it black (October 1956). After high school he got a job as a truck driver for the Crown Electric Company. He asked local bands to let him sit in, like the time he sat in with the Shelby Follin band. Paul Burlison remembered:

> We were broadcasting live from a car lot, J and S Motors, on a Saturday afternoon on KWEM, West Memphis. We were on a flatbed truck with steps coming up. They were paying us to play, and they had big old speakers to stop the crowd, get them to come into the car lot to sell cars. Everybody parked out there, had an audience all out there in front, besides it was going through the air, too, and people driving around would come down and watch. And he [Elvis] used to come down and stand around and watch. I worked with him at Crown and knew him just casual. Somebody there—it was Lee Denson, who [later] had a song out on Vik—was with Elvis and said, "he sings, let him sing a song." I told Shelby, "this guy can sing." So he got up to sing and sang "Birthday Cake." It's an old blues song: "Take your finger out of it, it don't belong to you." You get right down to the end and it says "I'm talking about your birthday cake." It goes good.[2]

During this period Elvis started hanging around Sam Phillips's studio. In the summer of 1953 and again early in 1954 he paid to make a custom ten-inch acetate, a single-copy record with two sides, crooning pop songs to hear how he sounded. He made enough of an impression to get his phone number noted. Some time later he was called in to try out a song Phillips had in mind. It did not work out, but Phillips suggested that Elvis rehearse with guitarist Scotty Moore. Phillips then asked the two of them, along with bassist Bill Black, down to the studio to commit a couple of songs to tape. The details of these events are worth knowing, but since the story is one of the most often recounted, with slightly conflicting elements, I will not elaborate on it.[3]

In any case, the first session started on July 5, 1954, and continued the next day. The first song recorded was the conventional ballad "I Love You Because." It wasn't what Phillips was looking for. During a break, as the story goes, Presley started fooling around with "That's All Right," a song by bluesman Arthur "Big Boy" Crudup from 1947.

When Black and Moore joined in, Phillips saw something in it, encouraged them, and got it on tape. Elvis used the first verse and one line each of two other verses, ignoring a fourth verse. The scat singing at the end is found in the source record, but Elvis ignored the rhythmic stops employed by Crudup and his bassist and drummer.

Moore and Black were the only musicians invited to Presley's first session. Phillips either had this trio instrumentation in mind or came to like it, for no one else was called. Presley strummed acoustic guitar, Black played and slapped the strings of his upright bass, and the studio echo and Moore's fluid leads and fingerpicking filled out the texture.[4] The instrumentation proved to be very satisfying and was used on all five of Presley's Sun singles, with the artist credit acknowledging the contributions of all three. The labels read "Elvis Presley, Scotty and Bill." In live shows Moore and Black were called the Blue Moon Boys.

Along with the ten songs on Presley's singles, nine more titles (including a rehearsal of "How Do You Think I Feel") survive from his Sun sessions.[5] How many of those nineteen songs are truly rockabilly, that is, genuine country and western R&B, the blending of black and white elements? My count is six: both sides of the first single, "That's All Right" and "Blue Moon of Kentucky," plus "Good Rockin' Tonight," "Milkcow Blues Boogie," "Baby, Let's Play House," and "Mystery Train." These are all songs from black sources, except the drastically reworked "Blue Moon of Kentucky." Of the other songs, some have similar energy to the ones just named (and some do not) but use the tonalities of pop, country, or blues.

None of the rockabilly songs uses drums—thus the concept of rockabilly's classic trio lineup—although six of the others do, and two more use bongos.[6] "Trying to Get to You" even has Elvis playing piano. Few sides by others maintain the trio format; usually at least drums are added. Charlie Feathers advocates the trio idea, sometimes performing that way. Sleepy LaBeef recorded some of his first songs with this instrumentation and has been known to use it in a portion of his live show. This configuration was being used on records as late as 1957, in Bob Luman's "Make up Your Mind Baby," and returned in the revival.

"Blue Moon of Kentucky" became the flip side of "That's All Right," but getting the sound Phillips wanted from the musicians took some time and probably some coaxing. It is quite conceivable that Phillips played records and tapes of other artists who approximated what he was looking for, as he did with Billy Riley (playing him Billy "the Kid" Emerson's "Red Hot") and with Roy Orbison (playing him Arthur

Crudup 78s).[7] Phillips may have played Sun blues and R&B songs by Ike Turner, Rufus Thomas, James Cotton, or Junior Parker or songs by Harmonica Frank or Charlie Feathers. I discuss the possibility of Feathers's influence in these matters in chapter 13.

Presley's released version is very different from anything previously known. Tosches calls it "daring to the point of insanity."[8] "Blue Moon of Kentucky" was a classic and famous bluegrass song, recorded in 1947 for Columbia by Bill Monroe and the Bluegrass Boys: Monroe (vocal, mandolin), Lester Flatt (guitar), Earl Scruggs (banjo), Chubby Wise (fiddle), and Cedric Rainwater (bass). They played it at a stately tempo of 104 beats per minute in waltz time (3 beats to a measure). Monroe sang with sincerity and emotion in his high, keening tenor and played a melody solo on mandolin using his signature tremolo picking, a hallmark of the bluegrass sound. The Sun gang altered the meter from 3/4 to 4/4, increased the tempo, changed the intro chords, added words to the intro (which changed the symbolic role of the moon), changed the key from B-flat to E, sang and played aggressively, used only three instruments, and wrapped it in an eerie echo. What they did not do was change the song's chord progression, form, or lyrics.

An earlier Sun take reveals that this large stylistic distance was traversed in stages. That take has Presley strumming in quarter notes and Scotty Moore playing along unobtrusively; no bass is heard. The meter is already changed to 4/4, and the tempo is moderate at 158 beats per minute. Although tentative and incomplete, it is a simple and flowing rendition. Phillips sums it up nicely in the preserved studio talk: "Hell, that's different. That's a pop song now little Vi, that's good."[9] The issued version moves at a much faster tempo (M.M. 223): Black now furiously slaps his bass, Presley strums passionately, Moore solos and fills in brilliantly, and the echo blends the instruments and enriches the mix. Monroe's intro featured a fiddle; Presley sings his intro with new words:

> Blue moon, blue moon
> Blue moon keep-a shinin' bright
> Blue moon keep on-a shinin' bright, you gonna bring-a
>   me back my baby tonight
> Blue moon keep-a shinin' bright

This moon is now an agent that will return the sweetheart, not the passive reminder of loss that it was for Monroe. Although Elvis retains the rest of the original lyrics, he sings in the pushy, rhythmic, and high-density vocal style that became so characteristic of rockabilly. Words and syllables are added—"I said," "oh well-a," and so on—in an attempt for more sound and rhythm for the voice. The enunciation is exaggerated ("hit" for "it") and words are dropped: "[the] stars shinin' bright, [the] wind whispered on high, [your] love [has] said good-bye."

In showing a new way to fuse black and white components, Presley's first single was a major achievement. This momentous occasion "just happened" because of a fortuitous combination of people, mood, and opportunity, and its effect was unbelievably far reaching. As Dave Marsh points out, Elvis integrated black and white music. Indeed, some people found it offensive because he "acted out our lip-service belief in equality before our very eyes."[10]

The two songs were featured on *Red Hot and Blue,* the radio show of local deejay Dewey Phillips (no relation to Sam), beginning on July 10 (nine days before the record's release), where Sam Phillips had taken it to gauge the reaction. From the first night the feedback was extremely positive—so much so that Elvis was fetched from a movie theater to be interviewed on the air. Dewey made a point of asking him which high school he had attended, thereby informing the audience that Elvis was white, schools being segregated at that time. The record became a regional hit, selling approximately 20,000 copies in six months and charting on the national western jukebox chart in *Music Guild* magazine.

Six weeks after the record's release its success prompted Bill Monroe to rerecord his song. On September 4, in Nashville, Monroe did a version that shows the influence of Presley's record: after the intro and thirty-two bars in 3/4 time, the remaining sixty-four bars are in 4/4 time. Monroe played the waltz portion faster than his original, at M.M. 123, and the 4/4 portion faster than Presley, at M.M. 235, but breakneck tempos are common in bluegrass. Presley's influence is felt in no other way. Monroe featured a fiddle trio. Later versions of "Blue Moon of Kentucky" by rockabilly veterans are occasionally done in this 3/4-followed-by-4/4 arrangement; this is how Sleepy LaBeef recorded it (1977) and Marcus Van Story performed it (Memphis, 1982). Doc Watson, who played some rockabilly before getting known for his folk music, also performed it this way (1993).

Also from Presley's first session are the pop songs "Blue Moon," by Rogers and Hart from 1934, probably inspired by a version by Billy Eckstine or Ivory Joe Hunter, and "Harbor Lights," later a hit for the Platters, although Presley's version did not surface until years after.

On Friday, July 30, 1954, the trio played an outdoor show at the Overton Park Shell in Memphis, opening for country stars Slim

Whitman and Billy Walker. Walker recalled that Elvis "really knocked them out . . . they hadn't seen anything like him before; he was just so different."[11]

In September 1954, after a bit of local gigging with both Malcolm Yelvington's band and the Starlite Wranglers, the trio's second session yielded another single—"I Don't Care If the Sun Don't Shine" and "Good Rockin' Tonight"—plus the Shelton Brothers' "Just Because," which came out on Presley's first RCA album. Roy Brown wrote and recorded "Good Rockin' Tonight" in 1947, but it was a bigger hit for Wynonie Harris soon after. Brown remembers that an as yet unrecorded Elvis Presley heard his band in Tupelo, Mississippi (Presley's birthplace), a dry town, and bribed the alcoholic guitarist with a big bottle of moonshine; "Elvis was on the bandstand just playing and singing with them, nobody paying any attention to him, but he followed us, Tupelo, Indianola, Memphis."[12] A few months later Brown heard a hillbilly singing his song.

Later in September Presley appeared as a guest on the *Grand Ole Opry,* during Hank Snow's regular time block. Apparently Presley was popular with the audience but not with the management, and he did not fare any better at his second (and final) *Opry* appearance less than a month later. Between them, on October 16, 1954, he made his debut on the *Louisiana Hayride,* where reaction was so great that he soon signed a one-year contract. It was later extended six more months, although on December 17, 1955, the contract was terminated in an agreement negotiated by Col. Parker in exchange for a benefit concert Presley did for the Shreveport YMCA.

One of the early *Hayride* shows was recorded. Presley sang both sides of his first single and LaVern Baker's "Tweedlee Dee," and the group was augmented by piano and steel. Between songs Frank Page, the master of ceremonies, said, "I'd like to know . . . how you came about that rhythm & blues style, that's all it is, that's all you can say."

> PRESLEY: "Well, sir, to be honest with you, we just stumbled upon it."
>
> PAGE: "Well, you're mighty lucky you know, they've been looking for something new in the folk music field for a long time, and I think you've got it."
>
> PRESLEY: "We hope so."

The next sessions came in November or December 1954.[13] "Milkcow Blues Boogie" and "You're a Heartbreaker" made the third single. Bluesman Kokomo Arnold's "Milkcow Blues" was a staple in western swing repertories. Presley learned "You're a Heartbreaker" from a local songwriter's demo. "I'm Left, You're Right, She's Gone," written by Stan Kesler and Bill Taylor, white musicians who recorded at Sun, was subsequently used on the fourth single. Alternate, bluesy versions of this exist, subtitled "My Baby's Gone." This session also may have resulted in a version, unissued at the time, of Lonnie Johnson's 1948 hit "Tomorrow Night."

From sessions in 1955 came the other side of the fourth single, "Baby, Let's Play House," done the previous year by Arthur Gunter on the Excello label. "Baby, Let's Play House" was Elvis's first hit record, reaching number ten on the country charts. The unissued "Trying to Get to You," another cover of an R&B record from the year before, was originally by a group called the Eagles. Country singer Jimmy Wakely's "I'll Never Let You Go" was covered. Shows and demos recorded in Texas and Louisiana indicate that the following were in the band's repertory: "I Got a Woman," by Ray Charles, the Clovers' "Fool, Fool, Fool," Chuck Berry's "Maybellene," and Big Joe Turner's "Shake, Rattle and Roll," also popularized by Bill Haley.

A session in July 1955, likely Presley's last at Sun before the informal Million Dollar Quartet, yielded "Mystery Train" and "I Forgot to Remember to Forget." The latter was written by Stan Kesler and learned from Charlie Feathers's demo (whether Feathers earned his cowriting credit for helping to finish the song or just for recording the demo is unclear). "I Forgot to Remember to Forget" is a song with two sections, each one with a different rhythmic feel. The first section's shuffle beat is a Memphis specialty: a stiff, hard, medium-tempo beat, with no fills, accenting the offbeat. The second section changes to a more typical slow rock feel accenting the second and fourth beats.

"Mystery Train" is an R&B song recorded in 1953 on Sun by Little Junior's Blue Flames. Herman "Little Junior" Parker sang his own composition, although the line "train I ride is sixteen coaches long" is to be heard at least as far back as Memphis bluesman Furry Lewis's "Good Looking Girl Blues" of 1927.

Presley's train (at M.M. 242) not only was moving faster than Parker's (M.M. 196), but it built its momentum by increasing the vocal density from verse to verse. As if doing a call and response with himself, by the last verse Presley sings,

Train train, coming round round the bend, round round the
   bend
Train train, coming round and round the bend, round the
   bend
Well it took my baby, but it never will again, never will again.

This last line is the only alteration he made to Parker's lyrics: the forceful assertion of "never will again" contrasts with the sense of inevitability Parker expressed when he sang that the train "took my baby, it's goin' do it again." Neither is the fatalism of the original song's mood shared by Presley, who ends his recording with joyful laughter after singing wordless falsetto notes.

"Mystery Train" uses a variation of the standard blues progression: the first chords are the IV chord instead of the I chord.[14] This progression was used for two other Sun R&B recordings that relate to Elvis's version. Pat Hare's guitar solo on James Cotton's "Hold Me in Your Arms," from 1954, is the model for Scotty Moore's solo with Elvis, and Rufus Thomas's "Tiger Man," a local hit in 1953, was joined in a medley with "Mystery Train" in Presley's later concerts.

"Mystery Train" backed with "I Forgot to Remember to Forget" was Presley's fifth and last single for Sun. Issued in August 1955, the disc (both sides) soon became a national country number one, staying on the charts for a total of forty weeks, his biggest success to date. Presley was signed to RCA later in the year, and RCA rereleased all his previous singles in November. He never recorded for another label.

What the Bopping Hillbilly (as Presley was sometimes known) achieved on the Sun sides in those first sixteen months was a fiery and personal synthesis of influences. Others tried the blend but missed the passion; Larry Donn copied six of Elvis's Sun songs almost note for note, but they lack fire. That the synthesis of styles was different and viable was recognized by Phillips, who with his staff producers recorded performers in a similar style in the next few years, eclipsing the styles previously recorded at Sun: blues, R&B, gospel, and conventional country. Rockabilly's difference was also recognized by an audience whose enthusiastic response spawned a wealth of recordings on hundreds of labels across the country by thousands of artists.

The Sun sessions reveal the range of Elvis's influences and the seeds of the direction he would take in the RCA days. Although Elvis wrote none of these songs, the fact that he chose them (or accepted them if he was directed to them) can be at least somewhat indicative of his endorsement of their contents as statements. There are the blues and bluegrass songs, but there is more here than just "come on and rock." We also can find a little bit of gospel, albeit in a secular context, in the last verse of "Trying to Get to You," a song about traveling to meet his sweetheart—

> Lord above he knows I love you
> It was He who brought me through

> When my way was dark as night
> He would shine His brightest light

—not to mention the "blue moon" that heard his prayer for "a love of my own."

Elvis always aspired to pop music, frequently naming singers like Dean Martin, Pat Boone, Bobby Darin, Kay Starr, and Patti Page as favorites. Along with admiring their vocal assets, he was not alone in being attracted to their high-class image and high level of social acceptance. He recorded pop throughout his career, even back to the songs he cut as vanity items. The first song Elvis put down on tape for Sam Phillips was the sentimental, sincere-styled "I Love You Because," with a spoken monologue. In "I'll Never Let You Go" there are banal pop images: "the stars would tumble down . . . the moon would hang its head and cry." Even his movie roles are foreshadowed in the following lyrics from "I Don't Care If the Sun Don't Shine":

> Well that's a-when we gonna kiss and kiss and kiss and kiss
> And we're going to kiss some more
> Who cares how many times we kiss, 'cause at a time like this
> Who keeps score?

His macho posturing is also evident in "Baby, Let's Play House," where he sings "I'd rather see you dead little girl than to be with another man" (which, incidentally, crops up as a line in the Beatles' "Run for Your Life"). At the Houston show Elvis introduced "I Got a Woman" by saying, "this one's called little darlin' you broke my heart when you went away, but I'll break your jaw when you come back, did you ever hear that one?" One of the lines in this song is "a woman's place is in the home." This posturing is by no means exclusive to Presley. Other rockabilly examples are Roy Duke's "Behave, Be Quiet or Be Gone," Jerry Reed's "I Have Had Enough" ("and I might get rough . . . you're my private property"), and the line about the baseball bat in the Rock 'n' Roll Trio's "Honey Hush." In "My Way" Eddie Cochran sings "when I say 'frog,' you jump" and

> don't let me hear you talkin', just be there when I call,
> 'cause what I do, I do my way or it won't be done at all,
> oh little girl, better hear what I say,
> I'm an easy-going guy but I always gotta have my way.

The more socially conscious revival bands of the 1980s avoided this type of song like the plague.

Presley had a profound impact in the South in the year and a half before he went to RCA. The band toured relentlessly from the first Overton Park show through 1955, doing over 200 dates in Louisiana, Tennessee, Georgia, Ohio, New Mexico, Florida, Virginia, North Carolina, Mississippi, California, Missouri, Arkansas, Oklahoma, and Texas, regularly racing back to play the Saturday night *Louisiana Hayride* in Shreveport. Many country artists who shared the bill on these shows later recorded rockabilly, notably Marty Robbins, Johnny Horton, Rose Maddox, Wanda Jackson, Eddie Bond, Bobby Lord, Glenn Reeves, Dean Beard, Onie Wheeler, and Johnny Carroll. During dates in Texas Buddy Holly shared the program with Elvis; the experience changed Holly's musical direction.

Promoters were affected by the Elvis phenomenon. After Presley galvanized the audience at the *Big D Jamboree* in Dallas in the summer of 1955, promoter Ed McLemore booked Sid King and the Five Strings and other local boppers, later bringing in Gene Vincent (whom he was to manage for a while), Jerry Lee Lewis, and Carl Perkins.

Many musicians will readily admit Presley's early influence. When asked whether Presley had influenced him a lot, Paul Burlison replied, "Yeah, he did, sure he influenced. He had a different sound. . . . Of course, we were already playing country and doing a lot of country honky-tonk songs. . . . But it wasn't any trouble at all to just go right into that type of stuff because it was the same feeling. . . . He put a lot more personal feeling into his songs and a little bit different rhythm, different feeling."[15]

Eddie Bond stated that his music changed after hearing Presley. He said that after hearing Presley, he "just sung it a little bit faster, maybe, a little bit louder, a little bit crazier guitar."[16] Ray Harris was a country fan working at the Firestone plant until he was invited by coworker Bill Black to attend the recording session for "Good Rockin' Tonight." Not only did the experience convert him to rockabilly music—he recorded a handful of intense, primal examples of rural southern rockabilly at Sun in the next two years—but being in the studio that night converted him to the record business, and he went on to form his own labels, notably Hi Records.

Other indications of early Presley influence are found in early cover versions of his first records, often on major labels. Although not showing a tremendous musical debt, these versions demonstrate that his records affected musicians. Marty Robbins, in December 1954, five months after Presley's version of the song, recorded a subdued and countrified version of "That's All Right" using only acoustic instruments, including fiddles. It sold more than Presley's, partly because of Columbia's distribution system and Robbins's already established reputation. Cliffie Stone (on Capitol) and Phil Gully (on Decca) both did 1954 versions of "Blue Moon of Kentucky" in the wake of Presley's; both have drums and saxes, and neither is rockabilly.

On the local level Presley was obviously exerting considerable influence in the first few months of his recording career. One telling artifact is a private live recording, made in late 1954, of a charity show at the Kennedy Hospital in Memphis. Although I am not familiar with any of the musicians, the six issued songs are probably indicative of the repertory of contemporary bands.[17] They play two songs by Hank Williams, "If You Ain't Lovin', You Ain't Livin'" and his Luke the Drifter narration "I've Been down That Road Before," an original instrumental ("Three Way Boogie"), a cover of Lucky Joe Almond and his Hillbilly Rockers' "Gonna Roll and Rock" (just released on the Trumpet label of Jackson, Mississippi), and two covers of Presley songs ("Blue Moon of Kentucky" and "Good Rockin' Tonight"). The band is hillbilly in style, albeit with drive, but Red Rolison's vocals on the Presley songs have rock 'n' roll and rockabilly inflections not evident even in the Almond cover.

Rockabilly did not become a craze until 1956, when Elvis was on TV and on RCA. Discographer Terry Gordon, discussing the preceding years, states:

> In the early fifties, country was chic. Hank Williams's songs would be covered by pop singers and you'd have square dancers on TV. By '54, '55, rhythm & blues was the "in" thing, and that was at the expense of country. Radio stations would change format from country to rhythm & blues. Rockabilly and rhythm & blues cover versions [by country artists] was an attempt to either reverse that trend or cash in on it. So at the same time that you have people like Elvis Presley and Sonny Fisher doing a very distinctive, very raw type of sound, you have very unspirited, slavish cover versions of rhythm & blues tunes, like Pee Wee King doing "Tweedlee Dee." You listen to the record and wonder why it happened. It's a case where, instead of taking black music and adding something to it, they take black music and take something away. They take [away] the spirit and just use the tune in the belief that maybe it's the lyrics or something that is selling the record. But throughout '55 there are more of those records than there are [of those showing the influence] of Presley.[18]

In looking at records made in 1954 and 1955 that we can label true rockabilly, we invariably see a connection to Presley: they are made by artists who we know saw Presley perform in person or can be safely surmised to have seen him. "Love Me," by Jimmy Lee (Fautheree) and Wayne Walker, recorded January 1955 for Chess, is a strong example of early rockabilly, featuring harmony vocals and stinging lead guitar accompanied by steel guitar. It has a tough intensity rarely found at this date. These two were regulars on the *Louisiana Hayride* and surely saw Presley there. From Memphis comes "All Messed Up," Jess Hooper's only single, on Meteor in 1955 and strongly influenced by Elvis's Sun sound, with the same trio instrumentation. The electric guitar playing sounds like Scotty Moore, but it is not: Hooper worked at times with Billy Riley and named him as the lead guitarist on this cut. The vocalist was at one time mistakenly thought to be Charlie Feathers.[19] Hooper, from a town about sixty-five miles south of Memphis, was working at a radio station in Clarksdale, Mississippi, where the song was a regional hit. Although seven or eight original songs were recorded at the session, only one record was released. Hooper left the area shortly after and moved to Texas, soon retiring from music. Bobby Lord's "Beautiful Baby," recorded twelve days into 1956, has a freely improvising bluesy lead guitar over a stiff shuffle provided by strummed acoustic guitar locked with a walking bass (one note on every beat) and percussion with lots of echo. Lord, later a *Grand Ole Opry* regular, had been part of package shows with Elvis. Incidentally, Lord's "No More, No More, No More!" from 1954, for which he claims cowriter credit, is a direct copy of Munroe Moe Jackson's "Go Away from My Door" from 1949, which can be heard on *Country Blues Classics vol. 1* (Blues Classics 5).

Other records from these years, although presented under the banner of rockabilly on compilation albums, are more accurately seen as late western swing and country boogie styles, such as Jimmy Heap's "Sebbin Come Elebbin" from 1955 on Capitol *Rockabilly Originals* and Eddie Zack and Cousin Richie's "I'm Gonna Rock and Roll" from November 1955 on *CBS Rockabilly Classics*, volume 2.

Presley's Sun records initially were reviewed and charted in the country field, and Presley toured the South playing in country settings. His new manager, Col. Tom Parker, shrewdly placed him in a distinctly noncountry setting: prime-time national TV. The first appearance was January 28, 1956, on Jackie Gleason's *Stage Show*, where Presley sang "Blue Suede Shoes" and "Heartbreak Hotel." In less than a year he would be on TV twelve times: five more times on Gleason's show, twice on the *Milton Berle Show*, once on the *Steve Allen Show*, and three times on *Toast of The Town*, hosted by Ed Sullivan. Each time Elvis was backed by his regular band of Scotty Moore, Bill Black, and D. J. Fontana (who had been a staff drummer on the *Louisiana Hayride*); from June onward he had (off-camera) backing vocals by the Jordanaires, a male vocal quartet.

D. J. Fontana was added to the band in the spring of 1955. Levon Helm, who became the drummer for Ronnie Hawkins and later for the Band, recalls a gig in Arkansas from those days. Fontana was "building up to the solos, riding the solos in and riding them out again. He had incredible technique and fast hands . . . he played like a big-band drummer—full throttle. Now Elvis had a real foundation, some architecture, and he made the most of it. D. J. set Elvis *free*."[20] Helm also observed that Bill Black played electric bass that night, which anchored the rhythm section even more, giving Scotty Moore extra freedom in his solos.

"Heartbreak Hotel," recorded in Nashville on January 10, 1956, at Presley's first RCA session, included Presley's band members plus pianist Floyd Cramer (also previously on staff at the *Hayride*) and guitarist Chet Atkins. Released the same day as Presley's first TV show, the song soon reached number one on the pop and country charts and number five on the R&B chart. By March 3 the record, plus the five previous singles now rereleased on RCA, made RCA's list of its twenty-five best sellers. In addition, that month RCA released Presley's first album, an unusual occurrence so soon in the career of a relatively new performer, fleshing it out with four of the Sun masters. All this sensation, commotion, and success served notice to legions of eager hopeful singers and money-conscious record company executives that the gold rush was on.

Audiences were buying Presley's personality as well as his music—and they were definitely buying. The market was flooded with Presley product in 1956: eleven singles, eight EPs, one double EP, two albums, a movie, and tons of Presley trinkets. Despite the fact that many of the records were simply repackages (only the beginning of a tradition), no apparent saturation point was reached.

But there was a backlash. Elvis's two-week booking at the Frontier Hotel in Las Vegas in April 1956 was shortened to one week because of audience dissatisfaction, low attendance, and unsavory behavior by underage fans. One saving grace was Elvis's latching onto "Hound Dog" after he saw Freddie Bell and the Bellboys do it down the road at the Sands Hotel. "Hound Dog," written by Jerry Leiber and Mike Stoller, a successful songwriting and production team, had been recorded first by Willie Mae "Big Mama" Thornton four years earlier. A number-one R&B hit, it had wide appeal: by April 1953 it had been covered six times by country artists.[21] Although Presley sings the same lyrics as

Freddie Bell did, certainly he would have been familiar with Thornton's hit, a relaxed, smoky blues that has her howling away with the band at the end. After a review of Elvis's Las Vegas performance likened him to a "jug of corn liquor at a champagne party,"[22] he no doubt found good reason not to howl at the end of his version.

Besides the disappointments in Las Vegas, there was controversy about the gyrations of "Elvis the Pelvis" on TV. The taming of Elvis went alongside the selling of Elvis. When the detractors made enough noise, changes were made: he performed in a tuxedo, he sang "Hound Dog" to a basset hound, and he was filmed from the waist up. Still, his amazing charisma shone through. Nevertheless, Elvis, the young man with real talent, real looks, and real personality, was not in control. His manager was.

Col. Parker and his team manipulated, directed, and marketed that talent, and probably no act in any field had management to compare. Certainly no other rockabilly act had anything remotely close except perhaps Ricky Nelson, in 1957, who was managed by his father, Ozzie. In the 1950s Col. Parker ushered his moneymaker through four halfway-decent movies, the domination of the record market, and once the youth market was conquered, into mainstream respectability via two years of duty in the U.S. Army. Discharged in 1960, Presley was sheltered from the changes of that decade by his isolation from the public. The fans had several long years with only a succession of records, many of them shoddy and most of them endlessly recycled, and a numbing series of basically vapid movies to keep them connected to the "King of Rock 'n' Roll." Somewhere along the way Presley seemingly lost his desire and merely acquiesced to being the figurehead of a giant corporation that fed off his talents, wasted though they were. His fans were numerous enough and devoted enough to keep it all in motion.

With the 1968 television special and the subsequent return to concert stages, Elvis added something to his legacy, but despite flashes of brilliance, he seemed to become a parody, a victim of his own image, recycling himself, like his records, until it all became an empty show. If music, art, and life appear to be without effort, meaning, interest, desire, or hope, why continue? Nonetheless, Elvis made many fabulous records (not just rockabilly) in the 1950s and later, and the story of rockabilly is tied to his story.

Although the band of Moore, Black, and Fontana went with Presley to RCA, the company was unable to duplicate the full Sun sound attained with the slap-back echo. On most of Presley's RCA recordings the band was augmented by the Jordanaires and various additional guitarists and pianists. At the beginning this was partly to compensate for a sound that otherwise lacked the fullness characteristic of the Sun records, which the RCA engineers, despite phone calls to Sam Phillips for technical advice, were at a loss to replicate. In addition to the fuller ensemble, the drums were miked separately and mixed higher and, since the slap-back echo's blending of sounds was not happening, the instruments were heard more clearly as individual elements. It was a new sound that came out of the frustration of being unable to make an old sound, and as it became the new version of rockabilly, it also moved away from being strictly rockabilly toward a clearly defined, white version of rock 'n' roll—"white rock," if you will.

In white rock the country elements and acoustic lightness are absent or diminished, and the sound is tougher, more assertive, more calculated, and more coolly confident. Tempos may be faster. Compared to its blues sources, rockabilly is hyperactive; compared to rockabilly, white rock can seem frantic. White rock is the white musicians' own style, less of a hybrid. As in 1954, when Elvis crystallized rockabilly, a mixture of country and R&B, in 1956 he crystallized white rock 'n' roll, a mixture of evolved rockabilly with evolved R&B, notably of the Little Richard and New Orleans variety, with its strong drums and prominent piano. We can clearly hear the differences by comparing Carl Perkins's "Blue Suede Shoes" with Presley's or by listening to any of the four Presley covers of Little Richard hits: "Tutti Frutti," "Rip It Up," "Long Tall Sally," and "Ready Teddy." In other words, when rockabilly, in the form of Perkins's record, was first hitting hard in the marketplace, the style was already evolving into something else. White rock eventually superseded rockabilly after a period of coexistence, because the conditions were not so specific: for one, the musicians did not need to have country music origins or any direct or strong indirect influence from black music. In fact, most of them just needed the influence of Elvis himself.

Great artists—Duke Ellington, Muddy Waters, Bill Monroe, and the Beatles, to name a few—are able to evolve through existing styles into the creation of a unique body of work, thus making their indelible mark. Presley did not achieve either the rockabilly or the white rock crystallization alone. They happened because of who he was, who he was with, and who was encouraging him. At Sun he was an untested country boy with two local musicians on a small label that had a precedent of recording pure country and pure black music and that could hope to aim him toward the regional circuit. Sun could allow him to be idiosyncratic. He and Sun created a personalized hybrid style. At RCA he was a seasoned performer with a large band of stage and studio professionals on a major label with a pop approach and a manager aiming him for mass acceptance. They put him in a more formulized environment. He and they created a purely white style that could stand alone. That Elvis was capable of being involved in such revolutionary musical movements is a testimony to his versatility, and since he did not achieve these single-handedly, it is also a sign of his malleability. This, as we know, in time turned from strength to weakness.

As I mentioned, one component of white rock 'n' roll as defined by the RCA Presley was the backup vocal group. Gospel and doo-wop were certainly sources, as were well-known pop vocal groups like the Andrews Sisters, the Mills Brothers, and the Ink Spots. The Jordanaires were originally a gospel group, as their name indicates. In gospel music, both white and black, there is a long tradition of quartet singing. The Presley-Jordanaires combination (adding them apparently was his idea) was influential to the point that singing background groups became almost mandatory for all but back-shack record makers. Gene Vincent even toured with two male backup singers.

Presley's gospel background was legitimate; he had sung informally with such quartets in Memphis.[23] Aside from being audible on his religious records, that background appears in the revealing moments captured on tape of the so-called Million Dollar Quartet. In late 1956 Elvis paid a visit to the Sun studio while Carl Perkins was recording and Jerry Lee Lewis, backing him up, was doing one of his first sessions. The three men started singing informally—a few current hits, country songs including Bill Monroe's "Little Cabin on the Hill," and a surprising number of traditional gospel songs, such as "Down by the Riverside," "Farther Along," and many more. Sam Phillips, sensing a historic occasion, called a photographer and reporter, and part of the music making was recorded. Johnny Cash was also present (he appears in the photo and is acknowledged in the name given to the group by the reporter, but he left early and was not recorded). After years of curiosity, the tapes—at first just portions on bootlegs—were released in the 1980s. Besides getting backstage, so to speak, listeners become aware of just how close to the surface was the shared gospel background of the participants.

The other source of chorus singing is the doo-wop style of New York vocal rock 'n' roll, itself influenced by gospel singing. Doo-wop makes great use of syllables without inherent meaning—"dip-dip-dip," "rama-lama," "shoop shoop," and so on—whereas rockabilly makes one notable use of nonsensical syllables with meaning. In rockabilly the popping of syllables is a favorite device of more intense, raw singers. This works particularly well on the singing of the words "baby, baby, baby" or just "ba-ba-ba-baby." Presley's version of "Baby, Let's Play House" is likely the source of this device, and it had a strong influence. The effect is used in "Where'd You Stay Last Night" by Ray Harris and "Let's Go Baby" by Billy Eldridge (1959). "Oh Baby Babe," by the Rock 'n' Roll Trio, and "Cool Off, Baby," by Billy Barrix, are really just "Baby, Let's Play House" with new words, but both keep the vocal device. This popping of syllables underscores a sense of self-mockery: it's fun and it's not intended to be taken seriously. These qualities are present in doo-wop, but doo-wop actually had scant effect on southern rockabillies. Texans for some reason paid more attention to it, such as Sid King and the Five Strings and Johnny Carroll, whose "That's the Way I Love" has the background singers going "bop-bop-a-diddle-it."

If we closely observe songs Elvis recorded in 1956, even from his first sessions for RCA, we see, as noted, the emergence of white rock in the hard push and drum-heavy sound of songs like "Blue Suede Shoes" and "Heartbreak Hotel," but we see too that neither rockabilly nor earlier styles were yet abandoned. "I Got a Woman," with its slapped upright bass and Sun-type guitar playing, is mature, evolved rockabilly, as is "Money Honey." "I'm Going to Sit Right Down and Cry (over You)" is a song that mixes the two styles. There is a great fingerpicked guitar solo, but the song is too fast for the emotional content of the lyrics, with a pushy, almost frantic feel. Genuinely fast and frantic is "Tutti Frutti," with all holes filled in, including tom-toms entering during the guitar solo. Another track that mixes styles is "One Sided Love Affair," a real standout. It mixes rockabilly singing with gospel-styled singing and a boogie piano solo, played not by Floyd Cramer but by Shorty Long.

Many ballad songs, such as "Love Me" and "I'm Counting on You," mix pop, country, gospel, and doo-wop elements into a style we can only call pop. That blending became a homogenization, a formula that shortly took over much of Elvis's repertory, leaving only traces of the distinguishing and obvious features of the other styles. By the time of his second RCA album, recorded in September 1956, the bulk of the songs were this kind of pop music. The Arthur Crudup blues tune ("So Glad You're Mine") and the rocker from the pen of Otis Blackwell ("Paralyzed") retain much of their character within this formula, and white rock is represented by the three Little Richard covers, but the pop music formula dominates the rest of the songs. There would be other white rock songs, "Hound Dog" and "Jailhouse

Rock," of course, but of rockabilly we hear little else besides echoes (pun intended).

Records by Presley soundalikes were inevitable and numerous. One was Marvin Benefield from Atlanta, Georgia, who changed his name to Vince Everett, the name of Presley's character in his third movie, *Jailhouse Rock,* from 1957. Everett's recording of "Baby, Let's Play House" turns Presley's drummerless Sun-era song into an Elvis-on-RCA song. His voice is less southern than Elvis's, but so was Elvis's on RCA. Everett realized the dream of Presley imitators: an Elvis name, an Elvis song, Elvis's band—Scotty Moore, Bill Black, and D. J. Fontana—and Elvis's producer, Felton Jarvis. Add the Jordanaires (or Jordanaires imitators), and voilà, it's Almost Elvis. Elvis soundalikes were sometimes successful in the marketplace, although most were not.

Sun Studio, 1982 (photo by the author).

Elvis Presley (from the collection of Wayne Russell).

Malcolm Yelvington at home in Memphis, 1983 (photo by the author).

Carl Perkins promo photo (from the author's collection).

Billy Lee Riley, Memphis, 1983 (photo by the author).

Sonny Burgess (from the collection of Wayne Russell).

Ray Smith in concert, Eindhoven, Holland, 1979 (courtesy of Tommie Wix, the Ray Smith Fan Club).

Ray Smith promo photo (courtesy of Tommie Wix).

Paul Burlison shows how he plays the double-octave licks in "Train Kept a-Rollin'," at home in Walls, Mississippi, 1982 (photo by the author).

Pianist, guitarist, and producer Jim Dickinson leading his band in a festival performance, Memphis, 1983 (photo by the author).

SIX

MEMPHIS
"Red Hot"

The musicians profiled in this chapter came from or worked in the Memphis region. All but the Rock 'n' Roll Trio recorded for Sun, and aside from Roy Orbison, who recorded first in Texas, they all made their recording debuts with Sun.

MALCOLM YELVINGTON
Born September 14, 1918, Covington, Tennessee

After Elvis Presley's debut with two singles issued consecutively, Malcolm Yelvington was the next singer with a release on Sun.[1] He sang in the direct manner of honky-tonk singers: "people said I sounded like Ernest Tubb; I wasn't too proud of that."[2] Nevertheless, his material and his musicians' instrumental work show a working country band arriving at an artistically successful and personal style within the emerging rockabilly climate. Yelvington had not paid much attention to black music; it was the country stars of the 1940s who were his chief influences, particularly his idol, Red Foley.

Yelvington was a generation older than most of the Sun artists when his recording career began. In November 1954, when "Drinkin' Wine Spo-Dee-O-Dee" was released,[3] he was thirty-six years old, whereas Presley was nineteen. Mr. Yelvington, as Elvis called him, was impressed with the teenager's personality and music and learned to "snap" out his lyrics from hearing Elvis's first record, although Bill Haley's music impressed him more.

Yelvington started playing hillbilly music (although he never con-

sidered himself a hillbilly), mostly as a solo act or with another guitarist, around 1933 in his hometown of Covington. In 1953 he moved
to Memphis, thirty-five miles to the south, commuting to Covington every weekend to play dances and a Sunday radio program with
his band. They played western swing, country, country boogie, and
honky-tonk songs. Later they included songs they had recorded,
Chuck Berry tunes, and pop instrumentals like "September Song."
Yelvington's band, the Tennesseans, formed in the 1940s. In 1952
they merged with another band, the Star Rhythm Boys, to become
Malcolm Yelvington and the Star Rhythm Boys. Despite Yelvington's
star billing, everyone took an equal share of the money. All were
friends, and some of the members had been with him since 1942. In
the spring of 1954 a demo disc recorded at Sam Phillip's Memphis
Recording Service plus a contact via the Home of the Blues record
shop on Beale Street resulted in Yelvington, but not his band, being
offered a contract with RCA. He turned it down out of loyalty to the
band, later wondering whether he had done the right thing.

Since Yelvington was an experienced musician, I asked him about
any changes in style that may have come about during recording:

> When I first learned about that recording company, I went down
> and I just asked him [Phillips] for an interview, asked him for
> an audition, just like, I guess, most all the rest of them did. . . . "I
> don't know exactly what I'm looking for but I'll know it when
> I hear it," he said. "That's the reason I listen to everyone that
> comes in. One of these days somebody's going to come in here
> and do something that I'm looking for." And lo and behold, it
> turned out that Elvis was the one that walked in and did what
> he was looking for. And then, of course, after he released Elvis,
> then that started giving all the other guys that had been going
> down some idea of what he was looking for. I had to change
> my style, it was either change or just forget it [recording], one
> of the two. You've heard "Wine Spo-Dee-O-Dee" and the flip
> side, "Just Rolling Along." Both had a steel, and you noticed
> the other stuff I cut, like "Rockin' with My Baby" etc., didn't
> have a steel. I dropped that right away, 'cause when you men-
> tion steel, you're talking strictly country.
>
> [Presley] hadn't [yet] made that much of an impression on
> country music. I was still playing on radio shows, still playing
> nightclubs and stuff like that, but in order to cut a record that
> at least had a chance, I had to drop the steel. I didn't drop him
> from the band, I just dropped him from the sessions. After the

sessions we were still playing country music: we'd play the stuff that we'd cut in the studio, but we'd have the steel on the gigs.[4]

Note also that Yelvington's 1954 and 1955 recordings have no drums, but they are present in his 1956–58 recordings.

At the first session Yelvington and his band played several songs for Phillips but failed to come up with one with a beat to his liking until they pulled out "Drinkin' Wine Spo-Dee-O-Dee." It took six or more hours of working on it, with the addition of four or so background singers, to get a take he could accept. There were no overdubs; they did it until it was right. "Drinkin' Wine Spo-Dee-O-Dee" had been an R&B hit in 1949 for Brownie McGhee's brother, "Stick." Yelvington had been doing it for years. "The guy that used to play steel with me, back in the late forties and early fifties, he learned it somewhere and he sang it, and I learned it from him. He quit the band and I got another steel player, so I started singing the song. It was for dancing, or, you know, for what we call honky-tonks. Back then it was a real popular song; it was more of a boogie than it was anything else."[5]

A single on Meteor, "Yakety Yak" and "A Gal Named Joe," was released under the pseudonym Mac and Jake and the Esquire Trio.[6] Mac was Malcolm, and Jake was bass player Jake Ryles, who slaps rhythmically toward the end of the latter song, one that had been recorded (but unissued) in a more country version at Sun some months previously. Both songs use an almost identical melody for the first six bars of the verse: a walking bass pattern.

Pianist Reece Fleming, who had first recorded in 1930 as part of a duo, worked with Yelvington for years. Fleming's compositional skills were a real asset to the band and are a major factor in the high esteem in which the Yelvington repertory is held today. Fleming recorded only four titles with the band, three of which he wrote: "Just Rolling Along" (where Yelvington and Fleming shared the vocals and Fleming's wife, Lavern, played the piano), "Yakety Yak" (cowritten with lead guitarist Gordon Mashburn), and "Blues in the Bottom of My Shoes" (also known as "Way Down Blues"). Fleming was no longer with the band for the Meteor version of "Yakety Yak"; Frank Tolley played the boogie piano. Nonetheless, Fleming's songs were still a part of the repertory: "A Gal Named Joe," "It's Me Baby," and "Goodbye Marie" (written in 1942). Fleming, who died around 1958, even wrote "Gonna Have Myself a Ball," according to Yelvington (to whom it is credited).

"Rockin' with My Baby," Yelvington's only recorded composition,

lists numerous song titles in the verses: "Sixteen Tons, Rootie Tootie, and Birth of the Blues, Blue Suede Shoes." Backed with "It's Me
Baby," its 1956 release marked his third single in as many years, and
it was his last issued work for quite some time.

Louie Moore, a songwriter from Alabama, came to Sun to drum
up interest in his material. Yelvington sang six of his songs, the lyri-
cally clever "Trumpet" being one of the best he ever cut. It derives
its momentum from drummer J. M. Van Eaton's relentless pattern and
its hypnotic minor-to-major tonality from low notes on the electric
guitar.

Yelvington explained that often recording was done midweek during the day, causing musicians to be absent from their jobs. Apparently, unless they were staff musicians, performers were paid (from
royalties) only for issued material. Like almost all rockabilly artists,
he reaped no direct financial benefits from reissues. He stated, with
only slight bitterness, that he made forty-eight dollars out of his recording career in the 1950s.

Retiring from the music business in 1961, Yelvington did not per-
form again until the Memphis festival concerts started featuring rock-
abilly in the late 1970s. In 1974 he recut "Good-bye Marie," presented
on the *Get With It!* anthology on Flyright. In 1976 he recorded "Shim
Sham Shimmy" and "Shotgun Boogie" for Marcus Van Story's album.
In 1980 a new version of "A Gal Named Joe," misnamed "Goin'
Downtown," appeared on *Johnny Burnette's Rock and Roll Trio and Their
Rockin' Friends from Memphis*.

In 1983 Yelvington retired from his work as a pipefitter and welder, satisfied that he had provided for the education of his five children. In the spring of 1988, at the age of sixty-nine, Malcolm Yelvington played in Europe to great response, backed by the Dave Travis
band augmented by a pedal steel guitarist. That show became Yelvington's second album; his first album, collecting his 1950s output,
had been released the same year.

In 1991 he was recorded again in Memphis, at the refurbished
Union Avenue studio where he cut his first single.

CARL PERKINS

Born April 9, 1932, Tiptonville, Tennessee

One of the most talented rockabillies, Perkins is a strong vocalist, a
creative composer, and one of the best guitarists in the field.

Perkins was born poor. The Perkins family sharecropped, working
among black sharecroppers, and Carl's first guitar lessons and inspi-

ration came from one of them, "Uncle" John Westbrook. By the late 1940s a band made up of the three Perkins brothers was getting popular in the honky-tonk bars of Jackson, Tennessee. Carl played electric guitar, his older brother, Jay B., played acoustic rhythm guitar, and his younger brother, Clayton, played upright bass and the role of the clowning showman, commonly reserved for this instrument in traditional country bands. Carl did most of the singing, although Jay occasionally sang lead or harmony. Without the usual fiddle or steel, for a while they fulfilled the later concept of the classic trio, but eventually they added drums and piano.

The Perkins brothers' band was surely one of the first to play rockabilly. In 1954 pianist Jerry Lee "Smoochy" Smith, then fourteen years old, was playing in the clubs with the band. Smith said that Carl was a better cotton picker than he was and that Carl was "into rock 'n' roll actually before Elvis Presley. He did a lot of good rock 'n' roll tunes back before Elvis ever cut his first record."[7] Drummer Tony Austin, a cousin of the Perkins brothers, joined the band in early 1954. He called Carl the "original rockabilly" and said that they played country music with a black influence, their local popularity due partly to the beat generated by the drums.[8] Shortly thereafter, a new drummer, W. S. "Fluke" Holland, became a permanent member, and he played on all the band's recordings done at Sun. When they saw Elvis perform, Holland said, "that was the first time we ever saw anyone play the type of music we were doing."[9] Carl stated that he realized he had a chance in the music business when he heard Presley's debut record because "it was exactly what I was doing."[10]

Although only eight singles were issued while Perkins was with the Sun company (one was on Sun's Flip subsidiary), he recorded forty-one songs between October 1954 and December 1957, twelve of them before Presley made his first live TV appearance, on January 28, 1956, with "Blue Suede Shoes," a Carl Perkins composition. Two days later Elvis recorded the song in RCA's New York City studio.

The first three songs that the Perkins gang recorded were bar-band country. Two songs, "Honky Tonk Gal" and "Movie Magg," are youthfully energetic with strong, confident vocals. Both are in the same key (E) with a bright tempo and an almost identical intro. They are nearly rockabilly, especially the aggressive, bluesy guitar solos on "Honky Tonk Gal." Malcolm Yelvington remembered meeting the Perkins brothers in 1953 when their bands both played in his hometown of Covington, noting that Carl was very unusual, with a style all his own, playing like a blues guitarist.[11]

As a guitarist Perkins has a variety of techniques and approaches at his command, employing fingerpicking, imitations of the pedal steel guitar, right-hand damping (muffling strings near the bridge with the palm), arpeggios (chord notes played in succession rather than simultaneously), advantageous use of open strings, single and double string bending (pushing strings across the neck to raise their pitch), chromaticism (using notes outside the scale), country and blues licks, and tritone and other tonality-clashing licks (short phrases that include notes from other keys and move in logical, often symmetric patterns).

Perkins has a rich chord vocabulary, incorporating sixth and thirteenth chords, ninth and add nine chords, and suspensions, which show up in both his rhythm parts and his solos. His strong rhythmic sense enables him to freely use syncopation (accenting a normally weak beat), chord anticipations (arriving at a chord change in advance of the other players, typically by one eighth note), and crosspicking (repeating a pattern of three eighth notes so that the accented notes of the phrase fall sometimes on upbeats and sometimes on downbeats).

The lyrics of "Honky Tonk Gal" tell of a woman who leaves her lover for the world of jukebox records and the honky-tonk hardwood floor. Carl gives a hint of yodeling on the title words, and in the last verse he scat sings one line in a way similar to Presley's scatting in "That's All Right." "Movie Magg" was Carl's first composition, written when he was fourteen, and it was popular with his relatives and neighbors. The song has many rural images. After plowing all week while dreaming of Maggie, the singer says, he will slick himself and prepare his horse for a Saturday night date. Despite a double-barrel shotgun that awaits him, he tells his girlfriend, "climb up on old Becky's back and let's ride . . . let me take you Maggie dear to a western picture show." In the reworked version issued as Perkins's first record, the aggressive lines directed to the girl's father (that "dog-gone man")—"so look out dad just back up boy 'cause you are in the way"—are eliminated; anyway, the singer wants only to hold her hand. "Turn Around," the third song of the first batch, was apparently written on the demand of Sam Phillips. Its theme is devotional love, and, with the added session fiddle and guitar player, its more conventional style is similar to that of Hank Williams. Both this style and the hopped-up country with rockabilly inflections are further represented at later sessions.

The band's July 1955 sessions, one year after Presley's first, produced Perkins's first real rockabilly recordings. The driving "You Can't Make Love to Somebody," with its Hank Williams–style intro, has a loose backshack feel with great energy. The drums are prominent, and the acoustic guitar and slap bass are clearly audible. Before his solos Carl contributes his first spoken interjection, the somewhat tentative "rock!" "Gone Gone Gone" is even stronger and more committed. It is the first Perkins recording to use the twelve-bar blues form, there is a lot of slap-back noticeable on the drums, the voice is very pliable, and Carl pops syllables, scats, and makes urging comments. It's relaxed and tense at the same time in an appealing way. The solo is fingerpicked and the guitar is miked closely and distorted, while the fiddle is all but inaudible.

The country material recorded at this session—"Let the Jukebox Keep on Playing" and "What Ya Doin' When You're Crying," with steel guitar and fiddle—is the last to show a strong Hank Williams influence. From the same period comes "Drink Up and Go Home." Written by Johnny Bond and Joe Maphis, it is the first nonoriginal song the band recorded and is unique in the Perkins brothers' recorded output: a moralizing, pure bluegrass performance in stiff waltz rhythm, featuring three-part harmony on the chorus.

"Blue Suede Shoes" was released January 1, 1956, less than two weeks after it was recorded; it was only the third rockabilly-styled song of Carl's to be taped. Many stories are told about it: that it was inspired by a real-life incident at a dance, that Carl wrote the lyrics on a potato sack in a fit of inspiration in the middle of the night, that the title was suggested by Johnny Cash, or that the band members were all drunk while it was recorded. One unoriginal aspect of the song is the intro; in 1953 Bill Haley sang "one for the money, two for the show, three to get ready and here I go" at the start of his "Whatcha' Gonna' Do?" on Essex. Part of the popularity of "Blue Suede Shoes" comes from the fashion consciousness and violent imagery of the lyrics and the immediacy of the blues form, the rhythm intensified by the forceful stops. It was Sun's biggest hit to date.

Presley's version of "Blue Suede Shoes," also a hit, shortens Perkins's intro by eliminating the pauses after "one for the money" and "two for the show" and has a clean, rehearsed ending. Perkins's ending, on all three takes, seems to fall apart, as is true of a great deal of his band's Sun recordings; it seems that Clayton's bass always tries to have the last word.

Besides Presley, others hastened to release versions of "Blue Suede Shoes." Boyd Bennett and his Rockets (their "Seventeen" made no. 5 the year before), Jim Lowe (soon to hit with "Green Door"), Lawrence Welk (the "champagne music" bandleader who had just started his long-running TV variety show), Sam "the Man" Taylor (noted saxophonist), and the Pee Wee King Band (he was a western swing bandleader, accordionist, and writer of the "Tennessee Waltz"), as well as Jerry Mercer, Bob Roubian and Cliffie Stone, Sid King and the Five Strings, and Roy Hall. Hall also did "You Ruined My Blue Suede Shoes," while Homer and Jethro did a clever parody in "Two Tone Shoes."

The success of "Blue Suede Shoes" put the Perkins band in great demand for live appearances. In March exhaustion was a factor in a car accident en route to New York for the Perry Como TV show. Carl and Jay were hurt, and their appearance was postponed while they convalesced in hospital. Carl recovered fairly quickly, apparently starting a *Big D Jamboree* tour one month later in Beaumont, Texas, but Jay was more seriously injured. The band recorded again within three months, with a replacement for Jay, who was able to tour again after about six months. The setback occurred at a time when national TV exposure would have boosted Carl's career tremendously. As it turned out, further success was elusive. The loss of momentum resulting from the accident is surely a factor, although probably not as big a one as it is often made out to be. The fact is, actual rockabilly by anyone had scant success on the charts.

"Honey Don't," the flip side of "Blue Suede Shoes," came from the same session. A warm-up take includes the line "I know you can even if you don't," which is not found in the issued take. Carl interjects "hang on children let's rock" before the guitar solo. This song contains a C chord (the bVI) in the key of E, Carl's first recorded use of a chord outside the standard few found in most harmonically simple music. He was to use uncommon harmonies in subsequent songs, like the descending chord progression found in his Sun recording of "Pink Pedal Pushers" from 1957 (B–A–G–F-sharp, two beats each, in the key of B). The progression was not used his Columbia recording of the same song the following year.[12]

In "Tennessee" the chorus is sung in two-part harmony: "let's give old Tennessee credit for music as they play it up in Nashville . . . in that old hillbilly way." The only Tennessee artist mentioned is Eddy Arnold. The last verse is surreal, reminding the "folks" that "they made their first atomic bomb in Tennessee." It is curious that Nashville's music scene, a pop country singer, and a bomb are the things a "country boy" from Jackson, recording in Memphis, would find to be proud of in his home state.

The rockabilly boom and his own initial success led Carl to write about their effects on others and himself. At a session in March 1956 (just before the car accident), each of the four songs—"Perkins Wiggle," "Boppin' the Blues," "All Mama's Children," and "Everybody's Trying to Be My Baby"—commented on these phenomena. "Perkins Wiggle," based on Glenn Miller's 1940 million-seller "Tuxedo Junction," is a celebration of rockabilly, the South, and a boogie-woogie-playing Tennessee woman with a "rhythm that rocks." He accurately gives himself a certain credit for the "red hot rhythm we don't understand." Stuttering is added to Carl's already large vocabulary of vocal embellishments when he sings "d-dixie bop" (a good contemporary description of rockabilly).

In "Boppin' the Blues," his second hit (no. 70), potent music (bop, R&B, and rock are named) provides a healing power: "the doctor told me, Carl you don't need no pills, just a handful of nickels, the jukebox'll cure your ills." This works not only for him but for grandpa, who "got rhythm and blues, he threw his crutches down," the lyrics thus contributing to the large body of songs on the theme of grandpas and grandmas trying to cope with young music or ways.

In "All Mama's Children" "they" (and sometimes "we") "want to roll, want to rock, want to bop 'til they pop." With the nursery rhyme image of the Old Lady in the Shoe, we see the effect of rockabilly on country folks and children. The drums are particularly interesting and well executed. Using no cymbals, W. S. Holland does strong snare work and tasteful fills on the tom-toms.

At this session Perkins self-consciously begins trying to solidify his commercial standing; in "All Mama's Children" there are two mentions of a "blue suede shoe." "Everybody's Trying to Be My Baby" has the same kind of intro as "Blue Suede Shoes," and both songs are twelve-bar blues with the same pattern of stops on the first three bars and a fill in the fourth.

Although Carl Perkins takes composer credit for "Everybody's Trying to Be My Baby," the song apparently originated with country singer Rex Griffin in the mid-1930s. A version by country stars the York Brothers, credited to Webb Pierce and Johnny Mathis, was recorded in 1957. Perkins's version was recorded the year before but not issued until 1958, when it appeared on his first album. His verses are about women vying for his attention, very likely not a fantasy. The lyrics tell of him being awakened at four-thirty in the morning by "fifteen women knocking at my door" who seem never to leave him alone; they are not after his looks or his brains, but, he figures, they probably want his heart, or at least a ride in his car.

The darker side of rocking—alcohol, intoxication, violence, encounters with the law—is seldom covered, and nowhere as sequentially as in "Dixie Fried," which describes a character who goes to the local night spot at 5 A.M., where he pulls out a quart of liquor from his pocket, urging on the party with shouts of "rave on! the cops are gone, let's get Dixie fried" (drunk). He gets excited and pulls out a razor. The people get out of his way because he has a reputation for violence. The shouting brings the police, and they take him away. The revelers admire his bravery at not being intimidated by authority. From jail he throws a note to his girlfriend claiming innocence. Still urging his listeners to continue to party, he admits to being "Dixie fried"—in this case not just drunk but apprehended.

In many of the recordings made subsequent to the accident, there are changes in approach. Not only is there a string of cover versions of country songs, but the band's sound is enlarged by the addition of a pianist and of cymbals to the drummer's kit. Also, Presley's influence is surely being expressed in three 12/8 ballads. One of them, "Keeper of the Key," has a recitation, constant closed high-hat triplets, increased echo, and arpeggiating cocktail piano; chorus singers are conspicuous in their absence.

With "That Don't Move Me" Perkins returned to original material in the piano-less rockabilly style, although the cymbals are retained. The famous "Matchbox" is credited to him, but it is just a blues that uses three traditional blues couplets; the matchbox couplet dates at least as far back as Blind Lemon Jefferson's 1927 recording and survived in many versions, including the 1938 recording by Roy Newman and his Boys, a western swing band from Jefferson's home state of Texas.

"Your True Love," recorded in January 1957 with Jerry Lee Lewis at the piano, was aimed and fired at the marketplace, hitting number sixty-seven, aided by the effect provided by speeding up the tape. A chorus of band members answers the opening phrases and sings "aaahs" thereafter. To date it was the most pop-styled song Carl had composed (with its AABA form and circle-of-fifths B section).

The session of January 30, 1957, was hot and wild, and the band delivered intense, fierce, rocking music, including "Put Your Cat Clothes On." Years later Perkins claimed that he had never heard the recording, that he did not know what the song was about or how it started, and that he had made it up in the studio while drunk with the band trying to follow along.[13] Maybe that's why it took them eleven takes to get it right, but right it was: it is one of his best songs, period. When it was finally released in the 1970s, it became a call to dress up for revival fans.

Perkins last Sun single was "Glad All Over" backed with "Lend Me Your Comb," released December 31, 1957. It failed to generate much interest. In 1982, when I was rooting through the piles of unsold Sun records in the dimly lit warehouse at the back of a Memphis record store, I found boxes and boxes of them.

In January 1958 Perkins joined Columbia, hoping that the change of company would lead to success. He signed a five-year contract at 6 percent. Johnny Cash joined then, too, and got the same terms. Jay Perkins played the first Columbia sessions, before his death from a brain tumor, a complication from the crash.

Carl's success with a footwear theme made him try again with additional fashion songs. After "Blue Suede Shoes" he had "Put Your Cat Clothes On," "Lend Me Your Comb," and "Pink Pedal Pushers." The first Columbia single was a remake of "Pink Pedal Pushers," and it had commercial success, but barely: a solitary week on the charts, hitting number ninety-one. With this small encouragement there followed "Levi Jacket" and back to footwear with "Pointed Toe Shoes," which again hit the charts, this time for two weeks: number ninety-three in 1959. Thus three of Perkins's chart entries were about apparel. More teen themes were tried, "Pop, Let Me Have the Car," "Rockin' Record Hop," and "Jive after Five," all classic Perkins rockabilly. A total of eleven singles came out on Columbia; only the first two hit the charts. The growing awareness that nothing much was happening in his career, coupled with grief over the loss of his brother Jay, led to a period of alcoholism.

His first Columbia album, *Whole Lotta Shakin'*, contains not one Perkins original. In fact, it could almost have been called *Carl Perkins Does Rock 'n' Roll Standards;* it was supposed to reflect his live show. There are four covers of Little Richard hits, two of Elvis's Sun sides, and "Whole Lotta Shakin' Goin' On," "Shake, Rattle and Roll," and "I Got a Woman." To round it out, there is a country standard ("Hey, Good Lookin'"), a blues standard ("Sittin' on Top of the World"), and a surprise: an obscure rockabilly gem, "Where the Rio de Rosa Flows," although Perkins completely missed out on the intense atmosphere of Jimmy Lloyd's original. Despite Perkins's enthusiastic performances, some of the tempos race along, and the songs come out with a sameness not found in the hit versions. There are only two keys used, A for seven songs and E for five. Eight of the songs use the twelve-bar blues structure, each accompanied by a walking bass. Almost everything is well placed and well played, aside from a missed cue here and there, and the band (the three brothers with W. S. Holland, their last time together in the studio) does fall apart on a few endings, with the upright bass trailing on a bit longer as usual. Added to the band is piano and, on half the songs, a tenor sax. It sounds as if they recorded it in an afternoon; actually all but two of the songs were recorded in a two-day period in June 1958. It reminds me of seeing Perkins in the 1980s, when he did a long medley of rock 'n' roll standards (some of the same ones from this album), rounding off their edges until there was little character left, just different lyrics sung over relentless repetitions of the blues form.

All is not lost on this album, however: on "Whole Lotta Shakin' Goin' On" and "I Got a Woman" everything fits into place beautifully. "Shake, Rattle and Roll," with its fine, authoritative guitar playing, is marred only by the unusual slant given to some of the lyrics: "I believe to my soul you're the devil and now I know" becomes "I believe to the devil you're the devil . . . ," and the "one-eyed cat peepin' in' in a seafood store" becomes the less sensible ". . . seafood door." The change in the last line, however, is intriguing: "*we* don't do nothing to save *our* doggone souls." Women, incidentally, are referred to as "chickens" on a number of songs.

One of the best songs recorded at these sessions was not released until the 1980s: "Because You're Mine," an original. Despite a teen slant ("too young to know the meaning of love"), it is classic Perkins rockabilly. It contains another of his unusual chord progressions: in the doubled (twenty-four-bar) blues progression in the key of A, two bars of the E chord (V) are followed by two bars of F (♭VI), and they stick out like a welcome visitor to the album's total reliance on the standard I, IV, and V chords. After this album, with few exceptions, Perkins recorded mostly country and pop songs—some excellent and some not—that need not be discussed here.

In 1963 his contract with Columbia ended, and Perkins worked for a series of other labels, returning for a second stint on Columbia. In the fall of 1964 he toured England (with Chuck Berry), where he recorded, appeared on TV, and met many loyal fans. He returned to England twice in 1965. The Beatles knew many of Perkins's songs, and three of them appeared on their albums, thus providing him with royalties. A very prolific writer, by 1978 he had published over 360 titles, many of them sentimental and autobiographical country songs.

Perkins joined the Johnny Cash show in January 1965, and in October he and Cash quit their addictions, to alcohol and pills, respectively, and became born-again Christians, each receiving moral support from the other.[14] The show toured all over the world. After Cash's guitarist Luther Perkins (no relation) died accidentally in 1968, Carl Perkins also became a member of the Tennessee Three on stage. His composition "Daddy Sang Bass" was a big hit for Cash. Perkins quit the show in 1976.

Perkins now performs with his sons Greg and Stan, carrying on the family band. Recent albums mix remakes of some of his better-known tunes with newer originals.

Carl Perkins's stature in the eyes of his fans and fellow musicians is evident in the 1986 concert video *Blue Suede Shoes,* where he was joined by, among others, George Harrison, Ringo Starr, Eric Clapton, Rosanne Cash, and Dave Edmunds. Perkins was inducted into the Rock and Roll Hall of Fame in 1987.

In 1991, right after finishing the album *Friends, Family and Legends,* recorded in New York and Nashville, Perkins was diagnosed with throat cancer and was cured through radiation treatment. The next year Perkins traded licks with Scotty Moore on *706 ReUnion: A Sentimental Journey,* a mostly instrumental album cut at the reopened Sun studios. Perkins compositions have done particularly well in the country market: "Restless," by the New Nashville Cats, "Silver and Gold," by Dolly Parton, and "Let Me Tell You about Love," by the Judds, were all hits, the last leading to nearly a year of touring alongside the Judds.[15]

WARREN SMITH

Born February 7, 1933, Humphreys County, Mississippi; died January 30, 1980, Longview, Texas

Warren Smith's limited success in the marketplace was not equal in measure to his attributes and ambition. His expressive voice—distinctive, dignified, and controlled—worked equally well in rockabilly or country (which he preferred). Although Smith was neither prolific as a writer nor notable as a guitarist, his nearly two dozen 1950s recordings nonetheless are highly regarded, for they carry his individual artistic stamp.

For more than a year Smith sang with the Clyde Leoppard Band at the Cotton Club in West Memphis, Arkansas. One night, on a tip from Carl Perkins, Sam Phillips and Johnny Cash came by to check him out. Cash mentioned that he had a song called "Rock 'n' Roll Ruby," and they invited Smith to record it. "I took my Ruby jukin' on the outskirts of town"; thus begins a portrait of a wild, independent woman who knows what she wants—to rock, that is, to dance—and cannot get enough of it. At 4 A.M. she wants to continue just a little bit more. No one at the juke joint can get enough of observing her. The catchy chorus of "rock 'n' roll Ruby, rock 'n' roll" no doubt helped the song to become a local number-one hit in 1956. Bob Neal, Elvis's manager at the time, booked Smith for personal appearances, and he put together a band with Marcus Van Story on bass, Al Hopson on lead, and Jimmy Lott on drums. The band stayed together for years, performing regularly on the *Louisiana Hayride* and doing countless one-nighters in package shows, touring throughout the South in a 1954 Cadillac.

Van Story, like others including Haley's bass player and Dorsey Burnette, performed antics with his instrument: riding it like a horse, spinning it, lying down and holding it above him with his feet, and stepping on the peg while the bass was lying on its side, causing it to rise into his awaiting hand. At some shows Van Story doubled as the master of ceremonies. He remembered selling color photos of Elvis in 1955 during intermission.

For performances of "Ubangi Stomp," the rockabilly side of Warren Smith's second Sun record, Van Story would hang a small skull from his bass. The lyrics of this song tell the story of a sailor who lands in Africa and watches dancing natives. Invited to participate, he beats a tom-tom and becomes so entranced with the all-night rocking and the chief's daughter that he wants to remain behind when the captain calls to return to the ship. Several other rockabilly songs talk about learning to dance or rock while in the company of beings in or from exotic locales, for example, Billy Lee Riley's Martians in "Flyin' Saucers Rock 'n' Roll" ("the little green mens [*sic*] taught me how to do the bop") and Hank Mizell's African animals in "Jungle Rock" ("a knocked-out beat and I had to move my feet").

Warren Smith's taste in songs reveals not only his country music leanings, with the traditional "Black Jack David" and songs learned from Hank Williams and Hank Snow (he was able to imitate both vocally), but also an involvement with black music. He covered songs by Big Maybelle and Slim Harpo and incorporated traditional blues lines in his composition "Miss Froggie."

One of Smith's best rockabilly songs is "Uranium Rock," composed by his guitarist, Al Hopson, who plays an insistent, repetitive riff. The singer, tiring of low-paying work, imagines finding a uranium rock with his Geiger counter, cashing in on the uranium prospecting fad in the mid-1950s atomic era.[16] His find provides him with a Cadillac (no red light can make him stop) and lots of

> Money, money honey, yeah the kind you fold
> Money, money honey, rock 'n' roll
> Rake it in, bale it up like hay
> Have a rockin' good time, throw it all away

Smith left Sun because of lack of releases, royalties, and promotion. Energy was being concentrated on Jerry Lee Lewis, and besides,

Smith wanted to do more country material. He moved to California and had seven country hits for Liberty (1960–64); during the same time he performed on the *Grand Ole Opry* for two years. In 1965 an auto accident slowed his career efforts, although he continued to record for small labels. In 1977 he recorded an album in Dallas, near his new home.

Smith had not played live in five years when he appeared (and was recorded) in 1977 at London's Rainbow Theatre. He was awed by the response of the thousands of British rockabilly fans there, who gave him his first standing ovation. Unfortunately, the characteristics that make his 1950s canon so interesting—vocal control, individuality, song selection—are not inspiring in these later recordings. His voice sounds tired and sometimes falters, and the repertory is primarily remakes of his earlier recordings and the most common covers. He returned to Europe but did not enjoy the revival for long, for he died of a heart attack in 1980.

BILLY LEE RILEY

Born October 5, 1933, Pocahontas, Arkansas

Billy Lee Riley is a versatile musical chameleon. He has been a session musician on harmonica, lead guitar, rhythm guitar, bass, and drums. He has composed and sung various shades of country, rock, and blues, and he knew his way around a studio and the record business enough to record for close to twenty labels, some of them his own.

Riley grew up in various Arkansas towns. After two stints in the army, where he started playing hillbilly music, he moved to Memphis in 1955. His association with Jack Clement, as members of Slim Wallace's Dixie Ramblers, led to a demo recording. It in turn led to both of them working for Sun, Riley as an artist and session musician and Clement as a producer who also recorded a handful of songs. Between 1956 and 1959 six Billy Riley singles were released (the Lee was added in the 1960s). His success with "Red Hot" led to touring in the United States and Canada. His band of Pat O'Neill (replacing Marvin Pepper) on bass, Jimmy Wilson on piano, Martin Willis on sax, Roland Janes on guitar, and J. M. Van Eaton on drums backed lots of Sun artists on tour and in the studio over several years. They never rehearsed for sessions, working up the arrangements in the studio with whomever they were backing. Janes called it "organized looseness."[17]

Riley and Sam Phillips had a lot of differences, particularly about promotion. One night Riley went on a rampage in the studio: "Sam and I fought all the time—we probably got along worse than anybody. . . . We still respected each other's talent but he didn't respect me enough to promote me. . . . After I wrecked the studio and we got to drinkin' and talkin' all through the night. . . . he said 'I can't let you get a hit record—if you do you'll take your band and leave.' He said it as a joke—but it was true. We were the band at Sun Records, and he didn't want to lose us."[18]

Riley's first three Sun singles transcend their influences and are the foundation of his reputation. His first single was "Rock with Me Baby" backed with "Trouble Bound," both original compositions, both showing Elvis's influence, and both using the uncommon shuffle beat mentioned in connection with Presley's "I Forgot to Remember to Forget."

The second single, in 1957, featured "Flying Saucers Rock 'n' Roll." The song's composer, Ray Scott, was inspired to write it after seeing a flying saucer. It was Phillips's idea to have the label read "Billy Riley and his Little Green Men." In this song Riley introduced his rasping voice, a sore-throat style of singing. The much-admired guitar intro is provided by Roland Janes. Piano is by Jerry Lee Lewis from his very short period as a session player. The flip side, "I Want You Baby," written by Riley on the spot, has an Orbison touch and does not sound as if it were sung by the hoarse man on the A side.

On the third single, also from 1957, Riley sings in a nervous, assertive, frantic, throaty rasp, almost an articulated scream. "Red Hot" originally was an R&B song from two years earlier by Billy "the Kid" Emerson on Sun; Riley made it a rockabilly standard. It has been covered by Bob Luman, Ronnie Hawkins, Sleepy LaBeef, and a host of revival bands. In the lyrics a man describes his partner's attributes to skeptical listeners. Riley kept only the following lines from Emerson's refrain (answering voices are in parentheses): "My gal is red hot (your gal ain't doodly squat) [twice] / She ain't got a lot of money, but lovin' she's really got a lot," (although he changed the last line to "she ain't got no money, but man she's really got a lot"). In Emerson's version the partner is appealing because she can dance and because she is obedient, smart, not too tall (five feet), and sexually experienced—*and* she is red hot. Riley, however, describes the girlfriend's negative qualities: she stays out all night, talks too much, wants her own way, is lazy and loose, is unusually tall (6'4": note the sixteen-inch difference in height between these women)—*but* she is red hot. Only one verse by Riley describes the woman favorably—"Well she's a one man's woman that's what I like, not a wishy washy woman change her mind every night." Compared to Emerson's song, Riley's compresses several elements—vocal range, melodic function, and timing—making for a very tense, forceful, charging performance. Emerson's vocal range spans two octaves, whereas Riley's spans only a tritone. Emerson's opening phrases were eight beats long; Riley's is only six. In the 1980s neither Riley nor drummer Van Eaton performed "Red Hot" using this elimination of beats: the longer form is easier.

The flip side, "Pearly Lee," is derived from "The Girl Can't Help It," by Little Richard, whom Riley used to impersonate in his stage shows. It features, not surprisingly on account of its source, the first appearance of saxophone on a Riley recording. Not only was it the last of the sessions to include Jerry Lee Lewis, who graced both 1957 singles, but it was probably the last one produced by Sam Phillips.

"Wouldn't You Know," the fourth single, never quite seems to gel, at times veering to one style and then to another. A brief sojourn on Brunswick yielded one single—"Rockin' on the Moon" backed with "Is That All to the Ball, Mr. Hall"—recorded in Nashville in May 1958. The latter is a fair rocker that exists primarily as a vehicle for delivering lines with triple rhymes, like the title. "Rockin' on the Moon," written by Vic McAlpin, is another outer-space theme, but this time Riley is there in a dream. A cute soprano sax chirps over a constantly trilling tenor sax. The queen of the lunar rockers has eyes in the back of her head: "couldn't tell where she was going, but she knows where she's been." A few months later Riley lifted the line for use in "No Name Girl."

His last Sun single coupled "One More Time," an excellent "rockaballad" that Riley considers to be the best song he recorded in the 1950s, with a hard-driving "Got the Water Boiling."

The search for success seemed to drive Riley to record whatever seemed to be commercial at the time. His first demos in 1952 were country, including a song by Hank Williams, then his idol. He recorded rockabilly from 1955 to 1957, and then in the next two years drifted toward instrumentals, rocked-up traditional songs like "Down by the Riverside" and "Swanee River," and lightweight songs like "No Name Girl." In the last he shows a penchant for modulating, a concept he revived with a passion for his derivative 1969 sides: soul, funk, and Creedence Clearwater Revival imitations. In between those periods Riley covered R&B hits, played blues, went on the road, did sessions, got into the record business, and moved to California.

The revival took Riley to Europe (1979), as well as to Memphis festivals, where I saw him in action. In the summer of 1991 Riley hit the road again for well-received shows in Maryland, New York, and

Arkansas. The next year was a big one. An acclaimed new album, *Blue Collar Blues,* was cut at Sam Phillips's Madison Avenue studio, with J. M. Van Eaton and Roland Janes from the old Little Green Men band backing him on a few tracks. The Smithsonian Institution filmed him for a documentary. Bob Dylan had him open several shows, introducing him as a favorite. The crowd went crazy for him.

In 1993 Riley played at the eleventh Hemsby festival in England, topping the bill along with Mac Curtis, Janis Martin, and Richard Berry (composer of "Louie Louie"). Riley also has been playing dates around Memphis and doing some more recording.

SONNY BURGESS

Born May 28, 1931, Newport, Arkansas

Albert "Sonny" Burgess is one of rockabilly's greats, another triple-threat performer: vocalist, lead guitarist, and composer of most of his recorded repertory. He grew up on a farm, and his birthplace, eighty miles from Memphis, has remained his home. His first guitar was a mail-order Gene Autry model from Sears and Roebuck. His first musical love was country music, and an early performance was on a Hadacol Medicine Show in Arkansas, headlined by Wayne Raney and Lonnie Glosson. As a teenager Burgess had a good collection of blues and R&B records. His first professional job in music, lasting about a year, was as lead guitarist in the band of (then unknown) country singer Freddie Hart. In 1954, after army duty in Germany, Burgess formed the Moonlighters with local musicians, playing country and western swing and adding rockabilly as it became popular. In October 1955 they were booked as the opening act when Elvis Presley appeared in Newport, which led to further engagements with him.

Burgess and his band, by then calling themselves the Pacers, first recorded on May 2, 1956, at Sun. Although Burgess never had a national hit, the first record, "Red Headed Woman" backed with "We Wanna Boogie," reportedly sold over 90,000 copies, and other releases were hits in regional markets. The six-piece band was very popular for its wild live show—a couple of times Burgess was decked out entirely in red: shoes, socks, shirt, suit, guitar, and dyed red hair—and toured extensively with label mates Johnny Cash and Roy Orbison (whom Burgess sounds like on "You're Not the One for Me"). The atmospheric "Restless," Burgess's second single, uses an eight-bar progression of C–F–G–C (two bars each) over which the piano plays a hypnotic figure, Burgess sings and whistles, and the band sings "aah" rhythmically.

Many of Sonny Burgess's recordings have an exuberant, fun quality, and the arrangements are often clever and effective. The Pacers were a great band: Ray Kern Kennedy on piano, Joe Lewis on guitar, Jack Nance on trumpet, John Ray Hubbard on bass, and Russell Smith on drums. (For recordings in 1958 and 1959, Burgess was backed by session players.)

Although many of the Burgess recordings use the common blues progression, the players bring such vitality and variety that these cuts are among the most enjoyable in rockabilly. For instance, "Ain't Got a Thing" has the trumpet, the band answering the humorous lyrics (common for Burgess but rare elsewhere in rockabilly), and a key change (from C up to F); "Fannie Brown" uses the quarter-note triplet figure found in Louis Jordan's "Caldonia."

Burgess's contract at Sun ended in 1960. When he joined Conway Twitty's touring band, first as a guitarist and later on electric bass, he rejoined former Pacers Jack Nance and Joe Lewis. Nance had played trumpet in the Pacers, but in Twitty's band he played drums, later switching to piano. In 1958 Nance had coauthored Twitty's breakthrough hit "It's Only Make Believe." Back home the Pacers continued under drummer Bobby Crafford.

Twitty was born in Mississippi in 1933 and died in 1993, a beloved superstar who saw more than forty of his recordings hit number one on the country charts. Under his real name, Harold Jenkins, he recorded (unissued) rockabilly for Sun. After leaving Sun (and changing his name) he recorded rockabilly for Mercury and then MGM. His warm and expressive voice, obviously influenced by Presley, was nevertheless distinct. "Long Black Train" is a strong, enjoyable performance. It has the intro of "Orange Blossom Special"; the theme, guitar style, group sound, and vocal delivery of Presley's "Mystery Train"; and the melody and words of his "My Baby Left Me."

Burgess soon left Twitty and teamed up with Larry Donn. In 1964 Burgess recorded four singles for Bobby Crafford's Razorback label with a band called Kings IV that included Kern Kennedy and also featured an organ. The uniform was Beatles-style collarless jackets. Later issued in France as Sonny Burgess and Bobby Crafford, *Country Rock,* selections include covers of rock 'n' roll standards, with "Lawdy Miss Clawdy" and "Willie and the Hand Jive" taken at rather fast tempos; the band sounds eager to get them over with in a hurry. There is a driving if basic blues instrumental and an uptempo remake of "Restless," which retains the whistling and adds an overdose of fuzz guitar. More successful are "Mary Lou," with driving eighth-note bass figures starting each verse, "School Days," and the 12/8 ballad "Lonely

Hours." "Is It Wrong" is a standout track, a country ballad that had been Warner Mack's first hit in 1957. W. C. Handy's "St. Louis Blues" gets a slow and bluesy treatment with the organ obviously influenced by the Animals' "House of the Rising Sun."

After recording in 1968 for Roland Janes's Rolando label, Burgess drifted into musical retirement and did not record again until 1976, when he was reunited with the Pacers for an album-in-a-day for Lake County Records of Switzerland. *The Old Gang* is mostly a run-through (perhaps "walk-through" is more accurate) of rock 'n' roll standards plus a couple of covers of country hits, one being "According to My Heart," a 1956 hit for Jim Reeves.

Burgess made occasional appearances at Memphis music festivals and shows in the 1980s. In 1984 he made his first visit to England for a festival appearance, returning the next year, when he recorded sessions backed by the Dave Travis Band. In the late 1980s Burgess became a member of the Sun Rhythm Section, which I discuss in chapter 13.

An album of home studio demos, called *I'm Still Here*, was made available about 1990 but does little for Burgess's reputation. The mix is strange (guitar is very distant), a drum machine spoils the proceedings, especially on "The Prisoner's Song" and "Red River Valley," and although Burgess again, as he had on Sun, does the original, "dirty" version of "One Night" ("of sin is what I'm now paying for" rather than "with you is what I'm now praying for"), the sax played through a distortion unit is quite superfluous. A superior effort is *Tennessee Border* from 1992, where Burgess is teamed with ex-Blaster Dave Alvin, who produced the record and played guitar.

JERRY LEE LEWIS
Born September 29, 1935, Ferriday, Louisiana

Jerry Lee Lewis is one of the most fascinating of rockabilly's pantheon. He is complex, charismatic, talented, unique, and tormented. He is tortured by the conflict between his religious beliefs and his love of music, women, and whiskey. For Lewis, only two possible destinations are available after death, heaven (the desired one, attainable only if he can change his way of living) or hell (the probable one, for he likely cannot).[19]

We know so much about him: the stories, the records, the concerts, the biographies, the movie. As a boy he watched black musicians at the local club, as a wild teenager he gigged in rough joints, and then came short tenures in Bible college and as a salesman. Pursuing his musical ambitions, he took an exploratory trip to the *Louisiana Hayride,* where he cut an acetate disc at an audition.[20] Following a short stay in Nashville, he went to Memphis and tried out for Sun, where he did sessions and his first record. Then came touring, TV shows, hits, marriages, England and the child bride scandal, and a boycott.[21] With great determination he went back to the club circuit and built his career again with country music hits. Along the way are the tales of pills and other excesses, erratic behavior, and deaths in the family and his own close calls. Later years have brought accolades, tax problems, exile and return, and continued touring.

Lewis's voluminous discography and huge performance repertory show him to be a living library of songs covering a vast spectrum of music from more than the last 100 years. While at Sun, from 1956 to 1963, he recorded more than 160 different songs. An examination of their sources reveals the following, in descending order of percentages: country and old-timey hits, rock 'n' roll hits, traditional songs (some dating to the nineteenth century), gospel songs, blues standards, R&B hits, and pop and jazz standards. Also well represented are songs written for him by Otis Blackwell (five, plus one cowritten) and by writers from the Sun stable of talent, especially Jack Clement (four), as well as by other writers of varied backgrounds.

Lewis himself composed only six (and cowrote two more) of the songs; he says that composing takes too much out of a person and claims it to have been the cause of Hank Williams's death.[22] Judging by Lewis's use of spoken language, he would have made a good lyricist, as evidenced by quotations such as "I am what I am and not what they want me to be. Why, I'm so unpredictable" and "I never heard a song I didn't like. I never seen a woman I didn't love."[23] Some of his sayings have been woven into lyrics for him by others. One song he did compose was "End of the Road," from his first session in November 1956: "what the heck we don't want no moon . . . don't give me no sass . . . I don't care if I never get home."

Lewis's musical heroes are represented by their songs in his Sun recordings: Hank Williams (ten songs covered), Jimmie Rodgers (two), and Gene Autry (two). Another of his musical heroes was Al Jolson, although Lewis, in this period at least, recorded no songs associated with him. Lewis did cover songs associated with the following artists: Elvis Presley (five songs covered); Carl Perkins (four); and three songs each by Fats Domino, Warren Smith, Chuck Berry, and Floyd Tillman.

Lewis is a stylist, an artist whose forte is an individual approach that can adapt all manner of songs. Although he requires his bands and

audiences to accept an incredibly diverse range of songs, he is so assured that he willingly takes on any number of clichés. Some fans feel
that a song has not really lived until it has had the Lewis treatment.

Guitar is usually the central instrument in rockabilly; bass is almost always present. Jerry Lee Lewis's work is an exception, however: his style is unequivocally based on his piano playing. Starting in
1957 his singles were credited to Jerry Lee Lewis and his Pumping
Piano. On various songs—"Great Balls of Fire" is one—there is only
the duet of Lewis's piano and vocal and J. M. Van Eaton's drums. Both
men usually are interesting rhythmically, whereas Roland Janes, who
often played electric guitar at sessions, is often hesitant and rhythmically mushy. Janes's musical ideas are good, just not terribly ambitious. The electric bass playing, where present, is generally func-
tional and supportive, although sometimes nearly inaudible.

J. M. (James Mack) Van Eaton, born in 1937 in Memphis, became
one of a small group of Sun studio musicians in the late 1950s. He
had played drums in the school band and in a student Dixieland
band, and while he was a senior in high school, another band he
was in paid to cut Presley-influenced demos at Sun. He, along with
bass player Marvin Pepper, was asked to come back. Van Eaton remembers his first session as Jimmy Williams's "Fire Engine Red,"
which dates it as June 1956. Six months later Van Eaton played on
Jerry Lee Lewis's debut record, "Crazy Arms." Thereafter Van Eaton
played on almost all Lewis's songs, as well as on much of the other
material recorded at Sun until the early 1960s; in the discography
he is listed on hundreds of sessions with over forty singers. He is an
extremely versatile and sensitive musician with a readily recognizable style, a simple but influential one that proved to be difficult to
copy. His drumming is the basis for much of the later rockabilly
sound at Sun. "My basic change and contribution to this stuff is that
shuffle on the cymbal. The patterns that I play with the right hand
doubling with the shuffle of the left hand was, to me, one of the biggest changes in rhythm in music for us down here, and fortunately
people liked it; it was a change for the better. We sold lots of records.
I guess that's my claim to fame if you want to call it that."[24]

On some songs Van Eaton plays his pattern absolutely consistently throughout, without any fills (e.g., Warren Smith's "So Long I'm
Gone"and Malcolm Yelvington's "Trumpet"), yet on other songs he
can be particularly inventive with his fills. His taste is remarkable,
as are his ideas. He is careful with the tone of his snare and bass
drums, preferring a slightly dead sound, laying his wallet on the snare
and using tape or towels to dampen both. The timbre he thus creat-

ed and came to prefer was actually a by-product of necessity: it was important to lower the drums' volume in the tiny studio to diminish the sound bleeding into other microphones. One microphone was used for both drums and acoustic or electric bass. Van Eaton's kit consisted of a snare, one floor tom, high hats, a ride cymbal, and a distinctive bass drum with a homemade calfskin drumhead, with black-and-white fur still attached.

Jerry Lee Lewis's piano playing is wonderfully fluid, rhythmic, musical, and full of flourishes. Some potent trademarks, especially for intros and turnarounds, come from various sources and his own invention. He has a number of pianistic devices at his command: arpeggios, tremolos, and glissandi, as well as blues licks and boogie bass figures. His playing exhibits elements of church music and honky-tonk influences of players like Moon Mullican. Lewis also acknowledges the influence and inspiration of Del Wood. Like most primarily self-taught pianists, he prefers certain keys: C, F, G, and less often, D and B-flat. His command of the piano and his confident, passionate playing contrast with his seeming contempt for the instrument as furniture: he hammers it with his fist, plays it with his feet, sits on the keys, walks on the keys, stands on it, kicks away the stool, and sets the piano aflame, so the legend goes. It is not that he despises the piano's traditional propriety; it is merely that the piano is a prop for his showmanship.

Lewis has been so prolific in the recording studio that three multivolume box sets have been released, each representing a different phase of his career. Thanks to the Sun Box collection, eleven CDs of Jerry Lee Lewis covering 1956 to 1963, we are privy to a great number of working sessions. For the privilege, we must accept those moments where the musicians are obviously feeling their way, making mistakes while reaching for an arrangement. In the multiple versions that exist for some songs, we can hear overdubs and changes in tempo, style, instrumentation, and key. Some are fully realized renditions, but in many cases the song is dropped before a first-class reading is achieved; nonetheless, some of these rougher or flawed takes have a fabulous feel.

Recordings by Lewis that I find to be artistically successful are those showing a certain intensity, sincerity, and commitment of delivery, combined with appropriate musical choices of tempo, form, instrumentation, and so on. Included in this large number are "End of the Road," "Deep Elem Blues," "Whole Lotta Shakin' Goin' On," "Great Balls of Fire, "Break Up" (single version), and "Hillbilly Music," released first in 1962 on Lewis's second album.

Lewis's free command of his voice is akin to the qualities of a jazz singer, although his vocal assurance and emotional involvement vary from song to song. As Lewis becomes more familiar with a tune, his delivery gets more confident and the phrasing gets more deliberate, as can be heard in successive takes of "It'll Be Me." His singing style is notable in his versions of two R&B hits. In the Dominoes' "Sixty Minute Man" he exhibits a large variety of expressive devices used very freely but always under control. Lewis is flexible and fluid with his rhythms and pitches, swooping up to notes and gliding down. Besides simplifying both the form and the lyrics, he changes bass vocalist Bill Brown's "look-a here girls" original opening line to "listen here boys"—from inviting to bragging. In Lewis's version of the Midnighters' "Sexy Ways," called "Cool Cool Ways," he growls, swoops, sings falsetto, fills up the spaces with excessive repetition of words and syllables (some unintelligible), and makes many interjections and comments ("honey I can't stand much of this, mmmmmm, well"). He probably did not remember all the words. Lewis is one of the few rockabilly singers to make use of falsetto singing or yodeling, although he uses these devices sparingly. As with those of other rockabilly singers, his melodic exaggerations seem to express a flamboyance and a devil-may-care attitude.

With "Crazy Arms," at his first session, Lewis and crew established a rocking approach to country songs. Although not exactly rockabilly as commonly accepted, the performance would have been perceived as such by the audience of its time. It was a definite departure from the conventional country of the day. To my ears, it is country with elements of rock 'n' roll: country rock, if you will. Many of his recordings can be described thus. Many others can be called straight country. The ones most likely to be agreed on as rockabilly—his first and biggest hits, "Whole Lotta Shakin' Goin' On," "Great Balls of Fire," and a handful or two more—are fast songs with a combination of characteristics: simple chord progressions with melodies that lend themselves to bluesy inflections, Lewis playing and singing with wild urgent intensity, complementary drumming (Van Eaton), and usually, a guitar solo (Roland Janes).

Lewis's star rose quickly. Those first hits from 1957 went into the top five on the pop charts. The next year "Breathless"—aided by a TV promotion on Dick Clark's show—was in the top ten, and "High School Confidential"—the title of a movie containing a memorable opening scene with Lewis and band performing the song on the back of a moving truck—almost hit the top twenty. Lewis also made appearances on the *Steve Allen Show* and was in the movie *Jamboree*, along with Carl Perkins and Fats Domino, and he made several tours across America, into Canada, and to Australia.

Months later Lewis's star fell even more quickly, after a tour of England was cut short by scandal. When British reporters inquired about the young lady he was traveling with, they found out that Myra was his bride, that she was only thirteen, that she was his cousin, and that he was not yet divorced from his previous wife. With the press frothing over the sinfulness of the baby-snatching bigamist who married a cousin, fans heckled in half-filled halls and concerts were canceled. It is clear now that marrying at age thirteen was not uncommon for females in his cultural corner of the world at that time.[25] Her father was on the tour with them; he was the bass player. Lewis, being a very popular, flamboyant, grimacing, sexually charged wildman, became a scapegoat in the backlash against rock 'n' roll. The Americans were no kinder in their judgment. He was blacklisted by the industry: radio stations dropped him, and TV would not touch him. He could still draw on the live circuit, however, although his fee dropped from $10,000 to a low of $250 a night. Aside from "What'd I Say" hitting number thirty-one in 1961, his records did poorly on the pop charts.

In 1962 the British welcomed him back as the world's number-one rock singer. America took longer to forgive him, and big success returned only in the late 1960s with a string of top-ten hits on the country charts.

The softening of rock in the late 1950s addressed the young adolescent mentality. Lewis avoided most of it, keeping his musical integrity even while the lyrics of some songs—"Milkshake Mademoiselle," for example—reflected the trend; in 1961, at age twenty-six, he was singing about high school romance in "Bonnie B." He never was a love-struck puppy, however. The image he projected and was projected on him is of a person arrogantly continuing to celebrate the joys of adolescent rebellion, refusing to learn from personal experience and resisting the pain of growing up, although in songs like "39 and Holding" and "My Life Would Make a Good Country Song," his writers tailored lyrics about the realizations and reflections of growing old.

Years of touring have kept up his name and fame and claim to rock 'n' roll's throne.

In *Great Balls of Fire* (1989) actor Dennis Quaid turned Lewis into a caricature. Lewis was reportedly depressed when the movie did poorly. He moved to Ireland, and news from overseas talked about missed dates, health problems, tax troubles, and superb shows. In 1994 he moved back to the United States, where the Internal Revenue Service had claims against him for unpaid taxes and penalties to the tune of four million dollars, later reduced to one-half million. To help raise money he opened his home to tourists. The same year he signed a deal with Warner Brothers and recorded new material.

RAY SMITH

Born October 31, 1934, Melbar, Kentucky; died November 29, 1979, Burlington, Ontario

Ray Smith was the seventh son of a seventh son. Married at age eighteen, he left the air force in 1956. Back home in Paducah, Kentucky, he did one-nighters, performed on the radio, and then had his own television show for more than two years, seven nights a week. He attracted a manager who arranged a contract with Sun, where Smith had five releases, three in 1958–59 and two in 1961. The manager stayed with him until about 1964.

Although Smith played guitar and piano, he only sang on his 1950s recordings. His later recordings reveal him to be a limited pianist. Charlie Rich played piano for the sessions, and his pen contributed many songs to Smith's repertory, including both sides of his first record. "Right behind You Baby" is one of Smith's best rockabilly songs. The stop-time accents in the verse get increasingly more rhythmic over four measures; other varieties of stops appear in subsequent Smith recordings. "So Young," the flip side, is pop rockabilly with a teen theme, intriguing for the tension between the fast tempo and the slow harmonic rhythm. Three more Rich compositions done by Smith are "Why Why Why" (an Elvis-style ballad), "You Made a Hit," and "Break Up." Smith's version of "You Made a Hit" is vibrant rockabilly, whereas Rich's demo version is lackluster. In Smith's version of "Break Up," however, he coasts on the surface of the song's emotion, whereas Rich, in his own rendition, dives in.

Ray Smith had a wonderfully expressive and pliable voice enabling him playfully to use all of rockabilly's vocal devices. Even when he is overdoing them, they are not placed or performed gratuitously. He is having fun with his voice, but he is totally in control. It does give a touch of parody to almost all his Sun material; it is difficult to take him seriously, but the lyrics don't call for that, anyway. He is at his most sincere on ballads, where his vocal control can shine more evidently, as in the cover of Carl Perkins's "Forever Yours." Something of a vocal chameleon, Smith's voice can take on characteristics of Elvis and Charlie Rich. When he wants to be dramatic, he can make you think of opera.

"Rockin' Bandit," overdubbed with gunshot sound effects, was probably influenced by the Olympics' hit "Western Movies." Big and little screens in the 1950s featured lots of Hollywood cowboys and Indians, and many examples can be found of that influence in music: the Lone Ranger is quoted in "Honey Hush" ("hi ho Silver, away!"), Elvis Presley's first movie is a Western, and the Everly Brothers' "Take a Message to Mary" is a ballad about a stagecoach robber in jail. In 1966 Roy Orbison was in a movie called *Fastest Guitar in the West.*

Smith composed two of his best-loved numbers, "Shake Around" (also recorded at Sun by Tommy Blake) and the atmospheric "Willing and Ready."

In 1960, between the two periods on Sun, Smith recorded for the Judd label, run by Sam Phillips's brother Jud, who broke away to start his own company. "Rockin' Little Angel" is a song that seesaws between two chords; momentum is provided by two modulations up a semitone. It hit number one in some cities and number twenty-two nationally. On a live recording from 1962 Smith introduced "Rockin' Little Angel" as one that "did pretty good for me thanks to payola" (*Live in '62*); apparently it sold three and a half million copies. An album followed containing yet another Charlie Rich composition, "Rebound." Smith appeared on Dick Clark's *American Bandstand,* and his extensive touring included sixteen weeks in Las Vegas with Wayne Newton. Ray Smith's vocal flexibility enabled him to do imitations of many famous singers, and he did very well as a nightclub entertainer.

The album and his early 1960s singles are infused with Elvis's influence, and Ray Charles's influence is felt in "Let Yourself Go." Smith's 1964 version of Billy Brown's "Did We Have a Party" is solid rockabilly, but by then most of his rockabilly impulses had evolved into a teen pop product. This general direction neither began nor ended with Ray Smith, but it was evident in his work right from his first record, "So Young" ("too young to love"), and it appears again with "Robbin' the Cradle" ("is it strange for true love to be so young?"), which is sung in Dean Martin's drunk persona: "they szay I'm-a robbin' a cradle." "That's All Right" is another suffering from the "honey-bee syndrome," a willingness to embrace the preteen element with cute, sometimes condescending, sometimes nursery rhyme–styled lyrics about honey and bees, sugar and spice and all things nice. More songs of this type are "Little Miss Blue" and "Blond Hair, Blue Eyes" ("pretty little dimple in her chin"). Square rhythms are sung by Jordanaires-type male choruses and whitewashed female choruses, sometimes intentionally (and annoyingly) sounding like eight year olds ("Nice Guy"). There is little of the rock 'n' roll sexuality from whence came the style's name.

Of the two other singles issued from the second period at Sun, "Hey Boss Man" become a staple in Smith's live repertory, whereas "Candy Doll" is better than the title suggests. *Live in '62,* preserved through radio station tapes and lovingly released after Smith's death by John and Tommie Wix of the Ray Smith Fan Club, offers a rare chance to hear a working band in action: a benefit concert in Smith's hometown of Paducah, Kentucky. Songs from Elvis, Gene Vincent, and Jerry Lee Lewis (including "End of the Road") are mixed with Hank Williams's "I Can't Help It," Hank Ballard's "The Twist" (popularized by Chubby Checker), and Charlie Rich's "On My Knees." Only "Four Precious Years" seems out of place in this repertory, a waltz about college romance that Smith tries to sing straight-faced, a feat that his harmony singer cannot manage.

Ray Smith moved to Ontario in 1966, continuing to play the Canadian show club circuit that he had been on since 1959. Conway Twitty had pioneered this circuit, and his recommendations helped open it up for Ronnie Hawkins, Gene Simmons, and Narvel Felts.[26] In the 1970s Smith worked steadily and recorded for many labels, doing mostly country pop, and enjoyed some hits in the Canadian country charts. On late 1970s recordings put out by the Ray Smith Fan Club, he races through sloppy versions of rockabilly standards and rocked-up country standards. A painfully under-rehearsed medley of Elvis songs takes up one whole side of the *I'm Gonna Rock Some More* album.

In 1979 the revival took Smith overseas. In Holland, with Dave Travis's Bad River Band, he reprised his Sun favorites and his big hit, as well as "Rebound" and "Did We Have a Party," rounding out the set with a few classics. Later that year he committed suicide at home with a handgun.

ROY ORBISON

Born April 23, 1936, Vernon, Texas; died December 6, 1988, Hendersonville, Tennessee

"Oh, Pretty Woman," "Blue Bayou," "Crying," "Only the Lonely," and "Running Scared" are just some of Roy Orbison's 1960s hits, cherished by millions. Recorded for Monument in Nashville, most were dramatic ballads. His first records, however, were rockabilly made between 1955 and 1957, and are very distinctive.

Like Buddy Holly, who recorded two of his songs, Orbison brought a classy, assured, gentlemanly touch and a wide vocal range to his rock 'n' roll. Both Texans played lead guitar, although neither is particularly remembered for that talent, and both went through a rockabilly phase (influenced by seeing Elvis), subsequently establishing a personal, softer, and more pop style, primarily with original compositions. Both recorded with the Roses vocal group and worked with Norman Petty at his Clovis, New Mexico, studio. Orbison and Holly saw each other perform many times.

Roy Orbison was raised in Wink and Fort Worth, Texas. Biographer Ellis Amburn portrays him as a social outcast who from an early age dyed his hair black and wore sunglasses to alter his homely looks. Orbison affected an egotistical attitude to mask feelings of inadequacy. After the first spoils of success, he showed off his new car as if to say "I told you so" to those who had belittled him.

Orbison's father gave him a guitar for his fifth birthday, and Roy learned how to play from him and from an uncle; by the age of eight he was singing in public and on the radio. Around age fourteen he formed his first band, the Wink Westerners. The name, Orbison clarified, represented "'west Texas' as opposed to 'western' music because we played all kinds."[27] They toured in west Texas and New Mexico playing standards and the hits of Hank Williams, Lefty Frizzell, and the like, although Orbison's pure and controlled pop voice never exhibits on record any particular country and western inflections. It is revealing that despite later living in Nashville, he never courted the country market. On the other hand, his voice shows no strong black inflections, and he does not dip into the repertory of rockabilly vocal affectations, aside from occasional growling.

While a geology student at North Texas State University, Orbison saw Presley perform in Dallas. After winning a couple of talent shows, Orbison and the band, now known as the Teen Kings, graduated to having a fortnightly thirty-minute television show in Odessa, Texas, on which Elvis appeared in early 1955.

Later that year the band went to Petty's studio to cut a record, probably the first rock recorded there. "Ooby Dooby" was learned from fellow students Wade Moore and Dick Penner, and "Trying to Get to You" was inspired by Elvis's performances.[28] "Trying to Get to You" is very smoothly sung, sparse with just acoustic guitar, bass drum, snare drum with brushes, and a shimmer provided by electric mandolin. "Ooby Dooby" became a regional hit on the Je-Wel label and was covered by Sid King and the Five Strings, who learned it from a demo Orbison had made for Columbia records in an attempt to get a contract there.[29] The success of "Ooby Dooby," however, did lead to Orbison's contract with Sun, necessitating the band's move to Memphis. There he rerecorded the two songs, as well as over two dozen more. Some of these are rockabilly, and others point to his later style. The Sun version of "Ooby Dooby" became his first national hit in 1956, reaching number fifty-nine and getting covered by Janis Martin. Note the worked-out and repeated guitar solo, played by Orbison. The flip side, "Go Go Go," his first original composition to be recorded, became known under the title "Down the Line" through recordings by Jerry Lee Lewis and Ricky Nelson.

"Ooby Dooby" led also to appearances on the *Big D Jamboree* and Ed Sullivan's television show (June 1956). Starting in July, and continuing until 1958, Orbison toured regularly on shows with Warren Smith, Faron Young, Carl Perkins, Johnny Cash, and many others, performing from Canada to Florida to Texas.

Although three more singles were released on Sun, none was a hit. The second one, from the fall of 1956, a double coupling of solid rockabilly, put Johnny Cash's "You're My Baby" with "Rockhouse," by Harold Jenkins (Conway Twitty). "Rockhouse" became a favorite of revival bands. The third single, from January 1957, coupled "Devil Doll" with "Sweet and Easy to Love," both credited to Sam Phillips but probably penned by Orbison. Both sides show a much more pop approach, with the Roses providing "oohs" and "aahs" and chanting syllables and phrases. "Sweet and Easy to Love" and "This Kind of Love," another rocking pop song by Orbison, were covered by Sun artist Vernon Taylor.

A mid-1957 split from the Teen Kings, a band Sam Phillips admired, meant that the next recordings were made with studio players. From these October sessions came Orbison's fourth and last Sun single: "Chicken Hearted," written and produced by Bill Justis, and "I Like Love," written by Jack Clement. The former is almost an instrumental in the familiar Justis mold, and the latter is good evidence of why Orbison was not cut out to be a rockabilly vocalist, although to be fair, he sounds more convincing on other tracks.

Some of his best rockabilly did not get released at the time. The poorly recorded "Domino" celebrates the exploits of a character of that name. "Mean Little Mama" is perhaps his most satisfying rockabilly performance all round. "Problem Child" also works well. As "Don't Be Runnin' Wild (Problem Child)," it was covered by Ken Cook, somewhat of an Orbison protégé. Cook's "I Was a Fool" was another Orbison composition, with the author singing harmony.

Additional Orbison originals were recorded. He cowrote both sides of a single recorded at Petty's studio by Teen King guitarist Johnny

"Peanuts" Wilson: the punchy sound and novelty character voice of "Cast Iron Arm" made it popular in the revival, and the pop ballad "You've Got Love" was also recorded by Buddy Holly. In addition, Holly recorded Orbison's "An Empty Cup (and a Broken Date)." In 1957 Warren Smith had his only pop hit (no. 72) with an Orbison composition, "So Long I'm Gone." Although Orbison never recorded it, it gave him his first composer royalties. In 1958 Orbison's "Claudette" was a number-thirty hit for the Everly Brothers, the flip side of their number-one "All I Have to Do Is Dream." Two other Orbison compositions appeared on Sun recordings by Johnny Cash and Jerry McGill.

It became clear to Orbison that he was having more success as a songwriter. Through the Everly Brothers, Orbison met Wesley Rose and subsequently obtained a songwriting contract with Acuff-Rose, moving to Nashville in 1958. To get out of his Sun contract, he signed over some of his copyrights to Sam Phillips, although that year and the next he returned to Sun as a visitor (as did other Sun alumni who had switched companies), helping to produce sessions, including ones where his own compositions were recorded. A brief and unsuccessful stay at RCA resulted in two singles.

Orbison's second hit as a performer—"Uptown"—was not until 1960, but it started a phenomenal string of twenty-eight hits that lasted until 1967. To cash in on this success, Sun released some of Orbison's earlier tracks with new overdubbed instrumental and vocal parts.

Although he was not fond of his 1950s recordings (many fans are), in later years Orbison carefully answered interviewer's questions about the period. He did acknowledge his rockabilly roots by sometimes performing "Ooby Dooby" and "Down the Line."

In 1987 Orbison was inducted into the Rock and Roll Hall of Fame. The following year, amid a tremendous surge of interest in the man and his work, with success as a member of the Traveling Wilburys and a new album of his own just recorded, Roy Orbison died of a heart attack after a concert.

THE ROCK 'N' ROLL TRIO

Paul Burlison born February 4, 1929. Dorsey Burnette born December 28, 1932, Memphis; died August 17, 1979, Los Angeles. Johnny Burnette born March 25, 1934; died August 14, 1964, Clear Lake, California.

The Rock 'n' Roll Trio was the Burnette brothers, Johnny and Dorsey, with Paul Burlison. Together they made one of the most celebrated rockabilly bands, along with Presley's Sun unit and Gene Vincent's Blue Caps. Johnny sang and played rhythm guitar, Dorsey played bass and sometimes sang, and Burlison was a superb lead guitar player.

At age ten Burlison was inspired and taught by a black man who was adept at the fingerpicking down-home blues style. Burlison would wait daily for this man, whose name he never knew, to pass by the house after work.

After discharge from the navy, Burlison played occasionally with Clyde Leoppard and the Snearly Ranch Boys and was on the radio in 1949 with Don Paul. The meeting of Burlison and the Burnettes came about in 1949, through their mutual involvement in boxing. "Dorsey said 'I heard your name called on the radio this morning' ('cause I'd picked an instrumental). 'I didn't know you played music. My brother and I play music, let's get together sometime.' But we didn't see each other for a year, until 1950, so we got talking about it again. We called each other a couple of times, one of them was playing in one group and I was playing in another, we didn't get together that year. It wasn't until 1951 until we started getting together."[30]

That year Burlison joined the Shelby Follin band, and for a few months he and bandmate-pianist Smokey Joe Baugh performed with legendary bluesman Howlin' Wolf on radio KWEM in West Memphis, Arkansas. Howlin' Wolf's radio spot followed the Follin band's daily late-afternoon half-hour show. Burlison performed with Follin until 1954, playing music influenced by Hank Williams and Ernest Tubb.

> Johnny would come and sing sometimes on our shows with Shelby on the radio, and Dorsey would start playing the steel guitar. The next year, '52, Johnny, Dorsey playing steel, Scotty Moore was playing lead, Bill Black was playing bass, and they had a drummer, I can't recall who it was, they got them up a group, a band. They were playing out at the Chatelone, and they had a big fight out there on a Saturday night, and Dorsey got stabbed. Scotty and Bill quit playing up there, that's about twenty miles east of Memphis in Oakland, Tennessee. It's an old club up there called Chatelone, whew! it's rough. They have a fight out there every Saturday night.[31]

From 1954 until February 1956 the Burnette brothers and Burlison were all members of the Doc MacQueen band, which played Friday and Saturday nights at the Hideaway club (mentioned in the Trio's "Rock Billy Boogie") in Middleton, Tennessee, twenty miles north of Memphis. "I had just started with Doc MacQueen and I said 'maybe I can ease you in.' So that's how they came in with Doc Mac-

Queen. Then we went down and cut 'Go along Mule' and 'You're Un-decided,' just the three of us."[32] (This was the Von label single mentioned earlier.) The band also had piano (MacQueen), sax, drums, and steel guitar and played honky-tonk and western swing, doing songs by Spade Cooley, Hank Thompson, and so on.

At the gigs with MacQueen, the Burnettes, Burlison, and the drummer would warm up the audience at the beginning of the night with uptempo numbers such as Johnny Lee Wills's 1950 hit "Rag Mop" and Chuck Berry's "Maybellene" before bringing on the rest of the band. In February 1956 the future Trio decided spontaneously to drive to New York and try to make it in the music business.

> We'd been playing with him for two years and just decided we were going to take off. We got up to Brownsville, fifty-nine miles east of Memphis, before we even called Doc MacQueen and said, "we're not going to be there Friday night." He said, "what's the matter?" I said, "we decided to go to New York." He said, "New York City?" I said, "yeah," and he said, "what for?" I said, "we're going to go up there and play." "Oh," he said, "play what?" We said, "we're going to play!" "Well okay," he said, "if you all hit it big, let me know."[33]

They immediately secured a spot on the nationally syndicated *Ted Mack's Amateur Hour* TV show and won three weeks in a row.

> They asked us what our name was; we just told him we didn't have a name. We'd just left Doc and went straight up there. Ted Mack introduced us as "the rock and roll boys from Memphis," and he told us after the show that we ought to get a name. Dorsey and I were working as electricians out on a job, and Johnny was running the elevator down at the Edison Hotel. Dorsey and I were out on the job the next day and we got to talking about it, and Dorsey wanted to call it the Burnette Brothers, and I said no, we'll call it the Burlison Brothers! [laughs] Dorsey said no. So we said let's ask John when we get back to the hotel. I said there's three of us, there was no drummer, I suggested the Rock 'n' Roll Trio. They said that's not bad. So we told Ted Mack the next week.[34]

Their wins brought them to the attention of big-band leader Henry Jerome, who became their manager, and brought them offers from five record companies. They signed with Coral and during the next year recorded in New York and Nashville with studio drummers. They toured as part of a Ted Mack package show. Tony Austin, Carl Perkins's cousin from Jackson, Tennessee, played drums for the tours. Austin later did sessions at Sun and toured again with Perkins in the 1960s, as well as with many stars of the *Grand Ole Opry*. Over the years he has been a nightclub owner and has had success as a songwriter. Burlison continued:

> Henry Jerome changed it [the name] when we got to the Fox Theatre in Detroit to Johnny Burnette and the Rock 'n' Roll Trio. Course we had a drummer, that made four, so we had to come up with something. But Dorsey didn't like that, no, uh-uh. That went over like a lead balloon. When we got to Detroit, I was driving, Johnny was in the back seat with the drummer, and Dorsey was up with me. We went to the theater. Dorsey read on the marquee: Johnny Burnette and the Rock 'n' Roll Trio. He turned around and said, 'Hey John, what the hell's going on?' John called Dorsey "Junior"—he was a Junior 'cause his dad was a Dorsey. He called him "June" for short. He said, "June, I didn't have nothing to do with that." We went in the lobby, and Dorsey called up Henry in New York and chewed him out bad. Johnny wasn't so worried about it; he liked it. But see, Dorsey was singing on every show too. But he had been too scared to sing on nationwide television. Johnny [sang but] wouldn't even talk the first week.[35]

They toured on package rock 'n' roll shows with the stars of the time—the Moonglows, the Flamingos, Clyde McPhatter and the Drifters, Frankie Lymon and the Teenagers, Lonnie Donegan (from England with his hit "Rock Island Line," a cover of Leadbelly's song that reached no. 8 in April 1956), LaVern Baker, Carl Perkins, Cathy Carr (who reached no. 2 in May 1956 with "Ivory Tower"), the Rover Boys (from Canada, whose "Graduation Day" hit no. 16 in June 1956), and Chuck Berry. Once they were the only white artists in a show at Harlem's Apollo Theatre. On shows they would play only three or four songs: always "Tear It Up" and often "Tutti Frutti," "Train Kept a-Rollin'," "Your Baby Blue Eyes," or "Blue Suede Shoes" (if Carl Perkins was not on the show).

Their tours took them mostly to the Northeast—Detroit, Philadelphia, Cleveland, Niagara Falls—the territory covered by their booking agency, G.A.C. (General Artists Corporation). Burlison believes that they would have been more successful had they toured more in the South. They never achieved more than a regional hit; "Tear It Up," composed by the band, sold well in cities like Boston, Baltimore, and New York, even warranting a sheet music edition. At the end of

1956 Coral released an album called *Johnny Burnette and the Rock and Roll Trio,* but it did not sell well.

Not all the songs were originals:

> We didn't have one song picked before we went to Nashville [to record]. Not one. We went to the record stores around Nashville and picked out a few songs that we liked. They had a turntable up on the counter, and we just flipped through the 78s. I'd say, "how do you like this," and Johnny would say, "well I could sing that alright." We just happened to like the songs. We bought the records and took them back to the hotel, where we had a little old record player, learned them that night, and recorded them the next day at the studio.[36]

They already knew one of the songs cut at this session, because it had been part of the Doc MacQueen band's repertory: "Blues Stay Away from Me," a huge country boogie hit by the Delmore Brothers from 1949. The brothers, Alton and Rabon, had composed it with Wayne Raney, one of two harmonica players at the session, and Hank Glover, a black house musician and producer at the King studio. Obviously a lot of care went into making their deceptively simple and integrated sound, highlighted by the boogie figure on guitar and the Delmores' very smooth, precise harmony singing.[37]

As in the source, the vocals on the Trio's version are shared by brothers, two acoustic guitars are strummed, and a guitar riff continues throughout. The Trio, as could be expected, is more rhythmic: the string bass is twice as active, and the tempo is slightly faster. Instead of expressive harmonicas, the studio drummer provides a strong backbeat. The integration of the rhythm found on the original model is not destroyed but becomes a "bed" over which the lead guitar has freedom, improvising throughout and soloing while a second guitarist maintains the riff. The Trio's version uses the more rhythmic of the two riffs found in the original, which appears only in bar 12, and ignores the one used for bars 1–11, a more harmonically intriguing riff, for it anticipates the chord changes the bar before they occur.

Johnny and Dorsey Burnette sing in harmony for the middle verses, but what had been the Delmore Brothers' first verse ("Blues, stay away from me / Blues, why don't you let me be / Don't know why, you keep on haunting me") becomes the first and last verse call-and-response pattern for the Burnettes. It is evidently rehearsed, as there is no variation. Johnny sings the lead (in the following lyrics Dorsey's responses are shown in parentheses):

> Well I say blues (well I say blues)
> Stay away from me (stay away from me)
> Ooh oh blues (oh lordy them blues)
> Why don't you set me free (why don't you set me free)
> Well I don't know why (I don't know why)
> You keep-a haunting me

"Drinkin' Wine Spo-Dee-O-Dee," a song that usually has an answering voice, as in the original Stick McGhee hit, or a chorus, as in Malcolm Yelvington's version, has Johnny as the only vocalist, although Dorsey easily could have joined in. Burnette omits most of the parts sung by other voices in previous versions, retaining only the nonsense syllables ("mop mop"), no doubt for rhythmic reasons, and leaving out the types of beverages. His intense delivery makes the song seem to be more a declaration of an antisocial serious drinker than a light-hearted invitation to a party. Also intensely serious, Dorsey sings a grim verse in "Sweet Love on My Mind":

> Well the river looks cold and the bottom is a long way down
> If you're really going to leave me that's-a where I'm-a going to
> be found
> Well if the mailman comes in the morning, there's a note
> upon my door
> Just bring my mail to the bottom of the river I don't live here
> no more

In songs like "Lonesome Train (on a Lonesome Track)" and "Rock Therapy," Burlison's solos show why he is so highly regarded as a lead guitarist. He employs rhythmic variety, chromaticism, microtones obtained by bending strings, hammer-ons and pull-offs (including pulling off to an open string), upward and downward slides, triplets, and creative use of double stops. Even when the solo is entirely in one position on the guitar neck, he exploits the entire available range. "Train Kept a-Rollin'," learned from Tiny Bradshaw's 1951 R&B record, and its flip side, "Honey Hush," learned from Big Joe Turner's 1953 R&B record, both feature one of Burlison's inventions, a technique that became a trademark: plucking the highest and lowest guitar strings simultaneously at the same fret.

After recording, the Trio appeared on other TV shows: Dick Clark's *American Bandstand*, Steve Allen's *Tonight Show*, and Perry Como's *Kraft Music Hall*. In 1957 the group was in the Alan Freed movie *Rock, Rock, Rock*, miming the recording of "Lonesome Train (on a Lonesome Track)." How many noticed the sound of drums but no drummer? At that time the band consisted of Johnny, Paul, and Johnny Black on bass.

Black was brought in when Dorsey Burnette quit the Trio in late 1956. Black was left-handed and had a custom-built upright bass; he was also the younger brother of Presley's bassist, Bill Black. Johnny Black had been working with Jack Earls, whose intense rockabilly was about as backshack as Sun ever got. Jack Earls and the Jimbos played mostly in Memphis nightclubs, where the members would make about $35 for three nights' work. When Dorsey rejoined the Trio in early 1957, Black went back to his job as a baker in Memphis, turning down offers to go on the road, although he did one more session with Earls and some local gigs.[38]

When the Trio disbanded in mid-1958, the brothers moved to California and had success as writers, notably for Ricky Nelson. *Together Again,* an album presenting demos by the Burnette brothers from around 1960, presents a variety of pop and country styles, as well as rockabilly on "Little Ole You" (by Wayne Walker), "I Wanna Love My Baby," and "Just Keep a-Going" (with slapped bass).

We're Having a Party is an album collecting more California recordings by the brothers. Rockabilly is evident in the urgent vocals of "Sweet Baby Doll" (a rewrite of "Swing Low, Sweet Chariot"), in the hot guitar solos of three 1958 songs sung throughout in harmony ("Warm Love," "Boppin' Rosalie" and "Do Baby Do"), and in the pop rockabilly of "Love Kept a-Rollin'," "That's All I Care," and "Kiss Me." Clearly, though, the Burnettes' rockabilly, like rockabilly in general, became subsumed, consumed, by pop music. Dorsey's "Great Shakin' Fever" of 1961 is a notable exception, but most of the lyrics are written and sung as if they do not portray real emotions or situations—"spend your life with me eternally" and "be my steady date." There is a bizarre fixation with honey, bees, and bears that appears in "Me and the Bear" (a hunting story), "My Honey" ("them bees done stole all of my honey"), "Honey Tree" ("I'm a little bee . . . watch out for the honey bear"), "Boppin' Rosalie" ("I like you like a bear likes honey"), and "Do Baby Do" ("honey baby"). These themes are mostly matched with lightweight music. Of course, we are not supposed to believe this is real. If it were, then "You're Sixteen," Johnny Burnette's biggest success at number eight in 1960, would be a twenty-six-year-old singer claiming ownership of a bright-eyed girl ten years his junior who is his pet, "all ribbons and curls." Actually, he was married with children, so it was just a song.

After a while Burlison, feeling that he had been a failure in music, settled down in the Memphis area and restored lost confidence by building a successful contracting business and enjoying his family. He turned down Johnny Burnette's offer to hire him back as an equal partner in the early 1960s when the success of Johnny's "You're Sixteen" and "Dreamin'" would have made it very tempting. In 1962 or 1963, however, Johnny was on tour sharing the bill with Jimmy Dean (having a hit with "Big Bad John") when his guitarist broke two fingers. Burlison filled in for two weeks, joining the tour in Montgomery, Alabama, and continuing to Jacksonville, Florida. Afterward he put his guitar back in the attic. Both Burnettes used "Tear It Up" as the final song in their stage shows; whenever either of them played in Memphis, they would call up Burlison from the audience to play guitar on the song.

Johnny died in a boating accident in 1964. Dorsey, who also had solo hits—"Hey Little One" and "Tall Oak Tree"—died of a heart attack in 1979. Burlison stayed in musical retirement until the 1970s, while continuing his contracting business, tending horses on his farm, and running a mail-order record business. His recording career was not resumed until 1980, when he organized a tribute record, *Johnny Burnette's Rock and Roll Trio and Their Rockin' Friends from Memphis.* A few years later he joined the Sun Rhythm Section.

When Coral released the Trio's album in the United Kingdom in the early 1960s to capitalize on the pop success of Johnny and Dorsey Burnette's solo careers, the album, and especially Burlison's guitar playing and the fuzz tone he got, were a major influence on groups like Johnny Kidd and the Pirates and on many of the budding guitar heroes. "Train Kept a-Rollin'" was covered by the Yardbirds[39] (and in the 1970s by Aerosmith and by Motorhead), and their "Stroll On," which they performed in the movie *Blow Up,* is also based on "Train Kept a-Rollin'."

In 1981 a version of the Rock 'n' Roll Trio—Paul Burlison, Johnny Black, and Tony Austin, authentic members all—performed in the United Kingdom, with Johnny Burnette's son Rocky singing. The year before, Dorsey's son Billy covered two Rock 'n' Roll Trio's songs on his debut album. Billy sang "Tear It Up" again on Mick Fleetwood's solo album of 1983 and brought a rockabilly flavor to Fleetwood Mac when he later became a member.

SEVEN

COUNTRY SINGERS AND
NASHVILLE ROCKABILLY

"I Got a Rocket in My Pocket"

During the rockabilly gold rush, country artists saw fewer studio sessions and gigs. Younger country singers dropped the steel and fiddle from their bands and added drums. With rock 'n' roll on the rise, some country stations switched over.

Certain country songs refer to the impact of rock 'n' roll. In "Country Cattin'," Jimmy Swan sings in honky-tonk style about how he and his date, "two cats on the prowl," are going to "round dance, square dance, and jitterbug, we're going to try that rock 'n' roll." Swan "ain't got no 'Blue Suede Shoes' or the [Heartbreak] 'Hotel' blues," he is "just a country boy wantin' to howl." In Bobby Helms's "Tennessee Rock 'n' Roll," Helms describes a dance where "the caller called 'let's promenade,' the fiddlin' man looked gone as he played, the old square dance had been remade." In Arlie Duff's "Alligator Come Across," a woman who is called Alligator is fascinated by a rockabilly singer who passes through town; some of his music passes through Duff's song in the form of a rockabilly section before the accompaniment reverts back to the fiddle, steel, and Carter-picking guitar. Bob Gallion sang about "my square dancin' mama (she done learned to rock 'n' roll)" in a song of the same title.

Rockabilly's success caused dissension in the ranks of the country industry, although it was quickly seen as a marketable trend. In an article entitled "Drop Petty Bickering," a *Billboard* writer commented on the friction caused by

> the exciting type of performance and material first brought to prominence by Elvis Presley on Sun Records (now on Victor).

Already a school of followers, artistwise and labelwise, has aris-
en to try to develop and put to best commercial and artistic use
what amounts to a rhythm and blues influence. The disk business thrives on excitement. Any new trend in repertoire should
be given a fair trial. If it has any merit, it is likely to add to the
all-round quality and stability of c. & w. music. To those who
would detract or belittle r. & b. as an influence in the country
field, let us caution them not to make the same foolish mistake
that embarrassed so many music men in the pop field.[1]

One response by the Nashville music industry was to dress up
country in younger clothes. Some songs marketed in the revival as
1950s rockabilly are more appropriately thought of as teen-oriented
country or hillbilly music suitable for jive dancing. As the decade
ended, it became apparent that the most successful new clothes for
country music were not the rocking kind but the uptown variety.
Besides the television version of the West (gunfighter ballads), a new
Nashville Sound was developed by producers, especially Chet Atkins
and Owen Bradley, for records by Patsy Cline and others.[2] The sound
was soft and inoffensive, characterized by twangless singing with orchestra and smooth vocal groups. This development was paralleled
in pop with the fabricated teen idols.

Before these sounds took over, however, Owen Bradley's Quonset
Hut studio was just one of the spots in Nashville where first-rate rockabilly was recorded. Vocalists often used a house band known as the
A Team: a group of highly skilled and flexible session players that
included drummer Murrey "Buddy" Harman; pianist Floyd Cramer;
guitarists Grady Martin, Chet Atkins, and Hank "Sugarfoot" Garland;
and the Jordanaires or Anita Kerr Singers. They made some of the
most musical rockabilly ensemble work ever recorded, although perhaps lacking the fire of stable performing bands. Rockabilly sessions
gave the studio players a new vocabulary—Garland, for example, listened to black R&B stations to get ideas, used lighter-gauge guitar
strings, and dialed more treble on his amplifier—so it is no surprise
that, under Atkins's production, Don Gibson's finely crafted pop
country songs contain many rockabilly elements.

Most of these players were the band for Don Woody, then a deejay in Springfield, Missouri (home of the *Ozark Jamboree*), at his Nashville session in December 1956. Four songs resulted, although two
remained unissued until 1976; all were cowritten by Woody. The
songs are musically strong, but they demonstrate a surface involvement with rockabilly and how quickly it became studied and formal-

ized. Woody is cute and gimmicky: he barks in "Barking up the Wrong Tree," whistles in "Bird Dog" (not the Everlys' song), makes bad puns in "Make Like a Rock and Roll" ("make like a tree and leaf"), and sings "Morse Code" (pronounced "mor-ris" code) to the sound of thumping tom-toms. "Bird Dog" has producer Owen Bradley's guitar giving a Paul Burlison soundalike intro copied directly from the Rock 'n' Roll Trio's "Sweet Love on My Mind" (produced by Bradley five months earlier).

Ronnie Self recorded several sessions at Owen Bradley's studio and at other studios with Bradley producing. "Bop-A-Lena," Self's only hit, was written by Webb Pierce and Mel Tillis and features Self's painful scream voice, but he also did rockabilly with a smoother voice in his 1956–58 recordings.

Born in Missouri in 1938, Self became a devoted and prolific songwriter whose self-destructive tendencies managed to foul up his career repeatedly. After "Pretty Bad Blues" and "Three Hearts Later" came out on ABC, both good rockabilly songs from his own pen, response to Self's wild stage act led to his recording for Columbia, where he produced some fine music, accompanied by many of the top studio musicians. He toured for a year and a half with the Phillip Morris Caravan as its only rockabilly, earning his nickname, "Mr. Frantic," and inciting crowds of screaming, clothes-tearing females. On news of the impending birth of his first child, he deserted the show. Temperamental, unpredictable, alcoholic, and dangerous, Self lost contracts and credibility and was often in jail for his wild stunts. He and his wife were married and divorced three times. Although most of his dozen rockabilly songs were written by others, he had success as a writer of Brenda Lee's first two top-ten hits in 1960. He died in 1981.

Joe Griffith was only a mediocre singer but managed to hire some of the previously mentioned session players for the six songs he did in 1958 in Nashville at RCA's studios. They and a vocal group, possibly the Jordanaires, provided him excellent backing—note a whole chorus of triplets on the snare during the guitar solo in "She's My Woman." Two singles were issued, one of them under the name "Joe Griffith and his Teenage Rebels," on the Reelfoot label of Rives, Tennessee, owned by his father.

As rockabilly evolved from a minimal trio, various elements were added to the list of available options—drums, backup singers, piano, saxophone, and so on—each changing and stretching what had crystallized as a unique style. With the addition of the Everly Brothers' distinctive close and smooth vocal harmony (not to mention their teenage romance themes), the expanding sound image of rockabilly burst. The Everlys' music is artistic and wonderful, but it is not rockabilly. The white elements (such as brother duet singing in the country tradition) and black elements (such as the Bo Diddley–influenced rhythmic figures of Don Everly's open-tuned guitar) are adjacent, not blended, even on a song like "Rip It Up."

Many established country acts recorded in rockabilly and rock 'n' roll styles, often at the urgings of producers. The artists, sometimes reluctantly, achieved varying degrees of success in trying to retain their popularity or to win a new audience. Curtis Gordon, a career country singer based in Mobile, Alabama, had been part of a New Orleans show with Elvis and Hank Snow. In 1956 and 1957 Gordon, encouraged by his record company (Mercury), recorded four credible rockabilly sides, including "Draggin'" and "Rock, Roll, Jump and Jive," both originals.

Buck Owens, one of country music's biggest stars, was born in 1929 in Texas and first recorded in 1956, when four singles by him came out on the Pep label of California. The third one, released under the name "Corky Jones," is rockabilly. Both sides, "Hot Dog" and "Rhythm and Booze," are now much admired. Owens had his first country hit in 1959; by 1971 more than fifty of his records had hit the charts, nineteen of them at number one, and Buck Owens and the Buckaroos honky-tonk sound had sold $40 million worth of albums. From 1969 to 1986 Owens was a cohost on the *Hee-Haw* TV show.

Leon Payne, a well-known country singer-songwriter from Texas who had done a stint with Bob Wills in the early 1940s, had a big hit with his ballad composition "I Love You Because" (covered by Presley at Sun). His "Lost Highway" of 1948 was a smash for Hank Williams the following year. Because of the clear distinction in image between country and rockabilly, and to avoid alienating his country fans, Payne chose to use a pseudonym for his rockabilly recordings. As Rock Rogers he made the excellent "Little Rock Rock" and "That Ain't It."

For the same reason, George Jones, born in Texas in 1931, did rockabilly as Thumper Jones. Considered in some quarters as country's greatest singer, he started recording in 1954 for the Starday label, and his phenomenal career saw its first hit the following year with "Why Baby Why." Apparently, while on a tour with Buddy Holly in January 1956, Jones started singing rockabilly backed on stage by Holly and his band. Thumper Jones's debut was released soon after: "How Come It" and "Rock It," both rockabilly. Added to the Elvis-on-Sun sound and instrumentation is what sounds like a woodblock and, on one side, a piano. Jones's later rockabilly was fuller, with drums and harmony vocals. On all his rockabilly songs (mostly self-composed) he sings exuberantly, whooping or coarsening his voice at times, dropping to a deep bass for a line in the chorus. The musicians on these songs are on fire, and the combination of the strong ensemble playing, interesting songs, and totally engaged vocals makes for wonderful music, among the best rockabilly ever. In "Maybe Little Baby" a girl has him all excited: "we're gonna dance, jump, hop, and holler whoopee." In "White Lightning," written by J. P. Richardson (the Big Bopper), the singer celebrates his daddy's shamanistic power in making an awesomely powerful moonshine, and the medicine man magic extends to staying beyond the law. On the other hand, the power of the law is celebrated in "Revenooer Man," where the man with the gun, badge, and authority brags about his ability to stop this kind of activity, although the action is limited to putting fear in the hearts of the moonshiners. George Jones is no stranger to alcohol, and it also figures in the lyrics of "How Come It," where he sings of "a bottle in my hand." White lightning is partly to blame for the murder in "Who Shot Sam." Powerful stuff, indeed.

Skeets McDonald, who was born in Arkansas in 1915 and died in 1968, was thirty-five when his first record came out. His 1951 release, "I'm Hurtin'," points to rockabilly with its bright tempo, strong backbeat, and barrage of syllables coming out in a succession of eighth notes ("nothin' would be neater than to call you Mrs. Skeeter"). The following year his eleventh single, "Don't Let the Stars Get in Your Eyes," was a huge hit. McDonald's claim to rockabilly fame is a double-sided gem on Capitol: "You Oughta See Grandma Rock" backed with "Heart-Breakin' Mama," recorded in May 1956, when he was forty. Inspired by a hot band, he puts aside his usual relaxed vocal style and taps into rockabilly intensity without losing his huge drawl. In the former song McDonald voices a classic interjection with "rock it but don't ruin it!"; in the latter he stutters "h-h-h-heart breakin' mama mama." In 1957 he recorded another, different "I'm Hurtin'." On this 12/8 pop ballad, with a Jordanaires-style male group, brushes, electric guitar, and piano, McDonald is like a twangy Elvis. A 1958 album called *Goin' Steady with the Blues* has a gentle charm and a gentle rockabilly feel on many tracks.

Jimmy Lloyd, born in Kentucky in 1922, was the rockabilly pseudonym for Jimmy Logsdon, an aspiring but unsuccessful country singer who fashioned himself after Hank Williams. After Logsdon opened the show for his idol in Louisville in the fall of 1952, Williams recommended him to Decca in Nashville. Soon Logsdon started recording, sometimes writing with Vic McAlpin, who had cowritten songs with Williams, and sometimes using Williams's band, the Drifting Cowboys. The second of Logsdon's eight Decca singles, all pre-1955, was "The Death of Hank Williams" backed with "Hank Williams Sings the Blues No More." Other singles on other labels followed, but his inclusion here is for the two singles he had on Roulette in 1957. McAlpin wrote "You're Gone Baby," decent rockabilly, and cowrote with Logsdon two songs that rank among rockabilly's finest. Cut in Nashville with lead guitar by Hank Garland and Grady Martin, they feature very effective bluesy piano playing. "Where the Rio De Rosa Flows" is a superb controlled rocker, but even greater is "I Got a Rocket in My Pocket." The lyrics convey arrogance ("I didn't come here to listen . . . ain't nothin' you can tell me I don't already know"), express impatience ("the fuse is lit"), brag of sexuality and power ("I got a rocket in my pocket and a roll [of money] in my jean"), and employ a striking choice of language ("Two-In-One's polish and Three-In-One's oil, a lot of lip-flippin' make my bad blood boil"). The arrangement is propelled by stinging guitar and forceful drumming, especially the three accents that follow the vocal phrases.

Despite his goofy enunciation and a tendency towards the commercial and the corny, Marvin Rainwater made a few good rockabilly records, especially "Hot and Cold" from 1956. It features the western swing device of a riff harmonized by steel guitar and lead guitar (played by Roy Clark). The next year he started a short string of country hits. Although promoted as a full-blooded Native American, in buckskins and headband, he has only a little Cherokee blood in his veins.

To the list of country singers doing token rockabilly we can add Little Jimmy Dickens ("[I Got] A Hole in My Pocket"), Webb Pierce (the self-penned "Teenage Boogie"), the Sons of the Pioneers ("Tennessee Rock and Roll"), Jimmy Newman ("Carry On"), Wynn Stewart ("Come On"), Autry Inman ("Be Bop Baby"), Patsy Cline ("Stop, Look and Listen," "Got a Lot of Rhythm in My Soul"), Red Foley ("Rockin' and Reelin'," "Crazy Little Guitar Man"), and Cowboy Copas ("Circle Rock"). The list continues with Carl Smith, Faron Young, Hank Thompson, Ferlin Husky (under his own name and as Simon Crum), and the Stanley Brothers.

MARTY ROBBINS

Born Martin Robinson, September 26, 1925, Glendale, Arizona; died December 8, 1982, Nashville, Tennessee

An excellent singer and songwriter, Marty Robbins enjoyed a varied career that included a successful rockabilly phase, more deliberate than any other established mainstream country artist. One of nine children, Robbins was raised in poverty. As a boy he was inspired by Gene Autry and other singing cowboys in the movies. He learned to play guitar and write songs while serving in the navy in the Pacific theater at the end of World War II. By the early 1950s Robbins and his band, the K-Bar Cowboys, first had a radio show (*Chuck Wagon Time*) and then a TV show (*Country Caravan*) in Phoenix, Arizona.

On the recommendation of Little Jimmy Dickens, who had been a television guest, Robbins was signed to Columbia in 1951. Persuaded to visit Nashville in 1952 by Fred Rose, who was instrumental in Hank Williams's success, Robbins signed a songwriting contract with Acuff-Rose. The next year he scored two top-ten country hits and became a regular on the *Grand Ole Opry*.

Once he started doing rockabilly, he incorporated it into his stage act alongside the ballads. The well-recorded polished musicianship and his nonaggressive, smooth singing are on the pop side of rockabilly, yet his output is convincing and dynamic. By being on a major label, Robbins increased respectability for rockabilly, and his touring and the sales of these records helped it to spread.

An interest in the blues side of country was already evident at his May 23, 1954, recording session. The unissued "Pain and Misery (Mean Mama Blues)," a Robbins original, is reminiscent of the Delmore Brothers' "Blues Stay Away from Me" in its use of the male vocal trio, moderately slow tempo, and subdued, controlled mood. The band includes two electric guitars, one to play a simple boogie-woogie rhythm pattern and the other for fills and the solo, supported by walking bass and brushed snare drum. A fiddle, present only for the second verse, provides blues fills.

On July 30, 1954, Robbins was on the bill when Elvis Presley debuted at Overton Park in Memphis. Months later, on December 7, Robbins recorded his version of "That's Allright." It was a country approach to the blues. The first solo is harmonized by twin fiddles, and the second is a rather bluegrass barrage of notes from the acoustic guitar. In the background an electric guitar plays mandolin-like muffled high notes. Robbins adds a fourth verse ("I ought to mind my papa, guess I'm not too smart / If I was I'd leave you girl before you break my heart") but abstains from the "dee dee" scat singing present in both Elvis's version and Arthur "Big Boy" Crudup's original, replacing it with ad-lib talking: "mama that's all right" and so on. Robbins garnered a top-ten country hit with this cut, no doubt encouraging him to pursue rockabilly.

August 9, 1955, was Robbins's most rocking session ever, driven by a hard-hitting snare beat. "Pretty Mama," one of the two original compositions, unfolds a sinister scenario of the protagonist, a tough, jilted lover, coldly premeditating the shooting of "old monkey boy." He has no need for sympathy, for he is willing to accept the consequence of prison: "gonna let no woman get the best of me." A remake of "Pain and Misery (Mean Mama Blues)," called only "Mean Mama Blues," is recast as rockabilly, now in the key of E (from A-flat). Robbins alone sings, with lovely sparse fills from the piano to augment the rest of the band. Chuck Berry's "Maybellene" and Hank Williams's "Long Gone Lonesome Blues" were also recorded. On the latter, the band lays down a relaxed groove, as Robbins gives a detached reading of this yodeled song of suicidal despair.

A session on November 3, 1955, yielded "Singing the Blues," written by Melvin Endsley. It was Robbins's fifth country hit and first number one, and his first pop hit, making number seventeen; Guy Mitchell's cover made number one. It's not blues; it's about having the blues. It is pop country, more melodic, less driving, drummer-less, and noticeably acoustic sounding, aside from steel guitar. From the same day comes Robbins's own "Tennessee Toddy." This one is rockabilly—the snare and electric guitar are back, the piano and steel are gone—but relaxed. Robbins takes a solo whistling through his teeth, refers to a female as a "cat," and uses falsetto to mimic a girl's voice.

Marty Robbins got back to rocking on March 13, 1956, with his cover of "Long Tall Sally," uncharacteristically diving aggressively into the vocal with a gruffness he sustains only part of the time. "Respectfully Miss Brooks" is a strong original showing his growing ability to compose firsthand detailed stories full of direct human emotion. He is very playful vocally and sings a wordless falsetto interlude. Lots of rockabilly feeling is still present in the delivery. Note the unusual inclusion of an organ.

Another Endsley composition, "Knee Deep in the Blues," was cut September 4, 1956. This fascinating combination of a country song with rockabilly underpinnings gave Robbins a country top ten, but it did not make the pop charts. It features a very prominent intro from the fiddle, which is never heard from again, a slapped bass, a strummed acoustic, a busy electric guitar chattering away with all the rockabilly blues licks, a piano playing boogie figures in the background, and a very melodic, controlled, and understated vocal. No drums were used.

The first recording of Robbins's composition "Sugaree" came out in 1957, but it took until 1959 to make the charts, when Rusty York's version on Chess climbed to number seventy-seven (pop). By early 1957 Robbins's own rockabilly phase was already behind him as "A White Sport Coat (and a Pink Carnation)," accurately pegged by a contemporary review as "styled to attract the crew cut and pony tail set," started its half-year residence in the pop charts, climbing to number two.[3] Robbins now aimed for more pop sounds and got them with the help of producer Mitch Miller and the Ray Conniff Singers. Robbins had a particularly successful phase with gunfighter ballads— "El Paso," from 1959, was a pop and country number one—and his versatility encompassed Hawaiian, Caribbean, and religious styles.

Robbins was elected to the Country Music Hall of Fame in 1982 and died of a heart attack later that year.

ROY HALL

Born May 7, 1922, Big Stone Gap, Virginia; died March 2, 1984, Nashville

A versatile pianist and singer, Roy Hall is remembered primarily for his 1955 and 1956 recordings for Decca, on the country boogie side of rockabilly.

Hall, nicknamed "the Hound," grew up in Big Stone Gap, Virginia, where, at age eleven, he was taught piano in the blues style by a black man named Smith Carson. Around the same time Hall became a drinker, but as he told me in his Nashville office, much later "the Lord come down here and took that booze away from me. I'd been drunk nineteen years but I don't know whether I should've quit drinking or not 'cause I haven't written too many hits since I sobered up. I had an imagination that was out of this world. You know a person taking pills and drinkin' will imagine anything. I wrote some crazy stuff while I was drunk that I'm even ashamed to talk about."[4]

As a teenager Hall played and sang in a popular band, doing "Stardust," "In the Mood," "Body and Soul," "Whispering," and "Sentimental Journey," the kind of songs now called standards. These made up much of his repertory in his later years as a solo pianist.

His recording career started in 1949 in Detroit, where Roy Hall and his Cohutta Mountain Boys recorded for Fortune. The label for "Dirty Boogie" credits the fiddler with the vocals, and another player is listed as playing "Take Off Guitar." At Fortune Hall also backed a young Skeeter Davis in the Davis Sisters. Their record's flip side was an instrumental played by Hall: "Going Down the Road Feeling Bad." By 1950 he had recorded for Bullet in Nashville (more country boogie), had toured with Tennessee Ernie Ford, and was performing regularly as a staff pianist on the *Grand Ole Opry* and on *Opry* touring shows. He backed Marty Robbins and Hawkshaw Hawkins in the studio in the early 1950s and played accordion on many of Red Foley's gospel records. From 1954 to 1957 Hall owned a nightclub in Nashville, where he met Webb Pierce, with whom he then toured and recorded for six years. It was Pierce's influence that secured Hall's own Decca contract. These records sound hillbilly with a Bill Haley–influenced rhythm section. In fact, the influence was not one-sided, since Hall's version of "See You Later Alligator" was recorded before the Bill Haley hit on the same label.

At his first Decca session in September 1955, Hall covered Fats Domino's "All by Myself," released only the previous month; "Move On," a cover; and two songs from his own pen, "Offbeat Boogie" and "Whole Lotta Shakin' Goin' On" (these last two were unissued at the time), cowriting "Whole Lotta Shakin' Goin' On" under the pseudonym "Sunny David."

In fact, some question his claim of authorship for "Whole Lot of Shakin' Goin' On." The first recorded version, by blues singer Big Maybelle, lists only D. C. Williams in the composer credit; subsequent versions list both Williams and David. Hall told me that in late 1954, he and Dave Williams, a black musician, wrote it while in the Florida swamps drinking their way through a snake-milking expedition, selling the "milk" (poison) for medicinal preparations. His motto at the time was "carry a bottle of whiskey in case of snakebite and always carry a small snake."[5] Six months after Big Maybelle's version was produced, Hall recorded his rendition and two other versions were made, all in 1955.[6] During this period Jerry Lee Lewis made a trip to Nashville from his home in Louisiana, in an attempt to start his career. He found Roy Hall's after-hours club, the Musician's Hideaway, and worked there briefly, where he probably heard Hall singing the song, although Lewis has said that he picked it up at a nightclub in Natchez, Mississippi, from a bandmate, drummer Johnny Littlejohn.[7] Sometime later, when Lewis was on Sun, he started playing "Whole Lotta Shakin' Goin' On" at gigs. After having great response to it, he recorded his own version in 1957. It was, of course, a huge hit, selling possibly twenty million copies worldwide. Interestingly, Roy Hall's recording has no piano on it, as is the case with three more of his Decca sides. Hall's use of the pseudonym Sunny David, he explained, was an attempt to avoid income tax. Not only did they catch him, but later his exwife was awarded the royalties in a divorce settlement.

At Hall's second Decca session, in December 1955, his piano playing is prominent in "Don't Stop Now," an enjoyable original. At his third session for the label, the next month, the piano is present but relegated to the sidelines. Hall, like others, jumped to cover "Blue Suede Shoes," doing so the same month as its release. "Luscious," a pop song with a Mills Brothers–type backup group, was also recorded.

Hall was dropped from Decca shortly after his fourth session, which produced two gems, neither with piano: "Diggin' the Boogie," a cover of Piano Red's 1950 original (Willie "Piano Red" Perryman was later known as Dr. Feelgood), and Hall's own "Three Alley Cats," about a hot band of piano, trumpet, and drums that showed up out of nowhere to rock a dance party:

> we stood flat footed, our eyes on their stems
> we dug the music looked straight at them
> we said "who are you fellows and where do you hang your
>   hats?"
> they said "we're three Georges they call the Alley Cats."

His next couple of tracks came out on the short-lived Pierce label: "One Monkey Can't Stop the Show," probably learned from Big Maybelle's recording (the flip side of her "Whole Lotta Shakin' Goin' On" release), although Hall later claimed it as his own, and Wayne Walker's "Flood of Love."[8]

Hall returned to Detroit's Fortune label, where his cover of Piano Red's "Rockin' with Red," claimed as an original and renamed "She Sure Can Rock Me," appeared on a Skeets McDonald album. Around 1958 Hall was in Memphis recording for Sun. His four tracks were finally issued during the revival.

In the 1970s Hall's Decca singles were fetching high prices in the collector market, and their appearance scattered through the *Rare Rockabilly* reissue volumes on MCA helped to secure Hall's place in rockabilly history, solidified subsequently by two LPs of newly recorded material, plus two similar LPs collecting his 1950s sides. *Rockabilly or Else,* on Barrelhouse, recorded in 1979 and 1980, contains his version of "Flat Foot Sam," a revival hit for him in Europe. "Is It Over George?" is the flip side of the single, a narration requesting his friend George Jones to give up alcohol. Another gem from the Barrelhouse album is "Bedsprings Motel," a remake of a song he cut in the late 1950s for Hi Q, a Fortune subsidiary. This superior version is a New Orleans–style piano solo with Hall narrating the story of his night out. As he played it for me on his office record player, he explained the story: "I'm trying to make out with this girl." On the record he says, "I come here every Tuesday night . . . boy I sure dig that piano

man, Roy Hall on the piano"; his comment to me was, "see I'm bragging on my own self." The song contains a classic Hall line: "I got a
bottle of that chicken whiskey: one drink and you crow and two
drinks and you lay." Hall said, "That's the old tune called 'After
Hours.' I didn't get sued over it, though." When he spun "One Monkey Don't Stop No Show," containing "I used to be young and simple, but brother I ain't that way no more," his only comment was,
"that guitar is out of tune a mile and half."[9]

Hank and the Hound, recorded in 1980, which Hall referred to as
Roll Over Hank and Rock with Roy, is an album of rocked-up Hank Williams songs. "Bless his heart, if he was living now, he wouldn't be
mad at me, but he wouldn't like what I done to his songs. . . . I murdered them."[10]

At the time of our meeting, just shortly before his death, Hall was
involved with his various businesses, including the monthly *Country Music Enquirer.* He was especially proud of his Talking Bible company, which offered the Bible on tape recordings. On his own label,
Judd, bought from Jud Phillips, he had "God Made a Little Corner
for Me," a successful gospel record. He was playing sober for senior
citizens on the riverboats, doing country and middle-of-the-road
music. Hall was bitter about being cheated out of money and songs,
proud about offers to tour in Europe (ruled out due to ill health),
hopeful about recording another album, and confident about his abilities: "I got a good band, I got the best. We could cut any of them
dry, as old as I am. I ain't afraid of them young rockabillies 'cause I
know what I can do and I ain't braggin' but I got the experience."[11]

GENE VINCENT

*Born Eugene Vincent Craddock, February 11, 1935, Norfolk, Virginia;
died October 12, 1971, Los Angeles*

Gene Vincent is another of the giants, and his name is said more often than not in the same breath as Eddie Cochran's. Although Vincent died before reaping much benefit from the emerging revival, his
music and approach were tremendously influential. He was an ambassador for rock 'n' roll and a keeper of the flame in periods lean
both for him and for the music. He created a personal, albeit narrow, style, and he left a legacy of many great recordings.

Raised in Virginia, he made his first and best-known recordings in
Nashville at the Owen Bradley Studios. Vincent toured extensively in
the United States, as well as in Canada, Australia, England, France, Japan, and Africa. For a while he was based in Texas, and moved to Cal-

ifornia for the last five or so years of his life. Vincent's major success came at the very beginning of his career, and he led a restless, unsatisfied life full of unstable relationships, sinking into alcoholism.

His family moved from the seaport city of Norfolk to the country community of Munden Point, Virginia, when he was seven. Vincent played guitar from an early age, hearing the *Opry* on the radio and gospel through the windows of the local black church; he played music with neighborhood black musicians on the porch of his parents' country store. After six years the Vincents moved back to Norfolk, and in 1952, when Gene was almost seventeen and in the ninth grade, his father signed papers allowing him to join the navy.

In the summer of 1955, although he had just signed up for six more years, a motorcycle accident took Vincent out of navy duty. It also left him with a crippled leg in a brace that bothered him the rest of his life. While in the hospital he played guitar and wrote songs. One of them was "Be-Bop-A-Lula," written with a marine from Michigan.

In September 1955 Elvis and the Blue Moon Boys played in Norfolk as part of Hank Snow's package show, and Vincent was impressed and encouraged. Early in 1956 Vincent won a radio station talent contest, and deejay Tex Davis was one of the judges. Billed as Gene Craddock and the Virginians, Vincent became a local star singing on live shows and the radio, putting "Be-Bop-A-Lula" in his act. Davis became his manager and bought the coauthor's rights to the song for twenty-five dollars. Davis and his partners, seeing Elvis's popularity, formed the Blue Caps band around Vincent and sent a demo tape to Capitol, which led to a contract shortly thereafter. In May Vincent and the band had their first recording session in Nashville, cutting "Be-Bop-A-Lula," "Race with the Devil," "Woman Love," and "I Sure Miss You."

Gene Vincent's music at that first session consisted of two main styles. These, with many variations, remained the foundation of his subsequent output. The first is punchy, aggressive rockabilly delivered with controlled frenzy, the bass fiddle walking, the drums up front (especially snare), and lots of virtuoso guitar solos (played first by Cliff Gallup and later by Johnny Meeks or Jerry Merritt), usually punctuated by screams. Vincent had lots of words to get out, and he delivered them sometimes in a stagy breathiness, even producing sound on the inhalation of air. A marginally softer version of this style has a lighter voice quality, brushes on the drums, and a slower tempo. In certain songs all this does not eliminate the frenzy; it merely controls it more.

The other style is the ballad, with sincere vocals and subdued musical accompaniment. "I Sure Miss You," from the first session, starts like this but drifts toward the punchy style as the song progresses. Variations and evolutions include male backup singers, handclaps, electric bass, occasional piano and sax, and more pop influences. Vincent's treatment of "Pistol Packin' Mama," Al Dexter's million-selling country hit from 1944, shows the evolution in style: the vocal is in harmony, the bass is electric and playing roots in eighth notes, the cymbals are prominent, and a piano and a tenor sax are present.

At the time of his recording debut, Vincent had a limited repertory and limited performing experience. His management tried to find suitable songs for him and came up with pop standards like "Up a Lazy River," "Ain't She Sweet," and "Peg o' My Heart." Vincent was willing, and these songs and others such as "Unchained Melody," "Over the Rainbow," and "Beautiful Brown Eyes" also became part of his repertory. Many other rockers, especially Bill Haley, mined vintage pop songs. Additional repertory sources were covers of country and R&B hits.

Vincent's voice is a wonderfully expressive, flexible instrument capable of many inflections. His pronunciation is influenced by Presley, and Vincent sometimes exaggerates the southern accent to the point of parody or unintelligibility.

"Be-Bop-A-Lula" became a top-ten smash and a rockabilly classic. The song's terrific atmosphere of restrained tension, influenced by Elvis's "Heartbreak Hotel," conveys more of a mood—sexual and intense, almost demented—than a message, but what message there is concerns observations and feelings for a girlfriend with the unusual name (apparently inspired by the comic strip character Little Lulu). Vincent reiterates "she's my baby" in no uncertain terms ("I don't mean maybe"); mentions her clothes ("red-blue jeans"), her status with others ("queen of all the teens"), and her dancing ability (she's "got that beat" and has "flying feet"); hints at her occupation ("walks around the store"); and claims that she loves him "so" and gives him "more, more, more." That success, plus Vincent's explosive stage show, charismatic stage presence, and a moderate second hit in "Blue-jean Bop," made him a major star.

Johnny Black, touring with the Rock 'n' Roll Trio in the second half of 1956, remembered how Vincent would capitalize on his injured leg: "his leg was broken and he had the cast, and they would announce him and bring him on stage . . . they would make sure and say that the young man had been in a motorcycle accident—he's going to make the show anyway . . . well that would . . . get the crowd.

'Hey! C'mon, this is great!' Well, we used to laugh and tell Gene after about a year your leg is gonna' run off if you don't get the cast removed."[12]

Things continued to happen quickly for Vincent; by the end of 1956 he had toured a lot, including Las Vegas and Toronto, released an album, divorced his wife, appeared in the film *The Girl Can't Help It,* and lost his manager and all but one of the original Blue Caps.

In 1957 there was a new band, with electric bass and two singers called the Clapper Boys doing dance routines, a second album, and lots more touring. A new booking agent was found in Ed McLemore, who ran the *Big D Jamboree* in Dallas. Vincent moved there with his whole family. "Lotta Lovin'," released in the summer, became a top-ten hit, and its flip side, "Wear My Ring," also did very well, generating more lucrative tour dates. The band appeared on Ed Sullivan's show, and Vincent alone mimed to his records on *American Bandstand.* By the time "Dance to the Bop," recorded at the Capitol Tower in Hollywood, became a decent-sized hit, his last in America, rock 'n' roll and Vincent were both in decline.

His image is of a wild, tough, hedonistic working-class man with a greasy hairdo and a mean streak who is dangerous with women and cars, a man who runs alone or with a gang (the band) and insists on doing exactly what he wants—dancing, cruising, and racing in cars—regardless of girlfriends' wishes or society's standards, while consuming and enjoying society's material comforts and toys. This appealed to certain fans, mostly male, the same ones taken by Marlon Brando in *The Wild One.* In real life, bad publicity about his drinking, tax evasion, money problems, and wild life scared promoters.

In late 1959 Vincent went to England to appear on Jack Good's *Boy Meets Girl* television show, and Good is credited with creating the all-black-leather image that became Vincent's trademark. After surviving the car accident that killed Eddie Cochran, Vincent retained and increased his popularity. He continued to tour regularly in Europe, South Africa, Japan, and the United States and had success on the British charts. A 1969 appearance as part of the Toronto Rock and Roll Festival was somewhat of a comeback. In the weeks before his death, from a bleeding ulcer caused by alcoholism, he recorded in Ronny Weiser's home studio and did a session for the BBC in London.

Gene Vincent's influence is far reaching and widely acknowledged. Interest in him and his music remains high. In 1993 Jeff Beck, with the Big Town Playboys, released *Crazy Legs,* an album of re-creations of Vincent's songs done as a loving tribute to him and his guitarists, especially Cliff Gallup.

In 1982 a British promoter contacted Johnny Meeks in California about the first Blue Caps reunion tour. Meeks called vocalist and Clapper Boy Tommy Facenda, who was doing his shift as a firefighter in Virginia. Facenda replied, "Damn, Johnny, I ain't never thought of stepping back onstage again, man, much less with you guys. Are we all still alive?" When the band opened in London, it "was very emotional, we actually had to stop . . . you turn around and there's the same guys, except for Gene."[13]

For a month in the summer 1993, the 1958 lineup of the Blue Caps played sold-out shows to rapturous audiences in France, England, and Germany. Meeks, Facenda, drummer Dickie Harrell, and Paul Peek (the other vocalist and clapper boy) were joined by guitarist Jerry Merritt (author of "She She Little Sheila"). Graham Fenton, from Matchbox, shared the lead vocals.

EIGHT

ROCKABILLY WOMEN
"Let's Have a Party"

Many female singers did rockabilly, but few received much recognition. The best known are Wanda Jackson, Janis Martin, Brenda Lee, Lorrie Collins, and Rose Maddox.[1] I discuss the first three here and the Collins Kids and Maddox Brothers and Rose in chapter 11. In the minds of collectors and fans, certain additional names carry associations, making them better known: Jackie Dee (her later success as Jackie DeShannon), Barbara Pittman (Sun label and friend of Elvis Presley), and Martha Carson and her sister Jean Chapel (their previous careers in country music). Of others, we know but little. Of Sparkle Moore we know her real name (Barbara Morgan), her origins (raised in Omaha, Nebraska), and how she came to record (an original song she sent to a local deejay led to a trip to Chicago in 1956 to cut four songs, all self-written) but not much else.

Compared to Brenda Lee, whose comings and goings were analyzed in the gossip magazines, the life and career of someone like Laura Lee Perkins stands at the opposite extreme: we know virtually nothing about her. What is known is that she recorded two sessions for Imperial, in 1957 and 1958, which yielded two singles and at least two more songs, all available on anthologies. The personality coming through is a woman who knows what she wants: what interests her is loving and dancing. All six songs are simple, driving rockabilly with aggressive lyrics. She growls and feathers her sore-throat vocals to the backing of a hot piano, an energetic rockabilly guitarist who knows how to fingerpick, a steady bassist, and a punchy drummer who likes to ride on the cymbals.

Robert K. Oermann and Mary A. Bufwack wrote an article on rockabilly women and the notes to the *Wild, Wild Young Women* album. They
point out similarities to the male rockabillies, namely, youthfulness,
songwriting, guitar playing, early careers as country radio performers, a
rockabilly phase, and a return to country music.[2] They conclude that,
unlike their male counterparts, female rockabilly singers "presented no
real threatening or radically different image to country audiences. . . .
Since most female rockabilly singers were quite young . . . they were able
to act wilder without worry of offending. . . . By being presented as performers of novelty songs . . . and as novelty acts themselves . . . they came
across as bouncing, enthusiastic (though alluring) young women."[3]

In this way the women retained respectability while infiltrating
country formats (barn dances in particular) with this new musical
form. They "performed, but did not live the musical style of open
sexuality and rebellion."[4] Thus it gave a niche for women in the country music world. One who saw this niche was Audrey Williams: a
photograph from a Nashville deejay convention in November 1957
shows her standing, with Webb Pierce, in front of a sign advertising
a talent search presented by "America's No. 1 Rockabilly Bombshell!!
Audrey Williams (Mrs. Hank Williams)."[5]

JANIS MARTIN
Born March 27, 1940, Southerlin, Virginia

Before her recording debut, Janis Martin already had many years of
singing experience on the radio and at local shows doing Ruth Brown
and LaVern Baker songs after she got bored with the usual country
and bluegrass material.

Martin started playing guitar at the age of six and soon started
winning almost every talent contest she entered. In the month of
her sixteenth birthday she recorded for RCA in Nashville, accompanied by studio stalwarts Chet Atkins, Grady Martin, Floyd Cramer,
and Buddy Harman. The producer was Steve Sholes, the man who
had bought the Presley contract from Sun. Attracted by her demo
song and appealing voice, Sholes saw that she also had a mobile stage
presence, played guitar, and wrote some of her own songs, "Drugstore Rock and Roll," to name but one.

With Presley's permission, she was marketed as the "Female Elvis,"
and the theme was continued with the song "My Boy Elvis." A ten-
inch album, now highly valued by collectors, was released in South
Africa with one side by Martin and one side by Presley. She met him
only twice, once in early 1956 when he signed an autograph after a
show and a couple of years later when they chatted briefly in a New

York studio. He wished her luck, but she did not have too much of it. The Elvis association may have been more of a curse than a blessing, inviting unnecessary comparisons.

She had talent, an image—a perky, pretty teenager with a blonde ponytail—and major label promotion. She also worked very hard: extensive touring, forming her own band, *Opry* and TV appearances, and a European tour with the Jim Reeves show to entertain the armed forces. Despite all this, only one song, "Will You, Willyum," made a brief chart appearance, and a few others sold well in certain markets: "Drugstore Rock and Roll," "My Boy Elvis," "Love and Kisses," and "Ooby Dooby." In general, the rockabilly songs that hit the charts (especially the ones that rose the highest) were the ones with more pop music characteristics in their structure, lyrics, or arrangement. Martin's recorded repertory has a high percentage of blues structures, which is rather unusual for a major label rockabilly artist. Although she had been married at fifteen, she managed to keep it a secret until her pregnancy, giving birth to a son in 1958. That did not fit the image RCA was promoting, and the label dropped her.

In 1959 Martin herself received a tribute in "Janis Will Rock" by the Rock-A-Teens of "Woo-Hoo" fame. With a young child and a second husband who objected to her career, she retired after a 1960 session that produced two singles on Palette. Her second marriage ended after her 1970 decision to resume performing. In 1976, with a new manager and her son joining the band as a drummer, she started to gain a lot of publicity and new fans. The next year Elvis died: "I just lost interest after that, I felt a part of me had died too."[6]

Her fans and overseas interest convinced her to carry on, however, and she made another trip to Europe in 1982. A Holland show, on her forty-second birthday, showed her in fine form, giving a good cross-section of her RCA recordings and paying tribute to Elvis with a cover of "My Baby Left Me." The enthusiasm of European fans and able backing by the Dave Travis Band inspired her to write "Hard Rockin' Mama," which she sang, again backed by Travis, on her return in 1985: "I'm a hard rockin' mama and I'm here to rock, I'm telling you fellas that I don't plan to stop." She didn't: a live album called *Here I Am* documents a show from Vienna in 1992. Backed by the Continentals from Germany, Martin is in fine form.

BRENDA LEE

Born Brenda Mae Tarpley, December 11, 1944, Lithonia, Georgia

Brenda Lee became a star while still a child. In Nashville she cut a wide variety of country, rockabilly, novelty, and standard songs all

leaning toward pop, courtesy of producer Owen Bradley and his band
of regulars. Her instantly identifiable voice, effortlessly flexible and
clear, conveys innocence and confidence. Although she never wrote
songs, she is a consummate interpreter. Raised in Georgia, Lee heard
a lot of gospel and R&B, citing Ray Charles, Fats Domino, and Ma-
halia Jackson as main influences. "I didn't have a record player or
anything so I listened to people that sang the blues that never were
stars, people who never were with a record label or anything . . . old
people who sat on the corner with a guitar and sang the blues."[7]

At age five she started winning talent contests and shortly thereafter had her own radio show. In early 1956 she had a spot on the
Red Foley network TV show *Ozark Jubilee,* and in July, at age eleven,
she did her first session for Decca. By the time she left the company
in 1970, she had placed fifty-one songs in the pop charts, twelve of
them in the top ten. Her first release—as Little Brenda Lee—was Hank
Williams's "Jambalaya" coupled with "Bigelow 6-200," written by Don
Woody. "Bigelow 6-200" was one of her most rockabilly-styled songs;
there were not many more. "Doodle Bug Rag" is exactly the kind of
a rockabilly song a child could be expected to sing: it's about insects
dancing and playing instruments. "One Step at a Time" from 1956,
more in the Haley mold, makes a possible reference to Elvis in the
line "every old hound dog once was a pup."

Her first major hits came in 1960 with "I'm Sorry" and "Sweet
Nothin's," both written by Ronnie Self. A 1962 concert series in England with Gene Vincent was called the King and Queen of Rock Tour.
During her tours of Europe in the late 1980s, she did some of her
many hits and several rock classics. Her English tour of 1992 saw most
venues sold out.

WANDA JACKSON
Born October 20, 1937, Maud, Oklahoma

Not only did Wanda Jackson stay with rockabilly longer than most
female performers did, but "her songs and performances came closer
to the independent, aggressive, rebellious, and sexual male stance."[8]
She is a powerful singer with a pronounced southern drawl and strong
country inflections, occasionally resorting to the sore-throat sound.

In the case of Jackson, one thing led to another. A radio show
brought her the encouragement of a country star, which led to a
record contract, which led to joining a TV show, which led to touring, where she met Elvis, who encouraged her to sing rockabilly. A
switch of labels brought her to a legendary producer, which led to

superb recordings. One recording that named Japanese cities resulted in her becoming a star in that country. A surprise hit for a rockabilly song recorded two years earlier caused her to pursue the style
further. A big country hit led to others and stardom and world touring. Excesses of that lifestyle led to a religious conversion and a move
to gospel. Sustained interest in her music permitted a long career.

When Jackson was a child, her family lived in California for a
while, where she was impressed by the radio shows of the Maddox
Brothers and Rose. By 1953, while in high school back in Oklahoma, Jackson had a daily half-hour radio show. Western swing star
Hank Thompson, also living in Oklahoma City, was at the station
for an interview when he met and heard her, inviting her to sit in
with the band. She could not tour with them because she was still
in school, but she became a featured attraction whenever the band
was in town. On Thompson's recommendation, Jackson started recording for Decca. Her first single, a duet with Thompson's vocalist,
Billy Gray, was a country hit.

Decca eventually released seven singles, all country. They are mostly slow honky-tonk songs, with a few rhythmically bouncy tunes in
moderate tempos, using electric guitar, steel guitar, fiddle, two-beat
bass playing (two notes in a bar: first the chord's root and then its
fifth), snare drum with brushes, piano, and a light echo. The lyrics
portray a strong, self-willed mature woman with deep religious feelings and country roots.

On the first single, from Jackson's debut session on March 24, 1954,
Billy Gray does a spoken performance, taking the part of a rich city
"cat" meeting an Oklahoma girl with sand in her hair who is working in a cotton field. He tries to woo her by impressing her with his
money, clothes, Cadillac, chauffeur, and promises. Jackson's image
of being her own woman is already present in this song written for
her by Gray, Thompson, and two others. The song is called "You Can't
Have My Love," and she flatly states, "I'm not the gal to shine your
shoes." The well-conceived guitar solo on the flip side, "Lovin', Country Style," leads the band into a nice rocking groove without dropping the two-beat bass line.

From that session came a second single; both sides are plodding
Hank Williams–styled numbers. Jackson, at age sixteen, sings plead-
ingly about youth not being denied in "The Right to Love," citing
authority in "Him above" with biblically derived phrases. In "If You
Knew What I Know," her first recorded composition, she sings in
overdubbed close harmony about telling a friend to drop a cheating
lover, an old flame whom the protagonist inexplicably wants back.

One single came from the second session in August 1954. Again paired with Billy Gray, she sings "If You Don't Somebody Else Will" with heavy country pronunciation. In her own composition, "You'd Be the First One to Know," she declares her sincerity. Subsequent sessions through the end of 1955 find her continuing in conventional country territory.

Shortly after graduating from high school (1955), her career was boosted when she became a regular on the nationally televised *Ozark Jubilee* show of Springfield, Missouri. She toured with the *Ozark Jubilee* for the next five years and performed in Las Vegas casinos. She also toured with Elvis from late 1955 to early 1956.

In the summer of 1956, at age eighteen, Jackson started to record for Capitol in Hollywood with producer Ken Nelson, one of the industry's finest. Backed by a series of excellent players—such as guitarists Joe Maphis, Buck Owens, Merle Travis, and Roy Clark; steel guitarists Speedy West and Ralph Mooney; Skeets McDonald on bass; and Big Al Downing on piano—she recorded country, rockabilly, and the occasional novelty item such as the cha-cha "Don'a Wan'a," whose lyrics, which she sings in a pseudo-Mexican accent, again tell of a woman not needing a man.

Of her rockabilly songs, one of her compositions is "Mean Mean Man"; this song portrays a woman who knows that she is a fool but, somewhat masochistically, will continue to love her man. Other Jackson originals are "Baby Loves Him," about a happy rockabilly couple, which shows Marty Robbins's influence in the phrasing, and "Rock Your Baby," featuring the band chanting "all night long" after her lines. Note the fingerpicked guitar solo against the triplets played on the piano.

"Honey Bop," despite the steel solo, and "Cool Love," despite the boogie piano solo, are songs that would have suited Gene Vincent. Both "I Gotta Know" (about a woman who wants to get married) and "I Wanna Waltz" (about one who wants to dance close) alternate a rockabilly section in 4/4 with a country waltz. In "Fujiyama Mama" (previously recorded by Anisteen Allen in 1955 also on Capitol), Jackson warns and brags about her awesome power "like the atom bomb." She did a successful tour of Japan, where I suspect that listeners were happier about the local place names (perhaps the only lyrics they could understand) than the memory of war-time destruction.

In 1957 Elvis sang "Party" in his second movie, *Loving You*. The Collins Kids covered it, and Wanda Jackson did a version under the title "Let's Have a Party." In 1960 her version became a surprise hit, her first pop success, making number thirty-seven on the charts. An album called *Rockin' with Wanda!* collected many of her previous rockers, and the next album, *There's a Party Goin' On,* continued the momentum with the title song and "Man We Had a Party."

Jackson kept recording rockabilly and rock 'n' roll songs until 1963, and they remained part her stage act. Many of them were previously sung by males. Besides singing "My Baby Left Me," which she likely heard Elvis perform, Jackson covered songs by Little Richard, Chuck Berry, Carl Perkins, Jerry Lee Lewis, the Coasters, and the Drifters, as well as George Jones's "Who Shot Sam." Her version of the Robins' "Riot in Cell Block Number 9" has interesting changes in the lyrics; in her version, after the state militia is called in, "each and every trooper, he looked so tall and fine, all the chicks went crazy up in cell block number nine." From 1961, with her own "Right or Wrong," Jackson began a decade of country chart hits, more than two dozen.[9] In 1971 she had a religious conversion. At the time she was a major star in North America (where she had her own TV show), the United Kingdom, Europe, and Japan and had realized her dreams of being a singer, making records, entertaining people, and traveling the world. "I started drinking hard, smoking and partying all the time . . . It was a pretty scary time to go through—to have everything you want and yet you don't want to keep living. . . . God forgave my sins, dusted me off so to speak, and gave my singing some real purpose."[10]

Her next album was gospel, but she was not allowed to record another, so she asked Capitol to release her from her contract, and in 1973 she switched to Word, a Christian label.

In 1984 she did a three-week tour of Sweden, where Jackson was rated as the number-one female singer. Besides being treated to some country, the noisy and appreciative audiences heard a mix of rockabilly songs from the 1950s, as well as new ones from an album she recorded there called *Rockabilly Fever,* containing covers of Connie Francis's "Stupid Cupid" and Brenda Lee's "Sweet Nothin's." Then, after sharing the story of her conversion and the importance of her faith, she sang songs from another new album called *My Kind of Gospel.*

Wanda Jackson continues to perform in North America, Japan, and Europe. "It just gives me pleasure to sing."[11]

NINE

LOUISIANA

"Let's Go Boppin' Tonight"

We can make a distinction between Louisiana rockabilly and rockabilly recorded by Louisiana singers. The difference is that the artists who stayed in Louisiana—Al Ferrier, for example—recorded for Eddie Shuler's Goldband label in Lake Charles or Jay Miller's operations in Crowley and retained a strong regional sound, very down-home, raw, and powerful. Louisiana artists who recorded outside the state, namely, Rusty and Doug Kershaw, Werly Fairburn, and David Houston, show less of their state's regional flavor in their rockabilly sides.

As for Shuler's and Miller's home-grown products, a lot of the material was poorly recorded, and the music on these labels often sounds muddy, with brittle treble. Calling much of this music raw is an understatement. The best of the idiosyncratic songs are full of creative ideas and unusual phrasing. It's like inspired amateurism carried out at a professional level, and it can be fascinating. At its worst—a fair amount of the time—this music is plainly formulaic and derivative; less often it is too weird (too creative?) to make aesthetic sense, even for a person who falls for the charm of the unusual. This, coupled with off-mike and out-of-tune instruments and bands falling apart, can make the listener wince. A zealous reissue program has spread this music widely, however, and it has its fans.

Shuler's label started in 1949 and was sustained by the tremendous popularity of his first signing, accordionist Iry LeJune. Rockabilly was only a small portion of the label's activities, which covered Cajun, blues, country, R&B, and rock 'n' roll. Shuler has writer or cowriter credits on a large number of the songs recorded at Goldband, and the label is still going.

AL FERRIER
Born August 19, 1935, Montgomery, Louisiana

Al Ferrier's powerful, rural sound justifies his latter-day title: King of Louisiana Rockabilly. He idolized Hank Williams, whose influence is audible in Ferrier's very intense singing, giving an idea of what Hank might have been as a rockabilly. Born into a musical family with eleven children, Ferrier had been playing guitar for five years when he quit school and went to work in a logging camp with his brothers. Al and brothers Bryan (lead guitar) and Warren (fiddle) first recorded as a trio, although many of these tracks have a studio electric bass player overdubbed.

Al Ferrier and his Boppin' Billies first issues were on Goldband in 1956, and like much else from that label, the sound quality is crude, the timing is loose, and the playing is primitive, unruffled by the lack of consensus in matters such as chord changes (but don't underestimate the intensity level achievable during a guitar solo when the musicians are playing different chords, as in the faster version of "Honey Babe"). Their early music is the antithesis of slick, but it is authentic nonetheless, full of life and unpolished talent and highly prized for all these qualities.

The brothers clearly came out of country music traditions. As well as performing rockabilly, they did conventional country songs with harmony singing in the refrains and soloists trading after a couple of bars. In all the songs the lyrics are direct and conversational rather than poetic. They portray a man who just wants love, who wants an honest and true girl like his mother; he will treat her right, like his daddy does. Unfortunately, relationships are difficult or broken: the woman has gone away, it's finished, it's too late. The protagonist wants to know why his woman doubted him, why she left him, why she was untrue, and what she thinks love is. He is ready and wants to find out. His honey just wants to help him spend his money (which Al keeps calling *mon*, rhyming it with *fun* and *hon*), when he has any.

Warren on the fiddle, sounding (and almost rhyming with) brittle, plays rhythmic motifs in the faster songs and uses Cajun-style double stops in some solos. Bryan is very adept and versatile on electric guitar, playing country boogie riffs and fluid fills, or fingerpicking. In his solos the guitar takes over in the mix. The bass usually walks but occasionally uses the standard country two-beat style. Al's rhythm guitar strumming acts like glue, holding it all together, especially on the songs without drums; you can hear foot taps in places.

The first session, in March 1955, yielded one single, "No No Baby" and "I'll Never Do Any Wrong," and some unissued songs. Nothing was issued from the second session in November, but many of these early songs were redone later with added piano and drums, sometimes at a faster tempo. A third session at the end of the year yielded the second single: "My Baby Done Gone Away," one that had been previously attempted, and "It's Too Late Now." Warren was absent at the last session for Goldband, in late 1956 or early 1957. The single that resulted has a new version of "Thing Called Love" coupled with "Let's Go Boppin' Tonight." It shows a strong Sun influence from Elvis, a Scotty Moore–type solo, and vocal interjections like those of Carl Perkins.

In 1957 the act moved to Jay Miller's studio, resulting in issues on Excello, Zynn, and Rocko. The writers' credits for "Let's Go Boppin' Tonight" had been Al and Eddie Shuler. When the song was re-cut for Excello as "Hey Baby," some of the lyrics were different, and Al and Jay Miller were credited. This version has an African-sounding shaker instead of drums. For the most part, Miller's studio provided a more conventional setting with session players, one of them being Katie Webster on piano. The passion has polish, and the songs are more in the "swamp" style. There is no fiddle here either, but Bryan is in fine form.

After many years of gigging, including four *Hayride* appearances, Al retired professionally but still played in a family setting. By the early 1970s collectors had latched onto his records, and he got to record again with his brothers (as well as nephews), although Bryan died in 1981. Al has performed many times at the New Orleans Jazz and Heritage Festival, finally making it to Holland in 1987.

RUSTY AND DOUG KERSHAW
Rusty born February 2, 1940, Louisiana; Doug born January 24, 1936, Louisiana

Doug Kershaw's eccentric showmanship, Cajun dervish image, and wild fiddling on songs like "Louisiana Man" and "Diggy Diggy Lo" gave him a place in the rock world of the 1960s. His 1950s recordings with his guitarist brother Rusty, sometimes in the company of pianist and vocalist Wiley Barkdull, cover many styles: boogie, country, Cajun, and rockabilly. The duo, known as Rusty and Doug, were real Cajuns from a French-speaking household. They first recorded in 1954 for Jay Miller's Feature label from Crowley, Louisiana, and through him, later for Hickory in Nashville. Coming from a musical family, they had early professional experience on stage, radio, and television and in 1955 appeared on the *Louisiana Hayride*. The Kershaw brothers' close harmony singing is reminiscent of the Everly Brothers.

Of the Kershaws' first recordings, most of them not released at the time, two rockabilly songs are noteworthy. "Stop Look and Listen" has Rusty's vocal accompanied by his own guitar, brother Nelson "Pee Wee" Kershaw on drums, and Louis Fournerat on steel. Together they create a delightful atmosphere, much more engaging than in the version of the song by Johnny Jano. Also a demo from Jay Miller's studio, Jano's version is sparsely recorded with only acoustic guitar, electric guitar, and something providing a monochromatic percussion sound. Jano, from Eunice, Louisiana (he died in 1984 at the age of fifty), delivered a strongly Elvis-inspired vocal.

The Kershaws sing on "Rattlesnake," harmonizing the verses and singing "bop bop" while Wiley Barkdull's lugubrious bass voice chants the title word over a blues form propelled by Clarence Reese's lead guitar and Gene Reese's drumming.

Of the Nashville recordings, their self-composed "Hey Mae" from 1958, produced by Wesley Rose and made with an all-star session band, is their finest rockabilly song. Here is the recipe for its haunting sound: take hypnotizing vocals, insistent eighth-note rhythms, and lots of the tonic chord. Blend in a fascinating interplay from three guitarists (Hank Garland, Ray Edenton, and Chet Atkins) and add a tasty dash of piano work (Floyd Cramer). Beat with powerful drumming (Buddy Harman) and cook over simple half-note bass playing (Floyd T. Chance). Serve beautifully recorded. Satisfies discriminating tastes.

The brothers joined the *Opry* in 1957, but the draft ended their tenure shortly thereafter. Their first country hit came in 1958. The duo split in 1964, and Doug carried on alone.

WERLY FAIRBURN

Born Folsom, Louisiana, November 27, 1924

Werly Fairburn was about ten years older than many rockabillies, experienced in country and honky-tonk and a veteran of the *Louisiana Hayride*. Around 1952 *Country Song Roundup* magazine noted that he did a daily fifteen-minute morning radio show in New Orleans, where his nickname was "The Delta Balladeer." A promotional photo from the period shows him wearing a fancy embroidered cowboy shirt, holding a large Epiphone *f*-hole guitar, and looking dapper with slicked hair, sideburns, and a mustache; after all, he was a barber by trade, the "Singing Barber," as he was known in his hometown.[1]

His 1950s recordings, always professionally played and still satisfying listening, are a microcosm of the evolution of rockabilly. With his hillbilly band he recorded one 78 in 1953 for the Trumpet label of Jackson, Mississippi. "Camping with Marie," an original composition, has Louisiana Cajun fiddling and rural imagery sung in the region's mix of French and English. The flip side shows a strong influence from the recently deceased Hank Williams, as do his Capitol releases such as "Prison Cell of Love" from 1954.

Fairburn's next label was Columbia, where his two records were local hits. One of them, "Everybody's Rockin'," from April 1956, is appropriately named, for "Blue Suede Shoes" was then hot on the charts for both Carl Perkins and Elvis. Fairburn's recording shows that he has dropped the fiddle and the steel for a strong early rockabilly sound with the classic trio instrumentation. Although there are no drums audible on this song, Fairburn declares in his composition that he is "a rockin' fool . . . a drum goes boom to a rockin' tune and man, I gotta go!"

His recordings on Savoy, primarily an R&B label from Newark, New Jersey, add an excellent piano player but wrap Fairburn's flexible if not totally distinctive honky-tonk voice in a cold-sounding echo. "All the Time," from late 1956, backed with "I'm A Fool about Your Love" (the only Fairburn composition among the six songs on Savoy), sold moderately well. That record and the next, "Speak to Me Baby" and its flip side, "My Heart's on Fire," from early 1957, show that his band was a very strong rockabilly unit. Besides piano, there is fine rockabilly lead guitar and a propulsive rhythm from the slapped bass fiddle blended with the barely audible acoustic guitar.

By late 1957, with "Telephone Baby," the band had dropped the piano but added drums, played very vigorously and placed very prominently. A strong influence of RCA Presley and the Jordanaires, especially "Hound Dog," is heard in the bar of triplets hammered on the snare at the end of many of the verses and the band intoning "doo wop doo wop" and "aah." The lyrics, although charming, are more contrived and consciously hip: the "telephone-a baby . . . ain't no square," with her "feet up on the wall, going over campus capers or the teenage ball." She even does her homework while on the phone.

Werly Fairburn and his band's style and instrumentation thus followed the trends of their times: passing from an ethnic and regionally specific sound (Cajun) and honky-tonk (Hank Williams's style), through regional rockabilly (Elvis on Sun) and national rockabilly (RCA Elvis), into the tendencies of white rock aimed consciously at the teenage market. In the 1960s Fairburn relocated to the West Coast, where he worked as a deejay and recording engineer and had issues on various labels. In 1964 Jim Reeves had a posthumous country number one with Fairburn's "I Guess I'm Crazy," which he had first heard when they were both on the *Louisiana Hayride.*

TEN

TEXAS

"Gonna Shake This Shack"

Texas was a breeding ground for rockabilly talent. In general Texas rockabilly has a light, polished sound, a legacy of the well-rehearsed western swing bands. The Dallas–Fort Worth area was a rockabilly stronghold, the base for Johnny Carroll, Mac Curtis, Bob Luman, Sid King, Ronnie Dawson, and Groovey Joe Poovey. Houston had the Starday label and Hal Harris, Link Davis, Rudy Grayzell, Bill Mack, Sonny Fisher, George Jones, and many others.

Hal Harris worked as a deejay in Houston and was a session guitarist at the Gold Star Studios, where many of the Starday records were cut. He backed George Jones, Joe Clay, Sleepy LaBeef, and Roger Miller, to name a few. Born in 1920, in Alabama, Harris started performing in the early 1940s. His two rockabilly vocals are "Jitterbop Baby" and "I Don't Know When."

Link Davis was another of Starday's staff musicians. A multi-instrumentalist who sang and played fiddle, harmonica, and tenor sax, he was adept at western swing, Cajun, blues, and rock 'n' roll. His sax is heard on Big Bopper's "Chantilly Lace" and Johnny Preston's "Running Bear." He also worked with Sleepy LaBeef, George Jones, Sonny Burns, and Sonny Fisher. A protégé of Cajun fiddler Harry Choates—famous for his "Jole Blon"—Davis's lengthy and prolific recording career started in 1937 with a western swing group called the Crystal Spring Ramblers and continued until the early 1970s. His son, Link Jr., continues the family tradition and was a member of Asleep at the Wheel. The senior Davis recorded on Gold Star in 1947, shortly after forming his own group. Almost two dozen singles were recorded under his name for various Houston labels, although it was 1956 before his tenor sax was recorded. His best rockabilly songs are "Grasshopper Rock," "Sixteen Chicks" (cowritten with Wayne Walker), and "Trucker from Tennessee," about Elvis: "he's got a load of something, must be TNT... swings a guitar but he doesn't play... when he gets going the hep cats roar... stole my gal from me, this fascinating trucker from Tennessee."

Rudy Grayzell was from San Antonio, where he had a daily radio show in 1957. Before his rockabilly on Starday, he had recorded country singles as Rudy Grey (on Talent) and as Rudy Gray (on Capitol) and also on the Abbott label. He had one hillbilly single on Starday and then went rockabilly with "Ducktail" backed with "You're Gone" in May 1956. Six months later he cut "Jig-Ga-Lee-Ga" and "Let's Get Wild" as Rudy "Tutti" Grayzell. Two years later he dropped the nickname for his only Sun release, "Judy."

Just across the state's western border, in Clovis, New Mexico, was an independent studio owned by Norman Petty. One of the few studios in the area, it attracted many Texas artists; their style was called Tex-Mex by some. The NorVaJak studio had top equipment, which was unheard of for an independent. The equipment was paid for by profits from the Norman Petty Trio's recordings of standards like Duke Ellington's "Mood Indigo," featuring Norman at the organ and his wife, Vi, at the piano.

Petty had experience as a country pianist and as a deejay and had done a stint at Jim Beck's studio in Dallas. In addition, Petty had an experimental nature that, coupled with Buddy Holly's own, was especially noticeable on Holly's solo records.[1] He had his own labels, but most of his recordings were leased to others. Petty's inclination and his artists—Buddy Holly, Buddy Knox, Terry Noland, the Fireballs—leaned toward pop, and with certain exceptions (Holly tracks from early 1956 and Sonee West's "Sweet Rockin' Baby" and "Rock Ola Ruby"), what was recorded at NorVaJak is pop rock 'n' roll rather than rockabilly.

SONNY FISHER

Born November 13, 1931, Tyler, Texas

Sonny Fisher is one of the earliest full-fledged rockabillies to have recorded, and his entire 1950s output consists of just eight songs recorded in 1955 and 1956. He did not record again until 1980.

Fisher learned to play on his father's guitar and from listening to the *Grand Ole Opry* on a battery-powered radio. His first nightclub work was playing country and western with a fiddler and a steel player. In his late teens he got interested in black music and teamed up with bassist Leonard Curry and drummer Darrell Newsome. Later they were joined by Joey Long, an excellent lead guitarist. They made a vital, strong, and confident ensemble.

"Everything we did came from R&B; we picked up the beat, the rhythm, everything from Joe Turner, Fats Domino, B. B. King, people like that. Then we heard Elvis and recognized it as something a little different just like everybody else."[2] Like other radio and jukebox listeners, Fisher was under the impression that Presley was black until he saw him perform in Texas in 1954 at clubs called the Texas Korrall and the Old Spanish Trail. Fisher paid for his first session in January 1955, at Bill Quinn's Goldstar Studio in Houston, consciously going for a sound like Presley's. Quinn called Jack Starnes, of the Starday label, to tell him that there was someone doing songs similar to Elvis's material, and Starnes came to hear the band. This led to Fisher's being signed to Starday.

All eight songs recorded in the 1950s share common elements: the same instrumentation, a walking bass line, a swing pattern on the cymbals, and freedom for the lead guitarist, who plays fluid and energetic fills and solos. All songs contain a small number of verses, from two to four, and in every song, some or all of them are repeated, often with slight variation of a word or two. Six of the eight songs use the twelve-bar blues structure, although two of these have another section using a different progression, and another song, "Hold Me Baby," has a twenty-bar blues form for the verses. There is also a similarity in lyrics. Each of the following lines is from a different song: "I love my baby and I love her fine," "I love my baby and my baby loves me," "I told little mama," "I told my baby I was leavin' town," "my baby told me I was her little daddy." Five of the songs are in the key of C, and two are in G.

The four songs from his first session became Fisher's first two records. The refrain in "Rockin' Daddy"—"I'm a rockin' daddy from Ding Dong Tennessee"—is an obvious nod to the state from whence came Elvis and the Blue Moon Boys. The lead guitar plays alternating choruses of fingerpicking, chord inversions played in horn-like accents on the backbeat, and single note soloing. Eddie Bond adopted the song as his theme song and its title as his nickname. "Hold Me Baby" is a slow swing blues variation with simmering intensity. The title is never actually sung; Fisher sings "a-hold me" three times in a row instead.

"Sneaky Pete," aside from the singer expressing a desire for a "big fat woman and a bottle of Sneaky Pete," describes the activities of barnyard animals while drunk: "Like the little white rat he got drunk on Sneaky Pete [twice] / told the big tom cat don't you even bat your eyes at me." The electric guitar is played in a style, and with a tonal setting, that closely approximates a steel guitar and mimics that instrument's characteristic role.

After singing the title in "Hey Mama," Fisher imitates the sound of the string bass with "doopa doopa doopa doopa doo." This swing rhythm is used on the words "give me give me give me" and "look-ey look-ey look-ey."

The second session was in late 1955. "Rockin' and Rollin'" is yet another song with thrice-repeated two syllable units: "roll it, roll it, roll it" and "rock it, rock it, rock it." "I Can't Lose" has its "ooh ooh ooh, little mama." In this song guitarist Joey Long plays choruses of Bill Haley–inspired rhythm shots.

Fisher's last session for many years took place during 1956. "Pink and Black" is his most aggressively energetic song. Influenced by "Long Tall Sally" ("I saw my baby coming and I jumped under the table") and "Good Rockin' Tonight" ("come on and rock, well rock, rock my blues away"), it is the only one of his blues songs to use stop-time rhythm. The odd one out of the eight songs is "Little Red Wagon," an old-fashioned thirty-two-bar AABA song form that shows a different style of Fisher's singing (aside from the tape having been obviously sped up). The band still puts its rockabilly touch on this pop structure.

Although the band did many shows, including appearing with Presley (who borrowed Fisher's drummer for the gig), George Jones, and Tommy Sands at shows in Houston and in Beaumont, Fisher and his band never toured outside Texas. Starday offered him a two-year contract, but Fisher declined, feeling that he was being cheated on royalties and lied to about record sales. He later said "that just might have been the worst decision of my career."[3] He hoped for a deal with a major label but it never came. Later in the 1950s Fisher started his own label, releasing a couple of records but none of his own. Around then he performed in white clubs backed by an all-black band. He left the music business in 1961 after getting beat up outside a club.

The revival took Fisher overseas, where he toured the United Kingdom, Holland, and France, recording an EP in 1980 in London. In an interview he explained that he had been in the flooring trade since he was eighteen and was self-employed with a small business. "I got married for the first time in 1951 . . . later I married a young girl who kept me out of music until now. . . . She really knew nothing of my musical history until Ted Carroll and Ray Topping came and found me. She thought she'd married a floor layer. I had no idea either, I never knew about bootlegs or anything. Now I hope to do more tours of England. . . . The way people have received me over here, I'm gonna go with rock 'n' roll as long as I can."[4]

In 1983 he recorded for the Big Beat label in France. The album, *King of Rockabilly,* has a strong opener in the rockabilly arrangement of Eddie Rabbit's "Drivin' My Life Away." The musicianship is solid, but some of Fisher's eleven new compositions are weak. He reveals a penchant for cloying sentimentality with lines like "the hours I spend with you are like words from a poet's pen" from "If You Leave Me Tonight," which also shows that slow songs are not his forte vocally. Despite variations in structures and instrumentation (occasional use of piano and sax), the project feels somewhat sterile and clichéd, although "Goin' Rockin'" and "Lonesome Train" are very worthwhile additions to the Fisher catalog.

In Holland in 1983, in front of an enthusiastic crowd, he led a crack band that included piano through burning versions of some of his 1950s recordings, songs from his recent recordings, and a few classics. Even though insufficient rehearsal caused the band (and Fisher himself, on a couple of songs) to falter occasionally, all concerned generally proved themselves very capable. "Shake It Around" was just one of several high spots of which they could be very proud.

SID KING AND THE FIVE STRINGS
Sid Erwin born October 15, 1936; Billy Erwin born May 1938

Sid and Billy Erwin are from Denton, Texas, forty miles north of Dallas. They formed a country band in 1952 while still in junior high school, with Sid on vocals and guitar, Billy on lead guitar, and Mel Robinson on steel guitar and vocals. About a year later, the lineup was completed with the addition of Ken Massey on upright bass and Dave White, a drummer who possessed a rich deep voice. This group stayed together for about five years, producing ten singles.

Although the band was influenced by Elvis Presley's records and stage show, another strong (and earlier) influence was Bill Haley's Essex recordings. In fact, there are many similarities between the Five Strings and Haley's Comets: both are extensions of the western swing tradition, highly polished and very versatile touring dance and show bands; their instrumentation was the same (although the Strings had one less member, with the steel player doubling on saxophone); both bands minimized the use of the steel guitar, featuring instead virtu-

osic guitar playing; both leaders had a smooth and light vocal quality nearly devoid of histrionics; both bands recorded for major labels
in their prime, having recorded earlier for local independents; both
bands got their early boost from doing radio shows; and for both,
their black influence was not direct but came from records.

Right from its inception, the Erwin brothers' band did regular live
radio shows and soon were on television and touring. A TV appearance in 1953 in Dallas led to a one-year contract with Starday. They
recorded later that year in Starday's home studio in Beaumont, Texas (at the same time as a young George Jones), but the band was not
happy with the results. Early in 1954 they went to Jim Beck's studio
in Dallas, later used for recording their first four Columbia sessions.
There they redid the two songs, plus recording two more, and sent
the tapes to Starday, which released the remade pair. It was issued as
being by the Western Melody Makers, a name that the band had in-
herited from their first radio show and one that they did not especially like. One side was a song the company had presented, "Who
Put the Turtle in Myrtle's Girdle," a novelty item complete with intentionally "wrong" notes. The other side was "If Tears Could Cry,"
a pop country song cowritten by Sid.

A rare insight into these early days of the band is provided by two
radio programs made available on an album called *Rockin' on the Radio*. One show is from Denton in 1954 and the other from Taylor,
Texas, in 1955. On these shows they played boogie instrumentals and
a backbeat version of the Carter Family's "Wildwood Flower" to show
off Billy's lead guitar; covers of current country hits by Webb Pierce,
Carl Smith and Kitty Wells; gospel songs with trio vocals, such as
"Rock My Soul" ("in the bosom of Abraham"); and the songs that
had appeared on their only single to date. But they also played "hillbilly bebop," as Sid called it: "Rock the Joint," by Bill Haley (a song
they had recorded in Dallas), and Presley's "That's All Right." They
had shared the bill with Elvis in shows at Dallas and Austin in 1955.
The rockabilly sound impressed them, and shortly thereafter they
added the R&B standard "Flip, Flop and Fly" and Chuck Berry's "Maybellene" to their repertory.

Since they received no money or royalties from Starday, nor were
they reimbursed for the Dallas studio costs, the band just waited for
their contract to expire so that they could sign with Columbia, which
they did on December 15, 1954, recording the next day. In all, six
sessions resulted in nine singles, among them a number of rockabilly recordings. Theirs is a restrained and controlled rockabilly, with a
certain hillbilly charm.

Their first Columbia session resulted in two records released under the name the Five Strings. Later it was decided that a personality up front was a good idea, so Sid Erwin became Sid King, and subsequent records were issued as being by Sid King and the Five Strings (the King Brothers). The implication that they were all brothers was easy enough, since there was a resemblance. The music produced at that first session still displays corny humor, an important element expected in the act of a top show band. In "I Like It" the novelty element shows through with a tympani playing an upward glissando, lyrics hinting at sex, and corny vocals. Nonetheless, the band rocks along with jazzy guitar fills and strong rhythm. "Put Something in the Pot Boy" is one of the band's most interesting songs, with stylistically contrasting sections. The verse, in a country style, uses a seventeen-bar progression; the stop on bar 15 is followed by a two-bar tag figure. During the blues-form solos the band cooks with a walking bass. The chorus is also over a twelve-bar form, with the band singing "we're gonna rock, roll, hey boy." "Drinkin' Wine Spoli Oli" is one of the few nonoriginal songs the band ever recorded. It is given a black R&B vocal group treatment, with drummer Dave White (who claimed authorship) chanting the title in his strong bass voice. (Apparently he never recorded as a drummer, only as a singer.) The band sings nonsense syllables like "doo wee, doo wah," and above everything is a wordless falsetto voice, in the style of the Ink Spots. The Five Strings are rare in rockabilly for exhibiting a definite influence of black R&B vocal groups, via the records of the Drifters, the Midnighters, the Clovers, and others.

The second session, in July 1955, produced two more singles. Two of the songs use blues forms, and the band used piano for the first time on a recording; both were used frequently thereafter. "Sag, Drag and Fall" is somewhat of a parody referring to both "Flip, Flop and Fly" and "Shake, Rattle and Roll." In "Purr, Kitty, Purr" the Haley influence is noticeable not only in the arranged rhythmic fills and solo introduction but in the lyrics as well. The song is similar to Haley's speciality—lightweight subject matter with catch phrases, here with frequent references to dancing and music: "I tamed my kitten and I did it with a tom cat beat." A fiddler is used on two songs, the only time in the band's recorded output. In "But I Don't Care" the band modulates up a tone to put the song in a key more suitable for the fiddler's country-style double-stop solo, modulating back down afterward.

The Five Strings quickly developed into a top draw in the Texas entertainment world, stars of stage, radio, and TV. Unfortunately, they never achieved national prominence. With their fancy pseudo-cowboy uniforms, they appeared often as headliners on the *Big D Jamboree* (where they helped a hopeful Buddy Holly to appear). Their custom-painted bus (with their name and "Columbia Recording Artists" on the side) took them to dates on the *Louisiana Hayride* and the *Grand Ole Opry,* and throughout the United States and into Canada.

For their third Columbia session, on January 31, 1956, they produced a cover of "Blue Suede Shoes," which had been on the market only thirty days. The band managed to put in "doo-dly yop bop bop bop" chorus figures, and some verses are sung by the bass voice.

Their March 1956 session, which included a cover of Roy Orbison's "Ooby Dooby," added sax (played by the steel guitarist) for the first time; the steel player must have felt his role diminishing as rockabilly exploded. "Booger Red" is another good example of the Five Strings' R&B vocal group approach to rockabilly.

That summer the two Erwin brothers recorded four sides in Hollywood, all originals, with bass and drums played by studio musicians. These recordings are without steel, piano, sax, or chorus vocals, and all are classic rockabilly, never frantic, with a strong Presley/Sun-era influence and Billy fingerpicking like Scotty Moore. Both "Good Rockin' Baby" and "It's True, I'm Blue" include the typical Elvis device of a word chanted on the key note over the I and then IV chords. The latter song is the most country of the four, and the drums are played with brushes. In "When My Baby Left Me" Sid sings the first two verses low and then moves up an octave for part of the next verse. The unexpected use of the ♭VI chord is a nice touch, as is the half-time, almost burlesque ending. "Gonna Shake This Shack Tonight" is notable for the sparse and effective use of only tom-toms and voice for the first four bars of the verses.

Fourteen months later the Five Strings recorded their last session, this time in Fort Worth. By then, September 1957, the rockabilly gold rush had peaked, and neither of the two issued songs is rockabilly. "I've Got the Blues" is a ballad inspired by "Blueberry Hill" with sax, piano, open high hat, and a bluesy guitar solo. "What Have Ya Got to Lose," a nonoriginal, is full circle back to pop country with a very corny piano solo and echoey handclaps.

In 1957 the band was as active as ever, with its own TV show in Houston and its own club in nearby Conroe, where it performed and brought in big-name western swing bands like Bob Wills and Hank Thompson. Later in the year, however, Columbia did not renew the band's contract, which had a six-month option, and the original band members drifted apart. The Five Strings broke up officially in 1958. Sid and Billy toured with Sonny James, and Billy toured for a year and a half with Buddy Knox. Around 1959 Sid and Billy formed a new band for touring, and it stayed together for five years. Sid had one single on Dot in 1961. He stayed in the music business full time until 1964 or 1965, afterward settling in Richardson, Texas, and opening Sid's Haircutting, which he still runs, playing music on weekends.

A 1970s recording of "Drinkin' Wine" by Sid with just piano and drums, was issued on a Rollin' Rock compilation in 1976. Interest in his music from Texas rockabilly fans and revival musicians, especially Jim Colegrove of the Juke Jumpers, led to an album by Sid King— *Let's Get Loose*—recorded in Dallas in 1979 and 1980 with Colegrove playing, producing, and contributing the title composition. It was issued by Holland's Rockhouse label in 1987. Among other backing musicians, Billy King plays guitar, and former Strings Dave White and Mel Robinson contribute background vocals. A satisfying, quality album that reveals careful attention to detail, it features a new version of "Drinkin' Wine Spoli Oli," some new compositions of Sid's, and fine versions of "House of Blue Lights," "Boogie Woogie Country Girl," and Flatt and Scruggs's "Don't Get above Your Raisin'." In Sid's rewrite of Chuck Berry's "Rock and Roll Music," called "Rockabilly Music," he sings:

> Don McLean sang "American Pie"
> He said the music would surely die
> But it never really went away
> You just don't hear it in the U.S.A.

In the 1980s Sid and Billy made at least three trips to Europe to play for the fans.

BUDDY HOLLY

Born September 7, 1936, Lubbock, Texas; died February 3, 1959, near Mason City, Iowa

Aside from Elvis, Buddy Holly is now the most well known of the 1950s rockers. His life and work have been presented and homage paid in articles, magazines, biographies, recordings, tribute songs, cover versions, memorial concerts, movies, and the Buddy Holly festival in Lubbock. The stage musical *Buddy* has been seen by two million people in London's West End, where it started in 1989. More than 2,000 performances have been logged, including six months on Broadway and on tour.

Neither rebel nor misfit, Holly was loved and supported by his family and integrated into the social life of the community; there is no scandal, no substance abuse, no handicap overcome. The appeal is

following the hero's journey, a story of a self-confident and deter-
mined young man joined by trusty companions, a mentor, a muse,
and a true love, only to meet the incomprehensible: death in his
prime.

The outline of his career contains family music making; hillbilly
music at local performances; influence by Presley; an unsuccessful
year with Decca; the fruitful association with Norman Petty, with
whom he developed his own style; hits under the Crickets band name
and under his own; touring in the United States, Canada, Australia,
and England; TV appearances; marriage to Maria Elena Santiago;
breaking away from Petty and the Crickets; recording with orchestra; moving to New York; and the plane crash while on the Winter
Dance Party tour.

The earliest known recording by Buddy Holly is from 1949, when
he was thirteen. It is a solo performance of Hank Snow's "My Two
Timin' Woman." Released in 1986 by brother Larry Holley (the original spelling of the family name), it presents Buddy before his voice
changed; needless to say, the voice does not sound familiar. Holly's
command of the guitar, although nothing fancy, is confident and
rhythmic, and he does venture a solo on the low strings. He had high
standards for everything he ever put on tape, and this is a performance, not just goofing off. From the same source comes the traditional "Let's Pretend" (listed as "I'll Just Pretend" in Goldrosen and
Beecher's definitive biography). Bob Montgomery, his first musical
partner, sings and plays guitar while Holly plays mandolin and sings
harmony.

Later, in 1954 or 1955, nine songs squarely within the conventions
of country music were recorded as demos by Buddy and Bob (the name
used for their act). The ensemble had fiddle (Sonny Curtis), steel (Don
Guess, Weldon Merrick), and bass (Guess, Larry Welborn). The songs
have a lot of charm, despite occasionally being blatantly derivative:
"Gotta Get You Near Me Blues" puts new words and melody on the
progression of "San Antonio Rose" by Bob Wills and the Texas Playboys, and the first section of "You and I Are Through" does the same
to the chords of "Five Foot Two." The only versions available have
additional instruments, which were overdubbed after Holly's death, but
they still allow the listener to hear the original harmony singing in
the brother duet tradition on every song. The harmony is continued
throughout in some songs, but more often the second section is sung
alone. All songs are composed by the participants—Holly coauthored
two—and the term "heart songs" would be accurate, especially since
the first word appears in four of the songs' titles ("soft place in my,"

"door to my," "flower of my," "I gambled my"). Actually, love and the dramas and emotions surrounding it are the theme of almost every one of Holly's compositions. It often figures in the titles—"Love Me," "Because I Love You," "I'm Lookin' for Someone to Love," "Words of Love," "Love's Made a Fool of You," and "True Love Ways"—and in the lyrics of many more of his originals, as well as the titles and lyrics of other writers' songs that he recorded.

Lubbock, "the City of Churches," was conservative and segregated. In their youth Holly and his pals had scant direct contact with blacks or their music, but like so many other young musicians, they were attracted to blues and R&B, heard on distant radio stations. Elvis Presley performed in Lubbock at least twice in 1955; Holly and his trio also performed on the shows. By all accounts, Holly was captivated, and he changed his repertory and style, learning many of Elvis's songs within a week.[5] The business card of Buddy and Bob soon spelled out "Western And Bop."

"Down the Line," a demo, is not only Holly's first recorded rockabilly song but also his most pure, original, and wild.[6] In it Holly sings of being stopped on the highway while speeding toward his sweetheart in Oklahoma. On seeing her photo, the policeman urges him onward.

Buddy Holly's "Rock-A-Bye Rock" (Holly actually sings "rock-a baby rock"), from early 1956, is a rockabilly version of the Midnighters R&B hit "Sexy Ways," with the words almost completely rewritten. In fact, a set list of Holly's from 1957, reproduced in the booklet in *The Complete Buddy Holly* box set, shows "Sexy Ways" but not "Rock-A-Bye Rock." Avoiding the original's focus on sex, as most cover versions did, he changed the subject to dancing. Holly's own electric guitar punctuates his singing and takes a basic solo, Sonny Curtis strums an acoustic guitar, and Don Guess plays roots and fifths in half and quarter notes on the upright bass. Jerry Allison's drumming is prominent and very active, and he plays rolls, triplets, and accents in addition to the backbeat. The overall feel, however, is stiff and self-conscious, although not in a calculated way. In singing a clear flatted third, rather than the microtonal third used by the Midnighters, Holly is clearly a country singer emulating a black style. Not originally issued, this cut first saw light in 1963 with additional accompaniment by the Fireballs overdubbed by Norman Petty the previous year. The original version surfaced on vinyl in 1983.

For all of Holly's later originality, his rockabilly songs are derivative of early Elvis. Elvis facilitated Holly's exit from country music, and I doubt that he ever would have gone back to it. The rockabilly blend of black and white styles came to Holly from Elvis's model. Although Holly heard black music on the radio, the recordings he made before he saw Elvis indicate that there was not sufficient black influence in his own environment for him to develop a blend along those lines independently. As Holly became more creative with his songwriting and arrangements, the rockabilly elements steadily diminished.

Playing in duos—first with Bob Montgomery and then with drummer Jerry Allison—helped to develop Holly's ear for arrangements. In the clockless freedom of Norman Petty's studio in Clovis, New Mexico, about 100 miles west of Lubbock, there were explorations with overdubbing and different sounds, including organ and even celeste ("Everyday"). Allison proved to be an extremely imaginative drummer, playing with taste and dynamics and doing what the songs called for, exploiting the sound colors of cowbell, cymbals, tom-toms, or whatever was available, including his pantlegs ("Everyday") or a cardboard box ("Not Fade Away"). He has even been known to scratch his beard into a microphone for a unique percussion sound. The smallness of Petty's studio, where a full drum kit was too powerful, may have been the necessity that mothered some of this invention. Allison's drumming skills later brought him session work with Johnny Burnette, Eddie Cochran, the Everly Brothers, Johnny Rivers, Buddy Knox, and Bobby Vee.

"That'll Be the Day," a song attempted while Holly was at Decca but redone in 1957 with Petty, was the first hit, and it made number one. "Peggy Sue" and "Oh, Boy!" soon followed it into the top ten. Buddy Holly and the Crickets raised their profile by touring in the United States, Canada, Australia, and the United Kingdom and appearing several times on television on shows hosted by Dick Clark, Ed Sullivan, and Arthur Murray, as well as on shows in London. Many other songs charted, more in Australia and the United Kingdom than in the United States, especially after Holly died.

In late 1958 Holly parted with the Crickets—Jerry Allison and upright bassist Joe B. Mauldin (guitarist Niki Sullivan had been a member in 1957)—and moved to New York. In his last months Holly's musical evolution completely passed through rockabilly into pop, especially ballads. He veered toward the smoother, lighter (and whiter) vocal sounds of the Everly Brothers, Bobby Darin, and Paul Anka and was mesmerized by Mickey and Sylvia's "Love Is Strange." Holly's last recordings—solo demos of a dozen new songs and favorites recorded in his New York apartment—are reflective and mostly slow in tempo. Given that he was a newlywed, a surprising number of them are about troubles in relationships.

When Holly left the band, just months before his death, the Crickets continued with a nucleus of guitarist Sonny Curtis, Joe Mauldin, and Jerry Allison and a succession of different vocalists. After a period back in Clovis recording for Petty and sessions in New York City, by 1959 their base was Los Angeles. They vacillated between reviving the Holly sound and following their own impulses, creating direct, uncomplicated, pure pop that at times eliminated all black elements and practically all country elements as well.

The Holly sound was a strong influence into the 1960s, carried on by the Crickets, Bobby Vee, Tommy Roe's "Sheila" (1962), the Bobby Fuller Four, and numerous cover versions of Holly's songs.

BUDDY KNOX AND JIMMY BOWEN
Wayne Knox born July 20, 1933, Happy, Texas; Bowen born November 30, 1937, Santa Rita, New Mexico

One of the biggest success stories in rockabilly concerns the debut recordings of the Rhythm Orchids, a group formed at West Texas State University in 1955. At the end of the next year, when it looked as though the band would split, they went to Norman Petty's studio to record a souvenir. "Party Doll" was written and sung by guitarist Buddy Knox, and "I'm Sticking with You" was written by Knox but sung by bassist Jimmy Bowen, who shared composer's credit. Don Lanier was the lead guitarist, and they met drummer Dave Alldred in the studio. After positive reaction from the initial pressing, 2,500 copies were made on the band's own Triple D label. Lanier's sister, a model living in New York City, sent a copy to a pair of music publishers she knew, resulting in the record coming out on the newly formed Roulette label. The company put the songs on separate releases, each credited to the singer's name followed by "with The Rhythm Orchids." In 1957 "Party Doll" was a number-one hit (no doubt the first with a drummer playing a cardboard box), and "I'm Sticking with You" hit number fourteen, the first million-sellers to come out of Petty's studio.

In "Party Doll" Knox's voice is high, clear, and unaffected, all typical Texan characteristics (note his drawl on the word "hair," which sounds more like "har"). His style is reminiscent of Buddy Holly and Ricky Nelson. Knox was about fifteen when he wrote "Party Doll," which may account for its simplicity. The invitation—"come along and be my party doll"—is repeated three times. The motive—"and I'll make love to you"—caused the song to be banned on some stations. The catchy tune is performed in a light rockabilly style, with a female choral group. The singing backup group, whether female or male, became part of Knox's style. The same guitar solo appears twice.

The public's dollars voted for this accessible, simple, gentle pop rockabilly: music that was less black influenced, less raw, less emotional. Even though Knox sometimes covered songs done by black artists, his style has little appreciable black inflection because he was relatively isolated geographically as a youth. He was not aware of black music until he heard it on the radio in his late teens.

Knox's music is easy and happy, neither pretentious nor profound, with major-scale melodies and rather childlike lyrics, as in "now my mind is troubled like an angry sea," "blues are like the weather," "my love is your love," and the hit "Hula Love." Among his more rockabilly songs are "Devil Woman" ("you do me wrong one more time and you go 'way"), "C'mon Baby" ("cuddle up, tell me, tell me true"), "Swingin' Daddy" ("crank up the band and let's get hot"), and "That's Why I Cry" ("on the sly another guy took your love from me"). The latter two were among Knox's ten hits, as was "I Think I'm Gonna Kill Myself," containing a rockabilly solo played by Sonny Curtis. Most of his material, however, is not rockabilly but rhythmic pop music, sometimes with country elements, other times more in the teen idol mold. A few songs use more than the usual one or two sections; for example, "Rock Your Little Baby to Sleep," the second of his hits, uses five. Incidentally, Knox greatly favors the key of A: on an album collecting the bulk of his Roulette recordings, he uses it for "Party Doll" and eleven more, whereas the album's remaining eight songs are divided between four other keys.

Jimmy Bowen also had a light voice, more crooning and less noticeably Texan, but also less appealing than Knox's. The success of "I'm Sticking with You" obviously led to a formula for subsequent recordings, again light pop rockabilly: Bowen's voice alone, a medium tempo, simple lyrics, lots of repetition, echo especially pronounced on the percussion, occasional rhythm stops, an arranged rhythmic motif or two for the instrumental section (often involving an exchange between two guitars, one played low and one high), a typical B section starting on the IV chord, and perhaps a modulation up a semitone.

Bowen did not play bass on any of his recordings but did on the road, and the band toured extensively in America and Canada. After the two split up in 1958, Knox continued on the road because, he said, "one-nighters was where I could make my best money . . . [we did] a 125,000 miles a year in my car. . . . Them little towns, maybe 30,000 population and up y'know we played 'em all. . . . We usta run into Jerry Lee and Perkins and all the guys on the road. . . . We were averagin' 400 to 500 miles a night for three or four months on a row. . . . It was a really weird scene but it was fun."[7]

Knox liked Canada, and after years of running successful nightclubs in Vancouver, he moved near Winnipeg. He still tours a great deal, including overseas, and places songs in the country charts.

Bowen became extremely successful as a record producer and executive, becoming president of MCA in Nashville, where he gained a reputation for taking care of artists and being a hard-working, aggressive, powerful, enigmatic, and controversial figure.

JOHNNY CARROLL
Born October 23, 1937, Cleburne, Texas; died February 18, 1995, Dallas, Texas

Johnny Carroll is a vocal chameleon, best known to the rockabilly world for a voice he was probably able to produce only under duress at his major label debut. That voice could inspire a Mad Magazine–styled caricature: the Wild Rockabilly Singer.

At nine years of age Carroll bought his first guitar with money he made working as a water boy for German prisoners of war. His mother played fiddle and showed him the basics of music, and he started to learn country music from the radio. When a cousin in the jukebox business handed down some worn 78s, Carroll got exposed to R&B. He formed a band with his high school buddies, and their opening set at a Ferlin Husky show in 1955 impressed Jack Goldman, a bearded local smooth operator who called himself Jack Tiger. With the aid of demos, Tiger landed a Decca contract for Carroll (not the band). Of the two surviving 1955 demos (issued thirty years later), one song is rockabilly and the second is a tortured reading of the 1940s standard "You Made Me Love You." "You Two Timed Me Two Times Too Often," the Carroll-composed rockabilly song, shows a lot of Presley influence. That's no surprise, since Carroll and his band had been working the *Big D* and *Hayride* circuit, sometimes sharing the bill with Elvis.

Carroll flew to Nashville for the Decca contract, and over two days in April 1956 cut six titles backed by the usual Nashville session musicians. "They kept telling me to sing harder, and I sang harder on those than I ever did live. And, of course, it wasn't my band . . . I'd no idea who the guys were."[8] Carroll pours out sheer energy, exaggerating most of rockabilly's vocal clichés and singing out of tune. Still, some people enjoy these extreme vocals contrasted with the solid but reserved backing. Besides his own "Crazy Crazy Lovin'" and

Tiger's "Hot Rock," the other four songs were cover versions, two from Sun and two from Atlantic. One month before Carroll's sessions Sun had released Warren Smith's "Rock 'n' Roll Ruby," and Elvis's "Trying to Get to You" had just come out on his first album.[9] The traditional "Corrine Corrina" is based on Big Joe Turner's version, and "Wild, Wild Women," although credited to Carroll, is actually a cover of Ruth Brown's "Wild Wild Young Men," which Rose Maddox also had done (1955). Moderate sales helped Carroll to get on touring shows.

In 1957 Tiger got Carroll in *Rock Baby Rock It,* a quickie rock 'n' roll movie. In it Carroll performed four songs (two from the Decca group) backed by his high school buddies, now called the Hot Rocks. Their live show was very popular and lucrative. When Carroll found out that Tiger had been swindling him out of many thousands of dollars, the dispute went to the courts. Before it was settled Tiger forced him to stop performing for six months.

Decca soon dropped him, but before the year was out Carroll was back on the *Louisiana Hayride* with Scotty Moore and Bill Black, who had quit Elvis that summer. Carroll remembered that they were "madder 'n' hell 'cos Presley was on $50,000 a week and they were getting $100 each."[10] Moore started Carroll playing lead guitar, and Black put him in contact with Sam Phillips, who eventually bought the four 1957 demos Carroll and the band made in Fort Worth. One single was issued on the Phillips International label, one of few masters that Phillips ever bought. Three of the songs were Carroll's own, and one of them, the strongest of the group, was the unissued "Rock Baby Rock It," not from the movie but named after it.

Back in Dallas, Carroll got a new manager in Ed McLemore, who ran the *Big D Jamboree* and managed Sonny James, Buddy Knox, and others. McLemore also booked Gene Vincent, then based in Dallas. The two singers became friends and shared some of the same back-up musicians. Vincent recorded Carroll's composition "Maybe." In late 1958 Carroll recorded two singles for Warner Brothers. On two songs he sounds very much like Vincent; another, a ballad named "Bandstand Doll," charted regionally and was Carroll's biggest hit. A 1962 single for a local independent label was his last for more than a decade.

To his collection of voices—straining ambitious rockabilly, emotional balladeer, and experienced Gene Vincent–styled rocker, not to mention the pop gospel of the 1962 single—an unissued song from 1957 called "Whiskey River" adds an unknown Johnny Carroll voice: dark, husky, and country, which is the voice that endured for him.

For all Carroll's label bouncing, manager changing, style hopping, voice manipulations, live reputation, and movie experience, he left the performing part of the business. He stayed in the nightclub business but left that too after getting wounded by a bullet.

Carroll credits Judy Lindsey, his singing partner, with getting him back into performing. In 1974 he recorded a single for Rollin' Rock entitled "Black Leather Rebel," a fine tribute to Gene Vincent. Three years later Carroll's three Decca singles were reissued on the first two volumes of the *Rare Rockabilly* series, eventually leading to many European tours, some with Lindsey. In between, the Judy and Johnny Band played a regular gig at the Hilton Hotel in Fort Worth. They have recorded a couple of albums and many singles, some charting in Texas.

Johnny Carroll's 1978 album for Rollin' Rock, *Texabilly*, recorded in one twenty-eight-hour marathon session, is artistically successful. Ray Campi supplies the bass, and Carroll, singing in his raspy, husky voice, does all the guitar work. He also wrote five of the songs.

Carroll made eleven tours to Europe and remained a popular draw on the festival circuit into the 1990s. He died in 1995 following an unsuccessful liver transplant.

MAC CURTIS
Born Wesley Erwin Curtis Jr., January 16, 1939, Fort Worth, Texas

Mac Curtis's rockabilly credentials were established with his seven singles on the King label, from 1956 to 1958. The earlier ones, despite the presence of drums and simple piano playing, are strongly based on the Presley Sun sound, and songs such as "If I Had Me a Woman" and "Grandaddy's Rockin'" are fine examples of prime rockabilly. Later singles with background singers and electric bass are less delightful to the purists.

Curtis grew up in the small town of Onley, Texas, where he was raised by his grandparents (a later single paired "Grandaddy's Rockin'" with "You Oughta See Grandma Rock"). A bass-playing uncle and the radio exposed him to western swing, honky-tonk, and gospel. In 1954 Curtis moved to just outside Fort Worth, where his hillbilly band played parties and social functions. That year he met Johnny Carroll when both were in talent contests. Two years later, aged seventeen, Curtis started his lifelong career in radio.

Curtis's early influences included Piano Red's "Rockin' with Red," which he bought unheard in a used record store, and Marty Robbins's "That's Allright," which Curtis heard before knowing Presley's version.

During a rehearsal, Curtis recalled, "a friend came in and said, 'Hey there's a guy who sounds just like you and he's got a record on the jukebox down at the Dairy Mart.' We went down and saw the name Elvis Presley and said 'Aw that's the way we ought to be doing it, it's got that good Chet Atkins/Merle Travis–type sound'."[11] While playing at the *Big D Jamboree* show, Curtis and his band saw that Elvis had added a drummer, so they did, too.

When a car dealership hired them as an afternoon attraction, the phenomenal response from the live radio broadcast led to a contract with King. At their April 1956 recording session Curtis went in the control booth during playbacks and saw the producer playing a copy of Elvis's first album, checking to see whether they were getting the right kind of sound.[12]

Touring and sales were confined to Texas and Louisiana, but by autumn "You Ain't Treatin' Me Right" (a sixteen-bar shuffle using a one-bar riff) rated high on Alan Freed's radio show in New York. This led to Curtis's performing in Freed's *Christmas Shower of Stars* package show: after a couple of weeks of doing five shows a day at the Brooklyn Paramount theater, they went on tour, interrupting Curtis's senior year of high school. After graduation he entered the army in late 1957, studying broadcasting and working in the Armed Forces Radio Network in Korea. He did his next session while on leave. After King had recorded the minimum number of songs required by contract, the label did not renew. "I was paid union scale for playing rhythm guitar on the sessions and that was all—no royalties, no statement or anything like that; I suspect [label boss] Syd Nathan [whom he never met] never even knew I existed."[13] Curtis recorded for many other labels, trying various things like the novelty dance song "The Squirm," and rejoined the *Big D*. From 1968 to 1970 he placed six songs in the country charts, one of them a cover of Carl Perkins's "Honey Don't."

In 1971 Curtis moved to Los Angeles and continued his work as a top country music deejay. Ronny Weiser soon found him and started recording him on Rollin' Rock. The *Ruffabilly* album, the first of several Curtis albums for the label, was also one of the first recorded in Weiser's home studio. It lives up to its title: it's rough. Too few players (Ray Campi plays bass and guitars) meant too many bounced tracks on the four-track machine, poor sound quality, and problems locking into a groove. The most focused moments are in the three-song tribute to Johnny Carroll. A later album, *Rockin' Mother,* mostly a collection of the singles recorded for Rollin' Rock in the 1970s, is far more successful. Campi still plays most of the instruments, and

Curtis still wrote very little of his own material (he had written only two of the sixteen or seventeen songs recorded for King), but the looseness works, the song selection is interesting, the sound, while still brittle, is acceptable, the style is authentic rockabilly, and the good fun that was had in making it is infectious.

Curtis first toured England in 1977. In 1979 he moved back to Texas to manage a radio station and work in radio jingles, continuing to make more overseas appearances, including a trip to Japan in 1992.

JOE POOVEY
Born May 10, 1941, Dallas, Texas

A man of many nicknames, Poovey had his first music lessons on the steel guitar, but he switched to guitar to be up front. His was a precocious talent, and his parents started teaching him about entertaining at age four. In 1950, when he was nine, he was recorded in a studio doing hillbilly. Three years later he formed his first band, and the next year he became a deejay. As a red-headed twelve year old with freckles and a big Gibson guitar, he started performing regularly on the *Big D Jamboree* show as "Jumping" Joe Poovey. In late 1955, at age fourteen, he took part in a session recorded at Jim Beck's studio in Dallas. Sharing vocal duties with Earney Vandagriiff, with the Big D Boys as the backing band, Poovey released two singles on the Rural Rhythm label. Three of the four songs had Christmas themes. "Be Bop Santa Claus" backed with "Atomic Kisses" was reviewed in the trade papers in 1957.

After seeing Elvis's live shows in Dallas, Poovey was converted to rockabilly. His rockabilly output from the 1950s consists of fewer than a dozen titles, many unissued at the time and all appealing. Most are jaunty with a natural ease. There is a certain amount of variety: note the piano rocker "Ten Long Fingers" ("on 88 keys") with a sax solo, the doo-wop-style background singing on "Sweet Louella," and the steel on "Careful Baby." "Move Around" is reminiscent of Sid King and the Five Strings, and "Part Time Hero" is backshack pop country. Although not relying on blues structures, other songs are more conventionally rockabilly in style.

Producer Jim Shell has been Poovey's songwriting partner for more than thirty years. One of their early efforts, "Silence Baby," is another of rockabilly's songs of male dominance. Inspired by "Honey Hush," from which it lifts the "yakety yak/ holding a baseball bat" rhyme, "Silence Baby" includes the lines "now if I tell you to git, then you sure better go, and if'n' I say rooster, that's the time for you to crow" and "when I start to talking, that's the time for you to stop."

Poovey appeared on TV programs and remained with the *Big D* show until its demise in late 1960. He continued to perform, record, and write songs—for George Jones, Wynn Stewart, and others—and work as a deejay. In fact, it was another deejay who coined his rockabilly nickname—"Groovey" Joe Poovey—while introducing "Move Around." Poovey decided to keep it as a stage name, although his first chart success, in 1966, was as Johnny Dallas; in 1975 he was "Texas" Joe Poovey. European interest and tours saw him reverting to the Groovey tag while overseas.

BOB LUMAN

Born April 15, 1937, Nacogdoches, Texas; died December 27, 1978, Nashville

Bob Luman was in the army when his 1960 pop smash "Let's Think about Living," a response to the fad for tragedy songs, hit the top ten. He never had another in the pop charts, but the song started a long string of country hits. He owes his rockabilly fame mostly to his 1955 and 1957 recordings.

Luman's hometown of Kilgore, Texas, is just over the state line from Louisiana, and the *Hayride* in Shreveport played a big part in his career. Its first broadcast came two years before he got his first guitar at age thirteen. His father, who played fiddle, guitar, and harmonica and later wrote songs for his son, showed him the basics, and in high school Luman formed a hillbilly band, imitating the singers he heard on the radio. When Presley, between *Hayride* dates, did nine one-nighters in a row in the Kilgore area, Luman went to every one of them. "That's the last time I tried to sing like Webb Pierce or Lefty Frizzell," he said.[14]

After failing a trial in professional baseball, Luman focused on music. His win at a Future Farmers of America talent contest (judged by Johnny Cash, Carl Perkins, and Johnny Horton) led to guesting on the *Hayride,* and he gained a spot as a regular when Cash left the show. Before long Luman had his own TV show in Shreveport, and later he was on the televised *Town Hall Party* in Los Angeles. Mac Curtis had also competed in that talent contest, and they became good friends; Luman used Curtis's band for six demos in Dallas in 1955. Five of them are hot rockabilly, with slashing, incisive guitar, and the sixth, "Let Her Go," is a triplet ballad intriguing for its meter—the vocal in 3/4 and then the solo in 4/4—and its intro figure: two bars in 4/4, which show up again in the middle of the 3/4 section. That intro helps to date the session more accurately, since the figure is no doubt lifted from the Platters's first hit, "Only You," which entered the charts in October 1955. Luman used the figure again two years later in "Amarillo Blues."

In 1957 Luman was signed to Imperial and brought his Shreveport band of James Burton (guitar), James Kirkland (bass), and Butch White (drums) to Hollywood. Before long, however, Ricky Nelson enlisted them.

James Burton, born in Shreveport in 1939, is one of the most important guitarists of his generation. At age fourteen, just one year after getting his first guitar, he became a staff musician on the *Hayride*. After doing "Susie Q" with Dale Hawkins and working with Luman Burton spent many years with Ricky Nelson, backing him on record and on TV. In the mid-1960s he was one of the Shindiggers, the staff band on the TV show *Shindig*. From 1969 to 1977 Burton played with Elvis; following this he did stints with Jerry Lee Lewis, Emmylou Harris, John Denver, and others, as well as playing on countless sessions.

The movie *Carnival Rock*, produced and directed by Roger Corman in 1957, offers some of the most wonderful rockabilly film footage in existence. Bob Luman and David Houston take turns fronting the band, and James Burton is in fine form. Houston is known to country fans for his lengthy string of hits from 1963 through the 1970s. Several of them, including "Almost Persuaded," made number one. Born in Louisiana in 1937 (he died in 1993), he is also a native of Shreveport and another *Hayride* veteran, starting there at age twelve. He recorded first for Imperial in 1955, and the next two years saw him with RCA Victor. In the movie Houston does a cover of Don "Red" Roberts's "Only One." Both Houston and Eddie Fontaine used the title "One and Only" on their recorded versions. Other songs Houston does in the film are "Sugar Sweet" and "Teenage Frankie and Johnny." He joined the *Grand Ole Opry* in 1972.

Although Bob Luman did very little songwriting, his rockabilly style comes in part from his choice of material.[15] His 1957 songs are much less blues oriented, showing his obvious liking for songs with eight-bar phrases, often arranged with a two-bar break (especially in B sections), with the stop occurring on the downbeat of bar 7. A number of songs use the classic pop thirty-two-bar AABA song form, including "Blue Days, Black Nights" (a cover of Buddy Holly's first release), "Whenever You're Ready" (by Dorsey Burnette, using the "I Got Rhythm" progression), "Bring Along Your Love" (Burnette-styled pop), and "All Night Long" (sung in the movie *Carnival Rock*). "All Night Long," with its piano triplets and a catchy guitar riff, is one of Luman's best rockabilly songs. Another one, "Your Love," has Burton's characteristic inventive hot licks chattering over the shimmering piano background (in the full band version). It has just one eight-bar phrase, although because the verse's melody differs from that of the chorus, the song follows an AAB form. Luman was listening to Sun—his cover of "Red Hot" is his most intense rockabilly—and people there were listening to him: Warren Smith covered his "Red Cadillac and a Black Mustache."

After 1957 Luman swam the pop-rock waters in the wake of Elvis, backed by the usual male backup singers, sax, handclaps, and so on, and his records sound more anonymous. In 1962, after his army discharge, he moved to Nashville, joining the *Grand Ole Opry* in 1965. He toured regularly and was popular in Las Vegas, where his ability at impressions came in handy. Luman's high-powered live shows mixed country and rockabilly, on which he never turned his back completely. In 1976, still in sideburns, he cut his version of "Mystery Train." One of the first veterans to become aware of the revival, he was, unfortunately, not able to take much advantage of it. In 1978, twelve days after a performance at the *Opry*, Bob Luman died of pneumonia at the age of forty-one.

JOHNNY HORTON

Born April 30, 1925, Los Angeles; died November 5, 1960, Milano, Texas

Johnny Horton was a flexible but not particularly ambitious performer who passed through country and rockabilly to become a reluctant star, famous for his folk-based story songs, dying when his career was at its highest point. Horton, known as the Singing Fisherman, was not good at handling money and preferred hunting and fishing. He was a basketball star in high school, dropped out of geology studies at Seattle University, packed fruit in California, worked in construction in Alaska, went fishing at every opportune moment and place, and picked cotton at home on the farm in Texas where he was raised. After winning talent contests, Horton tried to make a career in country music and made his first recordings in 1951. He joined the *Louisiana Hayride* in 1952, where he was photographed performing in a tuxedo; he later embraced full cowboy attire. After years of little reward, in 1955 he got a new manager in Tillman Franks, who got him on the Columbia label.

Horton, usually with Franks, wrote some of his repertory. Like Marty Robbins and Johnny Cash, Horton presented a storybook America, the kind seen on TV Westerns and imagined by kids in Daniel Boone coonskin hats. Besides treating patriotism and the gold rush, Horton sang about or from the perspective of the biker, trucker, train rider, migrant worker, dying prospector, Native American, Cajun, Gypsy, pioneer, bear, honky-tonk dancer, and lover (whether rooted in devotion or running toward or away from women).

Some of these songs, mostly the earlier ones before the Americana visions became more grandiose, are rockabilly. Horton defined a personal, more subdued rockabilly—country structures with bluesy guitar and pronounced rhythm—as befitting one who was older and had already started a career in country music. Making little use of rockabilly vocal devices, except for some feathering, he nonetheless had a rich, versatile voice, from a sincere ballad style to a go-get-'em growl to a clipped, intense, and controlled gospel. His songs, especially the later ones, have a cornucopia of orchestrations, making use of harmonica, banjo, jaw harp, Dobro, harpsichord, and tambourine and a variety of colors pulled from the conventional rockabilly instruments, as well as a surprising variety in the types of choral singing.

The imagery of "Honky Tonk Man," one of Horton's most enduring songs (since the patriotic Americana songs now seem so quaint), was continued in "The Woman I Need (Honky Tonk Mind)," and "Honky Tonk Hardwood Floor," although all are by different writers. Many more songs were cut from the same cloth as "Honky Tonk Man," and the weave includes images of a proud, passionate loner and wandering womanizer, medium tempo, acoustic rhythm guitar, busy low-string guitar, upright bass, drums, and an affection for the keys E and A. Certainly the low-tuned guitar with the trebly tone was a trademark, but there is imaginative use of guitar muting and harmonics ("Take Me Like I Am") and of rhythms—for example, the train beat and Bo Diddley touches in "First Train Heading South," a Horton composition.

Another of Horton's favorite devices was to stay on the I chord for long periods. "I'm Coming Home," with the exception of a mere two beats of the V chord in each verse, is a one-chord country boogie, with a guitar figure out of "Train Kept a-Rolling": tension is created by the use of the flatted third (in the guitar figure and in the melody) against the major chord strummed by the rhythm guitar. Additional examples of mostly static harmony are "I Got the Bull by the Horns," and the A section of "Lover's Rock," a Latin beat in a minor key. Its B section is a rare (for Horton) use of the blues progression.

Horton had major success with the saga songs "Battle of New Orleans," "Sink the Bismark," and "North to Alaska." They all made the top five in 1959 and 1960. Around that time Horton became obsessed with premonitions of an impending and violent death. While driving on a foggy highway after a gig in Austin, Texas, Horton was killed at the wheel of his car in a head-on collision with a drunk driver, leaving his wife, Billie Jean, the former Mrs. Hank Williams, a widow for the second time.

BUCK GRIFFIN AND ANDY STARR

Griffin born February, 1923, Corsicana, Texas; Starr born Franklin Delano Gulledge, October 21, 1932, Mill Creek, Arkansas

Both Buck Griffin and Andy Starr recorded first for the Lin label of Gainesville, Texas, in 1954; both had a number of their masters bought by and released on MGM in 1956 (their best rockabilly), and both went back briefly to the Lin label in the early 1960s. They never met.

A. C. "Buck" Griffin grew up in Oklahoma and Kansas City. As a guitar-playing teenager he formed a band with three friends and played local dances. He worked for years as an oil-field roughneck, digging ditches for pipelines. For a while he had his own radio show and later was a regular on the *Big D Jamboree*. Despite having a fine voice and strong material, his music career did not take off. Perhaps his sound was too rustic or too relaxed. With a wife and two children to support, he augmented his earnings by selling Bibles. Seven singles came out on Lin in 1954 and 1955; they comprise various styles, including country, western swing, boogie, sacred, and rockabilly. Griffin composed almost all his songs and wrote for other artists. "Let's Elope Baby" was later covered by Janis Martin.

Griffin's three 1956 MGM singles roll more than rock. His assured country vocals are pleasant, playful, and relaxed, at times reminiscent of Carl Perkins, and his few vocal devices are more effective for being rationed. A strong acoustic feeling comes from the band—two guitars, bass, and drums. Only the lead guitar is amplified, but its sound is clear in the traditions of western swing and jazz, unlike the style of the raunchier blues and rock 'n' roll guitarists who overloaded their amps or purposely tore speaker cones to achieve distorted and aggressive sounds. The drums often keep a steady swing feel on the cymbals.

Of the six songs on the three MGM singles, two are blues structures, and three songs stay on the I chord with brief visits to the V. The sixth, "You'll Never Come Back," has an unusual texture: in 12/8 time, it includes a woodblock tapping all twelve beats, the acoustic guitar strumming an even four to the bar, and the bass playing on all but the first and seventh beats. Above this, the electric guitar delivers the shimmering sound of two notes alternating in rapid succession, using the hammer-on and pull-off techniques.

The lyrics of these songs on MGM deal with feelings for a woman. If in all these songs Griffin is describing his own life and referring to the same woman—he may or may not be—we could assemble the following components of a story:

- He enters the infatuation stage: he is simply crazy about her and needs her ("Stutterin' Papa").
- Money becomes a sensitive issue: he has to work hard lifting heavy iron to make a decent living and wishes that she were more careful with the money ("Bow My Back").
- Disenchantment sets in: he gets fed up with her because she does not love him enough, and he wants to look elsewhere ("Old Bee Tree": "no honey left for me").
- He considers the possibility of separation: he feels powerless knowing that she might leave and take his money ("Watching the 7:10 Roll By").
- Separation occurs, and reconciliation is at a stalemate: although he wants her back, he is tired of trying to please her and too proud and stubborn to beg ("You'll Never Come Back": "if you wait 'til I beg you to come").
- He gets desperate: he breaks down and begs her, enticing her by saying that he has lots of money ("Jessie Lee").

It is probably just fancy to construct a coherent narrative in this way, although if I may continue, let's say it is the same woman Griffin addressed earlier in "Let's Elope Baby." A seventh song (unissued) from these sessions might conclude the history. It is titled "Broken Heart with Alimony."

Griffin's next single came only in 1961, again on Lin. Subsequent releases were on various other labels.

Andy Starr, whose real name is Franklin Delano Gulledge, came from a large musical family and was raised in rural poverty in Arkansas. He dropped out of school early after pulling a pistol on a teacher, and by fourteen he was hoboing around the country. He moved to Texas in the early 1950s after serving two terms in Korea (leading to a diagnosis of post-traumatic stress disorder). His initial recordings, made in 1954 as Frankie Starr and the Rock-A-Way-Boys, were two singles for Lin. The style is honky-tonk, the band is loose, the piano playing is from the back shack, the guitarist is jaunty, especially on "Tell Me Why," and Starr's voice is lugubrious. The chorus of "Dig Them Squeaky Shoes" is Starr yelling out "rock!" several times.

To avoid confusion with a Nashville singer of the same name, Frank Starr became Andy Starr. Four Lin masters were bought and released by MGM in April 1956, and another four in September. The first batch show a big influence of Presley's Sun records, with a copy of Scotty Moore's solo from "Good Rockin' Tonight" in "Rockin' Rollin' Stone." Also lifted from "Good Rockin' Tonight" is the chant of "let's rock" over a boogie figure on guitar, which Starr uses in "She's a Going Jessie." The second group of four songs adds a male chorus singing doo-wop-type syllables, and the drums are more prominent and powerful; these songs rock much harder.

Starr's music on MGM has a cohesiveness. The drums in some songs play a simple accompaniment without any fills; coupled with walking bass, this gives an almost hypnotic feeling. Similarly, in three songs the bass plays the chord roots in half notes or the country two-beat cliché of root to lower fifth, but in quarter notes; in both cases the result is the root played on the strong beats 1 and 3. Another hypnotic effect is achieved by the repetition in "I Wanna Go South": "well hello, hey hey hey, come on come on come on, with me with me with me, let's ride ride ride, this train train train, south south south." Starr wrote it as a fast, rocking song but had to go along with label boss Joe Leonard's wishes, and it came out slow and bluesy. All eight of the MGM songs use the twelve-bar blues progression, although "Old Deacon Jones" uses it only for the solos; the verse and chorus use an eight-bar structure.

Starr's lyric themes in these songs reflect three main concerns: people and things in motion, the psychology of money, and love worries. In "Round and Round" it is the little roulette ball that is in motion, and "all my cash, just like trash, goes down, down, down." In "Rockin' Rollin' Stone" Starr sings about how he is always on the go, in "I Wanna Go South" he is riding the train, and in "She's a Going Jessie" he admires a young A student ("to say the least, she's the most") who is also a real rocker on the go. The psychology of money is explored not only in the study of the gambler's psyche offered in "Round and Round" (the blonde manages to make his money disappear) but also in "Old Deacon Jones": the good deacon's so-called friends take advantage of his generosity and then desert him when the well runs dry. In the love worries department, there is "Give Me a Woman," where any kind of caring woman will do. In "No Room for Your Kind" the woman is stepping out and the lyrics express jealousy, and in "One More Time" the lyrics deal with the fear of being loved insufficiently.

Vocally Starr goes to the Elvis approach with the first four on MGM and "Give Me a Woman" from the second batch, but on the remaining three—"Round and Round," "No Room for Your Kind," and "One More Time"—he adopts a more straining, frenetic vocal style.

In 1959 Starr's riot-inducing live show landed him a six-month booking in Anchorage, Alaska, and he ended up staying five years, working also as a male stripper and flying back to Nashville regularly for sessions. Until 1962 Starr had other singles: on Kapp, on Lin again, two on Holiday Inn (a Sam Phillips label), and on Valiant. Those that I have heard are not rockabilly but ballads and white rock with saxophone and piano. "Knee's Shakin'" is particularly enjoyable.

Starr, a real rock 'n' roll Casanova (he estimates that he bedded 5,000 women once each, as was his rule), cleaned up his alcohol and amphetamine habits in the 1970s when he became a minister working with prisoners. Dissatisfied with organized religion, he started his own church (the Church of America, "an ultraprogressive, liberal, leftist, deprofessionalized church—the voice of the voiceless") and ran for political office.[16] One of his promotional posters, with a picture of him playing guitar and singing into a mike, bills him as Frank Starr, America's "Patriot Prophet, Theorist Rectifier, Killer of Favorites, Candidate for the Presidency of the United States of America."

In 1990 Starr was booked to appear in Europe, and a series of his letters appeared in *Now Dig This* magazine. Signing himself as Frank "Andy" Starr, "The Ultimate Rebel," he wrote from Byron, Arkansas, where he had recently moved his family and made his first public performance in ten years. Starr mentioned running as a "protest" candidate in the 1978 presidential elections, that he has several higher education degrees, and that he planned to urinate on the remains of the Berlin Wall as a political statement. According to Paul Barrett, the agent who was to coordinate a European tour, Starr backed out of it after his demands were not met for "a big time recording contract, not wanting to be restricted to Fifties [music] but wanting to expand into the 'XXX-rated contemporary adult market.'"[17] Starr's ten-page response to Barrett was not printed "due to libel laws."[18]

Reprinted in *Billy Poore's Rockabilly Revue* is a newspaper ad for a 1990 performance that reads in part, "Back By Popular Demand—Frank Starr and his White River Ramblers. The Ultimate Rebel—High Priest of 50's Rock & Roll." Poore reports, "from the video & cassettes he sent me I believe he's beyond the point of ever recapturing a glimmer of the excitement he had in those Rockin' songs back 36 yrs. ago. I could be wrong though . . . hope I am."[19] Starr's address is given as "in care of the International Association For World Peace in Elkins, Arkansas."

THE STRIKES

The Strikes were a group from Gainesville, Texas. It generally has been thought that Andy Starr was a member, but in correspondence with Toronto researcher Marc Coulavin, Starr stated that he was not even aware of them.[20] That the Strikes' guitarist is probably on Andy Starr's tracks may be the cause of the confusion. This sonic likelihood is supported by the fact that six of the eight MGM Starr titles were written by Don Alexander or Willie Jacobs; they account for three of the four titles by the Strikes where authorship is known.

In 1957 six songs by the Strikes were purchased by Imperial from Lin, resulting in two singles being released. Of these recordings, five were reissued on the *Imperial Rockabillies* trilogy—the sixth, a slow ballad, was passed over for reissue. The five songs are unique in rockabilly: almost all the words are delivered by three male vocalists, two singing the melody in unison with the third singing a harmony part a third above. The singing is very smooth, with many held notes at the end of lines, and at times background "aahs" are sung during a guitar solo. The parallel motion in the voices, and sometimes guitar, is hypnotic. In addition, there are maracas (on three of the five songs), acoustic bass, what sounds like the same drummer as Starr's September 1956 MGM sides, and a musical, chattery, and sometimes distorted lead guitar. This musician often builds a solo by taking a simple pattern and transposing it at each chord change. Rhythm guitar is virtually inaudible in all but one song where, barely audible, it plays half notes. Both sides of the Strikes' first single—"If You Can't Rock Me" and "Baby I'm Sorry"—were covered by Ricky Nelson on his first album, also on Imperial.

HUELYN DUVALL AND DANNY WOLFE

Duvall born around 1940, Stephenville, Texas

Huelyn Duvall recorded a handful of appealing pop rockabilly songs in Nashville and Hollywood in 1957 and 1958 for the Challenge label, owned by Gene Autry, the singing cowboy movie star. The Nashville tracks, cut at Owen Bradley's studio, included such familiar names as Grady Martin, Floyd Cramer, Hank Garland, Buddy Harman, and the Jordanaires, who provide firm and in-the-groove backing, which is at the same time somewhat subdued. In other words, the heat is on but not turned up too high. This is also true for the Hollywood tracks, backed by a band later called the Champs, who hit with "Tequila" on the same label. This actually suits Duvall's pleasant though rather plain voice, which has as its most distinguishing feature a reliance on vibrato. He is often unsparing in his use of many of the tricks that rockabilly vocalists exploited, although he uses them less forcefully. He was about seventeen when he recorded, and most of the lyrics are particularly teen oriented, such as "Teen Queen" ("high school princess"), "You Knock Me Out" ("I played it cool 'cause I ain't no square"), "Three Months to Kill" (about getting out of school for the summer), "Pucker Paint" (slang for lipstick), and "Friday Night on a Dollar Bill."

The last three of the songs just named were from the pen of Danny Wolfe, who met Duvall in 1956. They were both natives of Stephenville, Texas, a town not far from Dallas, where they had seen Elvis perform. Wolfe played piano, had a studio, and booked Duvall and Tooter Boatman in clubs and on TV shows to help to popularize his songs, for it was Wolfe's prolific songwriting that provided most of their material.

Boatman recorded excellent rockabilly in "Thunder and Lightning," "The Will of Love," "Susie's House," and "Big Deal," all written by Wolfe. William "Tooter" Boatman was born in 1936 and was killed in a hit-and-run accident in 1964. His wild exploits as a lover, fighter, and reckless driver are recounted by his drummer Clay Glover.[21]

Danny Wolfe also wrote Sanford Clark's "Modern Romance," Bobby Milano's "Life Begins at Four O'Clock," and three songs recorded by Gene Vincent, including "Double Talkin' Baby" (revived by the Stray Cats). Wolfe's "Fool's Hall of Fame" was recorded by Wolfe, Duvall, Johnny Cash, and Roy Orbison, although none of these versions was released at the time. Duvall performed and recorded in Holland and England in 1985, backed by the Dave Travis Band, which has made a concert staple out of "Let's Flat Get It," a song that Danny Wolfe recorded but did not write.

Marty Robbins (from the collection of Marc Coulavin/Top of the Bops Archives).

Roy Hall in his Nashville office, 1983 (photo by the author).

Gene Vincent and Jerry Merritt (on the left) with musicians in Tokyo, 1959 (courtesy of Rockhouse Records).

Werly Fairburn (from the collection of Wayne Russell).

Sid King and the Five Strings (from the collection of Wayne Russell).

Buddy Holly (from the collection of Wayne Russell).

Frank Starr (also known as Andy Starr) and his Blue Notes at the Hi-Hat Club, Anchorage, Alaska, 1963 or 1964 (from the collection of Marc Coulavin/Top of the Bops Archives).

Maddox Brothers and Rose (from the collection of Marc Coulavin/Top of the Bops Archives).

Glen Glenn, Era label promo photo (courtesy of the artist).

Eddie Cochran (from the collection of Wayne Russell).

The Collins Kids (from the collection of Wayne Russell).

ELEVEN

CALIFORNIA

"Summertime Blues"

California was alive with rockabilly music. The large number of out-of-state performers who recorded there, some settling there, includes the Maddox family from Alabama, the Collins Kids from Oklahoma, Missouri-born Glen Glenn, Ricky Nelson, born in New Jersey, and Minnesotan Eddie Cochran.

THE MADDOX BROTHERS AND ROSE

Rose Maddox born December 15, 1926, Boaz, Alabama. Fred Maddox born 1919; died October 29, 1992, Delano, California. Cal Maddox died 1968. Henry Maddox died 1974.

This versatile group of musical siblings became a top country show-band attraction in the 1940s and 1950s, ably performing country standards, gospel, blues, western yodeling, rich harmony singing, swing, country boogie, honky-tonk, and waltzes. Their delivery was often laced with a strong dose of novelty: ad-libs, comedy routines, acting out the lyrics during performances, sound effects, and laughter. Their rockabilly material shows less black influence than most, and the singing retains the unequivocal delivery common to older, experienced artists who added rockabilly to their vocabulary of styles.

The siblings came from a family of Alabama sharecroppers. Their father played the banjo, and their uncle was a music teacher and performer, sometimes singing in blackface. In 1933, their crops failing, the family sold their worldly possessions, raising all of thirty-five dollars, and with five children age six to seventeen moved to California by walking, hitchhiking, and riding boxcars. The trip took three months. Two married children, Cliff and Alta, both musicians, stayed behind. For a few years the Maddox family worked as "fruit tramps" (migratory field hands), picking cotton and fruit along the coast from California to Washington and playing music after work in the camps. Fred, the bass-playing brother, got fed up with the work and decided that they could do better in the music business. He hustled them onto a radio show in 1937. The station demanded a female singer, so Rose, the youngest and only eleven, became the featured singer. Starting as a trio with Fred, Rose, and Cal on guitar and harmonica (and a frequently heard maniacal laugh), they were soon joined by the other brothers, Henry on mandolin and Don on fiddle. Various "hired hands," present for live dates and recordings but not for the radio shows, included steel player Bud Duncan, guitarist Roy Nichols (subsequently with Merle Haggard), and later, Glen Glenn. The group performed for many years on the radio, starting in 1937 in Modesto, California, where they were heard across five states. Popular from the beginning, they received stacks of mail and drew large audiences to their live shows. The war caused the group to disband, for some of the brothers went in the armed services. The Maddox Brothers and Rose started again in 1945. They made their first recordings the following year for 4 Star in Pasadena, an association that lasted five years and produced several hits, one being a version of Woody Guthrie's "Philadelphia Lawyer."

Commercial recordings and radio transcriptions from 1946 to 1951 provide a good picture of their varied repertory, including songs showing that during this period they were on their way to something very close to rockabilly. In the instrumental "Texas Guitar Stomp" Fred's furious but controlled slapped bass is, as usual, prominently pushing the beat along; not too much later, Fred's style made a big impression on Bill Black. The repetitions of the sixteen-bar harmonized western swing theme are broken up by a pioneering rockabilly guitar solo, opening with a quote from "Reveille" over the blues form and urged on by enthusiastic whoops and hollers.

"Hangover Blues," with steel, fiddle, electric guitar, and a melody like a guitar boogie-woogie figure, is a honky-tonk song from around 1950 pointing straight to rockabilly. Rose sings of being broke, out of alcohol, and hung over and of her man not letting her in when she came home. This and many other of Rose's songs paint an image of a strong-willed, fun-loving, nobody's-fool type of woman, but this is undermined by the lighthearted hilarity of the delivery and the brothers' interjections. Indeed, this is true for a great deal of the repertory no matter who is singing, serving to let the audience know that even if the subject matter is direct, the family entertainment concept is maintained.

In 1949 the band made their only appearance on the *Grand Ole Opry* on the strength of their hit "Gathering Flowers for the Master's Bouquet." In 1951 they moved to Hollywood, where their uniforms got outlandish and they signed to Columbia. In the 1950s they were regulars on the *Louisiana Hayride,* where they helped Elvis to appear for the first time. Rose began to imitate him on stage. As the 1950s advanced, the group's recordings show less clowning around, less overt country instrumentation and vocal inflections, and a bigger influence of rock and pop.

Released under Rose Maddox's name only was her February 1955 recording of "Wild Wild Young Men," a cover of Ruth Brown's R&B hit about how popular the singer was with men. Later in 1955 she released another fast and hot blues-form rockabilly song, "Hey Little Dreamboat," with the uncredited brothers chiming in on the answering vocals.

In 1956 the group parodied "I Got a Woman." They called it "The Death of Rock and Roll," good-naturedly satirizing the amateur vocalist's stilted phrasing, poor time, and poor command of pitch, although the vocals are pure country. On "Stop Whistlin' Wolf," from 1957, Rose is the only singer, there is a punchy rhythm figure on the snare drum, and the novelty element is evident only in the whistles, with a couple of spoken comments and a laugh at the beginning of the guitar solo. The fiddle has been deliberately pushed into the background.

The group recorded together for the last time in 1957. Around then Rose was a regular on the *Grand Ole Opry.* Contracted to Columbia also as a solo singer, she continued with the label until 1958, moving to Capitol the following year.

Rose's 1959 recording "My Little Baby," which she cowrote with brother Henry, is an appealing pop rockabilly song with lots of stops, strong cymbal and snare work, a hot guitar solo, and a reference to *American Bandstand.*

From 1959 to 1964 Rose did very well in the country charts, sang duets with Buck Owens, and toured with Johnny Cash. She continued to make records, including a bluegrass album with Bill Monroe. In 1982 I saw her performing country songs at the Vancouver Folk Festival. In 1990 Rose performed in Europe for the rockabilly fans.

GLEN GLENN

Born Glen Troutman, October 24, 1934, Joplin, Missouri

Glen Glenn was thirteen when his family moved to San Dimas, near Los Angeles. His paper route earned him enough money to buy his first guitar two years later. By 1954, after winning a talent contest, Glenn and guitarist Gary Lambert, a high school friend, were appearing on barn dance shows and television as Glen and Gary, the Missouri Mountain Boys. On one show he met Fred Maddox, and after Glenn did a stint back in Missouri playing with his cousin Porter Wagoner, he joined the Maddox Brothers and Rose. Rose soon left to pursue her solo career and was replaced by her sister. The band then was billed as the Maddox Brothers and Retta with Glen Trout (as he was then known). At the insistence of Fred Maddox and under the influence of Elvis—hearing his music and getting to know him—Glenn was converted to rockabilly and did an Elvis impersonation in the act. Live and studio recordings from 1956 onward, unreleased at the time, show him copying Elvis, Mac Curtis, and Sonny Fisher.

Those derivative stylings pale beside Glenn's relaxed and charming original rockabilly songs: "Everybody's Movin'," "I'm Glad My Baby's Gone Away," "One Cup of Coffee," "Would Ya," and "Blue Jeans and a Boy's Shirt." There are a number of creative touches in those songs. The catchy descending slide on guitar that sets up a two-bar bass figure made "Everybody's Movin'" a favorite song with fans and bands in the 1980s. "I'm Glad My Baby's Gone Away" has an unusual stop on beat three (followed by a full bar of instrumental silence) and catchy rhythmic accents during the instrumental break. At the end of most lines in "Blue Jeans and a Boy's Shirt," Glenn sings a slow, continuous rising portamento, varying both the speed and the interval of the rise.

Glenn recorded, at his own expense, the first of those songs in January 1958, with a band that included Lambert and Connie "Guybo" Smith, who also played bass for Eddie Cochran. After shopping around for a deal, Glenn was signed to Era, a Hollywood independent that eventually released all five songs plus the nonoriginal ballad "Laurie Ann" on three singles.

Only modest commercial success resulted. A few months after his first record came out, Glenn was drafted into the army. He served for two years, recording while on leave. His Special Service status had him performing in Hawaii, Japan, and Korea but prevented an appearance on *American Bandstand*. Not only did he miss promotion opportunities, but changes at Era moved him to the Dore label. Their pop-rock-with-session-musicians approach was unsuccessful for him both artistically and commercially. After army service Glenn still did personal appearances and TV, but the recordings that he did with his own band in 1961, the year he married, were not issued till 1964. Around that time he lost interest in the music business and worked in a missile plant.

After a number of tracks were released on a 1977 rockabilly anthology, interest in Glenn led to an album of additional songs, alternate takes, and live recordings. In 1982 Glenn, Lambert, and Smith were reunited for an album-in-a-day of new recordings called *Everybody's Movin' Again*. There were regrettably few original compositions by Glenn in the 1950s, so it is disappointing that there is only one, the title track, on this set. On the album Glenn mixes standards with less often heard songs by Wynn Stewart, Bobby Lee Trammell, Wayne Raney, and the Maddox Brothers and Rose. The best tracks, where the band is not racing through the material or merely driving over familiar ground, are very successful. Although Glenn's voice is sometimes wrapped in a little too much echo, the ensemble of veterans is generally excellent, especially Gary Lambert on the custom Bigsby double-neck guitar he proudly displays in the liner photo.

In 1987 Glenn made his first trip to Europe to play the Rockhouse festival in Holland and dates in Scandinavia and Great Britain. A second tour in 1993 covered Germany, Switzerland, Holland, and Austria. In 1994 he played the Buddy Holly Tribute at the Surf Ballroom in Clear Lake, Iowa, alongside the Crickets, the Blue Caps, Don McLean, and Narvel Felts.

THE COLLINS KIDS

Lorrie born May 7, 1942, Talequah, Oklahoma; Larry born October 4, 1944, Tulsa, Oklahoma

Even though the Collins Kids were seen regularly on television, enjoyed popularity as a live act, and made a number of well-crafted records for a major label, this brother-and-sister act had no hits. Raised on an Oklahoma dairy farm, they attended a one-room schoolhouse. When Lorrie, age eight, won a talent contest run by Leon McAuliffe, Bob Wills's famous steel guitar player, he advised the parents to move to California. In 1953 the Collins Kids made their debut at the *Town Hall Party* in Compton, a suburb of Los Angeles. Larry became a protégé of country guitar virtuoso Joe Maphis and, like his mentor, got a double-necked guitar, the upper neck tuned an octave above the lower. Larry and Maphis performed and later recorded twin guitar instrumentals. The Collins Kids signed to Columbia in 1955.

The siblings became the family breadwinners, and their proud manager-father drove them around on tour in new Cadillacs and helped to groom their image. Lorrie was also a guitarist, and at first their names were written on the body of the instrument, Lorrie's reading "Lawrencine" (brother Larry was really a Lawrence). Later the names were inlaid on the necks of the guitars; hers read "Lorrie Collins," and Larry, like Maphis, had one name on each guitar neck. Their guitars' fancy pick guards were embellished with musical notes. Stage clothes, in the California fashion, were of the rhinestone cowboy variety with matching buckskin fringes. A little later Lorrie wore crinolines with a one-strap dress, and Larry had a jacket of the same material, a bow tie, and flashy cowboy boots.

Lorrie looked and sounded much older than Larry, although only two and a half years separated them. When harmonizing, commonly in the song's chorus, they were equivalent to a female version of the Everly Brothers, as Larry's shrill child's voice took the higher part. When there was only one voice, usually in the verse of a song but sometimes in whole songs, it was almost invariably Lorrie's, unless Larry played the younger brother in a dialogue; less often he took the boyfriend role or sang a song alone. Their songs, from a variety of writers but sometimes written or cowritten by the Kids, often play up their youth, mentioning, for example, the man in the moon, the sandman, and admiration for parents still in love. Around the Collins Kids, all kinds of things seemed to get rocked up: polkas ("Rock and Roll Polka"), insects ("Beetle Bug Bop"), the cuckoo of Hickory Dickory Dock fame ("The Cuckoo Rock"), and even food ("Shortnin' Bread Rock"). The rockabilly guy next door is not far away ("Hop, Skip and Jump"), and fourteen is just too young to get a hot car ("Hot Rod"). Even Duke Ellington's "Don't Get Around Much Anymore" was rewritten with a teen slant as "Soda Poppin' Around" by Joe Maphis, Johnny Bond, and Harlan Howard (who take full credit). In their version Lorrie plays the role of a girl who becomes a sugar junkie after her boyfriend leaves her, forlornly walking the streets searching for a friend who can buy her a sundae.

Their first two records cast Larry in the role of the pesky kid brother interfering with Lorrie's romances: "Hush Money" and "Make Him Behave." One of Lorrie's true romances was with Ricky Nelson, and the liaison was played up in the fan magazines. Although the two had a lot in common and feelings were strong, neither set of parents was particularly encouraging. A surprise ending came when Lorrie married Johnny Cash's road manager, who was nineteen years older than his teenage bride. A shocked Nelson found out about it through a newspaper gossip column.[1]

The Collins Kids' first records, from 1955 and 1956, typically have banjo, fiddle, and steel, although they are absent in subsequent records. Larry's low-string country boogie figures gradually give way to a more rockabilly style, and the drums (usually played with brushes), bass, and piano remain throughout. As the Collins Kids got a little older, the novelty songs diminished. Lorrie, singing alone, became a match for any female rockabilly in songs like "Mercy" and her cover of Edwin Bruce's "Rock Boppin' Baby." The Collins Kids also covered songs Presley had done: "Party" and the Shelton Brothers' "Just Because."

One of their best songs is "Hoy Hoy," their 1957 version of Little Johnny Jones's 1953 original. Jones was a Chicago blues pianist best known for his work with Elmore James. The fast tempo is perfect for the country boogie guitar, and the hot band, fired by brushes on the snare, uses the same rhythm figure found in the middle of "Rock around the Clock."

In the early 1960s, while Lorrie was busy as a mother, Larry had solo releases. Later that decade they toured again on the casino circuit. Larry had success in the 1970s as the composer of several hits, notably "Delta Dawn."

A lavish set of all their Columbia material was released in 1991. In 1993, backed by the highly regarded Dave and Deke Combo, they played a supremely professional set at the Tenth Hemsby Weekender festival in England to a rapturous audience of more than 3,000. Larry, ever the guitar whiz, danced around the stage playing his twin-neck Mosrite guitar. Lorrie, in fine voice and wearing a custom-made dress with an "Indian chief" design on the front that she wore in 1957 on the *Town Hall Party*, was visibly moved by the crowd's adulation. Afterward they signed autographs for more than two hours.[2]

RICKY NELSON

Born May 8, 1940, Teaneck, New Jersey; died December 31, 1985, DeKalb, Texas

Aside from Elvis Presley, Ricky Nelson was the most commercially successful of any artist who did rockabilly. In the years 1955 to 1959, according to Joel Whitburn's classification system, Elvis was the number-one artist and Nelson was number seven.[3] Over his career Nelson had fifty-three songs in the top 100, eighteen of them in the top ten. Songs such as "Poor Little Fool," "Hello, Mary Lou," and "Travelin' Man" are still in the public's consciousness today. Because almost a dozen of his charted singles and many of his album tracks are rockabilly, Nelson was responsible for spreading the sound to millions of people.

In the year after Ricky's birth, the Nelson family moved to California, and Ricky and his older brother David grew up in public, first on their parents' radio show, beginning in 1949, and then on their parents' TV show, *The Adventures of Ozzie and Harriet,* which ran from 1952 to 1966. Since the TV show portrayed the suburban life of an actual family, many of the estimated eighteen million weekly viewers were readily able to relate.

California TV star or not, Ricky was just the right age to be captivated by rock 'n' roll, and he particularly idolized Carl Perkins. Ricky was interested, and his dad was supportive. Ozzie Nelson had been the leader of a big band—Harriet had been his vocalist—and his musical experience, connections, and willingness made him a powerful manager. At his first session in March 1957, for the Verve label, Ricky recorded two ballads and a cover of Fats Domino's "I'm Walkin'." Well-known jazz guitarist Barney Kessel directed the session, and the musicians included guitarist Merle Travis and drummer Earl Palmer, thus beginning the Ricky Nelson tradition of having highly respected bands and accompanists. (Palmer, from New Orleans, not only had played on Domino's recording of the song, as well as on most of Little Richard's hits, but he was well on his way to becoming one of the world's most recorded musicians.) A couple of weeks later, in the last two minutes of an episode that had him sitting in on drums with a big band, Ricky made his singing debut with "I'm Walkin'" for a television audience estimated at twenty-five million. Response was immediate and sensational: sacks and sacks of fan mail arrived, and the single sold 60,000 copies in the first three days of release. Both sides made the top twenty, and the ballad side, "A Teenager's Romance," climbed to number two.

Nelson performed every week on the show. Not only did he have perfect skin, sleepy eyes, and neatly combed and greased hair, but he looked uncomfortable and self-conscious: truly and universally teenage. Except for the expressive mouth, his face was placid. Not knowing where to look, he would demurely close his eyes, or after singing a line he would look down at his guitar chords. Girls on the set at the party scenes where Nelson inevitably played looked fascinated, but in television viewer land they went crazy. Fan clubs sprang up by the dozen. A full-time publicist was kept busy. Ricky was in the teen magazines, and his conventionally handsome face graced his singles' picture sleeves. He was the first TV celebrity to become a rock 'n' roll star.

Ozzie quickly negotiated an extremely lucrative five-year contract for his son with Imperial, and a team of heavy hitters gathered around Ricky. The Jordanaires were flown in from Nashville; their backing became part of Nelson's trademark. They were sometimes more present than prominent, at times sounding more like Buddy Holly's singers than Elvis's. At the *Town Hall Party,* not only had Nelson met his first love, Lorrie Collins, but he was impressed with Joe Maphis and his double-neck guitar virtuosity. Maphis provided excellent lead guitar on the first Imperial sessions, but his place was soon taken by James Burton. Burton was in town recording with Bob Luman, also for Imperial, when Nelson heard and hired him. One year older than his new boss, Burton not only gave the records an exquisite, authentic touch, but he was also the perfect visual foil: during the television performances Burton, at Nelson's left, is perfectly relaxed, all smiles as he mimes his own effortless hot licks and, with the rest of the band, pretends to sing the Jordanaires backup parts.

The week Nelson made his first recordings, Johnny and Dorsey Burnette did their last session as the Rock 'n' Roll Trio. Shortly afterward the brothers, their parents, wives, and children moved to California. One of their first moves was to meet Nelson, who was soon recording Burnette brothers compositions: "Waitin' in School" and "Believe What You Say," Dorsey's "It's Late," "A Long Vacation," and "My One Desire," and Johnny's "Just a Little Too Much." Most of them were big hits. In October 1957 Nelson met with Elvis and was greatly moved by his encouragement; at that time Ricky Nelson's first album was climbing to number two.

Despite all this genuine southern talent contributing, Nelson's style was ever smooth and pop oriented, unmistakably white and urban. He was actually a bit of a crooner with a rockabilly band. Furthermore, the band, full with guitars, drums, bass, distant piano, and background singers, was light and clean. Emotionally subdued, even distant, Nelson would understate lyrics with good diction rather than emote them. His voice is usually restrained, often tinged with regret and melancholy. His rockabilly was neither threatening nor rebellious. Sam Phillips said he "made rockers sound like ballads."[4] Nelson had a pleasant vocal tone, but he occasionally had pitch problems and trouble with high notes. Nevertheless, from his shy beginnings he gained in confidence; Roy Orbison noted that Nelson "learned to sing on million-selling records."[5]

Ricky Nelson's fast reading of "My Bucket's Got a Hole in It" is pure rockabilly. He starts verses unaccompanied in a light but urgent singing style, and the stop-start effect serves to push the momentum of his fine-tuned, powerful band even more. The dynamic drumming turns up the heat, and the arrangement builds in excitement: during the hot guitar solo the piano spews out hammered triplets. Harmony singers appear for the next refrain. Handclaps with lots of echo are then introduced, and to build it further, Nelson, like Sonny Burgess did in his version, sings an octave higher at the end. Nelson retains the verses about holding the empty bucket while waiting for an unattached woman and looking from the mountain to the sea, watching "the crabs and the fishes doing the be bop beat," but ignores the verse about having a woman in the boss man's yard, replacing it with one about intending to tell his woman, this very day, that he is leaving town. For Hank Williams, the hole in the bucket meant he "can't buy no beer," although for performances he sometimes sang the inoffensive "can't buy no milk." Nelson, aiming for accessibility, sang that the bucket "don't work no more."

Many of Ricky Nelson's songs emphasized his youth. There were songs about being in school and summer vacation, coming in late, going steady, "young emotions," and being "old enough to love." He came to rebel against this: on his twenty-first birthday he dropped the "y" and became Rick Nelson. He sought recognition as a contemporary pop singer, but not before confessing the loneliness of being a "teenage idol." In the late 1960s and early 1970s Rick Nelson and the Stone Canyon Band were one of the first country rock groups, and their music influenced California cowboys and Hollywood hillbillies. Nelson's last chart hit came in 1973. "Garden Party," his own composition, refers to the time he was booed off the stage at an oldies concert in Madison Square Gardens for his hippie appearance and current repertory. He sings "you can't please everyone so you got to please yourself."

In the 1980s he pleased himself by again playing hot rockabilly and newer songs by John Fogerty and Graham Parker, and he and the band did 200 dates a year. Hard work and professionalism helped his music to be belatedly recognized for its integrity and honesty. At forty-five he was still baby-faced and clean shaven, still looked nervous while strumming rhythm guitar or gripping the mike with both hands, and still looked like a kid next to the Jordanaires' definite adultness. While flying to Dallas for a New Year's Eve gig, his plane caught fire and crashed. Although both pilots survived, all passengers were killed: Nelson, his fiancée, the road manager, and the four band members.

For too many people, his television beginnings and huge success clouded critical estimation, and he was unfairly judged. For some, Nelson's death while on tour finally gave him rock star credibility. In 1986 he was voted into the Rock and Roll Hall of Fame. He is the subject of at least three biographies.

EDDIE COCHRAN

Born October 3, 1938, Albert Lea, Minnesota; died April 17, 1960, near London, England

At the time of his death at age twenty-one, singer, writer, producer, and multi-instrumentalist Eddie Cochran was a touring rock 'n' roll star. He became an icon.

In 1952 the Cochran family moved from Minnesota to Bell Gardens, a suburb of Los Angeles. There Eddie soon met Connie "Guybo" Smith, who played steel guitar (subsequently switching to bass). Together they did a few gigs, and later Smith would record and tour with Cochran a great deal. Although he was doing well, Cochran left school in January 1955 at sixteen and teamed up with Hank Cochran, one year older. That they were not related did not deter them from calling themselves the Cochran Brothers. They played pure hillbilly music with harmonized vocals in the brother duet tradition, including a tribute to Jimmie Rodgers and Hank Williams ("Two Blue Singing Stars"). Their first recordings were on the Ekko label: of the two singles released in 1955, the youthfully energetic "Guilty Conscience," written by the pseudo-brothers, contrasts with the three plodding songs the boys did not write. Instrumentation was the standard fiddle, steel, and electric and acoustic guitars (and no drums). That year they appeared on the *Big D Jamboree* in Dallas. Elvis Presley deeply influenced Eddie, and the duo added rockabilly to their act and even auditioned unsuccessfully for Sun.[6]

In late 1955 Eddie met Jerry Capehart in a music store. Capehart was a songwriter and drummer looking for someone to demo his songs. They became close friends and began writing together. Early the next year the two Cochrans backed Capehart on his own single, and then the three of them wrote both sides of the duo's third and final Ekko single, released in early summer 1956. "Tired and Sleepy" and "Fool's Paradise" are both good examples of the rockabilly influence on the "brothers'" sound. Against bass fiddle, Eddie's rockabilly lead guitar, and very powerfully played piano and drums, the vocalists alternate between trading lines and singing in harmony.

The duo toured a lot, doing shows in California, among them the

Town Hall Party and the *California Hayride* television shows, as well as working in Oregon, Washington, Kansas, Arizona, and even Hawaii, where they did shows with Lefty Frizzell.

Around this time Hank Cochran sang on unreleased songs produced by Capehart. "Latch On" (later recorded by Ron Hargrave for MGM) uses the classic trio instrumentation; Eddie's backup singing has him doing the Elvis "baby baby baby" bit. "I'm Ready" is a real gem written by the Cochrans and Capehart. Hank's solo vocal on it is controlled and relaxed despite the fast tempo, furious bass slapping, and stinging guitar. The drums may be Capehart doing the cardboard-box-with-lots-of-echo routine. He did play on a box at some sessions, but only once did he play drums on stage with Eddie. It was during a two-week engagement at the Sands Hotel in Las Vegas, the trio completed by Smith on bass. The Cochrans and Capehart also came up with "Pink Pegged Slacks," demoed in April 1956. It is probably the first song where Eddie sings solo, and it shows that his rock 'n' roll singing style was well formed. Not long afterward the Cochran duo split up because Eddie continued into rock and Hank preferred country. Hank Cochran later moved to Nashville, where he became one of country music's most successful songwriters.

Jerry Capehart and Eddie Cochran became a songwriting team, and Capehart became Cochran's manager, getting him involved first with a small label and later in 1956 with Liberty. Cochran's first single under his own name came out on the Crest label in September of that year: "Skinny Jim," written by the pair. Cochran's voice is clearly his own, with the growl and confidence familiar from his later work, but it is obvious that he has been listening to Carl Perkins and Gene Vincent when he sings "be bop a lula Skinny Jim." Of the two versions that I have heard, one has very safe ordinary piano, whereas the other one, a later overdub I believe, has a flamboyant pianist. The flip side, "Half Loved," presents Cochran's "sincere" persona in a rather melodramatic ballad. The singing is over the top to the point of parody.

In October 1956 Cochran signed with Liberty and hit the charts the next year with "Sitting in the Balcony," a "rockaballad" written by John D. Loudermilk and also released by him under the pseudonym "Johnny Dee." Cochran's version toys with an excess of echo and was atypical of his style, but it got him on the charts finally, as he had predicted, and led to lots of touring and TV appearances.

The second Liberty single died, but the third provided a minor hit in "Drive In Show," another rockaballad about going to a movie on a first date, complete with a ukulele (probably played by Cochran) and a male chorus delivering "doo doo doodly-doodly doo doo doo." Neither song was written by Cochran, and the songs and the time directed him toward the teen idol approach. His lack of total involvement in the singing is noticeable.

A demo of "Twenty Flight Rock" had helped to get the Liberty contract, and Cochran sang it in the film *The Girl Can't Help It,* one of the first color rock 'n' roll movies. Cochran's song was held back to coincide with the film's opening and became his fourth Liberty single. It was not a hit. Cochran appeared in two other films: *Untamed Youth* in 1957, singing "Cotton Picker," and *Go, Johnny, Go* in 1959, singing "Teenage Heaven."

The fifth single on Liberty produced another minor hit with "Jeannie Jeannie Jeannie," but the next two bombed. Finally, in an inspired moment brought on by the pressure of a recording session the next day, an intense desire for success, and no decent songs on hand, Capehart and Cochran wrote "Summertime Blues." Cochran did all the guitar parts, Capehart and Sharon Sheeley did the handclaps, Connie Smith played bass, and Earl Palmer played drums. "Summertime Blues" was Cochran's biggest hit, a top-ten smash in the summer of 1958, and it clarified the territory for which he is now so well remembered: spokesman for the teenage experience—parties, parents, weekends, movies, summer jobs, cars, and the opposite sex. Aside from Chuck Berry, no one articulated the details, desires, and pressures of teenage life as well as Eddie Cochran did. Other songs in the same vein were "C'mon Everybody" and "Something Else," both hits, as well as "Weekend," "Nervous Breakdown," and "Rock and Roll Blues." His success led to still more touring, even to Australia with Little Richard and Gene Vincent.

Rhythm is the prime component in most of Cochran's songs. Whatever the size of the ensemble, all instruments interlock into an infectious groove. Some constants in the sound are Cochran's distinctive voice, bass (usually electric), acoustic guitar, and echo; in addition, we may find a variety of percussion sounds—rim shots, snare drum with the snare loosened, tom-toms, open high hat or no cymbals at all, tambourine, and handclaps. Sometimes present are piano, female chorus, male chorus, or saxophones. Despite the fact that Cochran was a great natural talent on guitar, many of his songs lack a solo.

A side of Cochran less often (and less fondly) remembered is his crooner persona, for he did not really have the voice for it. Did he aspire to the adult market, to music that was widely accepted and not denounced by the leaders of the community? Although the violins used on his "Hallelujah, I Love Her So" were added by the producer, Snuff Garret, apparently against Cochran's wishes, other songs show him in Las Vegas territory: the tinkly, pure lounge-style piano on "That's My Desire" and a live recording with big-band accompaniment of "I Don't Like You No More." That style was appropriate for Frank Sinatra and his ilk, but not for Cochran, although his use of it speaks volumes about how he saw himself. It was not an abandonment of his rocker persona—in the same set he did Chuck Berry's "Sweet Little Sixteen"—but like Elvis and Buddy Holly, he probably was testing the waters for a market beyond rock 'n' roll. Since rock 'n' roll was increasingly catering to a younger market, perhaps these singers felt that they were outgrowing it. On the other hand, given that he recorded so much in the crooning style, maybe he just liked it.

At Cochran's last studio session in January 1960, on the eve of the fateful tour in England, he was backed by Smith and two members of the Crickets, Sonny Curtis on guitar and Jerry Allison on drums.

In April 1960, while on his way to the London airport to return to the United States after a wildly successful tour with Gene Vincent, Cochran met his death in a car crash. Vincent was injured.

Cochran did many sessions as a guitarist, bassist, or producer, including a number of guitar instrumentals, and devotees are still unraveling and devouring everything on which he made a sound.

TWELVE

THE REVIVAL

"Jungle Rock"

Late 1959 saw a definite drop in commercial releases of rockabilly, and although a small number of these recordings continued to be made, generally by tiny independents, within a couple of years rockabilly all but died as a recorded style. Artists either retired or aligned themselves with other styles. By 1964 the musical British Invasion of North America led by the Beatles made it obvious to all that rockabilly held little promise as a marketable commodity. Its influence, however, is traceable in the repertories, instrumentation, and approach of some of the groups of the period.

The Beatles standardized rock's guitar band instrumentation: two electric guitars, bass, and drums. Modeled after rockabilly bands, especially Buddy Holly's, the only difference was the change from acoustic bass to electric. In a 1964 issue of *Cowboy Songs* magazine, the Beatles were actually called "redcoat rockabillies." In their early years, before 1965, their repertory, as represented by recordings (whether live or studio, officially released or not), contained a number of songs by rockabillies: Elvis Presley's "That's All Right," Gene Vincent's "Be-Bop-A-Lula," Eddie Fontaine's "Nothin' Shakin'," and the Rock 'n' Roll Trio's "Lonesome Tears in My Eyes." The Beatles did many Buddy Holly songs: "Crying, Waiting, Hoping," "Words of Love," "Mailman Bring Me No More Blues," "That'll Be the Day," "Maybe Baby," "Peggy Sue," "I'm Gonna Love You Too," and "Not Fade Away." In addition, Carl Perkins, who was sometimes present while the Beatles recorded his compositions, is represented by "Everybody's Trying to Be My Baby," "Honey Don't," "Matchbox," "Sure to Fall," "Lend Me Your Comb," "Glad All Over," and "Blue Suede Shoes." These records had been formative influences on the Beatles, and they played the songs in a style and spirit similar to those of the originals. Of the songs in this list that were not hits, some had been issued in England, and some had been brought to Liverpool by sailors who had bought the singles in the United States. Nonhits and flip sides account for numerous early Beatle cover songs. More of the songs they covered, however, came from black sources, including works by Chuck Berry, Ray Charles, Little Richard, Larry Williams, and Arthur Alexander and songs from Detroit's Motown label. Some of the Beatles' own songs reveal a debt to rockabilly, such as "What Goes On."

After the middle of the decade, it became rare to hear anything resembling rockabilly from the contemporary scene, although old songs from rockabilly musicians occasionally were redone by new groups in the popular styles of the day. The Bobby Fuller Four from El Paso, Texas, operating out of California, had strong connections with 1950s music, especially that of Buddy Holly and the Crickets. Both Fuller and Holly were songwriting, band-leading Texans who loved experimenting in the studio, and both died prematurely. Fuller consciously carried on and developed the Holly style: the Bobby Fuller Four had their biggest successes in 1966, the year of Fuller's death, with "I Fought the Law," written by former Cricket Sonny Curtis, and "Love's Made a Fool of You," by Buddy Holly and Bob Montgomery. Other songs from the Holly repertory done by the Bobby Fuller Four were "Think It Over" and "Baby My Heart." They also did Roy Orbison's "Rockhouse," and their "Saturday Night" is in Eddie Cochran's style.

In the 1960s the roots of rock often were obscured and ignored in favor of new technology and new influences. Those who covered rockabilly songs did the hits, although rarely in rockabilly style. Sam the Sham and the Pharoahs, recording in Memphis, had a hit with their version of Billy Lee Riley's "Red Hot," although the strong rhythmic grid of even eighth notes made it sound more like the group's own big hit "Wooly Bully" than rockabilly. They also recorded "Mystery Train." Blue Cheer, a San Francisco power trio, hit with their very heavy version of Eddie Cochran's "Summertime Blues" in 1968, as did the Who in 1969.

Veterans who recorded rockabilly in the 1960s usually did tame versions of the handful of rockabilly standards that their intended general audience would likely know. Even when the artist was willing, company personnel were not particularly interested in presenting rockabilly. During his run of country hits in the late 1960s, Mac Curtis wanted to get back to rockabilly and had disagreements with his producer, Billy Sherrill: "I laid back and let them take the ball but I felt . . . 'this ain't working too well. . . . I just don't feel comfortable . . . you are trying to make me too country which I'm not. . . . I think the time is right to do what I think I'd do best and we'd all be better off.'"[1] Curtis wanted to do a version of Carl Perkins's "Your True Love," but it was considered too obscure. A compromise was reached, "Honey Don't" was recorded instead, and it made the charts.

From the mid-1970s to the mid-1980s rockabilly came alive again as a fad, a fashion, a theatrical outlet, a way of life, an evocation of the past, an acknowledgment of musical roots, and a commercial bandwagon. The revival phenomenon received its momentum from the interplay of several factors.

First, the demand of a growing number of collectors led to the issuing and reissuing of thousands of 1950s rockabilly and related recordings by companies based in England, Holland, France, and Germany (but rarely in the United States). Each country seemed to focus on a different aspect: the British compiled anthologies by combing through the archives of established American record companies, the Dutch compiled rarities and obscurities from independent labels, the French focused on Gene Vincent and Eddie Cochran, and the Germans revived lesser-known performers such as Janis Martin, Bob Luman, and Sid King. Second, in cities in a dozen or more countries, many bands were formed by young musicians who took much of their inspiration and repertory from early rockabilly. Third, hundreds of 1950s rockabilly songs, both famous and obscure, were rerecorded (usually in rockabilly style), and new rockabilly songs were recorded by willing participants. Fourth, many rockabilly records new and old achieved chart success in various countries. Fifth and finally, curiosity about the lives of early performers increased (heightened by the intensification of interest in Elvis Presley after his death in 1977), leading to the renewal of the careers many 1950s rockabilly acts.

Rockabilly was rescued from the fate of being a discarded, misunderstood, localized music through a combination of the energies of four diverse groups of people. The first group was the discophiles, those concerned with recordings: dealers, collectors, reissuers, and operators of new labels. The second group was the media, those involved with the gathering and spreading of knowledge: scholars, reporters, and certain serious fans. The third group was the audience of consumers, and the fourth group was the musicians. I discuss the musicians of the revival in the next two chapters.

The revival started in England. The small group of collectors there in the mid-1960s were supplied by dealers bringing back records from the United States. Prices rose as interest spread to the Continent and as discs became rarer because more and more collectors/dealers were cleaning out warehouses. Some dealers broke, scratched, or otherwise damaged the records they could not carry, making some records artificially rare, hence more expensive. The early 1970s saw bootleg 45s and albums compiling rare originals being pressed in quantities on the West Coast of the United States. Some record dealers asked Cordell Jackson to repress the singles from her Moon label, but she refused when she learned of their intention to pass them off as 1950s pressings. Nonetheless, reprinted records sometimes were passed off as originals. Many collectors, however, jealously wanted to keep their troves of rare sounds to themselves and felt that bootleg and later legal reissues devalued the originals and undermined their pains in collecting.

In 1972, with the advent of oldies record shops in England, companies had an outlet for specialist products, and collectors had a reliable source for obtaining rare records. Rockabilly then was still a minority music, but shortly thereafter small companies like Record Mart started making arrangements with the original labels to use old master tapes, reissuing obscure 45-rpm records in quantities of 500 or 1,000. These second pressings also became rare. In addition, the mid-1970s saw companies such as Ace and Charly start major reissuing programs, offering selected catalog holdings of important and minor labels. By the time of Presley's death, well-produced reissues of major artists and strong lesser-knowns were available to the small but loyal international audience, which might buy 10,000 or 20,000 copies. Because few of the hundreds of rockabilly albums eventually produced were issued in the United States, American collectors had to buy American music from the import bins.

The 1950s in America were romanticized even before the 1970s began (Sha Na Na performed at Woodstock in 1969), but the English and Europeans, because of their distance, manifested their fantasies with an intensity the Americans could never match. This romanticism helped to create a large market for singles, often with a reprint of the original label or with a picture sleeve that took on iconographic significance: it was as if the collector were there in the 1950s with the (almost) real artifact in his or her hand. Surely this is a playful, theatrical, imaginative idea—even those old enough to have been around in the 1950s did not know much, if anything, about rockabilly at that time, and in any case, they almost never had access to the original discs—but the concept was taken to even greater lengths. There was, for example, besides the second pressings of Sun singles made to satisfy the collector market, an Elvis 45 on the Sun label but containing songs he never recorded there: "Tweedlee Dee" from a 1954 *Louisiana Hayride* performance backed with "Lawdy Miss Clawdy," an alternate take from the NBC TV special in 1968, released as Sun 526. The last official Sun issue was number 407 in 1967; these 1970s releases from France were in a series that started with number 500. Other new Sun records included titles originally unissued and discs originally issued on the Sun subsidiary, Flip.

Why was this appealing? The first answer is because people liked the music. There was probably more to it than that, however. Being part of the revival and able to buy new records, as Americans used to do in the 1950s, brought an affinity for the southern experience. The consumer could feel like a youth (a vital time of their lives) in America (the land of the free) in the 1950s (the good old days when life was simpler and more fun). Nothing to do with patriotism, the interest in rockabilly was about connecting to a mental scenery, to a mythical place where people are imbued with both white and black music traditions, feeling things deeply, and having a down-to-earth life. One could belong to a community where music making is acceptable and music makers are encouraged to express themselves in creative and idiosyncratic ways in a dignified environment—a land ruled by Good Authority, where talent is rewarded (sooner or later) and life is celebrated.

The Charly record company began leasing original masters from Sun in 1974 and later issued in France a series of ten-inch albums (the same size as 78s but playing ten songs at 33rpm) that were presented (intentionally unconvincingly) as 1950 issues; "This brand new sound that only Space Cats have used before in their Satellite Hops will make you feel like rockin'!" from *The Swingin' Blast* is a sample of liner-note writer Ding Dong's stylized prose. The ten-inch fever reached absurdity with special issues duplicating LP versions except for having two fewer tracks. Less is more, indeed!

Amid this activity the audience widened, and new labels devoted exclusively or extensively to rockabilly were started. These had a major effect on the revival. One of the most important was Rollin' Rock in California, whose letterhead proclaims "sexy, slurpy, saucy, spicy, savage, succulent, American rockabilly." It was started in 1971 by Ronny Weiser, the "Hebrew Hillbilly," an Italian who had emigrated to Los Angeles six years earlier after being mesmerized by rock 'n' roll and the image of America, a passion ignited by seeing an Elvis

Presley movie. Rollin' Rock started by issuing vintage material but soon concentrated on newly recorded works by veterans—particularly Ray Campi, Mac Curtis, Johnny Carroll, Jackie Lee Cochran, and Gene Vincent (his last recordings)—revivalists such as the Magnetics, Colin Winski, Johnny Legend, Jerry Sikorski, Billy Zoom (who backed Gene Vincent before joining X, the noted L.A. punk band), and roots rockers such as the Blasters. Weiser also produced a Rollin' Rock magazine that served to promote the label. December 1977 saw the first package tour of Rollin' Rock artists concertizing in England. The first recordings were marred by mousy sound, lots of hiss, and spotty performances, but recording techniques were noticeably improved by the time of the Magnetics' 1981 debut. That year Weiser reported that he was receiving 100 letters a week from Finland alone, a hint of how important and successful his label was in Europe.

In Holland in 1974 Bert and Frances Rockhuizen started recording revival bands, English ones at first and then bands from all over, for issue on their Rockhouse label, a vital component of the revival. Both passionate about the music, Bert was a former jazz musician who had been a producer with EMI, and Frances had skill in business and a personal touch. In 1973 they had opened a 1950s record store in Holland. It became a focal point, and sales by post worldwide led them to develop the largest mail-order business of its kind in Europe. To the list of what was available they added items from their own label. From offering first issues by the likes of Matchbox and Crazy Cavan and the Rhythm Rockers, the label has developed the biggest catalog of neorockabilly in the world.

In the early 1980s Rockhouse was presenting a tight gang of British musicians under various names. The following provides some idea of the various permutations and affiliations within this group: the Edwards brothers, Carlo and Stef, of the Blue Cats, played with Dave Phillips in the Blue Cat Trio, but he had his own band, Dave Phillips and the Hot Rod Gang, which included Mark Harman, who led Restless, whereas Shotgun included Wild Bob Burgos, from Matchbox, and featured Ray Neale, who led the All Stars.

Certain Rockhouse items have been licensed to Japan, their second largest market after Europe. As well as marketing discs by the neorockabilly bands, the company released vintage material and recordings by veterans appearing at its large biannual "International Rock & Roll Meeting," a 1950s festival. In 1993 Rockhouse celebrated its fortieth festival.

From Rotterdam, Holland, comes the prolific White Label, put out by Collector Records, a company run by Cees Klop. Since 1967 Klop has been making several trips a year to the United States and Canada to track down people nobody else can or will find.

Richard Weize started Bear Family Records in West Germany in 1975. Three years later he began leasing and issuing out-of-print and unissued country, rock 'n' roll, and rockabilly from major American labels. With careful attention to sound quality, packaging, discographical details, and liner notes, Bear Family's releases are gorgeous and treasured artifacts.

The media group was made up of deejays, writers, researchers, and the like. Specialist radio shows with knowledgeable deejays provided detailed information on the style and the artists, spreading the influence of rockabilly and giving it respectability. One such show debuted in 1976: *It's Only Rock and Roll,* hosted by Stuart Colman on BBC Radio One. Colman also played bass in Dave Travis's band, compiled reissue albums, wrote liner notes, and produced recording sessions.

Specialist magazines printed articles, biographies, interviews, concert and record reviews, and discographies. For years *New Kommotion* from England, published by Adam Komorowski, was the main rockabilly forum. Often the authors were those who compiled and researched reissues, among them Bill Millar, Ray Topping, Colin Escott, Wayne Russell, and Derek Glenister. Glenister also had the Record Museum, a mail-order business that lived up to its name.

Now Dig This, a 1950s rock 'n' roll monthly also from England and edited by Trevor Cajiao, passed the hundredth-issue mark in 1991. Its professional look and informed content have made it the focal point for fans around the world.

American magazines *Time Barrier Express, Rockin' '50s, Record Exchanger, Goldmine,* and *Discoveries* all featured articles about rockabilly. Many fanzines (magazines produced by fans) emerged in the 1980s. *Cat Tales* was put out by Greg Milewski of Virginia from 1989 until his suicide in 1994. *Blue Suede News,* run by Marc Bristol of Washington State, started in 1986 and grew to receive international distribution in record stores and newsstands. *Red Hot Express* comes out of New Jersey and is run by Anthony Sturiale. All have presented valuable information about rockabilly.

One of the most influential of these fanzines is *Kicks,* a sporadically appearing, idiosyncratic, well-researched project of Billy Miller and Miriam Linna. Their band, the Zantees, played an exaggerated, heavy-handed variety of rockabilly showing influences of the hard-hitting mid-1960s garage music about which they also write. They later formed the A-Bones and issued records by Link Wray and many others on their Norton label. *Kicks* has provided details on many formerly obscure artists like the Phantom, who made rockabilly history with his only release, "Love Me."

Rockabilly Revue started in 1989 as a labor of love for editor Billy Poore. He draws on a lifetime of promoting concerts, producing sessions, managing performers, and countless other activities in the music business. Within its photocopied pages Poore writes reviews, career overviews, and anecdotes of his favorite acts, with a special emphasis on his friend Charlie Feathers. Poore relocated from Maryland to Nashville, and his mission of championing rockabilly and its artists, whether legendary, underrated, or unknown, reaches a wide audience.

From Alberta comes *Nervous Breakdown,* a publication of the Eddie Cochran Canadian Fan Club, which features articles about many different rockabillies.

In California Alan Clark has put out several booklets of clippings from vintage sources (trade magazine articles and ads, sheet music covers, etc.) mixed with a few recent items. Titles include *Rock-A-Billy and Country Legends, Rock and Roll Legends, Legends of Sun Records,* and *Gene Vincent: The Screaming End.*

Original Cool, from Virginia, emerged in 1993 as a bimonthly fanzine (or "zine") devoted to rockabilly, neorockabilly, and psychobilly. Interview-based articles are featured, plus reviews and news of American and overseas talent.[2]

Books covering rockabilly started to appear in the 1970s. *Mystery Train* (1976; revised 1982) by Greil Marcus has insights on Presley, and *Catalyst* (1975) by Colin Escott and Martin Hawkins gives a history of the Sun label. A revised edition came out in 1980 as *Sun Records: The Brief History of the Legendary Record Label,* and another take on the subject by the authors came in 1991: *Good Rockin' Tonight: Sun Records and the Birth of Rock 'n' Roll.* Peter Guralnick's *Feel Like Going Home* (1971) contains chapters on Sam Phillips and Jerry Lee Lewis. Guralnick's *Lost Highway* (1979) has chapters on Sleepy LaBeef, Charlie Feathers, and Elvis Presley. Nick Tosches's book *Country: The Biggest Music in America* (1977; revised 1985) contains a lot of detail, irreverence, and information on rockabilly.

The general media in the United Kingdom became aware of the revival in 1976 when an obscure song recorded in 1957—"Jungle Rock," by Hank Mizell—hit number three on the national pop charts. It had been acquired by London deejay Roy Williams on a collecting trip to the United States. He featured it on his radio show and at discos (record hops), creating enough demand for a bootleg issue that sold around 3,000 copies before the record was reissued legally by

Charly. Voted record of the week on London's Capitol Radio, it went into the charts and sold 250,000 copies.

Its originator, William "Hank" Mizell (1924–92), was a country singer who started playing music in 1949. Florida-born and North Carolina–raised, in 1956 he moved to Chicago, where he played in low-life redneck bars, adding rockabilly to keep up with the market. He recorded country but produced only one other rockabilly recording, retiring from music in 1961. With the left-field success of "Jungle Rock," he immediately was brought back into the studio to cut a new album. The original song, which came out on Chicago's Eko label in 1958 and subsequently was acquired and released by King, is on Hank Mizell's album, but the rest of the songs were recorded in March 1976. The material is heavy on the jungle theme, including the new songs "Singing in the Jungle," "Kangaroo Rock," and "Animal Rock and Roll," as well as a cover of "Ubangi Stomp." Additional songs came from the Sun catalog—not surprising, for it was recorded by the Shelby Singleton organization, owners of Sun—but the album, also not surprisingly, lacks spark. A couple of subsequent singles by Mizell went absolutely nowhere, and his promotional visits to England totally removed the mystique of the obscure.

This amazing story was fueled in part by the romantic appeal of the distant, exotic artist. The fact that many of the greatest rockabillies were dead only fueled the myth. On the other hand, this romanticism is less readily projected onto, and may even have worked against, someone like Carl Perkins, a certified rockabilly star who cut a less mystical image due to his survival and prominence.

The audience sustained the revival by consuming the records, frequenting the discos that featured rockabilly, attending the live shows, and living a rockabilly lifestyle. Fifties rock has never totally gone out of fashion overseas, where Gene Vincent and Eddie Cochran have remained cult figures. It was kept alive in England through the 1960s by Teddy Boys, so named for the Edwardian touch in their jacket styles. The Teds were tough, antiestablishment, antimaterialistic, wild motorcycling folk who liked leather, tattoos, beer, and rock 'n' roll. They were looked down on by the upper classes and the university crowd, who associated Teds with violence and who sneered at the working-class background of their music.

The importance of image to Teds and to the fashion-conscious English and European consumers was another factor in the revival. Stores in London like Ted's Corner offer a wide range of 1950s-inspired clothing: circle skirts, dresses, petticoats, pants, jackets, shoes, T-shirts, belts, buckles, patches, and badges. Jack Geach's London shop has a mail-order catalog picturing Eddie Cochran, Buddy Holly, and Gene Vincent on the cover. Modeling the clothes is a Ted with a great head of greased and perfect hair and sideburns almost to his chin. In several poses he is holding a vintage guitar, singing into an old microphone, or combing his hair using both hands. The catalog offers peg and drainpipe trousers (black), drape and box jackets (in any color or black velvet), creeper shoes with real crepe soles (in black or blue suede), chukka boots and shoes, and winkle-picker (pointed-toe) boots. The cardigans and pullovers (in black, blue, or red) and box or striped panel shirts (black with blue, red, pink, or white contrast) come with designs of flecks, diamonds, guitars, or musical notes. Socks are lurex or fluorescent (in green, yellow, pink, orange, or purple), and ties are slim jim, maverick, or bootlace style. The bootlace (bolo) ties come with designs showing a dancing couple, a steer, a gun and holster, or a skull and crossbones. All their jackets, drapes, and suits are tailored individually, down to the handmade button holes. As "makers of hot rags," Jack Geach celebrated twenty-five years of business in 1994.

Around 1977 the market expanded from Teds and collectors to include young kids who became "Rockabilly Rebels." These were not casual rock fans. Bored with the musical status quo, they became volunteer urban anachronists, devotees of the sound and image of rockabilly. They spent their time and money on clothes, records, and going to dances. Their wardrobe was inspired by images of America as it never was, except on film and in imagination. Exaggerated duck-tails, sideburns, hairdos, and tattoos completed the look. At dances they appreciated records by the likes of Ray Campi and Mac Curtis because they were suitable to a form a dancing unknown in the 1950s: a solo dance that took advantage of the springheel effect of crepe-soled shoes. In the 1950s, dancing, sometimes called "bopping" or "jiving," involved the traditional couple. Aside from being young and frustrated, the new audience was not similar to the original audience.

Sadly, some rockabilly fans belonged to the racist National Front and identified rockabilly with the Confederacy because of its southern origins. After all, both Presley and Orbison were cast as Confederates in movies. These fans expected American musicians to share their racism. In general, the Confederate flag, with its stars-and-bars pattern, became a symbol for rockabilly, sported on T-shirts, belt buckles, tattoos, and so on. In the group Matchbox it was painted on the back of the upright bass.

The Rock 'n' Roll Chart, published in U.K. music papers and representing sales and discotheque popularity, shows that the majority of records consumed by this audience were either original 1950s songs reissued or new recordings by veterans known through their concerts. A top-twenty chart from 1978 shows over half the places were held by veterans recently seen on tour, evenly split between their 1950s recordings and recent recordings (mostly of songs from the 1950s). The other places were filled by a few vintage obscurities, a couple of lesser-known songs by venerated deceased artists, and a couple by revival groups.

THIRTEEN

VETERANS

"Everybody's Movin' Again"

Most veterans were surprised by the revival. They had little or no idea of what they had achieved in the 1950s, and they had been through a period when the style was unacceptable and they were ashamed of it. Some had been real rockabillies, and some had only dipped into the rockabilly style. Whatever their status, almost none had played (or probably heard) that music in years. Some of the veterans were reluctant; they had not only retired from the style but also turned their backs on what it symbolized to them. Religious and social conflicts were solved by not performing at all or by involvement with gospel music. There were also opportunists, capitalizing on marginal credentials. For the committed veterans, the revival gave new life to old careers: chances to tour, to record, to get famous, to make money, and to justify to themselves an allegedly misspent youth.

Contrary to the young revival bands, which generally avoided playing rockabilly's big hits, the veterans aimed to reinforce their associations by performing standards (as many of them had in the 1950s), even doing whole albums of well-known tunes and medleys of others' big hits, for example Carl Perkins's *Ol' Blue Suede's Back,* Billy Lee Riley's *Vintage,* and Warren Smith's and Buddy Knox's 1977 performances in London.

Virtually all the veterans did not consider themselves solely as rockabillies; their revival performances have been influenced heavily by their perceptions of audience expectations. In the 1950s a few artists played rockabilly more out of commercial necessity than from a personal attraction to the style; being versatile and eager, they were recorded. They became known for their rockabilly involvement and more than twenty years later had to face a revival that asked them to perform again in a style that was not their first choice from the start. When I asked Malcolm Yelvington whether he ever considered himself to be a rockabilly performer, he said, "Well, I do now, more or less, because that's the only thing that I'm ever contacted to do. I'm never asked to be on a country show. To tell you the truth, I'd rather sing country than sing rockabilly, but if that's where the money is, that's more or less where you've got to go."[1]

The label *rockabilly* is a marketing term. It is for the participants to decide how bound they are by definitions. Musicians associated with or billed as rockabilly performed in other styles. Records identified as rockabilly in their title or in another way—maybe period fashions on the cover—often contain a wide variety of musical styles. These definition issues are commonly found in music revivals, whether of Dixieland, western swing, blues, psychedelic rock, or what have you. For fans, the story of the Sun label is so fascinating that the power invoked by the name seems to have borrowed a little of the energy-giving properties of the sun itself. At the very least, it became the leading brand name in rockabilly. Even the logo used on the record label—a rooster crowing in front of a stylized sunrise—was used for its evocative powers on T-shirts, reissue albums, and business cards and in band names such as the Screamin' Roosters from Edmonton and the Rattled Roosters from Vancouver. "The Memphis Rooster" was used as a nickname by Don Ezell, the late Memphis collector and friend of the music. A photograph of a rooster sitting on an old motorcycle graces the cover of the Boston Rockabilly Music Conspiracy's album.

Johnny Cash is an artist who recorded extensively for Sun, knew and toured with all the rockabilly stars of the area, but shied away from rockabilly until it was big in the revival. Even at Cash's most rocking, for example, on "Get Rhythm" and "Big River," his music is at the farthest reaches of rockabilly. His understated vocals (virtually devoid of the characteristic rockabilly histrionics), his understated instrumental sound, and his ability to sound unhurried at any tempo are elements of his personal and successful country style. The instrumentation on many of his Sun records is the classic acoustic guitar, electric lead, and acoustic bass. If Cash had any intention of being a rockabilly, he certainly had everything at his disposal, but about the closest he ever got was to string a few syllables together rhythmically and flat the third note of the major scale on occasion, in imitation of his guitarist. Although he is credited with the author-

ship of "Rock 'n' Roll Ruby," a hit for Warren Smith, Smith stated
that a number of people, including George Jones, told him that
Johnny Cash bought the song from Jones for forty dollars.[2] Cash,
nonetheless, at least in later years, affirmed his awareness of rockabilly by titling a 1980 album *Rockabilly Blues*, although only the gen-
erous would claim that it contains any rockabilly music. The *Survivors* album refers to the Million Dollar Quartet: since Elvis's death,
Cash, Carl Perkins, and Jerry Lee Lewis were the survivors. Although
Cash does not appear on the recording of that expensive quartet, a
picture exists proving that he was there that day in 1956, at least
before he left to do some shopping. His underlying attitude appears
in his song "I Will Rock and Roll with You." The sentence is completed by the phrase "if I have to."

New interest lit a spark under the veterans, and sometimes their
new recordings could stand up to their 1950s best. Certain veterans,
however, proved to be interested in not much more than re-creating
old sounds, and the market and the tastes of the audience permitted
this attitude, if they did not demand it. Most veterans rerecorded at
least some of their 1950s songs. Sonny Fisher was one of the few to
record primarily new compositions of his own.

The usual setting where Europeans see legendary figures of American rockabilly is the weekend festival. Usually a couple of veterans
and several revival bands are featured, as well as record stalls and discos playing 1950s music and old rock films. In almost every case the
Americans are backed by European bands at these shows. One of the
first and most important of these bands was led by Dave Travis,
profiled in the next chapter.

The list of veterans who have played European festivals is a long
one: Carl Mann, Mac Curtis, Janis Martin, Sleepy LaBeef, Andy Ander-
son, Eddie Bond, Barbara Pittman, Warren Smith, Jack Scott, Larry
Donn, Groovey Joe Poovey, Ronnie Dawson, Brenda Lee, Jimmy Wag-
es, Buddy Knox, Charlie Feathers, Ray Smith, Billy Lee Riley, Wanda
Jackson, Carl Perkins, Gene Summers, Ray Campi, Al Ferrier, Terry
Noland, Sonny Fisher, Bobby Lee Trammell, Hayden Thompson, Rudy
Grayzell, Marvin Rainwater, Huelyn Duvall, Gene Simmons, Glen
Glenn, Fred and Rose Maddox, Jackie Lee Cochran, Tommy Sands,
Eddie Fontaine, the Comets, the Jodimars, the Blue Caps, the Crick-
ets, the Jordanaires, Scotty Moore, D. J. Fontana, Sonny Curtis, Sid
and Billy King, Johnny Powers, Teddy Redell, Sonny Burgess, the Sun
Rhythm Section, Malcolm Yelvington, Narvel Felts, Curtis Gordon,
Vernon Taylor, Pat Cupp, Joe Clay, and the Collins Kids. Europe is
"a fantasy land for old rockers," says Johnny Carroll.[3]

Veterans concertizing for the faithful for the first time in Europe—the circuit includes Norway, Sweden, Finland, Germany, Austria, Luxembourg, Belgium, Holland, France, Spain, Italy, and the United Kingdom—were usually underprepared for the audiences' expectations in terms of repertory and performance. Following the opening set in a typical show, the veteran, backed by eager young musicians who usually have had insufficient rehearsal time with the singer, does a set of his 1950s tunes, having added classics to round out the repertory. Among the most obvious and most frequent choices are "Blue Suede Shoes," "Whole Lotta Shakin' Goin' On," and "Blue Moon of Kentucky." The usually enthusiastic audience demands at least one encore, in which case the artist, often not having more tunes, has to reprise his best-known song. Veterans were awed by the sight of Europeans dressed in a caricature of American 1950s fashion, speaking a foreign language, and enthusiastically responding to the music that reinforces their special way of life. It was a kind of audience never encountered before.

Needless to say, each artist's first European show was usually shaky. For the featured singers, it was a big change from their then-current style, whether country, lounge, or gospel—if they were still performing at all. The audience itself often had mixed feelings at the first meeting, too, misgivings that preconceived images based on a handful of old records and photographs might be shattered. Advertisements for these shows use photographs from the 1950s for illustration. Natural aging aside, European concerts diminished some legends but created others by exposing audiences to authentic and dedicated figures previously obscure.

RAY CAMPI
Born 1934, New York City

One of the first and most important of the veterans to affect the British in the revival was Ray Campi, a name hitherto almost completely unknown outside of Texas and record collecting circles. He released four singles in the 1950s, all on different labels, that enjoyed local sales and recognition in the press; he even had fan clubs. That promising period soon dissipated, and his passion and ambition were met with disappointments. Years later and an ocean away, some took him to be the living king of rockabilly, and his fame was solidified by energetic performances and his newly recorded Rollin' Rock singles on the charts. His fans expressed their feelings by writing graffiti: "ROCKABILLY REBEL, RAY CAMPI," and "ROLLIN' ROCK RULES."

The Campi family moved to Austin, Texas, when Ray was ten, and he absorbed country music from Del Rio border radio. By age twelve he was playing steel guitar and soon took up acoustic guitar. In 1948 Ramblin' Ray and his Ramblers broadcast a Saturday noon-hour radio show called *Ready or Not* (he joked that they often weren't). The following year he began writing songs and making home recordings, and in 1951 he made his first studio recordings. Some of his early demos, made in various Texas locations, were issued in the 1970s.

After graduating from high school in 1952, Campi auditioned unsuccessfully for the *Louisiana Hayride* and for Capitol Records, returning to Austin for a job installing telephones. A year later he enrolled in the drama program at the University of Texas, subsequently earning his B.A. Black music was readily accessible on Austin radio, and after hearing "Rock around the Clock," Campi's songwriting started to show these new influences. His first record, "Caterpillar" backed with "Play It Cool," did well locally. A session in New York came as a result of a family contact, but although one record was issued on Dot and Campi appeared on Dick Clark's show, nothing more came of it.

In 1971, several years into a career as a Los Angeles high school English teacher, Campi heard that his old records were fetching fifty dollars in the United Kingdom, so he went back in the studio. He recorded prolifically in the next years for Rollin' Rock. That label's first album presented Campi's 1957 recordings, mostly originals. They not only revealed his credentials but showed the relaxed beat, fluid delivery, and sense of humor that mark all his work.

The wide-eyed, goofy grimace he presents on most of his album covers shows his tongue out more often than not; when he sings, his tongue is just as often in his cheek, as it were. Not only is he one of the few rockabilly vocalists to play bass, but Campi is able to exploit the bassist's traditional role as the guy who provides corny comic relief, exaggerating his vocal inflections to the point of caricature. In "Once Is Enough" he sings both parts of a male-female dialogue. On most of his albums he is almost the only instrumentalist, taking assistance only on piano or harmonica. These talents made him the house "band" for Rollin' Rock productions.

His first U.K. tour, a double bill with Mac Curtis that played Teds' clubs exclusively, came in 1977. On subsequent tours he won many new fans opening for the Clash and George Thorogood. On stage, wearing wild red, white, and black western clothes and multicolored cowboy boots, he slaps, plucks, rides, and climbs his bejeweled white bass fiddle. Both player and instrument sport neckerchiefs. In his records, besides playing his originals and an interesting selection of obscure rock 'n' roll covers, he gives tribute to his boyhood, pre-Elvis country idols by doing songs by Bill Carlisle, the Delmore Brothers, Hank Snow, Jimmie Skinner, and Merle Travis.

Campi's humor, sense of history, showmanship, versatility, and engaging manner have made him a natural ambassador for rockabilly. Later albums have appeared on Bear Family and Rockhouse.

SLEEPY LABEEF
Born Thomas Paulsley LaBeff, July 20, 1935, Smackover, Arkansas

Another Texan who came out of obscurity to amaze the Europeans was Sleepy LaBeef. Although he had recorded with little success for countless labels, Europeans recognized him as a living repository of a whole tradition. Covering the entire history of rockabilly and beyond with his huge repertory, in live performance he moves effortlessly, almost in a stream-of-consciousness manner, from song to song, some lasting only a verse or two, and doing medleys of other performer's songs at the drop of a hat or the suggestion of a name. Also, to the delight of purists, he may ask the drummer and pianist not to play for a few songs, leaving the early trio instrumentation. To the delight of researchers and collectors, he is a fanatic about music and has a phenomenal memory for events. His awareness of music is evidenced in his 1979 rendition of "Red Hot," where he incorporates bits of lyrics from three differing versions: Billy "the Kid" Emerson's, Billy Riley's, and Ronnie Hawkins'.

LaBeef was the youngest of ten children in a farming family of Cajun ancestry. He attended a Pentecostal church and went to school until the eighth grade. The nickname comes from his heavy eyelids. In 1953, at eighteen, he moved to Houston, worked as a land surveyor, and began his musical career when his band had a gospel music radio show. He cites gospel music as a major influence on rockabilly, and the records of Sister Rosetta Tharpe as an influence on him in particular.

His first recordings were gospel in 1955; they remain unissued. The first Sun record to come to his attention was white guitarist Howard Serratt's solo gospel record "I Must Be Saved," which LaBeef stated was the model for his own "All Alone." Like LaBeef, both Tharpe and Serratt were from Arkansas. Other influences were honky-tonk, western swing, local black artists, seeing Elvis Presley, and bluegrass: "a little bit of all of it inspired what I do," he told me while we sat in his motor home behind a Toronto nightclub.

LaBeef toured the South and had his first release in late 1956 on Starday. Like Leon Payne, George Jones, and a number of other Starday artists, he recorded soundalike versions of best-sellers by Elvis, Fats Domino, the Everly Brothers, Hank Thompson, and Johnny Cash for budget-priced and jukebox EPs. These were released under pseudonyms on labels such as Top Western Hits and sold by deejay Wolfman Jack and his cronies over border radio stations.

Two of LaBeef's best rockabilly tracks are "All the Time," very much like the intense rockabilly George Jones was doing for the same label, and "Little Bit More." Both were written by LaBeef, with Hal Harris coauthor on the former. Harris, staff guitarist for Starday, was LaBeef's manager at the time.

In the late 1950s LaBeef was on the *Louisiana Hayride* and the *Houston Jamboree*. In the early 1960s he moved to Lake Charles, Louisiana, where he played regularly with his band, the Versatiles, on the *Saturday Night Down South* TV show and recorded for Crescent and Wayside, for the latter billing the band as Tommy LaBeff and his Versatiles.

In 1964 he moved to Nashville and recorded country during a four-year contract with Columbia. In 1969 Shelby Singleton bought the then-dormant Sun label from Sam Phillips (for an undisclosed sum) and revived it in Nashville. Sleepy LaBeef was quickly signed and stayed for ten years, putting out several albums of rather undistinguished cover versions. A fire that almost destroyed his motor home on the way to a gig in a club north of Boston led to an invitation to extend that engagement, and his eight months there in 1977 brought him publicity. Baron Records, a local label, released *Sleepy LaBeef: Early, Rare, and Rockin' Sides.* Starting in 1979 his many tours of Europe gave him international fame. Although he impressed with his rare deep baritone (sounding at times like Johnny Cash) and his 6'5" 265-pound frame topped with a cowboy hat, his live shows devastated audiences.

Behind LaBeef's calm and friendly demeanor is a man in motion, a man who never retired from music. In 1984 he did 200 to 300 shows, as he has done since 1964. In the 1980s he made albums for the Rounder label of Massachusetts. Living out of his mobile home with his wife and two children, he continued to tour, especially in the New England area.

Do not let his nickname fool you: Sleepy is wide awake. The fifteen to twenty cups of coffee he drinks every day may or may not have anything to do with the fact that his renditions of songs are usually faster than the source versions. Taking his "living encyclopedia" role seriously, LaBeef charges through repertory like the nomadic man he is, and his live shows are more a case of "do you remember this one," or "here's another song by the same artist," or "this will get the dancers going" than a chance to hear who Sleepy LaBeef is as an artist; unfortunately, he rarely composes or presents his own material.

LaBeef's intense singing and overpowering lead guitar command an audience and a band. Usually it is more or less a pickup band, and with repetitive drumming and relentless walking bass lines, they round off the corners of the songs, jackhammering through the material. Whether it's Bob Wills's "Faded Love," Wayne Raney's "Jack and Jill Boogie," Bo Diddley's "Gunslinger," Clarence "Frogman" Henry's "Ain't Got No Home," Tony Joe White's "Polk Salad Annie," Hank Ballard's "Tore Up" (one of LaBeef's signature tunes), or any of a host more, known and obscure, it drives audiences crazy.

His 1994 album, *Strange Things Happening,* finally captures him at his glorious best, with sympathetic backing and everything just right.

ROCKIN' FRIENDS FROM MEMPHIS AND THE SUN RHYTHM SECTION

The revival stirred interest in the careers of the Memphis veterans. In that city one of the first post-1960s events involving the old Sun performers was a 1976 outdoor performance featuring Sonny Burgess, Charlie Feathers, Carl Perkins, Dickey Lee, Ray Smith, and Warren Smith, who was reunited with his old band. The next year the death of Elvis and the phenomenal worldwide reaction to it jolted Memphis into reevaluating its musical heritage. Most people there had no idea that for some fans, the adulation of Presley and his music reaches religious proportions. They still come by the thousands to see the places where their idol walked, the eternally young and youth-giving star of one of America's dearest dreams—the rise from poverty—who became, even in life, a genuine folk hero.

One result of Memphis's reawakened interest in its own musical culture, not to mention its marketability, is the rehabilitation of the famous Beale Street area. Another result is the establishment of an annual award—the Distinguished Achievement Award for the Creative and Performing Arts in memory of Elvis Presley—for a leading member of the Memphis artistic community. This award is given by the University of Memphis at a prestigious event—a banquet, with speeches by civic and academic officials, as well as by peers and friends of the recipient, and media coverage. Sam Phillips, Jerry Lee Lewis, Charlie Rich, and B. B. King were among the first so recognized. It is rare (happily it is becoming less rare) to find such praise for local musicians in their home communities, especially practitioners of indigenous American music. After the first few years of the award, however, the focus has shifted to recognize visual artists, actors, concert singers, and so on.

Since 1976 there have been two or three events per year involving a loose group of veteran rockabillies, sometimes billed as the Rockin' Friends from Memphis, most of whom recorded for Sun in the 1950s. Many of them took part in the *Tribute to Johnny and Dorsey Burnette* album, organized by Paul Burlison in 1980. It was recorded in one day on the original monaural equipment from the old Sun studio.

A casual group, banded together for a 1983 festival and billed as the Original Sun Rhythm Section, solidified as the Sun Rhythm Section and launched a new career, recording, touring, and staying together for years. Joining Sonny Burgess, Paul Burlison, Stan Kesler, and J. M. Van Eaton (replaced by D. J. Fontana) were two more veterans: Marcus Van Story and Jerry Lee "Smoochy" Smith.

Memphis native Marcus Van Story (1920–92), a welder by trade and the oldest of the group, sang, played bass, harmonica, and guitar, and acted as the master of ceremonies, as he had in Warren Smith's band. In 1977 Van Story made an album for Barrelhouse and backed up Roy Hall on his album for the same company. Two years later Van Story, along with Smith bandmate Al Hopson and pianist Smoochy Smith, backed up Vern Pullens on a decent mini-album. Pullens, a bricklayer from Picayune, Mississippi, had cut rockabilly in 1956 for the Spade label of Houston. On this set Pullens takes a follow-my-phrasing-boys approach on "Elvis Stole My Baby," and Hopson comes up with a guitar riff for "Rock on Mabel" and then uses it again on "Jitterbugging Baby." Van Story's last session was the 1992 *706 ReUnion* album of Carl Perkins and Scotty Moore at the refurbished Sun studio.

Jerry Lee "Smoochy" Smith is the youngest member of the Sun Rhythm Section, born in 1939. In 1953 Smith was working with a religious quartet and had a radio show with a country band in Jackson, Tennessee. The next year, at age fourteen, he played with Carl Perkins, joining after drummer Tony Austin, who played with Perkins the same year, but Smith was too young to go to Memphis to record. He did make it to Sun a couple of years later with Kenny Parchman and did a few more sessions. In 1961 Smith was a member of the Mar-Keys, who hit with the instrumental "Last Night."

For their 1994 appearance at England's Hemsby Festival, the Sun

Rhythm Section consisted of just Smith, Burgess, Kesler, and Fontana, for Burlison declined to tour and Van Story had recently died.

Criteria for membership in these formal or informal groupings are not just musical; they include rockabilly credentials, residency in the area, willingness to be associated with rockabilly (not the preferred style for some), and willingness to perform. These artists have legitimate rockabilly credentials, although most are not well known as individuals. Malcolm Yelvington's comment was, "the ones you see on these rockabilly shows are the ones that didn't make it."[4] The better known generally perform their own old songs, and the lesser known generally perform standards. A couple of the singers, who had recorded for Sun but not as vocalists, sang the hit songs of famous Sun artists. Some of the others backed up new singers on songs they had originally performed as band members, functioning as backup musicians then and now. Overall the performances are aimed at reinforcing the association with rockabilly and Sun, and frequent mention is made of famous artists. At local festivals monetary gains are minimal and are not an important part of the musicians' motivation.

Aside from Elvis impersonators, landmarks, exhibits, and the occasional festival or club appearance by veterans, there is practically no rockabilly scene in Memphis currently.

GLENN HONEYCUTT
Born May 2, 1933, Belzoni, Mississippi

One of the Rockin' Friends from Memphis was Glenn Honeycutt, and his story is similar to that of many unheralded veterans. He is a singer, guitarist, and pianist who worked in country, rock 'n' roll, and pop styles for dances in Memphis and the surrounding area. Honeycutt's versatility and wide taste in music mean that rockabilly is only one small part of his style. His boyhood hero was Hank Williams, and he picked up guitar from family members at an early age. While stationed in Pennsylvania during armed service duty, Glenn became attracted to pop music. Returning to Memphis in 1955, he started regularly performing in nightclubs. Armed with a couple of original songs, he auditioned for Sam Phillips and recalls being rejected for being "too country."

From 1956 until around 1963 Honeycutt was the lead vocalist in Slim Wallace and the Dixie Ramblers. Just after joining the band he got a job as a mail carrier, which he still held when I met him in 1982. Ronald "Slim" Wallace played the bass and did the bookings, and for a couple of years, until about 1958, Jack Clement was the drummer in the band, also doing some guitar playing and singing. Clement and Wallace converted the latter's garage into a recording studio. Honeycutt made a demo, and Clement, who was working for Sun, took it to Sam Phillips, leading to a session in the last days of 1956. Honeycutt wrote all the songs, mostly dramatic ballads, two appearing on the single. The record did not sell, and having it out did not change much for Honeycutt. He did not even perform the songs live, for people wanted to hear what they knew. There was one rockabilly song done at that session, "Rock All Night" (also known as "All Night Rock").

The two takes of "Rock All Night" show how it was worked on in the studio. The differences in most regards are minimal except one adds a boogie piano solo and the other has a rhythmic figure between Roland Janes's guitar and J. M. Van Eaton's drums in the first part of the guitar solo. Despite coming up with a solid effort, the song was not on the market until the 1970s; Sam Phillips apparently thought the song too risqué for release. The intro and chorus are chanted variations of the title: "gotta rock, bop, bop . . . we're gonna rock it up right, we're gonna rock all night . . . 'til the broad daylight." Verse 1 shows that the coast is clear by enumerating the missing family members' whereabouts, and verse 2 describes the woman in question as lace wearing and the singer as jealous to the point of murdering an interloper. In verse 3 we find that others may have their proper homes, but this woman is homeless because "she just rocks around." In the last verse, despite their brief relationship and his implied youth, the singer can no longer go home because "I sure do like to go." All in all, it is a sinful package of hedonism, corruption, living outside the family and society's mores, and not sleeping at night.

For Honeycutt, there was one more session at Sun and subsequent recording into the 1960s for Memphis labels such as Fernwood, started by Clement and Wallace. In the mid-1960s Honeycutt retired from playing except as a hobby.

In the early 1980s that hobby meant performing pop and gospel at old folks' homes and rock 'n' roll and country at parties and joining his Sun cronies at some of the Memphis music festivals. Seeing him in action at one of them, I marveled at his wonderfully powerful voice and his relaxed manner and charismatic presence on stage. He did a blistering version of "Boogie Woogie Man from Tennessee," a dramatic rendition of "You Gave Me a Mountain" (Frankie Laine's hit, written by Marty Robbins), and a rocking "Rooster Blues," adopted from Jim Dickinson's singing at the Burlison tribute record session. Honeycutt himself sang one song on that record. About rockabilly songs he says, "none of the words are really worth a hoot, but if you throw enough hard rock 'n' roll feeling into them, and the musicians fall in there, you've got a song out of nothing. It really is amazing, making something out of nothing."[5]

EDDIE BOND
Born July 1, 1933, Memphis

Eddie Bond is a country singer from Memphis who, starting in 1956, aligned himself with rockabilly for about year and a half, reaping reward for it in the revival. Versatile and confident, he is a go-getter, a well-known figure in the Memphis region. He has been a recording artist, band leader, record-label owner, deejay and radio station manager, television show host, nightclub owner, chief of police, agent and promoter, and editor of a monthly entertainment newspaper. He is also quite involved in charity work and political campaigns. He has a family, and when he can get away, he likes to fish.

His smooth, expressive voice is adaptable to country, gospel, and rockabilly. Bond told me, "I never made out I was someone I wasn't,"[6] but he also has stated, "I didn't really like rockabilly... it actually broke my heart to do rockabilly. I used to tell the people when I'd get up there on stage 'Now, the more I shake my leg, the more it's gone cost you.'... I was ashamed to do rockabilly, but I wasn't so ashamed I didn't want to make my livin' out of it."[7] He was not the only one who felt that way, although few declared it as publicly or as baldly as Bond did.

In the mid-1950s he was a regular on the *Louisiana Hayride,* performing every Saturday night alongside Presley, Cash, Orbison, Johnny Horton, and others. Bond also performed on the *Big D Jamboree* in Dallas and on package tours. Other gigs with Carl Perkins included performing during intermission at drive-in movies on top of the concession stand, with listeners honking their car horns instead of applauding.

Bond first recorded in 1955 at age twenty-two for the Hollywood-based Ekko label. While playing at the Palms Club in Memphis, he was "discovered" by someone from the label who took him to Nashville and chose the four country songs he recorded there. Two of them, "Double Duty Lovin'" and "Talking off the Wall," were also released in England and are still part of his live show. These are fast songs, always a part of the country musician's repertory. At dances in the 1950s, Bond recalled, fast songs were mixed in after every couple of slow ones. Nowadays at dances, it is more likely four or five or more fast songs before a slow one.

In the wake of Elvis's success, most record companies looked for similarly styled acts. The Ekko discs generated enough momentum to interest Mercury Records, and in early 1956 Bond and his band started recording for that company. He earned his rockabilly credentials with the songs "Slip Slip Slippin' In," "Boppin' Bonnie," "Flip Flop Mama" (which he coauthored), "I Got a Woman," and "Rockin' Daddy." The last song was learned from Sonny Fisher's record, and after receiving strong response at shows, it became Bond's theme song.

After three singles in 1956, the fourth and final Mercury record came in 1957. "Hershey Bar" was aimed at the teenage market. Needless to say, of the Mercury songs mentioned, it is the only one not part of Bond's current repertory. His recordings at Sun in 1957 and 1958 went unissued at the time. Bond then recorded for a number of small labels, some of which he co-owned.

In 1962 he got to fulfill the old ambition of having a release on Sun when he did the album *Eddie Bond Sings Greatest Country Gospel Hits*. He also recorded about twenty additional unissued titles, including another version of "Rockin' Daddy": rockabilly and rare for its time.

While rockabillies with similar backgrounds retired from music, Bond continued in country music, occasionally performing on the *Grand Ole Opry*. He was involved in the writing and the music for the movie *Walking Tall*, based on the story (and story-telling, as Bond was to learn) of Sheriff Buford Pusser.

Although Bond enjoyed only limited success in the 1950s, he has been able to reap a larger gain in the revival, more than many of his peers. This is due to his persistence and ambition: he has appeared on more than twenty labels and has recorded more than 300 songs.

The first time I met him was at the Mid-South Folk Life Festival in Memphis in 1982, where he performed as Eddie Bond and his Rockin' Friends from Memphis, which included Malcolm Yelvington, Marcus Van Story, Al Hopson, Glenn Honeycutt, and Smoochy Smith. The unwieldy ensemble was not generally successful in their attempt at a rockabilly sound. The two bass players, often playing at the same time, and two to three guitar players, as well as piano and a drummer insensitive to the style, sometimes produced a cluttered wall of sound. The overall performance, however, was a success in that the individual artists played and sang well and were appreciated. After the show I asked Bond whether he considered himself to be a country or a rockabilly artist. He replied, "I'm country really, but I still do rockabilly as good as I ever did, and when I go to London I'm strictly a rockabilly."

The first of many overseas visits was in 1982, when he played the Rockhouse Festival at Eindhoven, sharing the bill with Barbara Pittman. Both were billed as Sun artists (his Sun material had been recently made available), although Bond's more obvious rockabilly fame is from his "silly songs" (as he has called them) on Mercury. Pittman's 1956–60 output, which was one Sun single and three singles on its subsidiary Phillips International, plus unissued tracks, was released on a Rockhouse album around the time of her European debut. It included her best-known songs: "I Need a Man," "I'm Getting Better All the Time," and "Everlasting Love."

During the 1982 tour Bond recorded twenty songs backed by Dave Travis and the Bad River Band. With little time for rehearsing, Bond trusted Travis's familiarity with repertory and audience expectations, letting him chose the songs for the album. One song was remade from Bond's Mercury days, and Roy Acuff and Johnny Horton provided one each, but the bulk of the remainder Bond would never have heard before: five of Travis's compositions, at least four songs from obscure 1950s artists culled from Dutch and British reissue anthologies, and two by American revivalist Billy Hancock. Travis's input into Bond's repertory points out a new line of influence to the tradition: from revivalist to veteran. Bond was willing ("easy to work with"), the audience accepting—after all, that is how pop music is made—and the results were worthwhile. His subsequent Nashville-made record, the 1983 *Eddie Bond Sings Carl Smith*, which Bond felt was his best to date, was conventional country.

After seeing the fantastic response he was given overseas and positive response at the local festivals, he sensed that the revival could sustain an audience in Memphis. Starting in September 1982, Bond organized a regular Saturday night event called the Rockabilly Barn Dance. Despite a decent venue (Cook Convention Center), a sponsor (Busch Beer), advertising (radio, TV), great musicians (Charlie Feathers, Carl Perkins, and most of the Rockin' Friends), it did not draw a large enough crowd, and the project expired after six weeks because of lack of interest. Bond concluded at the time that only about 500 people out of the 750,000 who lived in Memphis really liked rockabilly. In addition, some of the performers expressed dissatisfaction at playing for a drinking and dancing crowd, preferring concert situations.

The second time I met Bond was in the spring of 1983 in his office and private radio studio in the penthouse of the Falls Building in downtown Memphis, overlooking the Mississippi River. He was broadcasting his morning radio show, one of two he was doing every day (for different stations). Bond said:

Memphis really don't give doodly squat about their own people. It don't impress them if Eddie Bond walks down through
the mall, or if it's Charlie Rich or Charlie Feathers, it just don't
turn their heads. They never did a thing at all for Elvis until he
died, and when he died everybody started talking Elvis Presley,
Elvis Presley. It's a shame that Elvis never even knew all the good
things people said about him. The city put a statue down here
for him, *after* he died. Somebody said, "Oh Eddie, you're so
lucky, you get to go to Holland, they love you over there." They
try to pull my rings off my fingers, just get any kind of souvenir, grabbing and running. I guess you would say that's lucky
except for one thing. It's a crying, heart-breaking shame to think
that you've got to go 6,000 miles roundtrip to make people appreciate you.[8]

CHARLIE FEATHERS

Born June 12, 1932, Myrtle (near Holly Springs), Mississippi

Charlie Feathers is a controversial figure in rockabilly—some say a
major figure, himself included. Others view him as a bit player, an
also-ran, a could-have been, a country singer who got side-tracked,
one who, as compensation for his lack of success, weaves stories to
place himself in a better light.

He has lots of stories. Some of them might be true. He recorded
rockabilly in 1949. He knew Elvis and went to shows with him while
the Presleys lived at Lauderdale Court, and that they worked together six months before Elvis's first session. It was hard to record rockabilly; he had tried it before Elvis, but there were problems with needles going into the red because of the ad-libs. They did not have
limiters or compressors then, but with the advent of the slap-back
echo, things could be cut a little hotter, because that took the edge
off; the slap-back cools down the needles. He was helping Sam Phillips out all the way back to 1950. He and Phillips discovered slap-
back, "and then we could record Elvis." Elvis copied Feather's demo
arrangements of "Blue Moon of Kentucky" and "Good Rockin' Tonight." He worked with Sam in the control room, coming out to
move microphones around for Scotty Moore and Bill Black. Not only
was the tape sped up for Carl Perkins's "Your True Love" (which is
well known), but tapes for Presley's "That's All Right" and "Blue Moon
of Kentucky" were sped up. Tapes of Johnny Cash were slowed to
make his voice sound low, and Feathers had a part in tuning the instruments higher so that they would sound in concert pitch when

the tape was slowed. "My Baby Left Me" was a song Feathers learned in the 1940s and used as a theme song, and Scotty Moore "played it behind me way back before we knew Elvis."[9] And Charlie has many other stories to tell.

Feathers is one of the people who started rockabilly, and he knows it. He will tell you so, and if you don't believe it, it doesn't change a thing for him.

Get comfortable, gentle readers. I am going to tell you a tale, one that you may have heard before. Once upon a time, Carl Perkins, Elvis Presley, and Charlie Feathers were chosen by the powers that be to deliver rockabilly to the world. Carl got the first spark and was the most musically articulate, but he was not geographically placed at the time to deliver the goods to a wider audience. Later the fireworks of his infrequent bouts of success dazzled him so that he craved their repetition, trying to second-guess the market, follow its trends, and polish the edges off his music's character. He eventually found his peace and settled down to the rockabilly equivalent of the Zen state referred to as "chop wood, carry water." Elvis got the brightest spark and was the most charming; he delivered the goods first and success came quickly. Later his drive and creativity got turned toward self-deception, and he withered in a world of artifice. Charlie got the hottest spark, marking him the deepest, and he was the most intuitive. Later he had little success to speak of, so he just continued what he was doing. True or false?

Feathers's recognition came finally in the revival. Despite being difficult to work with, suspicious when it comes to business, and inconsistent in concert, many fans regard him reverently as a prime keeper of the rockabilly flame, honoring him for his passion for music, for his unique style, and for remaining true to the spirit of the music, neither adopting nor acknowledging most of the subsequent stylistic innovations. He had the stamina—the courage of his convictions or just plain stubbornness—to persevere and the ability to amaze audiences when he so desired. Part of his power as a performer is the emphasis he places on spontaneous feeling and communication: "I have always been totally against practicing before we play. That's uncalled for. You hear second-hand stuff . . . you've got to sing to the people as they respond to it. . . . You can go out on a show tonight: all you can do is get people standin' up in their seat hollerin', that's all you can do. They don't have wings; they can't start flyin'."[10]

The spontaneous feeling behind Presley's delivery was one of the things Feathers admired about him: "Elvis would do tunes for a rea-

son, not just 'hey man, I'm singing a song and this is the way it goes.'
It'd build up inside of him 'til he really didn't know hardly what he
was going to do until he got in on the song. If he felt it that way, he
went that way. That's what made it happen."[11]

One of the first things I did on arriving in Memphis in 1982 was
to visit Professor David Evans at his office in the music department
of Memphis State University (now the University of Memphis). He
gave me several phone numbers, and I called Feathers immediately.
When I mentioned I was researching rockabilly and wanted to talk
to him about it, he said "come on over, we's doing it." At the Feathers's household Charlie, son Bubba on lead guitar, and a bass fiddle
player were rehearsing in the den. The first thing Charlie asked me
was whether I had a tape recorder. When I said yes, he told me to
leave it in the bag: I found out that he has a profound distrust of
bootlegging. But they were surely doing it: the music was authentic,
deep rockabilly.

He would not let me record our conversation that day either, but
when I visited him again, he relented after we had watched the last
innings of a baseball game on TV. Playing baseball is one of his hob-
bies. Amid talk of slap-back and his early years and tales about what
came before what and who got what from whom, he became aware
of the depth of my ignorance of his career: at the time I was familiar
only with his hillbilly songs (on Sun and Flip in 1955). For my edifi-
cation, he played me bits of his recent singles on the Feathers label,
explaining how he likes to change songs around. He sure does: "He'll
Have to Go" had barely a trace of the original melody. While Feathers was adjusting his video machine to show me a BBC documentary on himself, on the TV appeared the Fonz, the greasy rocker on
Happy Days. By then I knew that Charlie Feathers was a character, a
snowy-haired rocker with salt-and-pepper sideburns, starring in his
own show. When the video came on there was a surreal moment: I
was listening to the live Charlie Feathers talking while the filmed
Charlie Feathers was talking.

I had been told that Feathers was illiterate, and although he auto-
graphed some albums for me, I noticed that while looking for a particular song he played bits of his records rather than look at the labels. I had heard a story of how he once got incredibly off course
driving home in the middle of the night from a gig in Mississippi
because he could not read the road signs. I reflected on what not being able to refer to written words would mean: no song lyrics to read,
no references to look up, no newspapers, no diaries to keep or letters to write.

Several meetings later I came to see that Feathers, for whatever reason, lives through his senses and memory like no one else I have met. Living through senses and memory may have been an asset, possibly increasing the intensity of his connection to past events of farm life (listen to "Call Dog," where he recalls a childhood fear of mad dogs), his musical inspirations (the time he saw Bill Monroe, learning the "cottonpatch blues" from Obie Patterson and Junior Kimbrough, or hearing gospel singers), and a well of emotions when he sings. He actually sobs on a couple of his recordings.

Feathers knows, or seems to know, much detail, and although some of his descriptions appear to be not totally accurate, they seem to be derived from direct personal observation, an extremely vivid imagination, or more likely, a combination of both. Distortions may creep into one's memories for many reasons. As oral histories reveal, each person's version of past events is like an alternative reality. Feather's version of events is at times at odds and at times congruent with commonly accepted views of what probably happened. Although certain stories and claims seem readily refutable, even laughable, others are intriguing.

Consequently, perhaps his stories should be examined with an open mind. Let me explore the possibility that Elvis's arrangement of "Blue Moon of Kentucky" was actually learned from a demo tape made by Charlie Feathers. At this point, it is just armchair detective work: we have no such tape. Feathers was certainly involved with Sun at an early date. Scotty Moore says that Feathers was in and out of the studio all the time but denies him any musical influence on the Presley sessions.[12] Colin Escott does say that demos were recorded by Feathers in 1954; the first datable item in the Sun discography is February 1955.[13] That Charlie Feathers can be inaccurate about dates was pointed out to me by his wife, Rosemary. She illustrated it by reenacting the old argument the two of them have over the date of Hank Williams's death: they name dates one year apart (she picked the right one). Most of Feathers's demos (the evidence) were presumably destroyed by Phillips, who routinely recorded over master tapes when he lacked money to buy new ones. Demos that survived were sometimes found at the ends of tapes when the newer material did not use the entire length of tape.

I return to the case of "Blue Moon of Kentucky." First of all, Feathers is probably the most Bill Monroe–influenced of all the singers who did rockabilly, an influence heard in his high singing, so it is probable that this song would have been in his repertory. Second, Feathers has a penchant for drastically rearranging songs, including chang-

ing the meter of songs from 3/4 to 4/4, as Presley did on this song—
and to my knowledge never did again. On the other hand, maybe
Feathers learned to do this from the Presley recording and made it
part of his style. It is impossible to reach a definite conclusion, but
Feathers has thrown a wrench in the works, and (for those who see
it that way) that is a delicious vagary, a gift, for rockabilly's audience.
Unclear history allows for romanticism and fantasy for those who
come afterward.[14]

Speculation aside, I turn now to Feathers's recordings. Much of his
Sun work is heavily influenced by Hank Williams. Feathers did not
record rockabilly until 1956 because, he says, Sam Phillips saw him only
as a country singer. Feathers's rockabilly credentials stem from his highly
regarded releases on Meteor (Memphis) and King (Cincinnati).

A drumless 1956 single on Meteor was his first issued rockabilly.
A trio of Feathers, Jody Chastain (string bass), and Jerry Huffman (lead
guitar) recorded "Get with It," written by all three, and "Tongue-Tied
Jill" ("me got what me want when me got you"), written by Chastain
and Huffman. The latter became one of Feathers's signature songs, a
vein he later returned to with "Stuttering Cindy."

All eight songs that he recorded for King were written by the trio,
now billed as Charlie Feathers and his Musical Warriors, and backed
by a drummer. Feathers's first King session, in Cincinnati in August
1956, yielded two singles. "One Hand Loose" is now recognized for
the wonderful specimen it is. "Can't Hardly Stand It" is a rare example of slow rockabilly. "Everybody's Lovin' My Baby" and "Bottle to
the Baby" are dignified, almost stately, rockabilly. "Bottle to the Baby"
was a song that he had twice demoed at Sun, almost the only rockabilly he recorded there. The first version has Feathers with just piano accompaniment; the second has the whole band. The King version has new, less rural words.

At Feathers's second session for King, at the RCA Victor Studios
in Nashville in January 1957, the band was augmented by a male
vocal group, the Prisonaires (a group of black prisoners recorded by
Sam Phillips in 1953 and 1954), according to Feathers. All songs on
these two singles are confident but relaxed; only "Nobody's Woman" is rockabilly. In that song the vocal group only claps, but the
other songs would be country pop with or without their singing.

Feathers continued to record, for more than a dozen labels, never
retiring from music while working jobs outside music as well. European collectors tracked him down in 1967 and brought him back into
the studio after a four year hiatus. His 1973 album, *Rockabilly Rhythm*,
on the Cowboy Carl label, is essentially a duo with his son Bubba;

Charlie plays acoustic guitar and overdubs his own upright bass playing. Given the song list, this could have been a 1950s product, and when everything connects, when he throws himself into the material with total conviction and respect (on more than half the tracks), the songs, the sound, and the intensity make it seem like the Charlie Feathers Sun Sessions. Besides the songs from Presley, Perkins, Cash, Berry, and Hank Snow, note the gospel song "Working on a Building." Feathers is, as Peter Guralnick says, "a traditionalist in a music that sought to overthrow tradition."[15]

Months later Feathers recorded the *Good Rockin' Tonight* album for Barrelhouse. It is, like the two volumes that followed in 1979 on the Feathers label, less successful. These homemade sounding albums, laid back and under-rehearsed, are full of familiar songs bent into new and unusual shapes, some interesting on the hypnotic side, some boring on the lackluster side. Whether country songs, rock 'n' roll, rockabilly, new songs or folk songs, the sound is glued together by the strumming of his acoustic guitar. Charlie's voice changes registers at will, son Bubba is his constant foil ("work with it, child," Charlie urges), and his daughter Wanda sings a verse or harmony here and there.

Feathers's first trip overseas was in 1977, for the Sun Sound Show at London's Rainbow Theatre, organized by author and promoter Graham Wood. Feathers and Warren Smith were the Sun artists, and Jack Scott and Buddy Knox also headlined, with Crazy Cavan and the Rhythm Rockers as the opening band. One of the two nights was recorded, against Feather's wishes.

In the late 1980s Feathers was having problems with diabetes. Several benefit shows helped to defray hospital expenses. In 1990, backed by Stan Kesler, J. M. Van Eaton, and Bubba Feathers and his band, he recorded an album engineered by Sam Phillips' son, Jerry, for Elektra's Explorer series. Producer Ben Vaughn called him "an abstract thinker . . . he's so far into music, he's a genius like Sun Ra or Monk or Mingus."[16]

A month later Feathers did shows in England and Switzerland. Performing in a chair most of the time, he wowed his audiences, winning back some fans who had been soured by previous weak concerts. On his return to Memphis, a cancerous lung was removed. In 1991 he returned to England, performing for the first time in the year since the operation. Despite his goodwill and a tremendous reception, the visibly ill Feathers rested on his chair between each song and was barely able to finish his set. His health has since improved, and some time later, he accomplished the unlikely by performing and recording again, with Billy Poore producing. The album is called *I Ain't Done Yet!*

CORDELL JACKSON
Born July 15, 1923, Pontotoc, Mississippi

Cordell Jackson is a free spirit who ran an independent label out of her home in Memphis from 1956 to 1959. She started Moon Records to put out her own "Beboppers Christmas" and "Rock and Roll Christmas," but the other nine singles that the company released were by different artists. Around 1980, when she heard that the old records were collector's items, she revived the label to release an album of its best tracks and started to record her own songs again.

Jackson began with guitar in her father's band at age twelve and later played on the radio in nearby Tupelo. During World War II she moved to Memphis, where she gained more performing experience on the upright bass.

While holding down day jobs, she ran the label out of her home, acting as engineer, singer, writer, arranger, and promoter. The Moon studio was her living room, fitted out with a single-track Ampex tape recorder and four microphones. Singers were isolated in a padded booth, but not the instruments; the only way to control the balance was to move the microphones. Echo was added at the mastering stage by the RCA studio.

The songs that came out on Moon were rockabilly, rock 'n' roll, hillbilly, and instrumental boogies. Allen Page was the main artist and had four singles. He had come to Memphis from Florida, drawn by Sun records, but "instead landed on the Moon."[17] His two best songs—"Dateless Night" (written by Jackson) and "She's the One That's Got It"—had moderate success in their day but saw new life in the early 1980s when they were covered by Tav Falco's Panther Burns. Around the same time Jackson was often invited by the band to perform between sets.

When I visited Cordell Jackson in Memphis, she showed me where the studio had been and played a tape of her latest recording, an EP of instrumentals called "Knockin' Sixty." The only working cassette deck was in her yellow Cadillac. As we sat in the car in the driveway, she joked that she was pleased with the recording because it contained "lots of human error."[18]

Further songs, one called "Football Widow," were promoted with stickers, buttons, T-shirts, a video, and a monthly newsletter. In 1991, after dueling guitars with Brian Setzer in a Budweiser beer commercial, she got more exposure on the David Letterman, Arsenio Hall, *Nashville Now,* and *Entertainment Tonight* television shows. Playing an electric guitar and wearing her trademark hoop skirt, she said, "If I want to wang dang rock 'n' roll at 69 years old all dressed up in an antebellum dress, it ain't nobody's business but mine."[19]

HAYDEN THOMPSON
Born 1938, Booneville, Mississippi

Of the artists with Memphis associations, Hayden Thompson was one of the last to reap benefit from the revival, but his is one of its best success stories, vindicating his years of endlessly trying to make it in the face of little recognition or promotion. His recording history predates Elvis's debut by a few months (as mentioned in chap. 3). Hayden Thompson and his Southern Melody Boys made it to the *Louisiana Hayride* but soon evolved into the Dixie Jazzlanders. Through most of 1956 they toured the movie theaters of Mississippi playing rock 'n' roll hits on stage between showings of *Rock around the Clock.*

Thompson then joined the Slim Rhodes Band, touring neighboring states from their base in Memphis. Sessions at Sun yielded only one single on Phillips International—a cover of Junior Parker's "Love My Baby," with Jerry Lee Lewis on piano, backed with "One Broken Heart," a country song with a Latin beat. Other gems were unreleased at the time but did wonders for Thompson's reputation when they finally surfaced in the revival. Among them are "Rock-a-billy Gal" (with the Slim Rhodes Band), "Blues, Blues, Blues," and "Fairlane Rock," whose lyrics favorably compare a car's appearance to a girl's. Sometimes he plays with his pronunciation so much we know not to take it seriously, although other times he sounds harder and more confident, reminiscent of Sonny Burgess, with whom he toured. "Don't You Worry" was a song credited on a 1985 Sun reissue album (*Shake Around*) to the absolutely unknown Sid Watson, a name so unknown it sparked some sleuthing by Trevor Cajiao, leading to the realization that the song is another by Hayden Thompson.[20]

Disillusioned by Sam Phillips's indifference to his career, Thompson moved to Chicago, gigging at the Tally Ho club from 1958 to 1962 and doing lots of radio and TV shows while continuing to record. He drifted back to country music for 1965 sessions and an album but not before inserting a twist verse into "Brown-Eyed Handsome Man," singing about beach parties in "It Won't Be Long until the Summer," and getting stung by the honeybee syndrome in

"Queen Bee" ("I'm the loneliest bee . . . I'll buzz around your throne").
He recorded primarily originals, although in this period his influences
are rather obvious: Elvis, Charlie Rich, and Chuck Berry. His "Old Kris
Kringle" resembles a Johnny Cash tune enough for me to want to
call it "Ballad of a Teenage Santa."

In the 1970s Thompson's efforts for a successful music career
brought him little reward, and he made his living as a cab and limousine driver, but the Europeans raised his hopes. His first gigs in
Europe came in 1984. While in London he recorded an album with
Dave Travis. It is weighted toward country, but Thompson delivers
the rockabilly goods with thrilling versions of "Eenie Meenie Minie
Mo" and Billy "Crash" Craddock's "Ah, Poor Little Baby." Other newly
recorded and highly regarded albums appeared on the SunJay label
of Sweden.

JACK SCOTT
Born Jack Scafone, January 24, 1936, Windsor, Ontario

The rockabilly revival gave Jack Scott some of the recognition he deserved anyway. How could someone so successful be so unknown?
Is it because he was a lone wolf, seemingly not part of a regional scene
or community, or because there have been no notorious events, no
scandals? Jack Scott had a remarkable number of hits in a short time:
nineteen songs made the national charts between June 1958 and
November 1961, four of them in the top ten. Sixteen of those songs
were his compositions. At the time he was largely passed over by the
fan magazines, and today, for most people, he is as unknown as someone who had no hits.

Scott was the eldest of the seven Scafone children. When he was
eight, his guitar-playing father gave him a guitar. Two years later the
family moved from Windsor, Ontario, to Hazel Park, Michigan, near
Detroit, and he gained experience performing on the radio, at school,
and at dances. The band was called the Southern Drifters, and early
pictures show them in fancy cowboy shirts and neck scarves.

His first two singles are from 1957 on ABC Paramount. "Two Timin'
Woman" is a decent, albeit standard-issue blues. "My Baby She's Gone"
is more interesting. Playing more slowly than most rockabilly groups,
the band is intense with slashing guitar played by Dave Rohillier, who
opens the solo with the minor chord (against the major tonality) produced by barring the top three strings, a trick learned from Scotty
Moore. Elvis's influence is found also in Scott's voice and in the way

that he pops the "babys" while singing "my baby baby baby she's gone from me." Scott loves to sing low in his range, sometimes moving the melody up an octave for the next verse. Conway Twitty, himself greatly influenced by Elvis, is probably the influence behind Scott's penchant for dragging a low note, making it come out in sputters; drawn on the page, the note would look like a dotted line. It is an expressive device that implies but does not convey emotion.

Scott's music is subdued, controlled, moody, effective, simple, and repetitive. The repetition is often hypnotic, as in "Geraldine," which opens with the name chanted sixteen times, then "cutest gal I've ever seen," her name three more times, then the whole chorus is sung again. Another example of repetition is in "Goodbye Baby Bye Bye," where the title line is sung three times in a row in three of the verses (and with slight variations in the other verses), followed by a single new line: "I'm going to leave you now," "Johnny's going away," "please don't you cry," and so on. The repetitions of the title in "Found a Woman" are broken by laconic, unusual lines like "not too keen, just a teen, sometimes works on a sewing machine."

Scott's music came in two main flavors: medium and fast blues songs with stops, such as "Leroy," and ballads, often in 6/8 time, like his biggest hit, "My True Love." Exceptions are his cover of the Sons of the Pioneers' "Cool Water," the gospel "Save My Soul," and "Bella," with its Greek bouzouki-like guitar playing. His songs in that period are almost exclusively in the key of E or A, exceptions being "Never Felt Like This" in A minor, "Midgie" in F-sharp, and "Bo's Going to Jail" and "Cool Water," both in C. Song structures are eight, twelve, or sixteen bars, the sax playing is adequate, the guitar playing is good, the bass fiddle (almost an anachronism by 1960) and drums are solid but basic, and the sound is completed by the prominently featured male vocal quartet, the Chantones. The success of Jack Scott's circumscribed sound world illustrates the saying "if you want to talk to America, keep it simple."

In the revival the Cramps, Shakin' Stevens, Robert Gordon, and others covered "The Way I Walk" and "Leroy," which brought some attention to Scott, and he made trips to England in 1977 and Paris in 1981. In 1983 I saw him as part of a Toronto rockabilly festival. He was superbly accompanied by the Frigidaires, a local group. Scott opened his set with "Greaseball" (the original, unsanitized version of "Leroy") and with little fanfare or pizzazz re-created many of his hits.

In 1993 a five-CD set was released on the German Bear Family label collecting his work from several labels from 1957 to 1965.

JOE CLAY

Born Claiborne Joseph Cheramie, September 9, 1938, Harvey, Louisiana

As the revival advanced, more veterans surfaced. In Joe Clay's case, the delay was just because he was hard to find.

In 1982 I was watching a revival band's performance in a basement club in Toronto. A guy with an exaggerated hairdo—held together (he told me later) with Royal Crown ("the same stuff that Elvis used, you can still get it at Honest Ed's store")—started yelling for the band to play something by Joe Clay. Mr. Hairdo's friend said, "who the hell is Joe Clay?" I had no idea either, and obviously neither did the band. I felt like I was on the outside.

It turned out that Joe Clay sparked a lot of people's imaginations, although it took most of us a little longer to catch on. Nine pure rockabilly songs—two singles and five unissued tracks—recorded in 1956 are the basis of the legend. A couple of the songs came out on an RCA compilation, and later all nine were released. Laudatory reviews propelled the cause.

Clay started singing in nightclubs when he was twelve, brought by his parents to Sunday afternoon dances. He was eighteen when a New Orleans deejay, responding to a record company memo, suggested him for Vik, a subsidiary of RCA that released acquired master recordings. Propelled by a drummer playing brushes and Hal Harris's guitar playing, Clay recorded five songs in Houston at the Gold Star studio, among them a cover of Link Davis's "Sixteen Chicks" and "Ducktail," written and previously recorded by Rudy Grayzell. "Ducktail" is similar to "Blue Suede Shoes": "don't mess with my ducktails." Enunciating as if he had a hot potato in his mouth, Clay and the other musicians offer an engaged, confident, and involved performance. These songs are all in flat keys—B-flat, E-flat, F—perhaps indicating that the master tape was sped up (the next batch of songs— New York sessions—are all in sharp keys: A, D, E).

One month later, in New York with a black studio band featuring Mickey Baker on guitar and two drummers, Clay sang more aggressively and the band was on fire. These four songs were given to him by the producer just before the sessions. The unissued "You Look That Good to Me" was written by R&B star Ivory Joe Hunter and Mercury A&R man Clyde Otis, who also cowrote "Cracker Jack," one side of Clay's second single. The other side was "Get on the Right Track," written by R&B singer Titus Turner. Finally, the title alone justifies a mention of "Did You Mean Jelly Bean (What You Said Cabbage Head)."

Even though Clay made some of the most charged music of his
time and appeared on the *Louisiana Hayride* (where he was photographed alongside Elvis Presley) and the *Ed Sullivan Show* (where at
the last minute he was forced to sing a ballad and did "Only You"),
nothing clicked. Aside from a few record hops around New York, little was done in the way of promotion. He continued to perform
around New Orleans, once filling in on drums when Elvis's drummer was sick.

Clay had been a schoolbus driver for fifteen years and had retired
from music shortly before he was rediscovered in 1986 by promoter
Willie Jeffery after a search of nearly three years. Clay soon performed
in Europe and toured in North America to reviews raving about his
drive, his confidence, his undiminished voice, his turn on drums for
Little Richard's "Keep-a-Knockin'," and his ability to drive a crowd
wild. There is talk of a movie of his life.[21] In 1989 he recorded a single in Belgium.

Back in New Orleans Clay plays drums in a lounge band, mixing
in R&B and rockabilly with the middle-of-the-road repertory.

RONNIE DAWSON
Born August 12, 1939, Dallas, Texas

Ronnie Dawson was an only child raised in Waxahachie, Texas, by a
father who played western swing and a mother who sang in the Pen-
tacostal church the family attended. For a brief period he studied at
the Southern Bible Institute (at the same time that Jerry Lee Lewis
had his short stay there), but the call of rock 'n' roll was stronger.
Dawson's first band was called Ronnie Dee and the D Men. Their repertory of R&B and rockabilly made them area favorites, winning the
Big D Jamboree talent contest ten weeks in a row. Nicknamed "the
Blond Bomber" for his platinum crew cut, he had a couple of local
hits with his first two 45s: "Action Packed," written by Jack Rhodes,
and "Rockin' Bones," by Rhodes with Don Carter and Dub Nalls, the
same trio who penned Gene Vincent's "B-I-Bickey-Bi, Bo-Bo-Go."
Rhodes also wrote Vincent's "Woman Love," plus the country standards "Silver Threads and Golden Needles" and "A Satisfied Mind."
Dawson did a little recording with Vincent and was part of the Dallas rocking gang along with Johnny Carroll, Sid King, Mac Curtis,
and Gene Summers.

After touring in the Midwest and the East, Dawson recorded two
45s of wimpy pop (that he now disowns) for Dick Clark's Swan label. It was back to rocking for a single on Columbia (which dubbed

him "Commonwealth Jones" and whose staff thought that he was black), where he later did a stint as a country singer. Some other rockers on small labels came in between. For a while he played with the long-running western swing band Light Crust Doughboys and was a session drummer for Major Bill Smith's operations, taking part in two number-one hits, Bruce Channel's "Hey! Baby" (1962) and Paul and Paula's "Hey Paula" (1963). In recent years Dawson worked in TV and radio advertising.[22]

In 1989 his 1950s and early 1960s output was collected on an album titled *Rockin' Bones*. Wildly enthusiastic response to his overseas performances led to three new albums for No Hit Records of London. *Rockinitis* teamed him with excellent backup from the Planet Rockers from Nashville, the Playboys from London, and ensembles led by ex-Polecat Boz Boorer, who acted as a producer with label boss Barney Koumis. Dawson's shows, like the albums that reflect them, are consistently highly rated because he delivers the goods. With a gruff and powerful voice, he is also a guitar slinger, trading hot licks with the guitarist from his invariably well-rehearsed backup band. His intriguing repertory satisfies his audience's demanding taste because Dawson keeps it interesting by mixing in country, rockabilly, rock 'n' roll, and R&B, playing songs by composers ranging from Hank Williams to Joe Tex. Still sporting a blond crew cut, the fit and spirited Dawson is Mr. Rockin' Bones himself. Friendly and youthfully energetic, he bops around the stage in unpretentious outfits: running shoes, slacks, and short-sleeved or embroidered cowboy shirts, or all in black and white. Reviewers give him their highest possible praise, and dazzled audiences love him. With his forthright, non-nostalgic approach he has become one of the major attractions on the European rock 'n' roll circuit.

On a 1995 tour Dawson was backed by High Noon, an excellent band from Austin comprising Sean Mencher on lead guitar, Shaun Young on rhythm guitar and lead vocals, and Kevin Smith on upright bass. Drummer Lisa Pankratz rounded out the lineup, and this fiery ensemble, after a weekend of gigs in New York City, performed on national TV on *Late Night* with Conan O'Brien.

◆ ◆ ◆

Many other performers enjoyed a renaissance. Hasil Adkins, a musical primitive and character-and-a-half, makes music with wild abandon. It has been called bad, tasteless, incoherent, and mad. He is championed by Norton Records, the same people who produce *Kicks* magazine. Several albums of old and new material have been released for an audience with a taste for the bizarre. They get it in the Haze (his nickname) and his dance, the Hunch. After watching an Adkins performance, a friend's comment (meant favorably) was "it's like watching someone's drunk dad singing at a party."

Charlie Gracie surprised a lot of people in Europe. Born in 1936 in Philadelphia, he was influenced by seeing Bill Haley and the Saddlemen in 1952, with their cowboy outfits and drums. Gracie's early recordings, from 1951 onward, covered jump blues, swing, country boogie, and protorockabilly and featured his own excellent lead guitar playing. In 1957 he had pop success on the Cameo label: "Butterfly" hit number one (Andy Williams also took it to number one the same year) and "Fabulous" made number sixteen. He toured, performed on TV and in the film *Jamboree,* and did shows in England that year and the next. When he returned to England twenty years later, he exceeded expectations and won converts among the rockabilly community. Although dubbed a rockabilly star in the trade papers in 1957,[23] his style is not rockabilly but rather northern swing, more pop than country, more swing than rock. Neither his approach nor his repertory reflects involvement or inspiration from the Elvis school of music. The amiable Gracie still performs regularly around New Jersey's resort towns and is a frequent visitor overseas, where he is a well-loved major figure on the festival circuit.

Gene Summers, born in Dallas in 1939, formed his first band, the Rebels, just out of high school. His long recording career started in 1958 with "School of Rock 'n' Roll" backed with "Straight Skirts," a regional hit. He toured for the next few years and had his biggest-selling single in 1963, "Blue Diamond." In 1976 he recorded the first of several sessions for Lake County of Switzerland, and in 1980 he recorded in Nashville with the Jordanaires and well-known session players. He first hit Europe in 1980, recorded in Paris, London, and Sweden, and saw new and reissued material on labels from Norway to Australia. His recordings are more surface than substance, his style more pop than down-home, and his newer material is more rockabilly than are his old singles.

Jackie Lee Cochran was born in Georgia and raised in Alabama, Mississippi, and Louisiana; he now lives in California. At age six he got his first guitar from his father, who was then in jail for killing a man in a barroom fight; he was released when the killing was ruled self-defense. Of his childhood, Cochran said, "all I could think about was guitars and music. Most of my time was spent alone with my music and dreams."[24] In 1956 he cut his first records for the Sims label in Dallas, where he worked on the *Big D Jamboree* with Marty

Robbins, Carl Perkins, Groovey Joe Poovey, and Freddie Hart. Cochran did a couple of shows with Elvis and hung around with him at drive-ins in a certain pink-and-black 1955 Cadillac. With Mac Curtis and Johnny Horton, Cochran worked on the *Cowtown Hoedown* in Fort Worth. While performing in California on shows run by Spade Cooley and Tex Williams, Cochran was signed to Decca. In Los Angeles he recorded his only Decca single: "Ruby Pearl" (his wife's name; they were married for six months) and "Mama Don't You Think I Know," two of his best-known songs. Legal problems over contracts hampered his career, although he had other releases in the 1950s, one each on Viv, ABC-Paramount, Spry, and Jaguar. "I was known as 'Jack the Cat,'" he said. "We had a big laminated black cat and somehow they got lights in its eyes . . . they rolled this thing on stage before I came out and did my thing."[25]

Besides enjoying a lengthy career as a nightclub musician, Cochran has been a rodeo rider, an aircraft mechanic (he served four years in the U.S. Air Force as a jet specialist), and a movie actor (he played a cowboy in a Walt Disney movie and an Elvis imitator in a 1960 Marilyn Monroe movie entitled *Let's Make Love*). In 1973 Cochran began recording for Rollin' Rock, and he writes almost all the songs and plays almost all the instruments on these albums. His first of many visits to Europe was a 1981 gig in Finland. As of 1993 he had been playing rock 'n' roll, rockabilly, and country three nights a week for seven years at the Gaslight club in Santa Monica.

Johnny Powers, born in 1938 in Detroit, was greatly inspired by the rockabilly records on Sun. After two singles, including the regional hit "Long Blond Hair" on Fortune, he got to record for Sun himself, resulting in one release in 1959. Back in Detroit he became the first white artist signed to Motown. Even though Powers was produced by Marvin Gaye, Motown did not know what to do with him, and only one single came out on a subsidiary label. Powers found his success in the music business as a producer and publisher. Revival interest has caused his 1950s tracks to be collected on CD, revealing that his songwriting was more developed than his voice. Since his first visit to Europe in 1985, he has returned three or four times a year to perform. He has recorded new albums, including the acclaimed *A New Spark (from an Old Flame)* from 1993, mixing blues, rockabilly, and, on a couple of tracks where he is joined by George Clinton, funkabilly.

Larry Donn from Bono, Arkansas, is known for "Honey Bun" and "That's What I Call a Ball" from 1959 and his work with Sonny Burgess. In fact, it was a 1955 performance by Burgess that was Donn's first exposure to live rockabilly. Donn is capable on guitar, piano, and bass, and his energetic revival performances backed by the Playboys give tribute to his influences, mostly the Sun gang. His reminiscences of gigs, recording sessions, and encounters with contemporaries make his "Rockabilly Days" column in *Now Dig This* one of its most popular features.

A darker side of the revival is that some of the less appealing patterns of the 1950s were replayed, unfortunately to some of the same individuals. In the 1950s young performers hoped for a break, for a chance to record, for recognition, and for financial reward for their music. They seized whatever opportunities they could, which often involved grueling tour schedules, recording for hole-in-the-wall companies (or releasing their records themselves), giving up rights to royalties, and altering their musical style willingly or reluctantly. These things no doubt were experienced by young revival musicians, but many of the veterans, some of whom had retired from music, had their hopes rekindled yet felt many of the same frustrations a second time.

The situation is, of course, not identical. Few of these older musicians tour extensively—they may get a couple of trips to England or Europe—but they still are eager (or at least willing) to perform and record. Despite being more cautious and experienced, some still get involved with less than favorable business deals. Certainly these musicians derive satisfaction from the interest shown in their lives and their music, and they have made some money from performances and new recordings, but they also have seen their old records reissued at (usually) no financial gain to themselves. Anyone who has or can gather together a handful of records marketable as rockabilly can put out a reissue. Even legal reissues—and many were not legal—did not result in the artists getting royalties, for in many cases (especially with the small independent labels), the artists had lost, given up, sold, or signed away their rights a long time ago.

On the other hand, a crafty or hungry musician will keep trying whatever he or she can in the musical marketplace, which may account for the appearance of such items as "Orange Blossom Special" by Mac Curtis's Nashville Marimba Band, spotted on the in-flight play list on an airplane trip. Is it the same Mac Curtis?

FOURTEEN

REVIVALISTS

"Rockabilly Rebel"

The lasting value of the best rockabilly, or of any style for that matter, is in the original and personal way that musicians work within tradition. To internalize a tradition means to get inside not just the notes but also the underlying emotional territory, enabling the musician to be articulate within a style; to play it but also to play with it—to stretch conventions in an artistic way without violating the thing itself. There are many ways to do this. The best music made by revivalists—younger musicians who chose to do rockabilly despite their cultural distance from it—achieved this level of internalization and represents the continuation of the tradition of rockabilly.

We have seen revivals of many styles. They often take a similar path: extensive reissuing of sounds, research, fanzines, young bands, and veteran performers. Post-1970s rockabilly, although encompassing re-creation, is a product of different traditions. The fact that rockabilly was essentially dormant for so many years meant that the revivalist musicians learned the style from records and blended it with their own traditions, usually rock, to form new hybrids.

When rockabilly was reborn in the late 1970s, it was perceived as something that could evolve and affect the world at large. Young groups had hit singles and albums in the charts in the United Kingdom and elsewhere in Europe, and for the Stray Cats, in North America. Over the next few years rockabilly again became an influence on the mainstream, although the style was never a threat to the established artists of the 1980s like it was to the established country artists of the 1950s.

For younger musicians, the revival offered an escape from postmodernism via pseudonostalgia. It protested artificiality by exploring little-known roots. There were new acts, new audiences, fresh money, and a quality in the style itself that was welcomed and desired.

As a style it offered a common, simple, folksy touch, direct and energetic. Rockabilly's structures, melodies, and rhythms were intuitively familiar to its audience. The country component of rockabilly recently had been reintroduced to the rock scene through certain songs by the Byrds, Bob Dylan, Linda Ronstadt, Emmylou Harris, the Eagles, and others. Rockabilly, the punk music of the 1950s, shared similarities with the punk music that emerged in 1976: primal energy, rebellion, basic instrumentation, and (often) basic musicianship. For some musicians with a background in punk, rockabilly provided a place to continue along similar lines. Since it cut across established divisions, it appealed to musicians looking for a bigger audience. It even came with ready-made symbols and a dress code.

One band that came from the punk scene was Vancouver's Buddy Selfish and his Saviours. On tour in 1982 in Toronto, guitarist Colin Griffiths told me:

> Rockabilly was the only reasonable place for the punk energy to go. 'Cause with punk it was just flat out: the people could hit themselves or throw themselves around, energize. When we started doing this stuff they actually started dancing, you know, with each other, rather than in such an independent frame. We started calling it AOR: that stands for ankle-oriented rock. A lot of the punk boys started to dance with the girls, so all of a sudden you saw more couples on the floor and in the audience. And they turned on to the fashions, which was a big deal: lots of crinolines and sideburns.[1]

Certain hallmarks of 1950s rockabilly are almost universally used by revivalists: echo (which may be excessive); small string band combos of guitar, bass, drums (generally played in more of a rock style), and sometimes piano but rarely saxophone or unusual instrumentation; predominance of males; and the use of encouraging interjections, catch phrases, blues forms, and exaggerated vocal style. The differences were far less use of chorus groups, generally faster tempos, more use of stereo and modern studio effects, and less sexism in lyrics. Exaggerated clothing and hair styles, period props (especially cars), and vintage equipment (guitars, upright bass, and microphones) were also seen. This was serious business, however; few bands went further than flirting with parody, and even that was rare. Musicians characteristically came from rock backgrounds and infused their style with country inflections, in contrast to the 1950s players, who were from country backgrounds and infused their style with R&B and rock 'n' roll.

One sampler of revivalist approaches is *L.A. Rockabilly,* released in 1983. It shows that for the most part, revival rockabilly incorporated few new elements. Most songs were written by the performers—one singer does a song his dad wrote in 1959—but Johnny Carroll and Little Richard each get covered, a Cajun standard gets an instrumental treatment, and Johnny Meeks sings and plays lead guitar on "Say Mama," a song he wrote for Gene Vincent while a member of the Blue Caps. The subjects covered are typical, as the titles indicate—"Let's Bop," "Shake the Roof," "Double Datin'," "Cadillac Cruisin'"—and classic sounds are re-created: slapped bass, the-girl-with-the-sore-throat, Presley on Sun, and train-rhythm drums. Modern studio techniques provide stereo and various kinds of echo. Signs of the times are some faster tempos than generally found in the 1950s and a band with a female bassist and a female drummer.

Reverence for an earlier era has been mixed with the possibility of adding a personal imprint. Revival bands pay homage to 1950s material by re-creating it, but some display strong original writing in a rockabilly-based style practically devoid of post-Beatles influence. Britain had maintained a strong presence and influence on the North American music scene since the Merseybeat explosion, and ironically, much of the revival's impetus was imported from there.

Most of the first revivalists in Britain, France, Holland, Italy, and elsewhere were eager and young and had limited musical abilities. They imitated the records but tended to sound mechanical. In time, however, they improved as individual musicians and as ensembles. Once the revival generated enough of an audience to support the touring of veterans, the young revivalists got inspiration and insight from seeing (and sometimes working with) the past masters in concert, thus bringing more authority to their music.

Foreign players consciously copied Americanisms of accent and dress. Their compositions regularly referred to American imagery, place names, brand names, coins, and expressions. English is almost universal as the sung language of revivalists, although there are songs in French, German, Spanish, Finnish, and even Japanese. Even Americans emulated the poor grammar occasionally found in source versions, as in "all them cats is boppin' the blues" and "little green mens." The Stray Cats urged audiences to sing along with the words "you gots cat class and you gots cat style" ("Stray Cat Strut").

Ray Campi, with car, bass, and hat (courtesy of the artist).

Rockhouse Records' forty-first festival with Mac Curtis headlining (courtesy of Rockhouse Records).

Sleepy LaBeef promo photo (from the collection of Marc Coulavin/Top of the Bops Archives; photo by Kurt Stier).

Marcus Van Story in Charlotte, North Carolina, 1956, while on tour with Warren Smith. They were part of a show that included Pat Boone, Brook Benton, Johnny Guitar, Bill Haley, and Danny and the Juniors (courtesy of Tommie Wix).

Glenn Honeycutt on stage in Memphis, 1982. Johnny Black is on bass (photo by the author).

Eddie Bond, with Marcus Van Story and Al Hopson, Memphis, 1982 (photo by the author).

Charlie Feathers, around 1979 (courtesy of the artist).

Jack Scott (from the collection of
Wayne Russell).

Ronnie Dawson promo photo (courtesy of the artist; photo
by Rex Fly).

Crazy Cavan (center) and the Rhythm Rockers, with Paul Barrett (top), back home in Wales in 1981 after a tour of Finland, with the Gold Record awards received there for sales of 25,000 copies of the *Still Crazy* album (courtesy of Paul Barrett).

Dave Travis promo photo (courtesy of the artist).

The Sidewinders, with Handsome Ned (third from the left), in Toronto, 1983 (from the author's collection).

High Noon: left to right, Sean Mencher, Shaun Young, and Kevin Smith (courtesy of the artists).

The Bopcats trio lineup, in Toronto, 1983: from left to right, Teddy Fury, Zeke Rivers, and Jack de Keyzer (from the author's collection).

Ray Condo and his Hardrock Goners, 1994: from left to right, Peter Sandmark, Clive Jackson, Ray Condo, Eric Sandmark, and Edgar Bridwell (courtesy of the artists).

For the younger players, rockabilly was something new, not already the property of the rock establishment; the veterans for the most part had worked on its fringes. Before long, however, rockabilly songs appeared in the repertories of stars who had not recorded any before. The Rolling Stones did "Twenty Flight Rock" on their 1981 U.S. tour and subsequent live album. Rod Stewart did a version of "Tear It Up" in 1982. Elvis Costello, who surfaced in the United Kingdom in 1977 under the new wave banner, showed himself adept at several styles, recording a country album in 1981 in Nashville called *Almost Blue,* containing "Honey Hush" and a rocking version of Hank Williams's "Why Don't You Love Me Like You Used to Do?" A rockabilly composition by Queen, "Crazy Little Thing Called Love," a total departure from the band's usual style, was a hit in 1980. Neil Young did a rockabilly-styled album in 1983 called *Everybody's Rockin'.* All these new rockabilly recordings by popular artists were by British musicians (except for Neil Young, who is from Canada).

Some of the newer American artists took the rockabilly influence but not the revival imagery, such as the LeRoi Brothers, a Texas bar band that covered songs learned from Sonny Fisher, Johnny Carroll, and Ronnie Self alongside other covers and originals on their first album in 1983. Chris Isaak debuted in 1985 with a rockabilly-based sound that hit in 1990 with the song "Wicked Game."

What would it have sounded like if Elvis had lived to cover "Crazy Little Thing Called Love"? The answer has been provided by Orion, the stage name of Jimmy Ellis, an Elvis soundalike who has played up the theory that he is in fact Elvis. The idea, taken from a book, is that Elvis faked his death, got cleaned up and lost weight, and wanted to perform again. Since he could not change his sound, he decided to wear a mask so as not to be recognized. Some publicity was generated when a voice sounding uncannily like Elvis's was presented (overdubbed onto existing material) on the albums *Duets* by Jerry Lee Lewis and Friends, and *Trio +* by Lewis, Charlie Rich, and Carl Perkins. The identity of the unnamed singer was left to the imagination. Orion's first album was called *Reborn.* His publicity billed him as "Super Star of the 80's," and his records, on the reactivated Sun label, were on gold-colored vinyl. One of his albums is called *Some Think He Might Be King Elvis.* The "autobiographical" "Down in Mississippi" from *New Beginnings* explains how he was "just an old rock 'n' roller tired of coming back" and "a prisoner of my fame." Because he could not just walk away, the singer says, "I changed the way I looked, now no one knows me / everybody in the world believes the king is gone / but I'm down in Mississippi and it's good to be back home."

Orion has at least three fan clubs. One of his fans passed me a tape of Orion's songs to play on my radio show, adding, "There's a lot of mystery about Orion's recordings and even the performer himself. I've heard a lot of Presley imitators and to call him an 'imitator' would be an insult to his talent. The emotions and feelings he puts into a song clearly come from within, regardless of outside influences or similarities. Maybe he is the reincarnation of Elvis or whatever. I've never felt I needed to know all the facts in order to enjoy the music."[2] On an album called *Rockabilly,* besides performing the standard covers, Orion does a decent job of letting us hear how Elvis would have sounded on Matchbox's "Rockabilly Rebel" and Queen's "Crazy Little Thing Called Love." The answer to the question is, it would have sounded like Elvis.

The first revivalists go back to the 1960s. Hank C. Burnette is the pseudonym of a one-man Swedish rockabilly band who recorded in the style as far back as 1964. Sven-Ake Hogberg (his real name) had a hit in the United Kingdom with "Spinning Rock Boogie" in 1976. *Rockabilly Gassaroonie,* Burnette's 1977 album, is "stereo electronically processed to simulate mono." Sailing over appropriate rhythm section playing and a satisfying general feel are Burnette's trademarks of low, understated vocals and hot guitar playing. One song has the sped-up lead guitar sound that used to be a trademark of Merle Travis and Les Paul. It is obtained by recording the solo at half the tempo and then playing the tape at the tempo of the song: the guitar races along at superhuman speed. The number of overdubs and bouncing of tracks needed to make the one-man band (and one-man harmony singing group) work deteriorates the sound and makes for hiss, although not any worse than some of the obscure small-label 1950s recordings that Burnette covers. He also brings life to better-known songs, including a standout version of "Over the Rainbow" inspired by Gene Vincent's and a couple of originals.

Freddie "Fingers" Lee is a flamboyant pianist from Newcastle-on-Tyne who first recorded in 1966. In the 1950s his life was changed by hearing Lonnie Donegan; Lee started playing guitar at age twelve in skiffle groups. In addition to performing his rock 'n' roll repertory, he still plays American folk songs such as Leadbelly's "Midnight Special" and "Pick a Bale of Cotton" arranged in boogie-woogie style. In the late 1950s Lee began playing piano, joining Screaming Lord Sutch's band, famous for their outrageous stage presentation.

For several years in the early 1960s, Lee played the beat clubs of Hamburg, Germany, alongside the Beatles, the Searchers, the Big Three, the Fourmost, the Undertakers, Johnny Kidd, Cliff Bennett, and Tony

Sheridan. In Hamburg Lee played piano for Sutch, Vince Taylor, and Roy Young; then, as part of the house band at the Star Club and the Top Ten Club, he played with Chuck Berry, Little Richard, Ray Charles, Tommy Roe, Fats Domino, Gene Vincent, Johnny Burnette, the Crickets, and one of his biggest inspirations, Jerry Lee Lewis. Lee also fronted numerous bands, writing much of his own material.

In England in 1979 a revival of Jack Good's *Oh Boy!* television show brought Lee into prominence. The show was seen in Europe, Africa, the Middle East, and North America. Good got Lee to wear the now-trademark patch over his glass eye, which led to the epithet "one-eyed boogie boy," the title of his signature song.

After helping to pave the way for the revival, Lee has been able to enjoy it as an established performer. On stage he is a wild showman, ripping through his sets, attacking his songs with abandon and attacking his pianos with an ax or chainsaw. He has been known to play piano while standing on his head and to set his hat on fire (not at the same time!); fortunately, he has a license in explosives.[3]

Welshman Dave Edmunds loves the early forms of rock 'n' roll. On his 1981 album *Twangin'* he included a track he had recorded in 1968, a close copy of Presley's "Baby Let's Play House." This was one of a handful of covers he recorded as an affectionate tribute to Presley and the Sun sound, never intending them for release. While continuing his own career as an artist, he produced records by a long list of roots rock acts: Shakin' Stevens, the Stray Cats, the Polecats, and the Fabulous Thunderbirds, among others. Edmunds considers himself to be more of a traditionalist than a revivalist, taking inspiration from classic rock 'n' roll and exploring, continuing, and extending the tradition.

Nick Lowe, a former bandmate of Edmunds's, is another who takes inspiration from 1950s rock, although his sound is less close to it. He has covered tunes like Wayne Walker's "Bo-Bo Ska Diddle Daddle" and Moon Mullican's "Seven Nights to Rock."

Crazy Cavan and the Rhythm Rockers, also from Wales, established a loyal following in England and reached top chart success in Finland. The nucleus of the band, vocalist Cavan Grogan and guitarists Lyndon Needs and Terry Walley, has been together since the mid-1960s. Drummer Mike Coffey joined in 1970. One of the most popular of the Teddy Boy bands, they had already released albums on Rockhouse and Charly by the time of their *Live at the Rainbow* album in 1977 from the Sun Sounds Show. It featured primarily original material, and their status as Teds was underlined in "Teddy Boy Rock 'n' Roll" and "Teddy Boy Boogie." In the latter, Cavan sings:

a-standing on a corner, a-swinging my chain
along came a copper and he took my name
he put his dirty maulers on my long drape coat
so I whipped out my razor and slit his throat

A favorite sound for this band is a blues pattern in a medium tempo
with a walking bass, two-string boogie rhythms in even (not swing)
eighth notes, and chorus lyrics like "stomp, stomp, stomp, everybody," and "bop, a-bop, a-bop, pretty baby baby."

In London in 1994 Crazy Cavan and the Rhythm Rockers celebrated their twenty-fifth anniversary with a frantic show. With former
members and guests augmenting the lineup, they put on a party for
"easily 400, maybe more, rockers of all types . . . Teds, Cats, Hillbillies, Rockers and Bikers all rubbing shoulders without the slightest
aggro [aggression]. . . . The crowd erupts, cheering . . . the audience a
seething mass of waves, heaving back and forth, locked arm-in-arm,
tanked up and hungry for more."[4] Although the police came in during the encore, the band wrapped up with one of their anthems, a
rocked-up version of Stephen Foster's "Old Black Joe."

Many others in the United Kingdom with a love for rockabilly and
old rock 'n' roll carved reputations from constant touring and prolific recording. For some, it finally paid off with big hits in the early
1980s.

SHAKIN' STEVENS

Born Michael Barratt, March 4, 1948, Ely, Cardiff, Wales

Since the 1960s Shakin' Stevens and his band the Sunsets defiantly
carried the torch for rock 'n' roll, especially rockabilly, through the
United Kingdom and the Continent. Seven years after his first recordings, Shakin' Stevens's portrayal of a midcareer Presley in the 1977
London stage show *Elvis* helped to propel him to fame.

His musical tastes were influenced by older siblings; he was the
youngest of eleven children, which may be the source of his craving
for attention and admiration. Certainly Stevens has demonstrated a
lot of drive: to get his equipment to his first gigs, he pushed it in a
wheelbarrow. A few years later, in 1969, he took his pseudonym with
the acquisition of Paul Barrett as manager, and Shakin' Stevens and
the Sunsets toured steadfastly and steadily. Barrett, a dedicated fan
of the music he promotes, has had a long career as the United Kingdom's leading rock 'n' roll agent.

In 1983, five years after he ceased being Stevens's manager, Paul

Barrett wrote a book on Stevens, portraying him as a charismatic, naive, immature, charming, nervous, egocentric, boorish, semi-illiterate social cripple who nonetheless managed to have people—including Barrett—care about him as a person. Seeing Stevens as controlled by his new manager, insecure around his band about his talents (he never learned to play an instrument), angry that success took so long, and bored, Barrett dedicated the book in part to Stevens, "who got what he wanted but lost what he had."

Shakin' Stevens and the Sunsets made their first album in 1970. *A Legend*, produced by Dave Edmunds for EMI, delivers very credible versions of rockabilly, at times with bass fiddle, steel guitar, piano, or saxophone. Poor sales led EMI to drop the group. Although successful in Europe as a live act, with a repertory that included some of the greatest songs of the pre-Beatles era, they ended up label hopping for the next few years.

By the time that the band recorded *C'mon Memphis* in 1976, one of several recordings done in Holland, years of road work (not without personnel changes) had made the band even better and even more focused on rockabilly, still unearthing obscurities and even putting Jackie Wilson's "Reet Petite," complete with steel guitar, into rockabilly style.

The *Elvis* show ran for a year and a half and broke up the band. When it ended, Stevens appeared regularly on TV.

The *Take One* album from 1979 is one of his best, and the song selection is eclectic and inspired. Stevens is backed by a hot band of session players, Albert Lee, Geraint Watkins, and Stuart Colman (soon to be his producer) among them. That album gave him his first hit— "Hot Dog"—and he never looked back. By 1988 Shakin' Stevens had placed twenty-eight songs in the British charts. Four of them hit number one, and almost all were in the top twenty. Despite his success in Britain, America never embraced him. Only "Cry Just a Little Bit" hit the charts, making number sixty-seven in 1984.

Of his hits that are rockabilly, some are covers of 1950s tunes already in the style—"Hot Dog" and "It's Late"—and others are adapted to rockabilly, such as Stuart Hamblen's "This Ole House" and Jim Lowe's "Green Door." Stevens also had rockabilly tracks on his 1980s albums—"Revenooer Man" and his own composition "Let Me Show You How," for example. His tremulous voice is capable of expressing fragility and emotion, much like Elvis himself—in fact, the thought of a British Elvis is apt. On these songs the band of top musicians lifts the music; they chime in on the titles, and the atmosphere is like that of an upbeat party. The tunes are fun and uplifting regardless of the lyrics: "This Ole House, " for example, projects thoughts about being near death through the image of a worn-out building, and "Green Door" is about not belonging, not being in the know and desperately wanting in on the action.

From 1981 other styles were in Stevens's bag of tricks, but after 1984 the rockabilly component was left behind, on his hits at least. Obviously the public was buying Stevens, not any particular style, for he had hits with cha-cha, rumba, Cajun, R&B, Motown, 1970s soul, disco, Christmas songs, standards, and ballads.

Reports from 1994 have him back rocking on the live circuit, drawing rave reviews for shows in Germany.

DAVE TRAVIS

Whether in or out of the spotlight, Dave Travis is a major figure in the rockabilly revival. He wears many hats: singer, bandleader, composer, producer, compiler of anthologies, music publisher, and label owner. Based in England, he is well known throughout Europe as a performer dedicated to country and rockabilly music and as a recording artist with more than a dozen albums since his first in 1968. His voice is at times reminiscent of Johnny Cash, and most of his early albums are classic country, but some of his rockabilly compositions slipped in, starting with "Old Country Rock" in 1969.

Travis picked up a great reputation as a bandleader after backing Warren Smith, Buddy Knox, Charlie Feathers, and Jack Scott at the legendary Sun Sounds Show at the Rainbow Theatre in London in 1977. This led to extensive performing, recording, and producing for a who's who of veteran rockers.

Travis's first all-rockabilly album came in 1978: *Rockabilly Fever,* mostly a collection of earlier tracks. That year he made his first of many appearances at the Rockhouse Festival in Holland. The European success of his *Rockabilly Killer* album in 1980 boosted his career, and his touring took him to the United States, through Europe, including Hungary and Yugoslavia, and to more exotic locales like Trinidad and Tobago, the Faroe Islands, and the Middle East. In 1984 Eddie Bond encouraged him to come to Memphis, and Travis also played around Texas with Johnny Carroll and Joe Poovey.

At a typical show Travis and his band perform rockabilly classics and obscurities, original compositions, and usually an instrumental featuring guitarist Eddy Jones. When backing up veterans they open the show with a set of their own. Travis's style is true to the country roots of rockabilly, with a wistful quality in the vocals. The band can rock hard but usually displays a tasteful, light touch that serves them well when called on to back up the vets but also gives their own music a relaxed feel.

Travis has produced and had his compositions recorded by Sonny Burgess, Eddie Bond, Hayden Thompson, and Charlie Gracie. Several of Travis's best-known compositions are found on his own *Jukebox Cadillac* album: the title song, "All Change," "Don't Tear Me Up," and "Feel Like I'm Catching the Blues."

With his own Stomper Time label, Travis has issued compact discs of vintage tracks of Eddie Bond, Glen Glenn, and Carl Mann.

MATCHBOX

Matchbox, from England, were adept at re-creating original sounds and creating rockabilly-based music that integrated modern studio techniques. Key members were guitarist Steve Bloomfield, who favors rockabilly, vocalist Graham Fenton, who had toured and recorded with Gene Vincent and who favored his sound as well as Buddy Holly's and the Bobby Fuller extension of it, and bassist Brian Hodgson, who drew from a broad palette of 1950s and 1960s rock. The band blended these elements into a commercially viable style: eight songs made the United Kingdom top 100 between 1979 and 1982.

The band went through four periods. The first, with Bloomfield aboard, had Bert Rockhuizen producing in Holland. Their first album (*Riders in the Sky,* 1976), shows them at least as dedicated, if not particularly exciting, journeymen rockabillies. The originals, except "Undeclared," are weak, and the covers—some interesting choices—pale compared to their inspirations. The caliber of the compositions moves up a couple of notches with Bloomfield's 1978 solo album (totally solo, by the way, aside from drums by Rockhuizen).

The second period, marked by the presence of Bloomfield and Graham Fenton with Peter Collins as producer, lasted from 1979 to 1981 and yielded three musically rich albums, each one moving further from rockabilly. The lineup was stable: Bloomfield and bassist Fred Poke from the first album were joined by Fenton, rhythm guitarist Gordon Scott, and drummer Jimmie Redhead. Each of the three albums has 50 percent originals (all from Steve Bloomfield). On *Rockabilly Rebel,* the first of these albums, they give Ray Campi the nod by recording his "Rockin' at the Ritz." The title track and "Buzz Buzz A Diddle It," their remake of Freddie Cannon's 1961 hit, made the British top-twenty pop chart, giving Matchbox deserved recognition as pioneers of the revival. *Midnight Dynamos,* from 1980, the second album in this bunch, is the last with a rockabilly component, particularly the cover of "Sixteen Chicks." Their next, *Flying Colours,* has the confederate flag on the cover, and they cover three country classics and two songs by Buddy Holly. This is polished pop music with elaborate vocals and production. It is built from previous styles, but nothing here is rockabilly as such.

In period three Bloomfield and Poke are gone, leaving no one in the band who appeared on the first album. The records from this period contain only original material, and bassist Brian Hodgson is the author or coauthor of all the songs on the 1982 album *Crossed Line* and the later, undated *Going Down Town.* He produced them as well. The line they crossed in 1982 was to eliminate any reference to the 1950s in their image (although not in their music). The *Crossed Line* album cover shows them, against a background of geometric shapes on a grid, with ungreased hair, jeans, and running shoes; one member is even wearing red pants, red cap and a tartan vest. The next album, however, shows vintage American cars with what may be Swedish license plates parked at a restaurant.

In the fourth period in the band's evolution, they are called "Graham Fenton's Matchbox." A 1990 album recorded live in Yugoslavia takes it full circle. Joining Fenton is veteran member drummer Wild Bob Burgos (from the first album lineup), and the repertory is mostly 1950s rock 'n' roll covers. Their high standard is maintained. More recently, Fenton sang Gene Vincent songs on Blue Caps reunion tours.

THE STRAY CATS
Brian Setzer born April 10, 1959, Massapequa, New York; Lee Rocker born Leon Drucker, 1961; Slim Jim Phantom born Jim McDonnell, March 20, 1961

The Stray Cats, schoolmates from New York City, are the most popular and the best-known revival band in the world. They were young, lovable hoodlums offering carefree fun, singing about teenage frustrations and release, playing intensely, and goofing off, too, riding the bass and playing shirtless to show their skin and their tattoos. As befitted the recessionary times, the Stray Cats were simple: their stage setup was one amplifier and two drums (using wireless technology, the bass went straight into the PA system). Despite their youth, they were polished, professional, and steeped in 1950s music, favoring the harder side: Gene Vincent, Eddie Cochran, and the Rock 'n' Roll Trio. Their stated goal was to bring recognition for rockabilly as British bands such as the Rolling Stones had for blues in the 1960s.

At sixteen, after years of jazz guitar lessons, Brian Setzer was doing a solo gig as the Rockabilly Rebel, which eventually expanded to incorporate other musicians. In 1979 the lineup solidified; Setzer, by now a bonafide guitar virtuoso with a blond coiffure, was joined by drummer Slim Jim Phantom and bass fiddle player Lee Rocker, a classically trained cellist. Rocker and Phantom had been a team since they were thirteen. For a brief period Setzer played concurrently in a new wave band called the Bloodless Pharoahs.

In 1980, at the urging of a British bartender who became their manager, the Stray Cats moved to London. After scuffling and sleeping in parks, they found acclaim. Their music was approved by Jeff Beck, Robert Plant, and the Rolling Stones, and a recording contract came within three months. Music papers buzzed about their audacity at moving to London with no contacts or contracts, about their looks, and then about their success. Dave Edmunds produced their recordings, three singles made the English pop charts, and an album followed. They toured Europe and Japan and opened dates on the Rolling Stones 1982 U.S. tour.

The Stray Cats' second album, *Gonna Ball,* quickly recorded in the West Indies, was mostly self-produced and the worse for it. As much blues and R&B as rockabilly, the guitar is distorted in the George Thorogood style, and lack of direction is apparent. That album gave them another U.K. hit in "You Don't Believe Me," featuring Setzer's slide guitar playing in open tuning.

Their first North American album, *Built for Speed,* was not released until the summer of 1982. Aside from including the newly recorded title track, it was compiled from tracks off both U.K. albums. With the interest generated by their videos on MTV and a fifty-five city tour, sales steadily continued, and "Rock This Town" and "Stray Cat Strut" both made the American top ten. The media gave them lots of coverage, including the covers of *Rolling Stone, New Musical Express,* and *Guitar Player.*

The release of their next album, *Rant and Rave with the Stray Cats,* was delayed due to the continued sales of the first—more than three and a half million units as of February 1983. When it finally came out in August, again produced by Dave Edmunds, it also yielded a top-ten single, "(She's) Sexy + 17," and two others that hit the charts.

The band was well aware of the hazards of monochromatic texture. In the studio Setzer double-tracked the guitar, and songs sometimes got spiced up with saxophones, organ, harmonica, or piano—

one had 14-Karat Soul, a black doo-wop group. For a few shows, Setzer played a song on the banjo. In their show at the *Grand Ole Opry* in December 1983, broadcast nationwide on the radio, they made use of steel guitar, sax, and guest appearances by Carl Perkins and the doo-wop group.

The worldview that the Stray Cats express is that of the teenage, male delinquent. Cars are for album front covers, instruments are for back covers. Cars, even their mechanical features, are described in loving detail ("Built for Speed," "Rev It up and Go"), gangs are joyous and violent ("Hot Rod Gang," "Rumble in Brighton"), and rock 'n' roll is great, radio and jukeboxes have lousy songs, and disco sucks. Style is vital, and looking cool is important, as is being wild and proud and aggressive, looking for a fight, and drinking. Chuck Berry and Eddie Cochran painted the plight of the teenager, and some of that comes through in the Stray Cats' sympathetic look at homeless teenagers in "Runaway Boys," but observation is secondary to justifying and advocating delinquency: class-cutting, dropping out, scoffing at cops and authority—one song has lyrics about not having bothered to get license plates—and arguing with parents. Parents are portrayed as restrictive and critical and as asking for a contribution to the rent.

Although Setzer is a self-proclaimed ladies man, his lyrics give women short shrift: they are cheats ("I Won't Stand in Your Way"), a waste of time ("Little Miss Prissy"), or far away ("Lonely Summer Nights," which is in the typical style of doo-wop ballads of longing, sharing some similarities with "Long Lonely Nights," a hit in 1957 for Lee Andrews and the Hearts). When close, women are just dancing and sexual partners. When the Stray Cats altered the lyrics to Eddie Cochran's "Jeannie, Jeannie, Jeannie" ("first we fuck, tough luck . . . do what you're told . . . I won't leave you alone 'til I get some more"), the publishing company that controls the rights to the song tried to sue the band for five million dollars for changing the words without permission. It was settled out of court. In live performances they sang the original lyrics.

The breath of fresh air that the Stray Cats brought to the marketplace became stale after a while. They were not able (or allowed) to transcend the cartoon-character image they created for themselves. They were too teenage, too juvenile. As often occurs, critical backlash followed their phenomenal success. Audiences steadily diminished. In 1984 the band splintered. Setzer went for a solo career, exploring songwriting on an album with no rockabilly on it. The others, eager for a showcase for their own composing talents, teamed with Earl Slick as Phantom, Rocker, and Slick. Free of their restrictive image, Phantom played a full drum kit and Rocker played electric bass.

In 1986 the Stray Cats got back together and put out *Rock Therapy* with little fanfare and not much success. Half of its songs are covers, and the rockers are punchy and ferocious. "Broken Man" features Setzer's banjo, western imagery, and touches of Eagles-like harmony. Some maturity was brought back from their other projects; the lyrics express need and vulnerability ("I Wanna Cry" and a cover of Holly's "Looking for Someone to Love").

In 1987 Setzer played Eddie Cochran in a concert sequence in the movie *La Bamba,* the story of Richie Valens. The next year Setzer put out his second solo album, this time with rockabilly, and the Stray Cats did a U.S. tour.

In 1989 the Stray Cats reiterated their rockabilly stance with the self-produced *Blast Off,* singing about the music in "Gene and Eddie" and "Rockabilly Rules." In late 1992 they were touring again in the United Kingdom and released *Choo Choo Hot Fish,* with Dave Edmunds again as producer. The album is strong, musically mature, and nicely varied, mixing jazzy styles with rockabilly, originals with covers. Setzer's awesome guitar playing is better than ever.

The Brian Setzer Orchestra, a rocking seventeen-piece big band, was formed in 1992. Setzer prances the stage wearing skintight leather pants, an open-at-the-neck tuxedo shirt with ruffles edged in black, and a metallic blue jacket. He croons and growls, plays boogie lines, comps in a jazz style, and lets loose virtuosic solos in front of a rhythm section and thirteen horn players in Hawaiian shirts (they also have white tuxedos). The band sits behind music stands, reading charts for originals, old pop songs, jump blues, supper club jazz, and rearranged rockabilly tunes, including a few Stray Cats numbers. The middle of "Stray Cat Strut" has a few saxes stand up for a Latin section, followed by a upright bass solo (jazz, not slapped). The trumpet section plays their parts using plunger mutes, doing a coordinated waving movement between phrases. In another song, a horn player quotes an Ellington tune, and Setzer plays the solo from "Rock around the Clock." One very effective piece is their Clash-inspired version of Vince Taylor's "Brand New Cadillac," one of the best rock 'n' roll songs of British origin. The Setzer arrangement drifts cleverly into "Peter Gunn" in the middle, a logical move, as both are based on a similar riff. Included in their version of "Route 66" is the theme from the old TV show of the same name. Enthusiastic audiences of mixed generations give Setzer the room to croon a song like "There's a Rain-

bow around My Shoulder" ("by Bobby Darin, one of my favorite singers," he says) but respond most to the wide-screen R&B and rockabilly. Setzer has gone from minimal accompaniment to maximal.

The Stray Cats still exist and continue to tour, mostly in Europe
and Japan in front of huge and enthusiastic audiences.

Bands that take a similar name, and there is a long list, generally
do so by way of acknowledging their inspiration: Sun Cats (Sweden),
Teen Cats (Norway), Cadcatz Sun Quartet (Germany), Kat Squire, and
Skiprats (United Kingdom), Crocats, Square Cats, Rumble Cats, and
the Stacy Cats (all from Holland). Other band names I have noted
are Jump Kat Jump, Washington Dead Cats, Dixie Cats, Hellkats, Go
Katz, Alley Cats, and the Restless Cats.

LEVI & THE ROCKATS

In 1979, twenty-five years after Elvis made his debut on the *Louisiana Hayride,* Levi and the Rockats (whose name does not reflect the
influence of the Stray Cats) performed there and released an album
of the show. Not only were they introduced by Frank Page, the same
announcer, but they stayed at the same hotel and in the same room
that Elvis stayed in. The producer had worked with Gene Vincent,
and the album was mastered at Gold Star by an engineer who had
worked with Eddie Cochran. The band members, three from Britain
and two from Kentucky, were nervous, the playing was rough, and
they were not particularly well-received. As a publicity stunt it was
an excellent idea, but unfortunately the band could not pull off a
performance to match. To their credit, an article about the event that
is not totally favorable to the band is reprinted on the jacket. From
the article we learn that the *Hayride* name was bought by the afore-
mentioned announcer and a partner in the early 1970s and the show
was revived.

Levi Dexter, from London but working in Los Angeles, left the band
and later recorded a five-song EP called *The Fun Sessions* (wordplay
on "the Sun Sessions") containing confident, realized, well-played,
and well-recorded music. "The Other Side of Midnight," the best original song from the *Hayride* set, is retained, and the covers of Hal Harris's "Jitterbop Baby" and Sid King's "Let 'er Roll" are nice choices.
"I Get So Excited" is exciting, and "Victim of Cool" ("just stand back
and give me sympathy") pokes fun at the studiously serious image
cultivated by some fans.

The Rockats re-formed around bassist Smutty Smiff, whose tattooed
arms grace both Rockats album covers. The original songs on *Make*

That Move, a six-song EP done in 1983, are from new lead vocalist Dibbs Preston. A cover of Marvin Gaye's "One More Heartache" from 1966, which Smokey Robinson had a hand in composing, alerts the rockabilly fan that there is a wider net in use. The new wave portion of their recipe is found mostly on side 1, and the rockabilly portion is on side 2, where all three songs kick forcefully and the drums sound big. Open-minded listeners will appreciate their slick, carefully arranged and produced music, rich in detail and professional in execution and sound quality. Purists will find it too modern, too far removed from the simplicity of the 1950s.

In 1992 Levi Dexter resurfaced with a stunning new album called *Pomp!*

In 1993 Smiff, Preston, and guitarist Barry Ryan from the 1983 lineup reunited with a new drummer to tour Japan, resulting in a video and live CD. An album of new material was announced to follow.

THE POLECATS

Formed in London in 1977, the Polecats did their first gig the next year and were signed to Mercury two years later. By the time that their contract ran out in 1983, they had produced two acclaimed albums and several singles.

The Polecats were young, stylish, and talented. They hooked into the energy of punk while making imaginative rockabilly, incorporating harmony vocals and strong original writing by all members: Tim Worman (vocals, guitar), Boz Boorer (guitar), Phil Bloomberg (upright bass), and Neil Rooney (drums, later replaced by John Buck).

Dave Edmunds produced their first album, *Polecats Are Go!* in 1981. It shows that they had absorbed the vocabulary of vintage rockabilly, but their willingness to innovate set them apart from the Teddy Boy bands. Even their choice of covers was unusual: alongside a couple of obscure 1950s tunes was a song by David Bowie and the jazz standard "How High the Moon."

After their recording contract finished, the band drifted apart. Boz Boorer is now the guitarist and musical director for Morrissey, formerly of the Smiths. Tim Worman moved to Los Angeles and got into music videos as a production designer. As Tim Polecat, Worman released the 1994 CD *Virtual Rockabilly,* which shows him experimenting with technology: he produced and engineered it, played most of the instruments, and incorporated digitally sampled sounds from 1950s records.

The Polecats reunite for occasional festival appearances.

THE SHAKIN' PYRAMIDS

The Shakin' Pyramids, from Glasgow, Scotland, brought acoustic skiffle and an Everly Brothers influence to their rockabilly music. Alcohol and pills fired up most of the 1950s rockabillies, but the Shakin' Pyramids expressed their preference for marijuana in their "Reeferbilly Boogie" and "Reeferbilly Polka."

They started as buskers (street performers) and kept it up as a publicity vehicle while touring the United Kingdom, France, Poland, Scandinavia, Japan, and North America. Their first album, *Skin 'Em Up* from 1981, mixes five originals with seven covers of 1950s rockabilly and garnered highest marks in the *Rolling Stone Record Guide*. The next year their second album drifted farther from rockabilly as they broadened their horizons. This led them to more ambitious material and arrangements. The originals are less melodic than before, and the covers come from Elvis Costello, Phil Everly, and Gene Pitney. The sound palette has more variety; in addition to the harmonica, guitars, upright bass, and percussion on the first album, electric bass, mandolin, strings, piano, and two female backup singers appear on the second. A Cajun accordion is featured on their version of "Sugar Bee." One writer asked, "From neo-rockabilly to neo-schlock—this is neo-progress?"[5]

BILLY HANCOCK

Born 1946, Fairfax County, Virginia

Hancock was exposed to a wide range of music through his parents' record store, and he started his professional music career in 1959 at age thirteen. Through the next two decades he worked around Virginia and Washington, D.C., in bar bands and backing Gene Vincent, the Clovers, Amos Milburn, Dale Hawkins, Roy Buchanan, Charlie Feathers, and Big Joe Turner.

In 1975 Hancock played bass and sang on an album by Danny and the Fat Boys called *American Music,* covering R&B, combo jazz, disco funk, reggae, country, and rockabilly (one song). Danny was guitar wizard Danny Gatton, a legendary musician with awesome ability in several styles who went on to record acclaimed albums under his own name. He committed suicide in 1994.

On his 1981 album *Shakin' That Rockabilly Fever,* Billy Hancock and the Tennessee Rockets take old songs from various styles and give them a rockabilly treatment, thus continuing a tradition common in the 1950s but rare in the revival. Hancock and company transform songs by Dr. Ross, Muddy Waters, the Delmore Brothers, Arthur

Crudup, Jerry Leiber and Mike Stoller, and Hank Williams, artists whose songs—but mostly not these songs—have been done by other rockabillies. Hancock is at his best when he is unself-conscious, which is most of the time, and the confidence and sincerity of his performance place him in a sparsely populated category: less a revivalist, more an authentic tradition carrier. He is aware of what he is doing—Crudup's "Do It If You Wanna" is done as Elvis would have in 1954. In "Rockabilly Fever" Hancock pays homage to the music and names names like a fan, but it is on songs like "Trouble Ain't Nothin' but the Blues" and his own "Knock-Kneed Nellie" where he takes his place as a rockabilly performer.

The same year Hancock and band backed Tex Rubinowitz. One track—"Hot Rod Man"—became a popular song for revivalists to cover. In 1981 and 1982 Hancock toured Europe. *Hey! Little Rock and Roller,* released in France in 1983, is a middling album. There are a few stellar moments, but the song selection is less inspired. Added to the influences—notably Elvis, Conway Twitty, and New Orleans music—is the sound of the heavier side of the rockabilly revival; the result is a mixed blessing.

ROBERT GORDON
Born 1947, Washington, D.C.

Robert Gordon had a powerful early influence on the revival and has maintained an active career. A few years after gaining experience fronting bands in clubs around Washington and New York City in the 1960s and following a stint in a new wave group called Tuff Darts, Gordon's debut album in 1977 showed him to be one of the first Americans of his generation to commit to rockabilly.

Although the songs and image were somewhat updated, his devotion to the songs of the 1950s was strong, and his serious delivery was without parody. Gordon was also noticed for his strong voice and the impressive company he kept. His band, the Wildcats, has had a succession of legendary guitarists: Link Wray, Danny Gatton, and Chris Spedding.

The cover of his first album is unequivocally rockabilly: a head-and-shoulders photo all in pink (skin, shirt, and background) and black (a high pile of greased hair). Six of the ten songs are from the 1950s, including covers of "Red Hot" and "Flying Saucers Rock 'n' Roll," both from the repertory of Billy Lee Riley. "Red Hot" made a brief appearance on the charts, and both songs became concert staples for him. Gordon's versions are strongly hammered out, with drums to the fore, and driven by a relentless walking bass, played very precisely and sounding unmistakably electric. Of the remaining four songs, three were written by Link Wray, the famous guitarist whose first hit was "Rumble" in 1958. Wray played on the album and was part of the touring band. There are three 6/8 ballads on this album, one by Wray, one from Gene Vincent ("I Sure Miss You"), and one by the producer. On these songs Gordon reveals a lighter voice quality, whereas on the rockabilly songs he bears down hard. His controlled and flexible voice is widely admired, if not universally appealing.

On Gordon's second album, *Fresh Fish Special,* also from 1977 and featuring Link Wray, the majority of songs again come from the 1950s canon. The Jordanaires provide background vocals. A cover of Bruce Springsteen's "Fire" expands the scope of Gordon's repertory while helping to break down his purely rockabilly image.

Both sides of the cover of the third album, *Rock Billy Boogie* (1979), are full-frame shots of Gordon emoting splayed-legged in full rockabilly splendor between an old ribbon microphone and a stage curtain decorated with images of instruments and dice. Again the majority of songs are from 1950s artists (three from the repertory of the Rock 'n' Roll Trio), but the others include a pumped-up version of the 1920s standard "Am I Blue" (possibly learned from Eddie Cochran's version), Leroy Van Dyke's million-selling country song "Walk on By" from 1961, and two songs Gordon coauthored. One of these is "The Catman," a tribute to Gene Vincent, Gordon's biggest vocal influence. The album's sound world is broadened to incorporate moments of synthesized trumpet and violins, the sound of the electric sitar, whistling through the teeth, and sleigh bells on "Blue Christmas." On a couple of songs a sound reminiscent of slapped bass is created by drum sticks hitting the rim of the snare.

The next year's album, *Bad Boy,* has fewer 1950s songs on it, and by *Are You Gonna Be the One,* his fifth album, released in 1981 and featuring Danny Gatton, the 1950s component was reduced to a Don Gibson song and an obscure Dorsey Burnette demo, both country. The organ on some songs is reminiscent of 1960s garage rock and Elvis Costello's band. Marshall Crenshaw penned three tracks, including "Someday, Someway," Gordon's second and last chart entry.

Although Gordon moved, like most revivalists, into a more pop approach on these and subsequent records, it is his rockabilly image that has endured for him. In live shows rockabilly is expected, and it gets the most reaction. The two shows I have seen, in 1988 and 1992, both with Chris Spedding on guitar, were almost identical. At the second one Gordon looked sharp in a leopard-skin tux jacket over a black T-shirt and tux pants, his hair short and slicked tight, with brush-cut sideburns. The Montreal rockabilly gangs, mostly young francophones, were dancing up a storm wearing their colors on their leather jackets: Rolling Teds, Rebel Strutters.

The band's live repertory drew heavily from Presley, the Rock 'n' Roll Trio, Eddie Cochran, and standards from the 1950s: "It's Only Make Believe," "Black Slacks," and "Walk on By." The 1980s were represented by "Fire," "Someday, Someway," and a couple of Gordon's originals, all interspersed in the middle of the set. Strong musical moments were Johnny Cash's "There You Go" and the very effective dynamic changes that Spedding led the band through in the solo of "I Forgot to Remember to Forget." Gordon was very professional but detached. Like his predecessors, Robert Gordon hoped for more success in his career and wanted acceptance for more than just his rockabilly work. Maybe he had sung "Red Hot" a few times too often.

The *All for the Love of Rock 'n' Roll* album from 1994 shows Gordon diversifying while touching base with his rockabilly roots and reconnecting with the Tuff Darts repertory. Old mates Spedding, Gatton, and Wildcat bassist Rob Stoner took part in the sessions, and Gordon also acted as producer. His touring itinerary covers Australia, Japan, Europe, and North America.

• • •

Since 1981, when I first started seeking out rockabilly performances, besides getting to see several of the veterans in action and some of the revival bands already discussed, I saw many local and regional rockabilly bands in Toronto, Vancouver, Victoria, Memphis, Boston, and Montreal. Each of the revival bands exhibited a different approach to repertory, instrumentation, and presentation. The bands made more use of modern inputs and original material than, say, Dixieland revival bands. In other words, these musicians recognized and practiced rockabilly as a living idiom, and they usually were not intent on slavish re-creation. It was clear that too much authenticity could lead to artistic and commercial stagnation. That there was a self-consciousness in the evocation of a previous era's music was indicated by the revival musicians' penchant for pseudonyms or stage names, which were much less common in the 1950s, when Marty Lott was known as the Phantom.

One revival guitarist with the nickname "Whitey Black" spoke in 1982 of how he and his band were affected by the historical aspect:

> I'm living in the present, more or less, and I see it from a theatrical point of view. Which allows me to indulge in it totally

and walk around the streets with this kind of haircut, and it allows other people to engage very readily, 'cause it's very familiar. You know the fifties, everybody knows what happened in the fifties, so they can get into their nostalgia trip without having to leave home. It works on our own behalf as well, 'cause it gives me a profile as an entertainer. It allows us to play for five year olds to those in their eighties. It allows us to go anywhere, especially Elvis. Elvis is the common denominator for every audience that we play for.[6]

Elvis was overwhelmingly the most popular artist to cover for the revival bands that I saw. Doing any song by Elvis Presley, regardless of date, that fit the style indicated respect for rockabilly's founding father, although some bands avoided his repertory as being too obvious. For the same reason, some avoided all the big hits, by Elvis or anybody else.

In the 1950s most performers had only a handful of songs that rocked. In the revival more rockabilly was available than ever before. Revivalists had lots of choice when looking for repertory, and repertory therefore became crucial to their image.

After Elvis songs, a second repertory category of the bands I saw included any song from the 1950s by important artists such as Perkins, Lewis, Holly, Vincent, Cochran, and (especially) the Rock 'n' Roll Trio, thus indicating awareness of history and the major figures.

Third, any obscure song by any obscure old rockabilly from the 1950s indicated a band's depth of knowledge and involvement with the style. Obscure songs have the advantage of not being readily identified by most audience members, not likely to be played by other bands, and possibly being mistaken for originals.

Fourth, doing a slow twelve-bar blues, often an original, filled the need for tempo contrast at live gigs. Although such songs were common during performances by revival and veteran rockabillies, similar songs are rarely found on rockabilly records of any era.

In the repertory of a typical band, songs from the 1950s accounted for about half the list, with originals accounting for much of the rest. None of the bands I saw performed only originals, although some held that policy for recordings. The remainder of the repertory came from miscellaneous categories: pre-1954 songs (especially country), 1950s rock 'n' roll hits, post-1960s songs (pop, rock 'n' roll, or country), and instrumentals from any era. Some oddball choices were intriguing, such as the Jackson Five's "I Want You Back" performed by the Flying Tigers, of Lansing, Michigan, a straightforward revival act except for having a guitarist visually and sonically reminiscent of Jimi Hendrix.

Herald Nix, a Vancouver-based band, gave equal weight to the "billy" side of rockabilly. More traditional, less flashy, and more acoustic than most revival bands, they were one of the most authentic sounding and one of the best. Evolving from the Westernaires, who played rockabilly, blues, and western swing, they gained a reputation through touring the interior of British Columbia and Alberta and then moved to Vancouver, where they quickly became respected for their approach. The person who answered to the name Herald Nix (real name John Wood) plays very tasteful electric guitar and sings in a confident, understated manner. The band included not only drums and upright bass but also a real piano, played by Michael Van Eyes, which they hauled around to their gigs.

Herald Nix was able to reach to the core of the songs in their fascinating repertory, even when the song was well known in another version. As well as playing an interesting selection of rockabilly songs—they are the only band I ever heard cover Jimmy Heap's "Sebbin Come Elebbin," for example—they also covered songs by Lefty Frizzell, Patsy Cline, and Bob Wills (including his, not Presley's, version of "Milkcow Blues"), as well as songs by the Drifters, Chuck Berry, and Solomon Burke. They even did a terrific version of "Moon River" in 4/4 meter. In thrift-store clothes, they played with quiet determination and talent that could completely win over an audience. *One Night Only,* a mini-album, was released in 1983. A second mini-album left rockabilly behind.

The Sidewinders formed in Toronto in 1979, making them one of Canada's first revival bands. They were another band that let the "billy" side shine through. Their acoustic sound came partly from the electric bass player's ability to achieve a sound close to that of the slapped bass. Chief singer and songwriter was Handsome Ned (Robin Masyk), who performed country music at his popular Saturday afternoon solo gig (which lasted five years), becoming an important catalyst for Toronto's Queen Street music community. He shared his passion for country music on a radio show he hosted for three years. After the Sidewinders split, he called his new band the Handsome Neds. It included Rene Fratura on the upright bass, formerly of Herald Nix. After Ned's death from a heroin overdose in 1987 (he was twenty-nine), his recordings were collected onto an album by his bandmate and older brother Jim. *The Ballad of . . . ,* released on Virgin and containing recordings by the Sidewinders and the Handsome Neds, is an excellent album of original compositions, featuring "Rockabilly Girls," "Sun Rockin'," and "I've Come to Get My Baby" ("out of jail"). At least three different acts have written songs about him. Gone but not forgotten.

The Bopcats, like the Sidewinders, formed in Toronto in 1979 and began to tour Canada. Around that time their first recording, an EP, was climbing to number two on the British rock 'n' roll charts. They later wished that they had toured England then to capitalize on it. With the release of two albums (1981, 1982) and a heavy touring schedule, they were in their time the best-known Canadian revival band. Many of their recordings are originals, although they played more covers live. The Bopcats actually preferred not to be known as a rockabilly band because of the restrictions of being typecast, although their clothes and repertory made it hard to conceive of them as anything else. When asked how they compared to traditional rockabilly, they replied, "our music is not traditional at all, there's the same fire there, the same energy, but it doesn't sound the same."[7]

The Bopcats' albums were well recorded, and the band exhibited a strong musical identity and confidence. The songs on the first album are interesting rather than appealing, and although sometimes meandering, they are well arranged with an imaginative use of background vocals. The originals are from the pens of vocalist Sonny Baker and founding guitarist Duane Wayne. Midway through the sessions Jack de Keyzer, a veteran of Ronnie Hawkins's and Robert Gordon's bands, replaced Wayne. Wayne (as Jim "Duane" McTaggart) went on to form the Paladins (of Toronto, not the San Diego band); they played in London and at the Eindhoven festival in 1983 and recorded their only album, *R&R*, the next year. On the cover of the Bopcats album, only Baker, de Keyzer, and drummer Teddy Fury are pictured, with hair all piled up.

Bassist Zeke Rivers joined for the Bopcats' second album, *Wild Jungle Rock,* and de Keyzer took the role of the prime mover in the band, writing or cowriting (with band members) the ten originals on the record. He sang lead on three of the songs, and his fabulous guitar playing and its tone elevated the band. The Bopcats had a fantastic sound, only let down by their repertory, but their best songs are exhilarating: "Train Called Rock and Roll," "Stop Breaking up My Heart," covers of "Rockhouse" and "Apache," and their sardonic "Dressed to Kill": "I was dressed in black from my head to my toes / I had forty-two skulls hangin' from my clothes . . . / dressed to kill and it's killing me."

When Baker left the band, they performed as a trio with de Keyzer as front man. Perhaps unhappy that their name was always getting them compared to the other feline bands—Stray Cats, Polecats, Rockats, Blue Cats—they recorded their last under the undistinguished name "Rock Angels" in 1983, issuing a four-song mini-album. Jack de Keyzer carried on under his own name, often working with pianist "Mean" Steve Hocura from the Paladins. One of Toronto's busiest and most respected roots rockers, de Keyzer finally had his own album, *Hard Workin' Man,* in 1991. A second solo album with a new band and a horn section is in the blues and R&B vein he prefers.

The Toronto band called the Razorbacks (a New Jersey band also has that name) made their reputation by giving very energetic shows with a catchy visual component featuring a standing drummer, bass fiddle acrobatics, and a trademark of playing powerfully on only acoustic instruments, enabling them to attract publicity from street corner performances. At least one member came out of the Wise Guys, a band from Ottawa that got to open for the Clash at the Montreal Forum in 1984, where the singer fretted his guitar with his shoe in "Pointed Toe Shoes." *Go to Town,* the Razorbacks' first album in 1987, was produced by Chris Spedding. Excepting "Knock Knock Bim Bam" from Gene Vincent, the album consists of confident original songs on eternal themes—cars, girls, bars, nearly dying—by vocalist Tony Kenny. Kenny's appealing pop voice rides over a rhythmic train made from punchy and vigorous snare drum, bass, and acoustic guitar playing. Their sound is their own but risks monotony, avoided by occasional strokes from a palette of other colors: accordion here, claves or tambourine there, a bit of harmony singing, a touch of Bo Diddley rhythm, a song in 6/8 meter, a bowed bass, a few chords on piano, a couple of studio tricks. A second album, *Live a Little,* was released in 1989, again produced by Spedding, and included their rockabilly version of the Who's "My Generation."

Ray Condo and his Hard Rock Goners formed in Montreal in 1985 and were leaders in the area's music scene until most of the band moved to Vancouver. Working outside the usual formulas, they performed a repertory almost entirely of covers: mostly obscure 1950s songs drawn from rockabilly and the Louisiana swamp sound, although over the years they have widened their scope, interpreting honky-tonk songs and surf instrumentals. Rejecting consumerism and society's worship of the new, these inner-city hillbillies find value in music and culture generally viewed as politically and aesthetically incorrect. Condo's frenetic vocals and charismatic stage presence is backed by brothers Peter and Eric Sandmark, on drums and lead guitar, respectively, Clive Jackson's bass fiddle, and Edgar Bridwell's fiddle. Personnel has remained stable since their first album, *Crazy*

Date (1986), although periods of hiatus gave rise to members' side projects that explore even earlier styles. All members of the Condos (as fans call them) have worked in visual arts, and they have turned these skills to their advantage, creating their own posters, album art, and seven videos, enabling them to reach an ever-wider audience. Their interest in the pop tunes of the 1920s, 1930s, and 1940s eventually led them away from rockabilly, but an invitation to appear in England got them back into it. In 1992 Ray Condo and the Hard Rock Goners' festival performance in England was ecstatically received, leading to a return in 1993 and more recordings.

Jack Smith and the Rockabilly Planet, from Rhode Island, took a narrow stylistic approach. When Smith saw Elvis's television debut, it was an unforgettable experience for the eleven year old, although it took him until he was thirty-four before he started singing professionally. In performance his engaging, enjoyable, and well-seasoned unit covered songs by the big names of rockabilly, and Jerry Miller really shone with his excellent guitar playing.

In 1988, nine years after the band was formed, the same lineup I had seen four years earlier recorded a disappointing album of original songs. Despite a promising opener and some hot solos, the songs, from decent to aimless, are nothing new: this one sounds like "Mystery Train," that one sounds like "Train Kept a-Rollin'." Despite the musicianship, fine ensemble work, and acceptable sound, the total is characterless and pedestrian, compounded by the monotony of nine of the eleven songs in the key of E. The two that are not are both in A and are sequenced back to back on the album. Another chance at variety was lost by placing the sole instrumental at the end of the album. That piece is in E, proving that it is not just a necessity of vocal range that holds them to that key. In the live show I attended, four keys were used, although half of the songs were in E (actually E-flat, since the bass and guitar were tuned down a semitone).

Around 1990 they changed their name to Jack Smith and the Headliners. They backed Billy Lee Riley in 1992 in New York City at his first appearance there in more than thirty years.

◆ ◆ ◆

Other primarily rockabilly bands that I have experienced are listed here with a note on their own approach. Black and Blue, from Toronto, had a tasty choice of repertory. Also in Toronto, Johnny Dee Fury led a heavy-handed power trio, singing, playing guitar, and writing all the songs on his self-produced 1982 album. When the rockabilly vogue faded, Fury reincarnated as a glam pop star, added a keyboard player, and wrote a new bunch of appropriate tunes. Buddy Selfish and his Saviours, of Vancouver, had a rare sense of parody coupled with good musicianship.

In Boston both the Shakes and the Wandells took a hard-driving approach, and the Memphis Rockabilly Band mixed Jeff Spencer's Charlie Gracie–influenced vocals with Billy Coover's hot guitar and occasional sax playing; they stayed together long enough to record in 1981 and 1986 and to make it to Europe.

In Montreal the Hollywood Mufflers chose obscure songs to cover, while the Jim Dandy Trio, two guitars and a drummer, sang Memphis rockabilly with a French-Canadian accent. The Dixie Stompers from France did mostly originals but played Elvis with precision. Reverend Horton Heat (real name Jim Heath) from Texas, opening for the Cramps, hyped up the speed and intensity and did a bit of sermonizing. Several more bands did a few rockabilly songs as part of a broader rock 'n' roll repertory.

Many revival bands were formed in 1978 or 1979, and few survived after 1983. Most of those that did underwent a name or an image change. For most, the image had been more evocative than authentic: the hair, clothes, and tunes suggested the era without being slavish reproductions. Many bands did not use vintage instruments or an acoustic guitar or acoustic bass and had a rock-sounding drummer.

One place neorockabilly succeeded was in feeding new styles born on the lunatic fringe of the revival. Several names have been advanced for this kind of approach: trashabilly, thrashabilly, punkabilly, and most durably, psychobilly. Rockabilly was mixed in with other styles, and certain aspects are greatly exaggerated while others are minimized.

Some bands explored different ways to minimize elements previously thought to be givens. Some bands used standing drummers playing a cut-down drum kit (the Stray Cats, the Shakin' Pyramids, the Razorbacks) or no electric instruments (the Razorbacks), but in the psychobilly camp not only were the country and acoustic components diminished, but often there was no bass player at all (the Cramps, Deja Voodoo), no rehearsals, or at least no polish (Tav Falco's Panther Burns' first efforts). Montreal's Deja Voodoo coined the term *sludgeabilly* for their music and took minimalism further: the band consisted of only two members, a drummer with no cymbals and a guitarist with only four strings.

THE CRAMPS

Probably the first band in this lunatic fringe wave was the Cramps, who formed in New York City in 1976. Their music feels primitive. "Demented," "a mutant strain of rockabilly," and "music for misfits" was how one writer described them;[8] one of their record titles is *Bad Music for Bad People*. The style is a bizarre and original amalgam, a mixture of rockabilly, garage punk, psychedelic and surf music, comic books, primal scream, science-fiction, monster and gore movies, and theatrics. Precursors were Screamin' Jay Hawkins, Hasil Adkins, Esquerita, and anybody who had weird hair, clothes, or songs. Some people don't get it, but those who do find it to be irreverently charming, celebratory, hilarious, energetic, off-the-wall, punning, evil, and valuable. Selective cover versions emphasized the dark subconscious side, drawing out and exaggerating all the deviant, demonic elements of rockabilly. Deceptively simple on first look, their music is grungy, fuzz-toned, well played and sung, and well arranged, with lots of dynamics and other variation. It is energetically presented, seriously and without parody. Although rockabilly is only one component, it is a strong foundation: they have covered "Uranium Rock," "The Way I Walk," "Domino," "Tear It Up," "Rockin' Bones," "Lonesome Town," "Love Me," and Jackie Lee Cochran's "Georgia Lee Brown."

The Cramps are led by charismatic, crazed, leather-clad singer and songwriter Lux Interior and his spouse, lead guitarist Poison Ivy Rorschach, who wears fish-net stockings and a miniskirt. Nick Knox settled in as the drummer; a series of players took the second guitar spot. Lux Interior sings of skeletons, werewolves, zombies, a human fly, a gorehound, cavemen, jungles, natives, wig hats, muck, goo, and fuzz. "Thee Most Exalted Potentate of Love" contains B-movie scientist dialogue ("mad? you call me mad? I who have the secret of love!?") and their usual cleverness ("I can teach you how to read the book of life, you can just look at the pictures if you like"). "Garbageman" is an original seemingly inspired by an old, possibly traditional song recorded as "Garbage Man Blues" ("get out your can, here comes the garbageman") by Milton Brown's western swing band in 1934, among others. The Cramps sing:

> Yeah, it's just what you need when you're down in the dumps
> One half hillbilly and one half punk
> Big long legs and one big mouth
> The hottest thing from the North to come out of the South

The Cramps inspired many bands, each with its own slant, like the Gun Club, who reworked delta blues, not rockabilly.

TAV FALCO'S PANTHER BURNS

Tav Falco and his band also perform on the fringe of the revival, albeit without the horror-movie image of the Cramps. Formed in Memphis, Panther Burns was named after "a bit of local folklore—the slaying by fire of a panther that had terrorized a plantation in Greenville, Mississippi."[9] No matter who Falco enlists (Jim Dickinson and Alex Chilton have both been involved), the band retains their swampy, theatrical, outrageous sound rooted in southern traditions.

Their early work is also intentionally sloppy and sounds like the work of amateurs. Not worrying about being out of tune or time, they gloried in the spontaneity of one-take recordings to the point of falling apart. Aware of their tradition and yet bringing new energy, commitment, and a warped musical vision to performance, they created a cult following, recording prolifically and touring Australia and Europe, signed to the New Rose label of Paris.

I first saw them in 1983 in Memphis; a few years later they played in Montreal two years in a row. When they do Memphis rockabilly, the spirit and abandon come from the inside, infusing it with influences from all over and their perception of the modern world, giving the songs an absolutely inimitable treatment.

Their rockabilly repertory was mostly drawn from Memphis recordings, although they also covered Crazy Cavan's "She's the One to Blame." Their repertory draws also from the blues tradition and garage rock with oddball choices thrown in: "Brazil," Dinah Shore and Xavier Cugat's "Throw Your Mask Away" and the theme from the James Bond movie *Goldfinger*. Rockabilly is less represented on later albums, and although the band is more polished, they are true to their original vision.

For several years Tav Falco has been working in Europe, based in Vienna. An album recorded there contains "songs that tie into themes that Panther Burns are fond of . . . unrequited love, lost causes, brother against brother, burning mansions."[10]

THE METEORS

Although the Cramps have been called psychobilly, that term is more identified with the Meteors, who came along later. In fact, the Meteors are thought of as the originators of psychobilly. The difference is that the Cramps are American, older, and imprinted with 1960s music, and they mixed rockabilly with garage punk and psychedelic. They often slowed down their cover versions. The Meteors are British, younger, and imprinted with 1970s music, and they mixed rockabilly with punk. Songs they covered got sped up. Although both bands sing about gore, monsters, and so on, the Cramps are more camp about it, the Meteors more grim.

The Meteors formed in 1980, evolving out of a rockabilly revival band called Raw Deal that had been on the scene for years. Theirs is an intense but polished style of rockabilly: the songs are short and fast, often in minor keys. The Meteors manage a certain amount of variety, aided by being well recorded. Their ironically titled first album *In Heaven* is named after a drunken singalong (from the movie *Eraserhead*) that opens the record. A more apt title would have been the final song: "Rockabilly Psychosis." All the songs were composed by either guitarist P. Paul Fenech or bassist Nigel Lewis, with the exception of the Rolling Stones' "Get Off of My Cloud," given entirely new verses setting it in a mental institution. The Meteors project dread through songs about apocalyptic annihilation ("Teenagers from Outer Space": "we don't want to save the world, we want to kill the human race"), domination by aliens ("Attack of the Zorch Men"), madness ("Earwigs In My Brain") and the experience of being made a zombie by voodoo ritual ("Death Dance"). Love is not totally out of the picture; there is "Psycho for Your Love" and the literal, graphic violence of "Love You to Death" ("squeeze out your last breath"). What lingers is the sense of fatality; you'll get it in the end, which is the message of "In the Cards." The Meteors made many other albums; after Lewis left to form the Tall Boys, Fenech led the band.

Psychobilly now involves many young bands, including Guanabatz, Batmobile (Holland), and the Falcons (Japan).

Conclusion

What was once obscure has now been thoroughly documented. When rockabilly was first sold, it came on 78s and 45s, scatter shot at the marketplace in hopes of a hit. When songs were gathered up in the 1970s and 1980s for long-playing albums, they were often presented with researched liner notes. The success of the CD format made new editions possible. What was well-presented on vinyl often became definitive: now one CD, a double CD, or a box-set package can provide the complete works of many an artist, with better sound, more detailed and more accurate notes, and a discography. This is a wonderful accomplishment, but it wraps up years of collecting, interviewing, archive searches, and detective work. Just about everything worthy of reissue from the 1950s has been tracked down and made available. It is now history. Research energy has shifted to other styles, such as doo-wop.

Rockabilly-style guitar playing is now found in many country and rock songs, such as Albert Lee's work with Emmylou Harris and others. Rockabilly guitar styles have been well covered in guitar magazines, books transcribing solos and characteristic licks, and instructional videos.[1] These publications have been a boost for the reputations of many excellent players such as Carl Perkins, James Burton, Scotty Moore, Paul Burlison, Cliff Gallup, Brian Setzer, Danny Gatton, and Chris Spedding.

Rockabilly is now documented on film. Greg Wolske of Columbus, Ohio, producer of the Paul Burlison instructional video, made *Tear It Up! The Rockabilly Documentary* by combining interviews, footage from European and American events, and vintage clips.

Rockabilly songs are a little more evident in the general sound-scape, showing up in the repertories of a diverse group of artists: Paul McCartney at the MTV Unplugged sessions, NRBQ on a TV show, and even a local blues band doing Carl Perkins's "Jive after Five."

Of the rockabilly veterans who have been going over to Europe, most have been there several times and have shown what they can and cannot do in terms of ability, stage presence, drawing power, and reliability. The pool of still-performing authentic rockabilly veterans is not large, and it is unlikely that we will be surprised by others coming out of the woodwork. The ranks have thinned, and the survivors are aging. Our links with the 1950s are diminishing. Purist fans who have not embraced younger performers will soon have only their record collections to listen to.

Although they have a mystique different from that of their inspirations, the committed artists that came out of the early days of the revival are already veterans, on their way to becoming the next set of venerated ancestors. North America has Robert Gordon, the Stray Cats, and a handful of others whose fame is more regional. Among the bands from the United Kingdom that qualify were those presented at a 1993 Teddy Boy Rock 'n' Roll festival. Crazy Cavan and the Rhythm Rockers were the headliners, with support from the Riot Rockers, Graham Fenton's Matchbox, the Jets, Flying Saucers, Screaming Lord Sutch and the Savages, Freddie "Fingers" Lee, the Rapiers, and the New Sunsets (plus other U.K. bands and ones from the United States, Norway, and France). Although most of these ensembles have a strong following in the United Kingdom and in parts of Europe, they are almost unknown in North America. They did not succeed in piercing that market in their early years. Will they be headlining American festivals ten or twenty years from now, as American companies reissue British recordings and publish magazines full of interviews with the movers and shakers of European rockabilly? Stranger things have happened. The early days of the revival are already being packaged as history in the Rockhouse label's series *The Neo-Rockabilly Story*. Rockhouse has another series looking to the future, called *Rock 'n' Roll around the Turn of the Century*, featuring bands from all over the world.

The British Invasion of the 1960s is often seen as the force that killed rock 'n' roll. In the early days of the invasion, however, most bands did versions of 1950s rock 'n' roll songs, a few rockabilly ones among them. This not only validated the songs and their originators; it also showed ways in which the style could evolve, although the practice soon diminished. The Beatles recorded the last of their

1950s covers in 1965, presenting solely original compositions from then on. By the time of their *Sgt. Pepper's Lonely Hearts Club Band* in 1967, rock had dropped the roll. The roll part of rock 'n' roll, which has a lot to do with swing (triplet) rhythms, had been carried through the big-band era into the R&B and rockabilly combos that served as a large part of the British Invasion bands' formative inspirations. When these bands came to America, they found not only that their cherished early influences were largely out of favor but also that there were new influences to be had as they competed with the innovations of their peers. At this point, rock 'n' roll became a dated style.

Rock 'n' roll is still trying to escape its time. All styles carry coded images; rock 'n' roll is still tied to a caricature of the 1950s—greasy hairdos, happy days, hot rods, soda shops, and so on. Roy Williams, who runs Nervous Records in London, issuing music from young rockabilly bands, wonders whether rock 'n' roll can "unchain itself from '50s nostalgia and emerge . . . as a valid music form and exist in the same way that country music or reggae does. . . . The future is a bunch of spotty kids struggling with guitars in a kitchen somewhere. . . . If rock 'n' roll doesn't attract them, it will become a museum piece."[2]

To escape from being stuck in nostalgia, some revivalists evolved alternative, even elaborate approaches to material, instrumentation, and arrangements. In restarting the evolution of rock 'n' roll from an early fork in the road, ambitious revivalists attempted a new evolution; in the end, the ideas of a few were not sufficiently different to sustain a powerful thrust. That failure was a repeat of the failure of 1950s rockabilly to evolve past a certain point. This new attempt did evolve, but it failed because of the nature of the style itself: the further that revivalists strayed from rockabilly, always a limiting genre (like blues), the less their music was recognizable or relevant to rockabilly. Many of the musicians became absorbed in a more general roots-oriented, partially antitechnology movement that frowned on synthesizers, drum machines, and sequencers.

Whether rockabilly will continue to draw young people to play it and listen to it remains to be seen. It very well could, but first they must be exposed to the style. Blues has succeeded in attracting a huge audience, including young people, but blues is far bigger than rockabilly in every way: magazines, blues societies, radio shows, award categories, touring artists, and festivals. In Montreal blues is readily available, whereas rock 'n' roll is scarce. Blues has its own section in almost every record and CD store, whereas rockabilly or even rock 'n' roll is presented as such in just a couple of stores. There are lots of local blues bands but very few rock 'n' roll ones.

Rockabilly's recovery and revival parallels that of down-home blues in the 1960s (when it was more often called "rural blues" or "country blues"), although there are significant differences. Both styles originated in the same general area and spread to the same general areas. Performers from both styles shared some of the same tensions, including the struggle with the morality of the music. The "rediscovered" black country blues performers were old and had a young white audience; the "rediscovered" rockabilly performers were middle-aged and had a white audience of a wider age spread. The length of time from the original era to its revival was much shorter for rockabilly, and the cultural distance between the original performers and the new performers and audience also are much smaller.

One big difference between blues and rockabilly (or rock 'n' roll) is that the former has escaped from being tied to a particular era. No one asks for blues by naming a decade; you do not hear requests like "play some 1920s blues" or "play something from the 1950s." Although extensions of the Chicago blues style of the 1950s is a dominant strain, it is the city's and the current players' links to the legendary names, not to the decade, that are used to promote it. The reason is that the style never went missing, nor did it evolve into a style different enough to warrant a new name.

Semantics are important. Words heard to distinguish strains of blues include *acoustic, down-home, Texas, delta, jump,* and *soul,* words that broadly indicate variations due to instrumentation, context, region, and style. When you do hear a word that indicates a time period, it is something general, like *prewar* (i.e., pre–World War II). Aside from *Sun, Memphis, Louisiana,* or *Texas,* few words, whether they refer to instrumentation, context, or style, are well-applied beside the word *rockabilly.*

There are the hybrid names, the ones that end in "billy": psychobilly, thrashabilly, punkabilly. If we remove the prefixes, we have phrases like the following: "Are you ready for the billies?" "Billy Festival," "King of the Billies," "I got the billies," "Mystery Train Billy," "here comes a real billy man." It works for blues, so what's wrong here? The answer is that the blues is a feeling. Everyone relates to the feeling of having the blues. Of course, it is also a style and a heritage. Even if they have no handle on the variations of style and heritage, many people grasp what blues is, but most, even music fans, do not know what rockabilly is. I wonder whether that is likely to change. To grasp the style and heritage requires some experience and knowledge. To spread and develop, rockabilly needs more exposure and more of a community.

Rockabilly will survive. It has been recognized around the world as a still-vital style worthy of being played and heard, studied and enjoyed. Recognition and appreciation of passé indigenous music at close cultural, temporal, and geographical proximity is rarely in abundance. The revival's original and largest impetus was from European countries; there and in Japan the revival continues. In North America certain cities and regions retain a rockabilly scene, whereas the style has atrophied in others. It is to be hoped that the genuine and positive response to rockabilly indicates an increased general appreciation of the value of artistic expression and community wherever it occurs.

When skateboards are in vogue everybody has one, but when skateboards go out of fashion, only the people who really like them stay involved. In the same way, rockabilly is carried on now mostly by people who are deeply committed to the style. Thousands and thousands of bands, from the lousy to the truly excellent, are playing rockabilly around the world. It may take some digging to find it, but rockabilly still lives, breathes, and continues to evolve. The train keeps a-rollin'.

Notes

CHAPTER 1: THE NAME GAME

1. The instrument is known variously as upright bass, bass fiddle, double bass, bull fiddle, stand-up bass, and even doghouse bass. The slapped-bass technique was used in western swing and bluegrass but likely is an influence from jazz bands. Steve Brown, from New Orleans, artfully slaps his bass in "My Pretty Girl," by Jean Goldkette and his orchestra, recorded in 1927 on the Victor label, which also features the cornet playing of the legendary Bix Beiderbecke. The percussive slapping effect on upright bass is produced by pulling up on the strings, causing them to slap against the fingerboard when released, or by hitting the strings with the right-hand palm, causing them to rattle against the fingerboard. Some players slacken one of the strings so that it functions only for the slapping sound and not for the production of pitches.

2. *Billboard,* August 7, 1954, p. 39.

3. *Cashbox,* August 14, 1954, p. 25.

4. Charlie Gillett, in *The Sound of the City* (33–46), identifies rockabilly as one of five distinct styles in 1954–56 that collectively became known as rock 'n' roll. The other four are northern band rock 'n' roll (exemplified by Bill Haley); New Orleans dance blues and R&B (Fats Domino and Little Richard); Chicago R&B (Chuck Berry and Bo Diddley); and doo-wop, the New York vocal group style.

5. Yelvington interview, August 20, 1982 (see the bibliography for details of all interviews).

6. Phillips interview.

7. The authorship of this song is not clear. On its first appearance on LP, Thompson was credited, but Colin Escott states in the notes to *Sun Records: The Rockin' Years* (regrettably devoid of songwriter's credits) that it was com-

posed by the Colby-Wolf Combo, recording for the Flip label of Los Angeles. According to the Gordon discography, another artist named Jonathan Craig recorded that title on the same label in both a vocal and instrumental version. They were reviewed in the trade papers in April 1957.

8. Millar, "Johnny Carroll," 15.

9. Snow, *The Hank Snow Story*, 383–84, 391.

10. Burlison interview, August 11, 1982.

11. Smith interview.

12. Yelvington interview, May 20, 1983.

13. Feathers interview, August 19, 1982.

14. Kaye, "Very Large Legend," 32.

15. Dickinson interview, August 19, 1982.

16. Sherman, "The Blasters," 32.

17. Van Eaton interview.

18. "Rockabilly Rules," *New Kommotion* 18 (winter 1978): 28–29.

19. Gordon interview, August 23, 1982.

20. Ibid.

21. Ibid.

CHAPTER 2: INGREDIENTS

1. Tucker, "Rockabilly," 3.

2. "Feathering" is the name given to the falsetto grace notes often found at the ends of lines in folk and hillbilly songs. This definition appears in the notes to *Hank Williams*, a Time-Life box set (TLCW 1), 23. Judith McCulloh gives a more technical definition: "a sudden or forceful raising of the soft palate against the back wall of the throat and/or a sudden closing of the glottis at the very end of a given note, generally accompanied by a rise in pitch" (quoted by Charles Wolfe in the notes to *I'm on My Journey Home: Vocal Styles and Resources in Folk Music* [New World 223], 4). An R&B example is Ruth Brown's "Mama, He Treats Your Daughter Mean" from 1953.

3. Tucker, "Rockabilly," 2.

4. Ibid., 2–3.

5. Malone, "Elvis, Country Music, and the South," 127–28.

6. Yelvington interview, August 14, 1982.

7. Shaw, *The Rockin' '50s*, 187.

8. Tosches traces the history of the word in *Country*, 25–31.

9. The song "Have Myself a Ball" is incorrectly called "Rockin' with My Baby" on two Charly anthologies (CR 30123 and CR 30150).

10. Escott and Hawkins, *Sun Label Session Files*, 29; Escott and Hawkins, *Sun Records: The Brief History*, 58; Escott and Hawkins, notes to Sun Box 101.

11. That the song was performed in the key of E is verified by film. In 1989 *Night Music*, a television variety show on NBC, aired a vintage performance clip of "Your True Love" by Carl Perkins, his two brothers, and a drummer, presumably W. S. Holland. The source was not given, but the year was indicated—erroneously, it seems—as 1955. Carl is playing the Les Paul guitar pictured on the "Blue Suede Shoes" sheet music cover.

12. Tosches, "Rockabilly!" 230.

13. Skeeter Davis did this song both times I was at the *Grand Ole Opry* (1982 and 1983). Davis introduced the song (1982) by saying that she had only recently begun to perform it again. Nothing else indicated an influence of the rockabilly revival on *Opry* repertory, although rockabilly was heard on the show in the 1950s.

14. Phillips interview.

15. This passage is informed by Stan Kesler (quoted in Clayton, "Sam Phillips," 28) and the Dickinson interviews. For more details, see Escott and Hawkins, *Good Rockin' Tonight,* 15, 18.

CHAPTER 3: ORIGINS AND PREDECESSORS

1. Some barn dance shows on the radio were the *National Barn Dance* (Chicago, 1924–70), the *Grand Ole Opry* (Nashville, 1925–present), *World's Original Jamboree* (Wheeling, W.VA., 1933–?), *Louisiana Hayride* (Shreveport, 1948–early 1960s), and the *Big D Jamboree* (Dallas, 1947–1960). The *Big D* was broadcast locally in its four-hour entirety and nationally by CBS in a one-hour edited version.

2. Jones, "Wolfman Jack," 64.

3. Tucker, "The Louisiana Hayride," 192.

4. Ginell, *Milton Brown,* xxx.

5. Townsend, in *San Antonio Rose* (103, 289), credits Bob Wills with the introduction of drums to country music.

6. See Russell, *Blacks, Whites, and Blues,* and Malone and McCulloh, *Stars of Country Music.*

7. Morrison, *Rockabilly Music and Musicians.* This work analyzes and compares the following source songs and their subsequent versions: Bill Monroe's "Rocky Road Blues" with versions by Ronnie Self and Gene Vincent; the Delmore Brothers' "Blues Stay Away from Me" with a version by the Rock 'n' Roll Trio; Hank Williams's "My Bucket's Got a Hole in It" with versions by Sonny Burgess and Ricky Nelson; Little Junior's Blue Flames' "Mystery Train" with the Elvis Presley version; Billy "the Kid" Emerson's "Red Hot" with versions by Billy Riley and Bob Luman; the Royals' (Hank Ballard and the Midnighters) "Sexy Ways" with versions by Wayne Raney (as "Shake Baby Shake"), Buddy Holly (as "Rock-A-Bye Rock"), Jerry Lee Lewis (as "Cool, Cool Ways"), and Johnny O'Keefe and the Dee Jays (as "Shake Baby Shake"); Billy Ward and the Dominoes' "Sixty Minute Man" with the Jerry Lee Lewis version; and Stick McGhee's "Drinkin' Wine Spo-Dee-O-Dee" with versions by Malcolm Yelvington and the Rock 'n' Roll Trio.

8. Burgess, "Sonny Burgess," 19.

9. Burlison interview, May 25, 1983. West and Blair (in "Johnny Burnette," 6) state that it was produced by Buddy Bain—a deejay who recorded for Meteor—and that it was cut in early 1954.

10. Komorowski, "Warren Smith," 48.

11. Kaye, "Very Large Legend," 33.

12. Dickinson interview, August 19, 1982.

13. Marcus, *Mystery Train,* 13.
14. Poindexter interview.
15. Escott and Hawkins, "Sun Records: The Brief History," 4, 45.

CHAPTER 4: THE RISE AND FALL OF ROCKABILLY IN THE 1950S

1. Two radio commercials for these 1956 shows in Richmond, Virginia, and Memphis can be heard on the Carl Perkins box set Sun Box 101.
2. Cordell Jackson is profiled in chapter 13.
3. *Billboard,* June 23, 1956, p. 58.
4. Dickinson interview, May 19, 1983.
5. Charlie Feathers interview, May 17, 1983.
6. Ibid. In a phone call on June 15, 1994, Feathers told me that Onie Wheeler was also on that show and that they were taken to the jailhouse for signing autographs on girls' legs but not put in jail.
7. Escott and Hawkins, *Sun Records: The Brief History,* 25.
8. Barnes, "Sun Records," 30–31.
9. That rockabillies had to deal with disapproval for their involvement with black-influenced music was brought home to me during a meeting with Paul Burlison. Burlison was the first rockabilly veteran I ever met, the first one I called on when I went to Memphis. I was with Jean-Luc, a rockabilly fanatic with an Elvis hairdo on a musical pilgrimage from France, whom I'd hooked up with in New Orleans. The three of us were well into an afternoon of talking music when a neighbor came to Burlison's house to buy a horse. "Hey, Paul," he said, "are you telling these foreigners about that old nigger music you used to play?" When the neighbor went out of earshot, Burlison leaned over and said, "don't listen to him, people around here don't understand what we were trying to do."
10. Dickinson interview, August 19, 1982.
11. Ibid.
12. It can be heard on the Jerry Lee Lewis box set *The Sun Years* or read in Escott and Hawkins, *Sun Records: The Brief History,* 110.
13. Dickinson interview, August 19, 1982.
14. Ibid.
15. Komorowski, "Jack Clement," 46.
16. Dickinson interview, May 19, 1983.
17. Guralnick, "There's Good Rockin' Tonight," 44.
18. Cain, *Whole Lotta Shakin',* 12.
19. See Shaw, "Teen Idols."
20. White, "Jerry Lee Lewis," 24.
21. Escott and Hawkins, *Sun Label Session Files,* 331.

CHAPTER 5: ELVIS PRESLEY

1. DeWitt, "Memphis: The Obscure Years," 20.
2. Burlison interview, August 11, 1982.

3. Many books and articles on American popular music and its creators relate this story. I recommend Hopkins's *Elvis: A Biography,* Palmer's interview-based "Sam Phillips the Sun King," Carr and Farren's *Elvis: The Illustrated Record,* Carr's liner notes to *The Elvis Presley Sun Collection,* Peter Guralnick's liner notes to Presley's *The Complete Sun Sessions,* his biography of Elvis in the 1950s called *Last Train to Memphis,* Cajiao's "The Most Important Man in the World," and Escott and Hawkins's *Good Rockin' Tonight.*

4. In fingerpicking, a guitar tradition in blues, ragtime, and country playing popularized by Chet Atkins and Merle Travis, the thumb of the picking hand steadily alternates between bass strings while the other fingers dance more freely on the upper strings.

5. Rumored to exist are versions of Red Foley's "Tennessee Saturday Night," Bill Monroe's "Uncle Pen," and Jack Guthrie's "Oakie Boogie." Even though they are mentioned in various articles and discographies, there is no conclusive evidence that these songs were recorded. When asked by Trevor Cajiao about "Uncle Pen" and "Tennessee Saturday Night," Sam Phillips stated, "I know the songs. No, no, I don't remember him recording those. I would've been the only one that woulda' recorded it at Sun and I don't remember that." When asked about another contender, "Give Me More, More, More," Phillips said, "That doesn't ring a bell either" (see Cajiao, "The Most Important Man in the World," 17). Presley did record a rendition of Martha Carson's gospel song "Satisfied," but this was lost by RCA.

6. The songs with drums are "You're a Heartbreaker," "I'm Left, You're Right, She's Gone," and the rehearsal of "How Do You Think I Feel" (drums by Jimmie Lott); and "I Forgot to Remember to Forget," "Trying to Get to You," and "When It Rains It Really Pours" (drums by Johnny Bernero). Bongos are heard on "I Don't Care If the Sun Don't Shine" and "Blue Moon."

7. Riley reference from Cajiao, "Rappin' with Riley, Part One," 20; Orbison reference from Elson, *Early Rockers,* 100.

8. Tosches, "Rockabilly!" 226.

9. I am not sure who "little Vi" is—or "Levi," as Roy Carr wrote (surely not "nearly 'bout," as Guralnick wrote). Perhaps it is a nickname for Elvis. If this arrangement was in fact learned from Feathers's demo, that demo would have sounded more country; perhaps the words *different* and *pop* in Phillips's comment refer to the singing style, not to the 4/4 meter.

10. Marsh, "Elvis: The New Deal," 23.

11. Cajiao, "Billy Walker," 16.

12. Broven, "Roy Brown," 16.

13. Exact dates and those of later Presley Sun sessions are unclear.

14. At its simplest, the progression is as follows: IV–IV–I–I [repeats once] / V–IV–I–I. An early use is Hambone Willie Newbern's "Roll and Tumble Blues" (1929), where it is most clearly heard in his solo passages (he adds two more beats at the end of each line). The progression commonly supports a double-time feel, causing each bar to be counted twice.

15. Burlison interview, August 11, 1983.

16. Bond interview, May 20, 1983.

17. The band is Charlie Roach (steel), Charles Moore (narration, lead and rhythm guitar), Red Rolison (vocals, rhythm guitar), and Jimmie Rhodes (bass and comedy) on White Label LP 8810.

18. Gordon interview, August 23, 1982.

19. In Miller, "Jess Hooper," 32, Hooper stated he had never heard of Feathers.

20. Helm, *This Wheel's on Fire,* 37.

21. Morrison, "Hound Dog in the Country," 16.

22. Carr and Farren, *Elvis: The Illustrated Record,* 31.

23. See Wolfe, "Presley and the Gospel Tradition," 139.

CHAPTER 6: MEMPHIS

1. He has stated adamantly that he recorded before Elvis. "'Drinkin Wine' was cut and ready to go by the time Elvis's first record was made" (quoted by Martin Hawkins on Sun LP 1010). The Escott-Hawkins discography contradicts this claim, giving the recording date as October 10, 1954, months after Elvis's first release.

2. Yelvington interview, May 20, 1983.

3. Yelvington's recording of "Drinkin' Wine Spo-Dee-O-Dee" has had the misfortune of being presented on most albums in a wobbly version that has been taken from an off-center disc, as well as being too fast, so much so that the key is one semitone too high. *The Sun Country Years* box set contains, finally, a version that is correct in both regards, in the proper key of F.

4. Yelvington interview, August 20, 1982.

5. Ibid.

6. Actually, that credit was used only for "Yakety Yak." The other side was credited to Mac Sales and the Esquire Trio.

7. Smith interview.

8. Austin interview.

9. Quoted in the notes to the Carl Perkins collection *The Sun Years,* Sun Box 101.

10. Ibid. Also note: "Sam considered the uptempo numbers performed by Carl [at his audition] to be too similar to Elvis" (quoted in Komorowski, "Carl Perkins, Part One," 22).

11. Komorowski, "Malcolm Yelvington," 40.

12. An earlier use of this descending progression is found in "Do What I Do," by Slim Rhodes, where it is used as an intro and as a four-bar turnaround replacing the last two bars of a standard blues.

13. Komorowski, "Carl Perkins, Part Four," 15.

14. Each has written about his religious beliefs. Perkins's book is *Disciple in Blue Suede Shoes.*

15. Information in this paragraph is from Cajiao, "The Return of the Rockin' Guitar Man."

16. The fad is referred to in the notes to the soundtrack of the film *Atomic Cafe* (Rounder 1034).

17. Cajiao, "Whole Lotta Shakin'," 4.

18. Cajiao, "Rappin' with Riley, Part Two," 30.

19. White, "Jerry Lee Lewis," 24.

20. Tosches, *Hellfire,* 88. Long rumored, the acetate has finally been issued; see under "Jerry Lee Lewis" in the discography.

21. For details, see the book written by Myra Lewis, his exwife (*Great Balls of Fire*).

22. White, "Jerry Lee Lewis," 24.

23. Greenblatt, "Jerry Lee Lewis," 22.

24. Van Eaton interview.

25. Priscilla Beaulieu, the future Mrs. Elvis Presley, was fifteen when she first came to stay at Graceland. She had her parents' permission. Roy Orbison married Claudette Frady when she was fourteen, but it never became an issue: she looked so much older, and he was not nearly as famous then as he would become.

26. Felts, "Stars on Stars."

27. Clayson, *Only the Lonely,* 16.

28. Presley recorded "Trying to Get to You" in 1955, but it was not issued until March 1956, on RCA, by which time the Je-Wel single had been issued and Orbison was already at Sun. Orbison's "Ooby Dooby" from the Petty studio was not reissued on Charly/Sun CDX4 in 1984, despite the claim.

29. Amburn, *Dark Star,* 42.

30. Burlison interview, August 11, 1982.

31. Ibid.

32. Ibid.

33. Ibid.

34. Ibid.

35. Ibid.

36. Ibid.

37. Escott and Hawkins note that Scotty Moore uses a riff derived from this Delmore's song in the unissued take of Presley's "I'm Left, You're Right, She's Gone" (a slow and bluesy version sometimes called "My Baby's Gone") (*Sun Records: The Brief History,* 6). It is not present in Presley's issued take, which uses a different arrangement. Another example of the popularity of this riff in Memphis is found in Malcolm Yelvington's "I've Got the Blues (Way Down Blues)."

38. Cajiao, "Johnny Black," 9–13.

39. The Yardbirds were recorded at the Sun studio by Sam Phillips during the Memphis stop on their 1966 tour.

CHAPTER 7: COUNTRY SINGERS AND NASHVILLE ROCKABILLY

1. "Drop Petty Bickering," 53.

2. See "The Development of Country-Pop Music and the Nashville Sound," in Malone, *Country Music U.S.A.,* 245–67.

3. The review dated March 9, 1957, is reproduced in Clark, *Rock-A-Billy*

and Country Legends, 22. The trade magazine from which it is taken is not indicated.

4. Hall interview.

5. Ibid.

6. Tosches, in *Country,* 69–70, prints a photograph of the original Big Maybelle OKeh release listing Williams as the sole composer, although in the text he acknowledges Hall, under the Sunny David pseudonym, to be the cowriter. According to Tosches, the two post-Hall versions from 1955 are by bigband singer Delores Fredericks and the Commodores (not the 1970s group).

7. Guralnick, *Feel Like Going Home,* 181.

8. In a letter to the editor of *Now Dig This* (no. 89 [August 1990]: 10), Paul Waring postulated that Hall learned both sides of Big Maybelle's record and subsequently claimed that he had been involved in writing them.

9. Hall interview.

10. Ibid.

11. Ibid.

12. Cajiao, "Johnny Black," 11–13.

13. Smallwood, "'58 Blue Caps," 14.

CHAPTER 8: ROCKABILLY WOMEN

1. The first three are discussed at length in Bob Garbutt's book *Rockabilly Queens.*

2. Oermann and Bufwack, "Rockabilly Women," 65–94.

3. Ibid., 71.

4. Ibid., 88.

5. *Journal of Country Music* 13, no. 1 (1990): 37.

6. Garbutt, *Rockabilly Queens,* 37.

7. Newcombe, "Little Miss Dynamite," 24.

8. Oermann and Bufwack, "Rockabilly Women," 80.

9. Whitburn, *Top Country Records 1948–1971,* 37–38.

10. Nunn, "The Wanda Jackson Story, Part Three," 27.

11. Ibid.

CHAPTER 9: LOUISIANA

1. Uncredited liner notes to Werly Fairburn's *Everybody's Rockin',* WALL 100.

CHAPTER 10: TEXAS

1. Laing, *Buddy Holly,* 30–31.

2. Millar, "That Rockin' Daddy," 16.

3. Ibid.

4. Ibid.

5. Goldrosen, *The Buddy Holly Story,* 35–40.

6. An undubbed version is found on a bootleg on the Cricket label.

7. Taylor, "Buddy Knox Interview," 17.

8. Millar, "Johnny Carroll," 15.

9. Carroll may have been inspired, as Roy Orbison was, to record "Trying to Get to You" after seeing Presley perform the song live or by Orbison's first single with this song on the flip side. Orbison's release predates the Elvis release.

10. Millar, "Johnny Carroll," 15. In the notes to Carroll's *Crazy Hot Rock*, on Charly, Adam Komorowski states that Scotty and Bill each made $150 a week, or $250 while on the road.

11. Millar, "Mac Curtis," 5.

12. Ibid.

13. Ibid.

14. Notes to Bob Luman's *Wild Eyed Woman*.

15. For the six 1955 demos, Luman is credited with authorship of one and coauthorship of two or three more: four songs appear, with songwriters' names, on *More Rock-A-Billy Rock* on White Label; all six are on Luman's *Wild Eyed Woman*, on Bear Family, but the only one of them that has a credit is inconsistent with that given on the White Label album. Of the remaining ten songs (seven with credits) on the Bear Family album, Luman wrote none.

16. Coulavin, "Andy Starr," 46. Other information on Starr comes from correspondence with Coulavin.

17. Paul Barrett's response and Frank "Andy" Starr's letter are both in *Now Dig This*, no. 86 (May 1990): 11.

18. Cajiao, editor's response to a letter in *Now Dig This*, no. 88 (July 1990): 12.

19. *Billy Poore's Rockabilly Revue*, no. 8 (Spring 1992): 30.

20. Marc Coulavin in conversation, October 1991.

21. Notes to *For Tooter Boatman Fans Only*.

CHAPTER 11: CALIFORNIA

1. Selvin, *Ricky Nelson*, 84.

2. Information on this performance from Stafford, "Hemsby No. 10," 20, and eyewitness accounts from Marc Coulavin, Clive Jackson, and Eric Sandmark.

3. Examining songs that appeared on *Billboard*'s pop singles charts, Whitburn added up points calculated from chart position and number of weeks on the chart (weighted with certain bonus points). Between Presley and Nelson, positions 2 through 6 are filled by Pat Boone, Perry Como, Fats Domino, Nat King Cole, and the Platters (Whitburn, *Top Pop Singles*, 724).

4. Sam Phillips, interviewed on *A Tribute to Ricky Nelson*, a TV documentary on PBS.

5. Roy Orbison, ibid.

6. Guitarist Gary Lambert, who knew and played with Eddie Cochran, has stated that "Eddie never met Elvis or saw him perform, regardless of what you've read, believe me!" (letter to the editor, *Now Dig This*, no. 90 [Sept. 1990]: 23).

CHAPTER 12: THE REVIVAL

1. Millar, "Mac Curtis," 7.
2. For addresses, see the resource list in the bibliography.

CHAPTER 13: VETERANS

1. Yelvington interview, May 20, 1983.
2. Mean Mountain Mike, "Warren Smith," 30–31.
3. McNutt, *We Wanna Boogie,* 217.
4. Yelvington interview, May 20, 1983.
5. Honeycutt interview.
6. Bond interview, May 20, 1983.
7. Raiteri, "Eddie Bond," 6.
8. Bond interview, May 20, 1983.
9. Feathers's quotations and paraphrases in this paragraph are from the May 17, 1983, interview.
10. Ibid.
11. Ibid.
12. Cajiao, "Have Guitar Will Travel," 20.
13. Escott and Hawkins, *Sun Records: The Discography,* 55.
14. For further explorations of Feathers's claims, see Cockburn, "The Charlie Feathers Enigma."
15. Guralnick, *Lost Highway,* 112.
16. Gordon, "Charlie Feathers Squawks Again," 16.
17. *The 50's Rock on the Moon* (Moon label compilation) liner notes.
18. Jackson interview.
19. "Old-Time Rock 'n' Roller," G1.
20. Cajiao, "We've Found Sid Watson," 5.
21. Some of this information comes from Cajiao, "Claiborne Joseph Cheramie."
22. Information on Dawson from Koumis, "The Ronnie Dawson Story," with additional information from Russell, "Rockin' Ronnie Dawson."
23. Clark, *Rock and Roll Legends,* 31.
24. Kelemen, "Jack the Cat," n.p..
25. Cajiao, "A Chat with Jack the Cat," 24.

CHAPTER 14: REVIVALISTS

1. Griffiths interview.
2. Lee Novembrino in personal correspondence, June 6, 1989.
3. Much of the information on Lee is from Woodford, "The Freddie 'Fingers' Lee Story," parts 1 and 2.
4. Tomlinson, "Crazy Rhythm!" 10.
5. Scott Isler, in a record review in *Trouser Press,* November 1982.
6. Griffiths interview.

7. Bopcats interview.
8. Newton, "Cramps Make Music," 29.
9. Smallwood, "Tav Falco: Out of the Shadows," 8.
10. Ibid., 7.

CONCLUSION

1. Rockabilly guitar instructional videos have been made by Danny Gatton, Arlen Roth, and Brian Setzer (all for Hot Licks Video); Jim Weider, guitarist for the Band (for Homespun); and Paul Burlison (for Rebel Riffs). One book is *Rockabilly Riffs for Guitar,* by Mark Michaels, published by Amsco (New York) in 1985. An instructional video for upright bass players is *Slap Bass: The Ungentle Art,* by Mark Rubin and Kevin Smith (for Ridge Runner). Smith is the bassist for High Noon.

2. Roy Williams, letter, in *Now Dig This,* no. 126 (Sept. 1993): 12.

Bibliography

WORKS CITED

Amburn, Ellis. *Dark Star: The Roy Orbison Story.* New York: Lyle Stuart/Carol, 1990.

Barnes, Barbara. "Sun Records—An Insider's View" (intro. Martin Hawkins). *New Kommotion,* no. 15 (1977): 30–31.

Barrett, Paul, with Hilary Hayward. *Shakin' Stevens.* London: Star/W. H. Allen, 1983.

Broven, John. "Roy Brown." *Blues Unlimited* no. 124:16.

Burgess, Sonny. "Sonny Burgess: The Sun Recordings in His Own Words." *Now Dig This,* no. 102 (Sept. 1991): 19.

Cain, Robert. *Whole Lotta Shakin' Goin' On: Jerry Lee Lewis.* New York: Dial, 1981.

Cajiao, Trevor. "A Chat with Jack the Cat—Jackie Lee Cochran Interview." *Now Dig This,* no. 29 (Aug. 1985): 24–26.

———. "An Interview with Claiborne Joseph Cheramie." *Now Dig This,* no. 44 (Nov. 1986): 26–28.

———. "Billy Walker: A Time of Change." *Now Dig This,* no. 77 (Aug. 1989): 16–18.

———. "Whole Lotta Shakin' Goin' On—2: Roland Janes." *Now Dig This* no. 82 (Jan. 1990): 4.

———. "The Most Important Man in the World: Sam Phillips Talks to *Now Dig This,* Part One." *Now Dig This,* no. 83 (Feb. 1990): 15–21.

———. "An Interview with Johnny Black." *Now Dig This,* no. 99 (June 1991): 9–13.

———. "The Return of the Rockin' Guitar Man." *Now Dig This,* no. 112 (July 1992): 4–7.

———. "We've Found Sid Watson." *Now Dig This,* no. 120 (March 1993): 5.

———. "Rappin' with Riley, Part One." *Now Dig This,* no. 130 (Jan. 1994): 19–23

———. "Rappin' with Riley, Part Two." *Now Dig This* no. 131 (Feb. 1994): 29–31.

Cajiao, Trevor, and Gordon Minto. "Have Guitar Will Travel: Scotty Moore Talks to *Now Dig This,* Part One." *Now Dig This,* no. 131 (Feb. 1994): 19–22.

Carr, Roy, and Mick Farren. *Elvis: The Illustrated Record.* New York: Harmony, 1982.

Clark, Alan, ed. *Rock and Roll Legends: Special Rockabilly Issue,* vol. 1, no. 2. West Covina, Calif.: Leapfrog, 1982.

———. *Rock-A-Billy and Country Legends,* no. 1. West Covina, Calif.: National Rock 'n' Roll Archives, 1986.

Clayson, Alan. *Only the Lonely: The Life and Artistic Legacy of Roy Orbison.* London: Sidgwick and Jackson, 1989.

Clayton, Rose. "Sam Phillips: A Place in the Sun." *Mix,* August 1980, pp. 26, 28, 30.

Cockburn, Howard. "The Charlie Feathers Enigma." *Now Dig This,* no. 90 (Sept. 1990): 18–22.

Coulavin, Marc. "Andy Starr." *Kicks,* no. 7 (1992): 46.

DeWitt, Howard A. "Memphis: The Obscure Years 1948–1952," an excerpt from *Elvis: The Sun Years: The Story of Elvis Presley in the Fifties. Discoveries,* October 1993, pp. 20–28.

"Drop Petty Bickering." *Billboard,* March 3, 1956, p. 53.

Elson, Howard. *Early Rockers.* New York: Proteus, 1982.

Escott, Colin, and Martin Hawkins. *The Complete Sun Label Session Files.* 1978.

———. *Sun Records: The Brief History of the Legendary Record Label.* 2d rev. ed. New York: Quick Fox, 1980.

———. *Sun Records: The Discography.* Vollersode, West Germany: Bear Family, 1987.

Escott, Colin, with Martin Hawkins. *Good Rockin' Tonight: Sun Records and the Birth of Rock 'n' Roll.* New York: St. Martin's, 1991.

Felts, Narvel. "Stars on Stars: Narvel Felts on Ray Smith." *Now Dig This,* no. 119 (Feb. 1993): 26.

Garbutt, Bob. *Rockabilly Queens: The Careers and Recordings of Wanda Jackson, Janis Martin and Brenda Lee.* Toronto: Ducktail, 1979.

Gillett, Charles. *The Sound of the City: The Rise of Rock and Roll.* New York: Outerbridge, 1970.

Ginell, Cary, with Roy Lee Brown. *Milton Brown and the Founding of Western Swing.* Urbana: University of Illinois Press, 1994.

Goldrosen, John. *The Buddy Holly Story.* 2d rev. ed. New York: Quick Fox, 1979.

Goldrosen, John, and John Beecher. *Remembering Buddy: The Definitive Biography.* London: GRR/Pavilion, 1987.

Gordon, Robert. "Charlie Feathers Squawks Again." *Musician,* March 1991, p. 16.

Gordon, Terry. Unpublished discography of issued rockabilly singles from 1949 to 1963, n.d..

Greenblatt, Mike. "Jerry Lee Lewis." *Gallery,* no. 24 (1987): 22.

Guralnick, Peter. "There's Good Rockin' Tonight." *New Kommotion,* no. 18 (Winter 1978): 43–44.

———. *Lost Highway: Journeys and Arrivals of American Musicians.* Boston: David R. Godine, 1979.

———. *Feel Like Going Home: Portraits in Blues and Rock 'n' Roll.* New York: Vantage, 1981 (1971).

———. *Last Train to Memphis: The Rise of Elvis Presley.* Boston: Little, Brown, 1994.

Helm, Levon, with Stephen Davis. *This Wheel's on Fire: Levon Helm and the Story of the Band.* New York: Morrow, 1993.

Hopkins, Jerry. *Elvis: A Biography.* New York: Simon and Schuster, 1971.

Jones, Peter. "Wolfman Jack: Ah-Oooo!" *Goldmine,* September 6, 1991.

Kaye, Lenny. "The Very Large Legend of Carl Perkins." *Guitar World,* July 1982.

Kelemen, Steve. "Jack the Cat: An Interview with Jackie Lee Cochran." *Nervous Breakdown,* no. 3 (Oct. 1993): n.p.

Komorowski, Adam. "Carl Perkins: Boppin' the Blues, Part One." *New Kommotion,* no. 14 (Winter 1977): 22–23.

———. "Carl Perkins: Boppin' the Blues, Part Four." *New Kommotion,* no. 18 (Winter 1978): 12–17.

———. "Jack Clement." *New Kommotion,* no. 22 (1979): 46–47.

———. "Warren Smith." *New Kommotion,* no. 22 (1979): 48–49.

———. "Malcolm Yelvington." *New Kommotion,* no. 22 (1979): 39–40.

Koumis, Barney. "The Ronnie Dawson Story." *Kicks,* no. 6 (1988): 40–43.

Laing, Dave. *Buddy Holly.* London: Studio Vista, 1971.

Lewis, Myra, and Murray Silver. *Great Balls of Fire: The Uncensored Story of Jerry Lee Lewis.* New York: Quill, 1982.

Malone, Bill C. "Elvis, Country Music, and the South." In *Elvis: Images and Fancies,* ed. Jac L. Tharpe, 123–134. Jackson: University Press of Mississippi, 1979.

———. *Country Music U.S.A.* Rev. ed. Austin: University of Texas Press, 1985.

Malone, Bill C., and Judith McCulloh, eds. *Stars of Country Music.* Urbana: University of Illinois Press, 1975.

Marcus, Greil. *Mystery Train.* 2d rev. ed. New York: Dutton, 1982.

Marsh, Dave. "Elvis: The New Deal Origins of Rock 'n' Roll." *Musician,* December 1982.

McNutt, Randy. *We Wanna Boogie: An Illustrated History of the American Rockabilly Movement.* Hamilton, Ohio: HHP, 1988.

Mean Mountain Mike. "Warren Smith." *Mean Mountain Music* 4, no. 1 (1979).

Millar, Bill. "Mac Curtis." *New Kommotion,* no. 19 (Spring 1978): 4–8.

———. "That Rockin' Daddy: Sonny Fisher." *New Kommotion,* no. 25 (1980): 15–16.

———. "Johnny Carroll." *New Kommotion,* no. 26 (1982): 15–16.

Miller, Billy. "Jess Hooper." *Kicks,* no. 3 (1983): 32.

Morrison, Craig. *Rockabilly Music and Musicians.* Unpublished master's thesis, York University, Toronto, Ontario, 1984.

———. "Hound Dog in the Country." *Now Dig This,* no. 82 (Jan. 1990): 16–17.

Newcombe, Jim. "Brenda Lee: Little Miss Dynamite." *Now Dig This,* no. 52 (July 1987): 24–25.

Newton, Steve. "Cramps Make Music for Misfits." *Georgia Straight* (Vancouver), April 13–20, 1990, p. 29.

Nunn, Roger. "The Wanda Jackson Story, Part Three." *Now Dig This,* no. 56 (Nov. 1987): 26–30.

Oermann, Robert K., and Mary A. Bufwack. "Rockabilly Women." *Journal of Country Music* 8, no. 1 (May 1979): 65–94.

"Old-Time Rock 'n' Roller." *Montreal Gazette,* May 19, 1992.

Palmer, Robert. "Sam Phillips the Sun King: A Revised History of the Roots of Rock & Roll." *Memphis* 3, no. 9 (Dec. 1978).

Perkins, Carl, with Ron Rendleman. *Disciple in Blue Suede Shoes.* Grand Rapids, Mich.: Zondervan, 1978.

Raiteri, Charles. "Eddie Bond: A Reluctant Rockabilly Remembers." *Goldmine,* August 1, 1986, pp. 5–8.

"Rockabilly Rules." *New Kommotion* 18 (winter 1978): 28–29.

Russell, Tony. *Blacks, Whites, and Blues.* London: Studio Vista, 1970.

Russell, Wayne. *Footsoldiers and Kings.* Brandon, Manitoba: Wayne Russell, 1983.

———. "Rockin' Ronnie Dawson: The Blond Bomber." *Kicks,* no. 3 (1983): 30.

Selvin, Joel. *Ricky Nelson: Idol for a Generation.* Chicago: Contemporary, 1990.

Shaw, Arnold. *The Rockin' '50's.* New York: Hawthorn, 1974.

Shaw, Greg. "Teen Idols." In *The Rolling Stone Illustrated History of Rock & Roll,* ed. Jim Miller, 96–100. New York: Random House, 1980.

Sherman, Lee. "The Blasters." *Zig Zag,* no. 123 (March 1982): 32–33.

Smallwood, Sue. "'58 Blue Caps: They're Back and They're Proud." *Original Cool,* no. 1 (1993).

———. "Tav Falco: Out of the Shadows." *Original Cool,* no. 4 (April/May 1994): 6–8.

Snow, Hank, with Jack Ownbey and Bob Burris. *The Hank Snow Story: Hank Snow, the Singing Ranger.* Urbana: University of Illinois Press, 1994.

Stafford, John, and Dave Driver. "Hemsby No. 10." *Now Dig This,* no. 123 (June 1993): 19–21.

Taylor, Hank. "Buddy Knox Interview." *Not Fade Away,* no. 14 (1979): 17.

Tomlinson, Johnny. "Crazy Rhythm! Twenty-Five Years of Crazy Cavan & the Rhythm Rockers." *Now Dig This,* no. 135 (June 1994): 10.

Tosches, Nick. "Rockabilly!" In *The Illustrated History of Country Music,* ed. Patrick Carr, 217–37. New York: Dolphin, 1980.

———. *Hellfire: The Jerry Lee Lewis Story,* New York: Delacorte, 1982.

———. *Country: Living Legends and Dying Metaphors in America's Biggest Music.* New York: Scribners', 1985 (rev. ed. of *Country: The Biggest Music in America* [New York: Stein and Day, 1977]).

Townsend, Charles R. *San Antonio Rose: The Life and Music of Bob Wills.* Urbana: University of Illinois Press, 1976.

Tucker, Steve. "The Louisiana Hayride, 1948–1954." *North Louisiana Histori-cal Association Journal* 8, no. 5 (Fall 1977): 187–201.

———. "Rockabilly." Unpublished essay and notes for proposed reissue set of rockabilly recordings, 1983.

West, Dennis, and John Blair. "Johnny Burnette and the Rock 'N Roll Trio." *Record Exchanger,* nos. 26:4–7 and 27:20–25.

Whitburn, Joel. *Top Country Records 1948–1971.* Menomonee Falls, Wisc.: Record Research, 1979.

———. *Top Pop Singles 1955–1986.* Menomonee Falls, Wisc.: Record Research, 1987.

White, Cliff. "Jerry Lee Lewis: The Killer Speaks." *New Kommotion,* no. 24 (1980): 22–24.

Wolfe, Charles. "Presley and the Gospel Tradition." In *Elvis: Images and Fan-cies,* ed. Jac L. Tharpe, 135–150. Jackson: University Press of Mississippi, 1979.

Woodford, Chris. "The Freddie 'Fingers' Lee Story—1." *Now Dig This,* no. 68 (Nov. 1988): 28–30.

———. "The Freddie 'Fingers' Lee Story—2." *Now Dig This,* no. 69 (Dec. 1988): 23–25.

INTERVIEWS

Tony Austin. August 21, 1982, at his home, Jackson, Tennessee.

Eddie Bond. August 14, 1982, at the Mid-South Folklife Festival, Memphis; May 20, 1983, at the Falls Building radio studio, Memphis.

The Bopcats. November 13, 1982, between sets at a gig at York University, Toronto, Ontario.

Paul Burlison. August 11, 1982, at his home, Walls, Mississippi; May 25, 1983, by telephone.

Jim Dickinson. August 19, 1982, and May 19, 1983, both at his home, Colli-erville, Tennessee.

Charlie Feathers. August 19, 1982, and May 17, 1983, both at his home, Memphis.

Terry Gordon. August 23, 1982, and May 15, 1983, both at the Country Mu-sic Hall of Fame, Nashville.

Colin Griffiths. October 12, 1982, at my home, Toronto.

Roy Hall. May 23, 1983, at his office, Nashville.

Buddy Holobaugh. April 17, 1988, by telephone to his home, Waco, Texas.

Glenn Honeycutt. August 17, 1982, at his home, Walls, Mississippi.

Cordell Jackson. May 17, 1983, at her home, Memphis.

Sleepy LaBeef. October 8, 1982, in his motor home behind the Horseshoe Tavern after his gig there, Toronto.

Robin "Handsome Ned" Masyk. February 3, 1985, backstage at Club Soda, Montreal.

Sam Phillips. May 23, 1983, on the stage of Opryland, Nashville. Interviewed by Archie Campbell for Nashville Network TV.

Doug Poindexter. August 17, 1982, at his home, Memphis.

Smoochy Smith. August 18, 1982, at the Admiral Benbow Motel before a gig, Memphis.

J. M. Van Eaton. August 19, 1982, at Sam Phillips Recording Service, Memphis.

Marcus Van Story. May 18, 1983, at his home, Memphis.

Malcolm Yelvington. August 14, 1982, at the Mid-South Folklife Festival, Memphis; August 20, 1982, and May 20, 1983, at his home, Memphis.

RESOURCES

Magazines

Alan Clark publications: P.O. Box 1062, West Covina, Calif. 91793.

Blues Suede News: Marc Bristol, Box 25, Duvall, Wash. 98019.

Kicks: Billy Miller and Miriam Linna, Box 646 Cooper Station, New York, N.Y. 10003.

Nervous Breakdown: Steve Kelemen, P.O. Box 235, Stavely, Alberta T0L 1Z0, Canada. Published for members of the Eddie Cochran Canadian Fan Club.

Now Dig This: Trevor Cajiao, 69 Quarry Lane, South Shields, Tyne & Wear, NE34 7NW, England.

Original Cool: Sue Smallwood, 1533 Sea Breeze Trail, Suite 201, Virginia Beach, Va. 23452.

Red Hot Express: Anthony Sturiale, 100 Walnut St., Bloomfield, N.J. 07003.

Rockabilly Revue: Billy Poore, P.O. Box 100504, Nashville, Tenn. 37224.

Southern and Rocking: 117 Selhurst Rd., South Norwood, London, SE25 6LQ, England.

Record Mail Order

Hepcat Records: P.O. Box 1108, Orange, Calif. 92668.

Nervous: 7–11 Minerva Road, London, NW10 6HJ, England. Note: this company is unrelated to the New York–based company of the same name.

Rockhouse: Nieuwveenseweg 23, 2421 La Nieuwkoop, Holland.

Wax Trax Rockabilly: 638 E.13th Ave., Denver, Colo. 80203.

Film

Tear It Up! The Rockabilly Documentary: available from Greg Wolske, Lasso Productions, 706 S. Ninth St., Columbus, Ohio 43206.

Selected Discography

This list is necessarily selective, since this music goes in and out of print, gets repackaged in various configurations and formats, and is manufactured for different labels in different countries.

Artists are listed alphabetically, and their recordings are listed chronologically by recording date, as much as possible. Anthologies are presented in alphabetical order by original label (with subsidiary labels noted in parentheses), followed by the company's location, unless an anthology encompasses various labels. In that case, it is filed under the reissue company's name. For the anthologies, I give only the serial number if the release is on the same label as the category, but I provide the label and serial number if the release is on a label different from the original label.

All items listed are on CD unless the catalog number is preceded by "LP" (for vinyl albums), "EP" (extended play single), or "45" (for singles). Following the catalog number, the date of issue (not of recording) is given, when known. Recommended purchases are marked with an asterisk (*). Certain songs mentioned in the text are noted in the anthology section.

A basic collection of early rockabilly should include the Sun and early RCA recordings of Elvis Presley, as well as some work by other Sun artists, including Sonny Burgess, Billy Lee Riley, Warren Smith, Ray Smith, Malcolm Yelvington, Jerry Lee Lewis, Carl Perkins (plus his early Columbia recordings), and Roy Orbison.

A good starting place to hear a lot of the songs mentioned in the text is Rhino Records' two-volume CD *Rock This Town: Rockabilly Hits*, although some of the songs are not really rockabilly.

Anthologies are the best first approach for almost every artist, such as the following (although all have worthy full-length sets): Glen Glenn, Mac Curtis, Sid King and the Five Strings, Joe Poovey, Ronnie Self, Roy Hall, Johnny Carroll, the Collins Kids, and Janis Martin.

"Best of" albums that emphasize the rocking side are a good way to approach Eddie Cochran, Gene Vincent, Maddox Brothers and Rose, Bob Luman, Johnny Burnette and the Rock 'n' Roll Trio, Wanda Jackson, Ricky Nelson, Buddy Holly (plus *For the First Time Anywhere*), Charlie Feathers, and Marty Robbins. The complete 1950s works are the best bet for Joe Clay (nine songs) and Sonny Fisher (eight songs).

To understand where rockabilly came from, you need to hear Bill Monroe, Hank Williams, Moon Mullican, Bill Haley, some of the Sun blues artists, and a couple of collections of western swing, such as the series on Arhoolie.

Recommended revival albums by veterans include Jackie Lee Cochran's *Rockabilly Legend,* Ronnie Dawson's *Rockinitis,* and Mac Curtis's *Rockin' Mother.*

Among the best of the revivalist recordings are Billy Hancock's *Shakin' That Rockabilly Fever,* Hank C. Burnette's *Rockabilly Gasseroonie,* Handsome Ned's *The Ballad of . . . , Rockabilly Rebel* by Matchbox, and any "best of" set by the Stray Cats.

ARTISTS

The Beatles
Live at the BBC. EMI 7243 8 31796 2, 1994. Includes songs learned from Buddy Holly, Presley, and Carl Perkins and Eddie Fontaine's "Nothin' Shakin'."

Jeff Beck and the Big Town Playboys
Crazy Legs. Epic EK 53562, 1993. Gene Vincent's songs and style. Very well done, but hear the original versions first.

Steve Bloomfield
Rockabilly Originals. LP: Charly CR 30159, 1978. One-man band, all originals, good sound, hot guitar picking.

Tooter Boatman
Rockin' Tooter Boatman. LP: Collector CLCD 4408.
For Tooter Boatman Fans Only. White Label WLP 8895.

Eddie Bond
Rockin' Daddy. Bear Family BCD 15708 BH, 1993. Recordings from 1955 to 1962 for Ekko, Mercury, Sun, and Phillips International; mostly country but includes his 1956 rockabilly (if you want just that, get the *Mercury Rockabillies* anthology). This double CD also includes his 1962 album *Sings Greatest Country Gospel Hits.*
Rockin' Daddy. Stomper Time STCD 1. Covers the same period as the Bear Family issue but provides cuts from other labels.
Rockin' Daddy from Memphis Tennessee. LP: Rockhouse LP 8206. London recordings with the Dave Travis Band from 1982.

Bop Cats
Bop Cats. EP: Showtime Step 001, 1979. Four songs.

"Caroline"/"I Can't Help It." 45: Show Time 002, 1980.

Bop Cats. LP: Attic LAT 1113, 1981. Confident, nicely recorded, featuring well-arranged rockabilly covers and further explorations.

Wild Jungle Rock. LP: Attic LAT 1139. 1982. Strong band sound, still connected to the roots, still evolving.

As the Rock Angels: *Rock Angels.* EP: Attic ATT 1231, 1983. Four songs: big sound, more rock than rockabilly.

Boston Rockabilly Music Conspiracy

Get Goin'. LP: Black Rose BR 1003, 1986. Conviction and fire but mired by a stiff rhythm section.

Sonny Burgess

*The Classic Recordings 1956–1959. Bear Family BCD 15525. Sonny Burgess and the Pacers' complete Sun recordings on two CDs with a thirty-two-page booklet.

Sonny Burgess/Larry Donn. LP: White Label LP 8817. Donn sings ten (including six covers of Elvis's Sun songs and "Honey Bun"), and Burgess does "Brown-Eyed Handsome Man," plus three instrumentals.

Sonny Burgess & Bobby Crafford: Country Rock. LP: Caepe RZ-1001.

The Old Gang. LP: Charly CRM 2025, 1981. A few good tracks, but this reunion mostly lacks fire.

Spellbound. LP: Off Beat WIK 50, 1986. Decent but safe; with the Dave Travis Band in London.

Raw Deal. LP: Rockhouse LPL 8601, 1986. Almost the same album as *Spellbound.*

Tennessee Border. Hightone HCD 8039, 1992. Strong and tough, with a good band led by Dave Alvin. The voice is a little buried.

Hank C. Burnette

The Hank C. Burnette Sound. LP: United Rock Records 501. Early and sloppy; avoid it.

*Rockabilly Gasseroonie. LP: Sonet SNTF 750, 1977. Here Burnette has it all together; contains "Over the Rainbow."

Johnny Burnette/The Rock 'n' Roll Trio

*Johnny Burnette and the Rock-n-Roll Trio. MCA MCD 30489. The original Coral album with extra tracks: legendary and essential. Get this one or the next one listed.

*The Johnny Burnette Trio: Rockabilly Boogie. Bear Family BCD 15474. Superb.

Johnny and Dorsey Burnette: Together Again. LP: Solid Smoke SS 8005, 1980. Demos.

Johnny Burnette: We're Havin' a Party. LP: Rockstar RSRLP 1017, 1988. California recordings from 1958 to 1960, some with Dorsey. Upgraded with additional material on two CDs: *The Burnette Brothers* (Rockstar RSRCD 005, 1994) and *Johnny Burnette: That's the Way I Feel* (Rockstar RSRCD 006, 1994).

Ray Campi
The Original "Rockabilly" Album. Magnum Force CD MF 063, 1990. In 1973 this came out as *Rockabilly,* the first album on Rollin' Rock (LP 001). Contains recordings from the 1950s.
The Eager Beaver Boy/Rockabilly Lives. Bear Family BCD 15501, 1990. Repackage on one CD of Campi's second (1974) and fourth (1976) album for Rollin' Rock. The earlier is a one-man band effort and includes a tribute to Jimmie Skinner; the later has some backup.
Rockabilly Rebellion. LP: Rollin' Rock 6902, 1979. Selections from one-man band sessions, 1972–79.
*Rockabilly Music. LP: Rollin' Rock LP 023, 1980. Solid band, good recording, enjoyable set.
Rockin' at the Ritz. LP: Rounder 3046, 1980. Primarily one-man band approach.
With Friends in Texas. Flying Fish FF 70518, 1988. Ray's country album; some of the famous guests are barely audible.
Rockin' around the House (Ray Campi and the Bellhops). Rockhouse ROCKO 9313, 1993. Part country, part rockabilly, with a Dutch backup band.
Hollywood Cats. Part Records CD613.001, 1994. Rollin' Rock material from 1983.

Johnny Carroll
Crazy Hot Rock. LP: Charly CR 30241, 1985. Covers 1955–60.
Texabilly. LP: Rollin' Rock LP014, 1978. Home recordings.

Johnny Carroll and Judy Lindsey
Shades of Vincent. LP: Charly CR 30249, 1986. Lots of Gene Vincent songs. The band is good, Carroll's voice is fine, but Lindsey's thin voice is hard to take.

Johnny Cash
The Sun Years. LP: Sun Box 103. Three albums, which include "Get Rhythm," "Big River," and his demo of "Rock and Roll Ruby."

Joe Clay
*Ducktail. Bear Family BCD 15516, 1990. Includes the nine songs that make up his 1950s output, plus two alternate takes. The nine are also found on *Get Hot or Go Home,* an RCA anthology.
"Be Bop Boogie Bop"/"Rock Little Lily." 45: Mac 131. Recorded in Belgium.

Eddie Cochran
The Early Years. Ace CDCH 237.
Legendary Masters Series. LP: Liberty UAS 9959, 1971. Samples his whole career: early songs, session work, hits, and rarities.
*The Eddie Cochran Singles Album. LP: United Artists UAK 30244, 1979. His best-known work.
Singin' to My Baby/Never to Be Forgotten. EMI 07777-80240-26, 1993. Two classic albums on one CD.

The Eddie Cochran Legend. LP: Oxford OX 3179, 1980. Contains Cochran Brothers tracks, Kelly Four instrumentals, and live BBC radio recordings made just before his death.

Eddie Cochran and Gene Vincent: Rock 'n' Roll Heroes. LP: Rockstar RSR LP 1004, 1981.

Jackie Lee Cochran

Jackie Lee Waukeen Cochran: Swamp Fox. LP: Rollin' Rock LP 005.

*Rockabilly Legend. LP: Magnum Force MFLP 045, 1986. Satisfying 1977 recordings made for Rollin' Rock.

Collins Kids

Rockin' Rollin'. LP: Bear Family BFX 15074, 1981.

Ray Condo and his Hardrock Goners

Crazy Date. LP: Pipeline Pipe Dream 002, 1986. Their first.

Hot 'n' Cold. LP: Crazy Rekkids 001, 1988. Band's own label.

Condo Country. Crazy Rekkids CR003, 1990.

Come On! Fury FCD 3031, 1994. Manufactured in England.

The Cramps

Gravest Hits. LP: Illegal/IRS SP 501, 1977. Five songs recorded in Memphis; contains "The Way I Walk" and "Domino."

Songs the Lord Taught Us. LP: IRS SP 007, 1980. Includes "Tear It Up"; produced by Alex Chilton.

Psychedelic Jungle. LP: IRS SP70016, 1981. Contains "Rockin' Bones" and "Green Door."

*Bad Music for Bad People. LP: IRS 70042, 1984. With "Garbageman," "Uranium Rock," Charlie Feathers's "I Can't Hardly Stand It," and the Phantom's "Love Me."

Crazy Cavan and the Rhythm Rockers

Live at the Rainbow. LP: Charly CR 30139, 1978. Abundance of blues forms and walking bass.

Crazy Times. Instant INSD 5029, 1990. An anthology.

Mac Curtis

*Blue Jean Heart. Charly CD 264, 1991. All his King recordings.

Ruffabilly. LP: Rollin' Rock LP 002. Kind of rough.

*Rockin' Mother LP: Rollin' Rock Rad 22, 1979. Some of the best of his 1970s recordings for Rollin' Rock, accompanied by Ray Campi.

Ronnie Dawson

Rockin' Bones. No Hit CD 1, 1993. Collects his 1950s recordings.

*Rockinitis. LP: No Hit 004. Terrific set recorded in England.

Monkey Beat! No Hit CD 8, 1994. A new album plus the entire *Still a Lot of*

Rhythm album previously released on vinyl. Backed by members of the Planet Rockers, Big Sandy's Fly-Rite Boys, and the Tin Stars.

The Delmore Brothers
The Best of The Delmore Brothers. LP: Starday SLP 962, 1975. Includes "Hillbilly Boogie," "Freight Train Boogie," "Blues Stay Away from Me," "Pan American Boogie."

Levi Dexter
Levi & the Rockats: At the Louisiana Hayride. LP: Posh Boy PBS 126, 1981. Rough recording of a rough performance.
The Fun Sessions. LP.

Larry Donn: see under "Sonny Burgess"

Huelyn Duvall
The Challenge Masters. LP: Bear Family BFX 15200, 1987. His 1950s recordings.
Yesterday and Today. LP: White Label WLP 8923. One side contains tracks from Europe in 1985; the other has tracks from the 1950s.

Werly Fairburn
Everybody's Rockin'. Bear Family BCD 15578 AH. Good collection showing the varieties of his style.

Tav Falco's Panther Burns
Behind the Magnolia Curtain. LP: Rough Trade/Frenzi US16/FZ 400016, 1981. A festival of first-take raw energy to start a cult following.
Blow Your Top. LP: Frenzi 5000/Animal AEP 4001, 1982. Four more songs to add to the legacy of this unique character.
Red Devil. LP: Citadel CITLP 517. Great variety, weird songs; cool and wild.

Charlie Feathers
*Gone Gone Gone. Charly CD 278, 1991. The celebrated King recordings (all eight songs), plus seven Sun recordings (hillbilly) and eight lesser and later songs.
*Rock-A-Billy. Zu-Zazz ZCD 2011, 1991. Includes the four songs from the Zu-Zazz LP entitled *The Legendary 1956 Demo Session,* plus items from many other sessions between 1954 and 1973.
Rockabilly Rhythm! LP: Cowboy Carl CCLP 108, 1981. Drumless session from 1973; songs from the 1950s, 1940s, and the public domain; essentially a duo effort by Charlie (acoustic guitar, acoustic bass) and his son Bubba (electric guitar, electric bass). Half of it feels like a lost Sun album.
Good Rockin' Tonight! LP: Barrelhouse BH 03, 1974. Loose and homemade-sounding standards and originals, all idiosyncratic.
Volume 1. LP: Feathers FR 101, 1979. *Volume 2.* LP: Feathers FR 102, 1979. Beautifully packaged volumes. Two trips into Feathers territory. Takes a certain mood to get into much of it.

Original TV Sound Track NBC 1979: We're Getting Closer. LP: Lunar no. 2 L2M
    20015, 1981. Terrific; trio of father, son, and upright bass.

Uh Huh Honey. Norton CED-225. Late-1960s to late-1970s tracks; includes the
    Barrelhouse album *That Rockabilly Cat* and five songs from the preceding
    LP.

Charlie Feathers. Elektra Nonesuch American Explorer Series 7559-61147-2,
    1991. Typically inconsistent, with a supportive band of Sun all-stars. Some
    of it is just right.

Al Ferrier and his Boppin' Billies
The Birth of Rockabilly. LP: Goldband LP 7769. The title is inaccurate, but the
    album contains his best recordings.

Sonny Fisher
*Texas Rockabilly. LP: Ace 10 CH14. All his 1950s recordings.
King of Rockabilly. LP: Big Beat BBR 1016, 1983. Recorded in France.
Texas Rockabilly. Big Beat 7930722, 1990. Twenty-seven tracks, including half
    of the preceding album and others for the same label; five are live.

Johnny Dee Fury
Born to Bop. LP: Orient OLP 5, 1982. Cold and calculated.

Danny Gatton
Cruisin' Deuces. Elektra 9 61465-2, 1993. Virtuosic guitar playing, some rock-
    abilly.

Don Gibson
Rockin' Rollin'. LP: Bear Family BFX 15089, 1982. Excellent collection of pop
    country with a rockabilly tinge. Tracks from 1957 to 1961.

Glen Glenn
The Glen Glenn Story/Everybody's Movin' Again. Ace CDCH 403, 1992. A single
    CD reissue of two vinyl albums: the first (LP: Ace CH 57, 1982) is a nice
    set of alternate takes and live tracks; the second (LP: Ace CH 105, 1984) is
    1982 recordings, about half of which are just fine. First get the *Hollywood
    Rock 'n' Roll* anthology on Ace for his best songs.

Curtis Gordon
Rock, Roll, Jump & Jive. LP: Bear Family BFX 15181, 1985. Some rockabilly.

Robert Gordon
With Link Wray. LP: Private Stock PS 2030, 1977. His first album; the band is
    rock solid, bass is very electric, and Link Wray is forceful.

Fresh Fish Special. LP: RCA AFL1-3299, 1979. More 1977 recordings with Link
    Wray.

Rock Billy Boogie. LP: RCA AFL1 3294, 1979. Chris Spedding on guitar.

Bad Boy. LP: AFL1-3523, 1980.

Are You Gonna Be the One. LP: RCA Victor AFL1-3773, 1981. Danny Gatton on guitar.

*Robert Gordon Is Red Hot! Bear Family BCD 15446, 1989. An excellent overview, with songs from each of his first five albums, plus a couple of live tracks.

Black Slacks. Bear Family BCD 15489, 1990. A second volume collecting most of the remaining 1977–81 tracks.

Charlie Gracie

It's Charlie Gracie, It's Fabulous. Cotton Town Jubilee C7JCD2, 1995. Original recordings from 1951 to 1958. The hits plus the rarities.

Amazing Gracie. LP: Charly CR 30211, 1982. From sessions in England in 1981 with Dave Travis.

Buck Griffin

Let's Elope Baby. Bear Family BCD 15811 AH, 1995. All the Lin and MGM tracks, plus others into the early 1960s.

Bill Haley and his Comets

Hillbilly Haley. LP: Roller Coaster ROLL 2007, 1984. Contains tracks from 1948 to 1951, 1959 to 1960.

*Rock the Joint! Roller Coaster RCCD 3001, 1990. This CD replaces the label's earlier LP, which replaced an earlier ten-inch. Contains Essex cuts from 1951 to 1953, including "Rocket '88'," "Icy Heart," "Rockin' Chair on the Moon," "Crazy, Man, Crazy," and the title.

*Golden Hits. LP: MCA2 4010, 1972. Decca glory days.

*Mr. Rockin' Rollin': Essential Bill Haley. LP: Charley CDX 5, 1984. Contains material from the preceding issue, plus some different tracks.

Roy Hall

Boogie Rockabilly. LP: Rock & Country R&C 1008, 1981. His 1950s recordings.

Rock-A-Billy or Else! LP: Barrelhouse BH 016, 1981. Spirited sessions done in 1979 and 1980 in Memphis and Nashville; includes "Flat Foot Sam" and the remake of "Bedspring Motel."

Hank and the Hound. LP: Rock & Country R&C 1014, 1983. Hall rocks up the Hank Williams songbook.

"Flatfoot Sam"/"Is It Over George?" 45: Judd 1228.

Billy Hancock

*Billy Hancock And the Tennessee Rockets: Shakin' That Rockabilly Fever. LP: Solid Smoke SS 8015, 1981.

Hey! Little Rock and Roller. LP: Big Beat BBR 1013, 1983.

Handsome Ned

*The Ballad of . . . LP: Virgin VL 3064, 1989. A gem: find it, hear it, buy it.

High Noon
Show and Dance—the Rockabilly Trio. DOJCD 5013, 1990. Original songs, rockabilly and honky-tonk country styles, classic trio instrumentation.
Glory Bound. Cassette: Goofin' HN003, 1993. Hot sound, originals and rockabilly covers.
Stranger Things. Goofin' GRCD 6060, 1995. All original compositions, still in
rockabilly and country traditions.

Buddy Holly
Holly House. EP: Buddy Holly Memorial Society HH, 1986.
Live, Vol. 1. LP: Cricket Records C001000.
In Person, Vol. 2. LP: Cricket Records C002000.
*For the First Time Anywhere. CD: MCA CMCAD 31048, 1987. Undubbed re-
cordings, mostly from 1956; a treat.
*The Complete Buddy Holly. LP: MCA Coral CDSP 807, 1979. Six LPs.

Johnny Horton
*Rockin' Rollin' Johnny Horton. Bear Family BCD 15543. Excellent.

Wanda Jackson
Early Wanda Jackson. LP: Bear Family BFX 15109, 1983. The country record-
ings on Decca.
*Rockin' with Wanda. LP: Capitol CAPS 1007. Good selection.
Two Sides of Wanda. LP: Capitol T 2030, 1964.
Rock 'n' Roll Away Your Blues. LP: Varrick VR 025, 1986. A bit clinical; record-
ed in 1984 in Sweden.

Johnny Jano
King of Louisiana Rockabilly: The Legendary Jay Miller Sessions, Vol. 10. LP: Flyright LP 531, 1977. A few good ones.

George Jones
*White Lightning. LP: Ace CH 117, 1984. His rockabilly gems.

Rusty Kershaw and Doug Kershaw
With Wiley Barkdull: The Legendary Jay Miller Sessions, Vol. 22. LP: Flyright FLY
571, 1981.

Sid King and the Five Strings
Rockin' on the Radio. LP: Roller Coaster ROLL 2006, 1983. Fascinating time
warp: radio shows from 1954 and 1955. The band is talented and polished.
*Gonna Shake This Shack Tonight. LP: Bear Family BFX 15048, 1980. Their
1950s recordings.
Let's Get Loose. LP: Rockhouse LP 8701, 1987. Sessions from 1979 and 1980;
thoughtful arrangements and tasteful playing.

Buddy Knox
Party Doll. LP: Pye NSPL 28243. His 1950s best.
*The Best of Buddy Knox. Rhino R2 70964, 1990. The song selection on this is
   similar to that of the preceding LP; get one or the other.
Party Doll. Rockster RSRCD 004, 1993. Contains 1979 and 1982 recordings
   with backing by Dave Travis and his band, plus three more from 1987.
   Thirty-two tracks in all.

Sleepy LaBeef
Early, Rare and Rockin' Sides. LP: Charly CR 30181. The rocking ones are rec-
   ommended.
1977 Rockabilly. LP: Sun 1004, 1979. Decent.
Downhome Rockabilly. LP: Sun 1014, 1979. Heavy-handed.
Electricity. LP: Rounder 3070, 1982. A mix of decent and awful.
Nothin' but the Truth. LP: Rounder 3072, 1987. A live set with unappealing
   sound and unsubtle, under-rehearsed backing.
*Strange Things Happening. Rounder CD 3129, 1994. The one we waited for:
   good, energetic, well-recorded music.

Brenda Lee
The Early Years. LP: MCL 1792, 1984. Includes "Jambalaya," "One Step at a
   Time," and "Doodle Bug Rag."

Jerry Lee Lewis
The Ultimate. CD Sun Box 4. Complete (or nearly) sessions from 1956 to 1963
   on eleven CDs: 161 songs and 318 tracks, counting alternates. Recom-
   mended if you want to hear that much. A similar edition is *The Classic
   Jerry Lee Lewis* on Bear Family (BCD 15420), containing eight CDs. An ear-
   lier twelve-disc vinyl version is *The Sun Years* (Sun 102).
The Killer's Private Stash. Electrovert EV CD 3001. Contains two songs from a
   1954 acetate done in Shreveport, two songs from the 1968 production of
   Othello, and outtakes from the *Great Balls of Fire* soundtrack.
*Great Balls of Fire. Charly Classic CDCD 1153. Nice collection of mostly Sun
   tracks.
*All Killer, No Filler! The Jerry Lee Lewis Anthology. Rhino R2 71216. Double
   CD set with forty-two songs, from the 1950s to the 1970s.

Bob Luman
*Wild Eyed Woman. LP: Bear Family BFX 15268, 1988. The 1955 demos and
   1957 sessions.

Maddox Brothers and Rose
1946–1951, Vol. 1. LP: Arhoolie 5016, 1976.
1946–1951, Vol. 2. LP: Arhoolie 5017.
On the Air, Vol. 1. LP: Arhoolie 5028.
On the Air, Vol. 2. LP: Arhoolie 5033.

Rockin' Rollin'. LP: Bear Family BFX 15076, 1981. Choice set.
Maddox Brothers and Rose. LP: King 677.

The Magnetics
Rockabilly Fools! LP: Rollin' Rock LP 025, 1981. Good, not great.

Carl Mann
Rockin' Love. Charly CD 93, 1987. Sun material.
Gonna Rock 'n' Roll Tonight. LP: Charly CRL 5008, 1978. One side live: enjoy-
    able 1978 recordings with the Dave Travis band.

Janis Martin
*The Female Elvis: Complete Recordings, 1956–60. Bear Family BCD 15406, 1987.

Matchbox
Riders in the Sky. LP: Charly CR 30157, 1976.
*Rockabilly Rebel. LP: Sire SRK 6087, 1979. Has the hits.
Midnight Dynamos. LP: MCA 5246, 1981.
Flying Colours. LP: Magnet MG 5042, 1981.
Crossed Line. LP: Magnet MAGL 5052, 1982.
Going Down Town. LP: Sun Jay SJLP 570.

Memphis Rockabilly Band
Jeff Spencer—from Boston to Memphis. LP: Big Beat BBR 0016, 1981. Ten-inch
    EP of five songs representing their live show.
Betty Jean. LP: Blind Pig BP 2186, 1986. Good guitar playing, but the band is
    not well served by the mix or overall sound. All songs but one are origi-
    nal, but none is outstanding.

The Meteors
In Heaven. LP: Lost Soul LOST LP3001, 1981. Psychobilly roots.

The Million Dollar Quartet
The Complete Million Dollar Session. Charly 102, 1988. Legendary, informal,
    and worth hearing.

Hank Mizell
We're Gonna Bop Tonight. LP: Baron EP-801. The score: country, 5; rockabilly,
    3. Sessions from 1958 and from 1979 to 1981.

Bill Monroe
*Bill Monroe and his Bluegrass Boys: 16 All-Time Greatest Hits. LP: Columbia
    CS 1065. Has "Rocky Road Blues," "Little Cabin Home on the Hill," the
    original "Blue Moon of Kentucky," and other classics.
The Best of Bill Monroe. LP: MCA2-4090, 1975. Contains the post-Elvis ver-
    sion of "Blue Moon of Kentucky."

Moon Mullican
*Seven Nights to Rock, The King Years, 1946–56. LP: Western 2001.

Ricky Nelson
*Ricky Nelson. LP: United Artists UAS 9960, 1971. Well-chosen double LP of his best early work. Part of UA's Legendary Master series.

Herald Nix
One Night Only. LP: Record WRC 22703, 1983. Six songs that give an idea of how good they were live.

Roy Orbison
The Teen Kings: Are You Ready? Rollercoaster RCCD 3012, 1995. From 1956 TV broadcasts in Odessa, Texas. Ten vocal and six instrumental performances, plus a recent interview with band members.
*The Sun Years 1956–1958. Bear Family BCD 15461, 1989. All the Sun masters, none of the later overdubs.

Orion
New Beginnings. LP: Aron RDR 13, 1989. "Down in Mississippi" and a couple more of interest.

The Paladins (Canada)
R&R. Star SR004, 1984

The Paladins (U.S.)
The Paladins. Cassette: Wrestler WR1687, 1987.

Carl Perkins
*The Classic Carl Perkins. Bear Family BCD 15494. His greatest work on five CDs. An earlier vinyl look at his work is *The Sun Years* (LP: Sun Box 101), all the Sun recordings—1954–57—on three albums.
Whole Lotta Shakin'. LP: Columbia CL 1234, 1958. First Columbia album.
Ol' Blue Suede's Back. LP: Jet/United Artists UALA 856, 1978. Good set of rock 'n' roll standards.
Carl Perkins. LP: Dot MCA 39035, 1985. A couple of remakes and some strong country compositions.

The Polecats
The Polecats Are Go! LP: Mercury 6359 057, 1981. Mostly originals, plus "How High the Moon" and David Bowie's "John, I'm Only Dancing."

Groovey Joe Poovey
Yesterday & Today. LP: Dee Jay Jamboree DJLP 2054, 1986. One side is from the 1950s, and the other side is from the 1980s.

Elvis Presley
The King of Rock 'n' Roll: The Complete '50s Masters. BMG 660502-07863, 1992.
  Four-CD set of Sun, RCA, and live tracks. This instant library includes the
  songs from his first acetate and those from *The Sun Sessions CD* (RCA 6414-
  2-R), his first two RCA albums, other early hits, and more. The Sun material appeared on vinyl as *The Complete Sun Sessions* (RCA 6414-1-R, 1987)
  and *The Elvis Presley Sun Collection* (RCA KPMI 0153).
The Legend Begins. Magnum Force CD MF 086, 1992. Live from the *Louisiana Hayride* and two other locations, 1954–56, plus an interview. Not studio quality, but the energy is electric.
Elvis Country. LP: RCA AYL-1 3956, 1971. Contains "The Fool," "Whole Lotta Shakin' Goin' On," and songs by Bob Wills, Bill Monroe ("Little Cabin
  on the Hill"), and Ernest Tubb.
Reconsider Baby. LP: RCA AFL1-5418, 1985. Elvis sings blues.

Vern Pullens
Vern Pullens. LP: Rockhouse CEL 6308, 1985. Decent mini-LP with "Elvis Stole
  My Baby."

Marvin Rainwater
Whole Lotta' Woman. Bear Family BCD 15812-AH, 1994. The best of his rock
  'n' roll, with some hillbilly.

Razorbacks
Go to Town. LP: WEA 25 56961. The Canadian band: forceful and good.
Live a Little. LP: WEA 25 63731, 1989. Contains "My Generation."

Charlie Rich
Original Hits and Midnight Demos. LP: Sun CDX 10, 1985. Good collection but
  omits "Break Up."

Billy Lee Riley
Classic Recordings, 1956–1960. Bear Family BCD 15444, 1990. Double CD with
  all his Sun material, including unissued songs and alternate takes, plus
  four from Riley's own Rita label.
Vintage. LP: Cowboy Carl CCLP 105, 1980. Famous songs, ordinary versions.
Blue Collar Blues. Hightone HCD 8040, 1992.

Marty Robbins
Rockin' Rollin' Robbins. LP: Bear Family BFX 15045, 1982. Excellent, covers
  1954–58.

Rockats
Make That Move. LP: RCA MFL1 8507, 1983. Highly arranged, nicely recorded, very good. One side is new wave, and the other is rockabilly.

Rock 'n' Roll Trio: see under "Johnny Burnette"

Jack Scott
The Way I Walk. Roller Coaster RCCD 3002, 1990. All his released material
   from ABC and Carleton, plus three; contains all his best early material.

Ronnie Self
Bop-A-Lena. Bear Family BCD 15436, 1990.

The Shakin' Pyramids
Skin 'Em Up. LP: Cuba Libre/Virgin VL 2217, 1981. A breath of fresh air.
Celts and Cobras. LP: Cuba Libre/Virgin V2216, 1982.

Jack Smith and the Rockabilly Planet
Jack Smith and the Rockabilly Planet. LP: Flying Fish FF510, 1988.

Ray Smith
Rockin' with Ray. Sun 32, 1991. His entire Sun output, including the five song
   demo that led to his contract.
It's Great, It's Ray Smith. LP: Judd 75-002. Late 1950s and early 1960s record-
   ings.
Sun Recording Artist Ray Smith Live in '62. LP: Wix 1002, 1981. Interesting and
   worth hearing.
I'm Gonna Rock Some More. LP: Wix 1000. Tries too hard.
The Rocking Side. LP: Boot BOS 7182, 1979. Recorded live in Holland, 1979.

Warren Smith
Classic Recordings 1956–1959. Bear Family BCD 15514, 1992. Complete Sun
   , output.
The Last Detail. LP: Charly CRM 2026, 1981. Not much spark.

Andy Starr
Dig Them Squeaky Shoes. Bear Family BCD 15845 AH, 1995. Early gems up to
   1963. If you don't get this one, then get the MGM collection with his tracks.

Shakin' Stevens
A Legend. LP: EMI Nut 25, 1970.
Shakin Stevens and the Sunsets at the Rockhouse. LP: Magnum Force MFLP 004,
   1981. Contains "Reet Petite"; originally issued in 1976 as *C'mon Memphis*
   (Dynamite label of Holland).
Take One! LP: Epic EPC 83978, 1979. One of his very best.
You Drive Me Crazy. LP: Epic PEC 90672, 1981. Strong set with "This Old
   House," "Revenue Man," "Let Me Show You How," "Green Door," and "Hot
   Dog."
Shakin' Stevens and the Sunsets. LP: RCA KYL1 0525, 1983.
Greatest Hits. LP: Epic EPC 10047, 1984. For the rockabilly hits.

Stray Cats
Built for Speed. LP: EMI America ST 17070, 1982. What their reputation stands
on. Get this or a greatest hits such as *Back to the Alley* on Arista 260 963
(twenty songs) or *Rock This Town* on EMI USA CDP-7-94975-2 (ten songs).
Rant 'n' Rave with the Stray Cats. LP: EMI America SQ 17102, 1983.
Rock Therapy. LP: EMI America ST-17226, 1986. Heavy-handed.
Blast Off. LP: EMI E1-91401, 1989.
Choo Choo Hot Fish. Attic ACD 1341, 1992. Renewed energy.
Something Else. Receiver RRCD 184, 1994. Live tracks.

Gene Summers
School of Rock and Roll. Collector CLCD 4420, 1994. A "best of" collection
with tracks from the 1950s to the 1970s.
In Nashville. LP: Big Beat BBR 0011, 1980. A 10-inch LP of standards to cash
in on the revival, backed by some Nashville session musicians.

The Sun Rhythm Section
Old Time Rock 'n' Roll. LP: Flying Fish FF 445, 1987. More fun in concert than
on record.

Hayden Thompson
Rockabilly Guy 1954–1962. LP: Charly 30262, 1986. Half of it is great.
Booneville Mississippi Flash. LP: Charly CR 30245, 1985. The rockabilly is ex-
cellent, but there is more country. Appealing sound and atmosphere.

Dave Travis
Dave's Rock and Roll Album. Dial LP 005, 1978. Mixed bag of tracks from 1963
to 1977; contains "Old Country Rock."
Jukebox Cadillac. Tonpress Sx-T 174, 1990. Eighteen tracks selected from his
Rockabilly Killer (1980) and *Let's Flat Get It* (1988) albums: some of his best.

Conway Twitty
The Best of Conway Twitty, Volume 1: Rockin' Years. Mercury P2 49574, 1994.
"Long Black Train," "It's Only Make Believe," and eighteen others; a mix
of rockabilly, rock 'n' roll and pop on Mercury and MGM.

Marcus Van Story
Drinkin' Wine Spo-Dee-Oh-Dee! LP: Barrelhouse BH 011, 1977. Recorded in 1974
and 1976. Of the nine songs sung by Van Story, six are from Elvis's repertory; Malcolm Yelvington sings two, and they sing duet on one other. Spotty.

Gene Vincent
Bluejean Bop! LP: Capitol T764.
Gene Vincent and his Bluecaps. LP: Capitol T8111.
The Gene Vincent Singles Album. LP: Capitol EST 26223, 1981. Twenty of his
best.

Eddie Cochran and Gene Vincent: Rock 'n' Roll Heroes. LP: Rockstar RSR LP 1004, 1981.

Forever. LP: Rollin' Rock LP 022, 1980. His last four American recordings plus tributes and covers by Johnny Carroll, Ray Campi, and others.

Malcolm Yelvington
*Gonna Have Myself a Ball: The Complete 1950's Recordings. LP: Sun 1010, 1988. Sun and Meteor tracks.

Neil Young
Everybody's Rockin'. LP: Geffen, 1983. Neil goes rockabilly.

REISSUE ANTHOLOGIES

ABC-Paramount (and Dot): New York, N.Y.
Cotton Pickin' Rock. LP: ABC 5247. Contains Danny Wolfe's "Let's Flat Get It," Vince Everett's "Baby, Let's Play House," Lloyd (Cowboy) Copas's "Circle Rock," Jimmy Newman's "Carry On," and a less frantic take of the Phantom's "Love Me," plus one each from Jack Scott, Ronnie Self, Sanford Clark, and others.

Ace (various labels): England
*Rockabilly Fever. CDCH 218, 1987. Twenty-two tracks including Glen Glenn, Sleepy LaBeef, Pat Cupp, Hal Harris, Link Davis, and others.
Rockabilly Shakeout. CDCHD 191, 1987. Tracks from Starday (sixteen), various Memphis labels (eight), and one from Miami. The following three entries are all 10-inch albums with ten songs.
*Rockabilly Party. LP: 10 CH 17, 1978. Some great songs from Hal Harris ("Jitterbop Baby" and "I Don't Know When"), Link Davis ("Trucker from Tennessee"), Rock Rogers ("Little Rock Rock" and "That Ain't It"), Benny Barnes ("One of These Days"), and others.
Kings Of Rockabilly, Vol. 1. LP: 10 CH 18.
Kings Of Rockabilly, Vol. 2. LP: 10 CH 19, 1980. Features three great Sleepy LaBeef songs.

Bandera (and Laredo): Chicago, Ill.
Bandera Rockabillies. LP: JSP Records 1005, 1979. A few good ones, but little actual rockabilly.

Bop Cat (various labels)
We Wanna Boogie: Original Memphis Rockabilly. LP: 200. Sun gang.
Goin' Back to Memphis. LP: 400. Artists with Sun connections on cuts from Sun and other labels.

Bullet: Nashville, Tenn.
Nashville Country Rock, Vol. 1. LP: Redita LP 109. Honky-tonk and country

boogie; includes two early Roy Hall songs, as well as songs by Leon Payne ("Lost Highway"), Johnny Lee Wills, Ray Price, and others.

Capitol: Los Angeles, Calif.
That'll Flat . . . Git It! Vol. 3. Bear Family BCD 15624 AH. From the Capitol vaults.
Capitol Rockabilly Originals. LP: CAPS 1009, 1977. Country, boogie, and rockabilly, with Jimmy Heap's "Sebbin Come Elebin" and songs by Ferlin Husky/Simon Crum ("Slow Down Brother"/"Bop Cat Bop"), Rose Maddox, and others.
Rock 'n' Roll at the Capitol Tower, Vol. 1. LP: 2S15085029/30. Between this and the two further volumes, double albums each, we get lots of Skeets McDonald ("You Oughta See Grandma Rock" and "Heart-Breakin' Mama" are on vol. 1), Wanda Jackson, Tommy Sands ("The Worryin' Kind" is on vol. 1), Jerry Reed ("I Have Had Enough" is on vol. 1), a few from Jack Scott and Bob Luman, and one each from Gene Vincent and Johnny Burnette, plus others. Not much rockabilly.

Cascade (various labels)
Twenty Great Rockabilly Hits of the 50's. LP: Drop 1003. Great mostly, but not hits.

Chess (and Checker and Argo): Chicago, Ill.
Chess Rockabillies. LP: 9124213, 1978. Lots to like on this twenty-tracker, including "Look Out Mabel" by G. L. Crockett, Eddie Fontaine's "Nothin' Shakin'," Rusty York's "Sugaree," and "Love Me" by Jimmy Lee and Wayne Walker.

Columbia: New York, N.Y.
Rockabilly Stars, Vol. 1. LP: Epic EG 37618, 1981; CD: CBS Special Products A 37618, 1991. Read the title carefully: (almost) all these artists did rockabilly, but not everything they do here is rockabilly. Lots of it is, however, and anyway, almost everything here is great. This is the first in the series of double albums (single CDs), beautifully packaged with hand-colored photos. First album covers 1954–60; second covers 1960–78. Includes songs by the Everly Brothers, Little Jimmie Dickens ("Rockin' with Red"), Marty Robbins ("That's All Right"), the Collins Kids ("Party"), Carl Perkins ("Pink Pedal Pushers" and three more), later work by Mac Curtis, Bob Luman, Charlie Rich, Johnny Cash ("I Will Rock and Roll with You"), and more.
Rockabilly Stars, Vol. 2. LP: Epic EG 37621, 1981; CD: Columbia Special Products A 37621, 1991. Same format as the preceding with many of the same names, plus Rick Nelson, Sleepy Labeef, Sid King and the Five Strings, Johnny Cash, Billy Lee Riley, and others. Includes Carl Perkins's "Daddy Sang Bass."
Rockabilly Stars, Vol. 3. LP: Epic EG 37984, 1982; CD: Sony Music Special Products A 37984, 1993. Excellent selection, all from the 1950s, featuring many

famous names. Tracks include Carl Perkins's "Pop, Let Me Have the Car" and "Because You're Mine," Ronnie Self's "Rocky Road Blues," and Leon Smith's "Little Forty Ford."

CBS Rockabilly Classics, Vol. 1. LP: CBS 82401, 1977. With the Collins Kids' "Hoy Hoy," Cliff Johnson's "Go 'Way Hound Dog," Freddie Hart's "Dig Boy Dig," Bobby Lord's "Beautiful Baby," and Jimmy Murphy's "Grandpa's a Cat," plus songs by Marty Robbins, Johnny Horton, and others.

CBS Rockabilly Classics, Vol. 2. LP: CBS 82993, 1978. With Little Jimmie Dickens "(I Got) A Hole in My Pocket," Ronnie Self's "Rocky Road Blues," Bobby Lord's "No More, No More, No More!" Eddie Zack and Cousin Richie's "I'm Gonna Rock and Roll," and Rose Maddox's "Wild Wild Young Men," plus songs by Marty Robbins, the Collins Kids, Sid King, and others.

CBS, Epic & OKeh Rockabilly, Vol. 3. LP: CBS 83911, 1979. Good set with Ronnie Self, the Collins Kids, Sid King and the Five Strings, Johnny Horton, and others.

Decca (and Coral): New York, N.Y.

Rare Rockabilly, Vol. 1. LP: MCA 203757. All volumes in this series have twenty tracks. This volume includes four each from Johnny Carroll, Roy Hall, and Don Woody, plus Autry Inman's "Be Bop Baby," Peanut Wilson's "Cast Iron Arm," Arlie Duff's "Alligator Come Across," and more.

Rare Rockabilly, Vol. 2. LP: MCF 2789, 1977. Tracks by Jackie Lee Cochran, Roy Hall, Johnny Carroll, Billy Lee Riley, Eddie Fontaine ("Cool It Baby"), Bobby Helms ("Tennessee Rock 'n' Roll"), Wayne Raney ("Shake Baby Shake"), Roy Duke ("Behave, Be Quiet or Be Gone"), and others.

Rare Rockabilly, Vol. 3. LP: MCF 2833, 1978. More on the country side; includes Red Foley's "Crazy Little Guitar Man" and Autry Inman's "It Would Be a Doggone Lie."

Rare Rockabilly, Vol. 4. LP: MCF 3035, 1979. Tracks by Moon Mullican, Webb Pierce, Eddie Fontaine ("One and Only"), Patsy Cline ("Got a Lot of Rhythm in My Soul"), and others on the "billy" side.

That'll Flat . . . Git It! Vol. 2. Bear Family BCD 15623 AH, 1992. Contains thirty of the best tracks from the previous four albums.

Rare Rock 'n' Roll, Vol. 1. LP: Coral CDL 8507. Like a volume 5 in the *Rare Rockabilly* series but more on the rock side. Has Roy Hall's "Blue Suede Shoes," Bob Wills's "So Let's Rock," Billy Lee Riley's "Rockin' on the Moon."

Rockabilly Boogie. LP: MCL 1504, 1981. Twenty rockabilly gems, including songs by Johnny Burnette Trio, Johnny Carroll, and Buddy Holly, as well as Cowboy Copas's "Circle Rock," Webb Pierce's "Teenage Boogie," and George Hamilton IV's "If You Don't Know."

Rockabilly Classics, Vol. 1. LP: 25088, 1987. Just ten songs, all recorded at Owen Bradley's Nashville studio, including Clint Miller's "Bertha Lou" and Buddy Holly's "Rock-A-Bye Rock."

Rockabilly Classics, Vol. 2. LP: 25089, 1987. Another skimpy ten-song set; includes Roy Hall's "You Ruined My Blue Suede Shoes" and Brenda Lee's "Bigelow 6-200."

Eagle (various labels)
At the Rockhouse, Vol. 5. LP: 315, 1981. Competent white rock from 1957 to
1960 with some pop, rockabilly, and country touches. Lots of blues-form
variations. Andy Anderson is the best-known name.

Era: Hollywood, Calif.
Hollywood Rock 'n' Roll. Ace CDCHM 1, 1989. Glen Glenn is the star here with
six great songs; also includes Dorsey Burnette's "Great Shakin' Fever," Dick
Busch's "Hollywood Party," Don Deal's "Don't Push," one by Alis Lesley,
and more.

Erwin (and other labels run by Marshall Ellis): Memphis, Tenn.
Memphis Rockabilly. LP: Ace CH 167, 1986. Highlights include two by Eddie
Bond, Hoyt Johnson's "Eenie Meenie Minie Mo," Pat Ferguson's "Fool I
Am," and Ray Scott's "Boppin' Wig Wam Willie."

Esoldun (various labels): France
Rockin' and Boppin'. LP: RR 2004. Obscure rock and rockabilly from 1958 to
1961.
Groovie Boogie Woogie Boy. LP: RR 2014. Includes Roy Hall's "Dirty Boogie"
and "Okee Doaks"; title is by Webb Pierce.

Fernwood: Memphis, Tenn.
Fernwood Rock and Roll. LP: Redita RLP 119. Postrockabilly cuts by Glenn Honeycutt, Scotty Moore, Bill Black's Combo, and others.

Flyright (various labels plus first issues): England
Get with It! LP: 556, 1980. Subtitled "Memphis-style rockabilly and country";
covers 1954–78 with Marcus Van Story, Smokey Joe Baugh, Malcolm Yelvington, Howard Serratt, Charlie Feathers, and others.

Goldband: Lake Charles, La.
Swampcats Beat. LP: Goldband GCL-117, 1984. Four of Al Ferrier's best, one
by Johnny Jano, plus others.

Hickory: Nashville, Tenn.
Hillbilly Rock. Magnum Force CDMF 034, 1991. Tracks produced by Wesley
Rose in Nashville, 1954–60, plus one from 1965. Includes two by Rusty
and Doug Kershaw (one is the essential "Hey Mae"), plus songs by Melvin
Endsley and others in boogie, up-tempo hillbilly, and light rockabilly
styles. Backing by Nashville studio all stars (Atkins, Garland, Cramer, etc.).

Imperial: Hollywood, Calif.
Imperial Rockabillies. LP: UAS 30101, 1977. Decent set; includes Bob Luman's
"Red Hot," Roy Brown's "Hip Shakin' Baby," and songs by the Strikes, the
Burnette Brothers, Laura Lee Perkins, and others.

Imperial Rockabillies, Volume 2. LP: UAS 30173, 1979. More from the artists in volume 1 and others.

Imperial Rockabillies, Volume 3. LP: Liberty-United 2C 068-83096, 1981. More from Luman, the Strikes, and L. L. Perkins, plus Dorsey Burnette's "It's Late," Jackie Dee's "Buddy," and others.

King (and Federal): Cincinnati, Ohio

*King-Federal Rockabillys. LP: King 5016X, 1978. Celebrated King sessions of Mac Curtis ("Say So," "Little Miss Linda," "Grandaddy's Rockin'," and two more) and Charlie Feathers ("One Hand Loose," "Bottle to the Baby," and two more), plus Hank Mizell's "Jungle Rock," Joe Penny's "Bip a Little, Bop a Lot," Ronnie Molleen's "Rockin' Up," and more.

Mar-Vel: Hammond, Ind.

The Mar-Vel Masters: Get with the Beat. Ryko RCD 20126, 1989. Contains twenty-seven tracks from the 1950s and 1960s on Harry Glenn's independent label. Various flavors of country and rock.

Mercury: Chicago, Ill.

Mercury Rockabillies. LP: 6463, 1975. Featuring Eddie Bond (four songs), Conway Twitty, J. P. Richardson (the Big Bopper), Curtis Gordon ("Draggin'") and one more), and others.

I Want a Rock & Roll Guitar. LP: Redita LP 112. Features Eddie Bond (three songs), Curtis Gordon (two), Jimmy Edwards's "Love Bug Crawl," and others. No duplicates to the previous album.

Meteor: Memphis, Tenn.

Meteor Rockabillies. Ace CDCHM 484, 1993. Twenty-four tracks, with songs by Charlie Feathers, Malcolm Yelvington (as Mac Sales), Jess Hooper's only single, and others.

MGM: New York, N.Y.

*MGM Rockabilly Collection. LP: Super 2315 394. Eight great Andy Starr and six great Buck Griffin songs, plus Carson Robison's "Rockin' and Rollin' with Granmaw," Bob Gallion's "My Square Dancin' Mama (She Done Learned to Rock 'n' Roll)," and songs by Marvin Rainwater.

MGM Rockabilly Collection, Vol. 2. LP: Mid Price 2354147, 1981. Conway Twitty's "Long Black Train," plus songs by Marvin Rainwater ("Hot and Cold" and five more) and others.

Modern (and Kent and RPM): Culver City, Calif.

Modern Rock 'n' Roll and Rockabilly. LP: Ace CH 185, 1986. Highlights are the five songs by Pat Cupp, Johnny Todd's "Pink Cadillac," and two by Jesse James.

Moon: Memphis, Tenn.

The 50's Rock on the Moon. LP: MR 3010, 1980. Variety set from Cordell Jackson's label, some rockabilly. Inspired Tav Falco.

RCA Victor: New York, N.Y.

Victor Rock 'n' Rollers. LP: RCA INTS 5166, 1979. Twenty good ones, including four by Joe Clay, two by Janis Martin, and Pee Wee King's "Blue Suede Shoes."

Get Hot or Go Home: Vintage RCA Rockabilly '56–'59. Country Music Foundation CMF-014-D, 1988. Double album (or single CD) contains all nine of Joe Clay's 1950s songs, seven by Rick Cartey, and three from Janis Martin (two live at the *Opry* in 1957), as well as songs from Roy Orbison, David Houston, Martha Carson, Homer and Jethro's "Two Tone Shoes," and more.

That'll Flat . . . Git It! Vol. 1. Bear Family BCD 15622 AH, 1993.

Redita (various labels): Holland

The Sound of Rockabilly. LP: 102.

Memphis Rocks the Country. LP: 104.

Shelby County Country 1948–'74. LP: 110. Grab bag of mostly Memphis artists, plus Hank Williams with added echo ("Window Shopping").

Rhino (various labels): Los Angeles, Calif.

Rock This Town: Rockabilly Hits, Vol. 1. R2 70741; *Rock This Town: Rockabilly Hits, Vol. 2.* R2 70742. Almost ninety minutes of quality music from the known to the obscure, although a few selections do not fit under this title.

Roulette: New York, N.Y.

Roulette Rock 'n' Roll Collection. LP: Pye NSPL 28245. Contains three by Jimmy Lloyd ("Rocket in My Pocket"), plus songs from Jimmy Bowen, Johnny Rivers, Mack Vickery, the Rock-A-Teens ("Janis Will Rock"), and others.

Rounder (various labels): Somerville, Mass.

Wild, Wild Young Women. LP: 1031. Terrific set of female rockabilly with Janis Martin, Lorrie Collins, Rose Maddox, and others, including Sparkle Moore's "Skull and Crossbones" and the Davis Sisters' "Rock-A-Bye Boogie."

Starday (and Dixie): Beaumont, Texas

Starday-Dixie Rockabillys, Vol. 1. LP: Gusto GD 5017, 1979. Fine set of Texas rockabilly: Link Davis ("Sixteen Chicks"), Rudy "Tutti" Grayzell ("Ducktail" and "Jig-Ga-Lee-Ga"), Joe Poovey, Sonny Fisher, and others.

Starday-Dixie Rockabillys, Vol. 2. LP: Gusto GD 5031, 1979. Contains the same artists as does volume 1; also has "Grasshopper Rock" by Link Davis, plus Thumper Jones.

Best of Dixie: Super Rare Rock-A-Billy Recordings, Vol. 1. LP: Million 1. A set of custom-label cuts, of occasional interest. Various kinds of 1950s country, some rockabilly. Ditto for the other three volumes. Reissue from Holland.

Rarest Rockabilly and Hillbilly Boogie and *The Best of Ace Rockabilly.* Ace CD-CHD 311, 1991. Two albums on one CD: the first, from the custom series, includes Rock Rogers's "My Baby Left Me." The second is a great set, mostly from Starday (regular sessions).

Sun: Memphis, Tenn.

Sun material has been presented many times and by many companies. The Charly label in England issued series on vinyl: *The Roots of Rock* had thirteen volumes, the *Legendary Sun Performers* and *Sun Sounds Special* series both ran to at least seven volumes, *The Best of Sun Rockabilly* came in two volumes, and many other albums under other titles. Charly in France issued its own series, including a 10-inch format that carried ten songs each. For this discography, the only Sun vinyl records I list are two box sets.

*Sun Records The Rockin' Years. LP: Sun Box 106, 1986. Twelve LPs, deluxe notes, stars and unknowns, no songwriter credits.

*The Sun Country Years 1950–'59. LP: Bear Family BFX 15211 (11) VA, 1986. Super deluxe: ten albums, color (and colored) photo sleeves, 128-page booklet. Complete (or almost complete) Sun recordings of Warren Smith, Harmonica Frank Floyd, Malcolm Yelvington, and (obviously) so much more.

*The Sun Story, Vol. 1—Sunrise. Instant CD INS 5039, 1990.

*The Sun Story, Vol. 2—Rockabilly Rhythm. Instant CD INS 5040, 1990. On vinyl this was called *The Sun Box* (Charly Sun Box 100). The two CDs cover blues, country, and rockabilly in a good overview, if weighted toward Johnny Cash (seven of fifty-four tracks).

*The Ultimate Sun Rockabilly Collection. Disky DCD 5202, 1991.

*The Ultimate Memphis Rockabilly Collection, Vol. 2. Disky Memphis 04, 1993.

*The Ultimate Sun Rock 'n' Roll Collection. Disky DCD 5203, 1991.

*The Ultimate Memphis Rock 'n' Roll Collection, Vol. 2. Disky Memphis 06, 1993. All the preceding Disky items are two-CD sets, each with more than fifty songs; compiled by Dave Travis, manufactured in Holland. Companion sets cover country and blues.

*The Sun Records Collection. Rhino R2 71780, 1994. Three CDs giving a comprehensive overview. A good place to start.

*Memphis Rocks: Rockabilly in Memphis. Smithsonian 2705. Contains eighteen of the best-known songs, with Lewis, Cash, Orbison, and others.

WEA (various labels)

Red Hot Rock-A-Billies. LP: Cruisin' K 58344 (UK), 1981. Two each by Johnny Carroll, Teddy Redell, and others.

White Label (various labels): Holland

Real Old Tennessee Rock and Country Rock, Vol. 3. LP: 8810. Six by Joe Griffith, plus six from a charity show live in Memphis, 1954.

The Rockin' Masters. LP: 8811. From Ohio and Indiana, a nice mix of styles, from Hank Williams to surf instrumentals; contains "Grandma Rock and Roll," by Gene Sisco.

Aaaahhhh Rock-A-Billy. LP: 8821. Misnamed: not much rockabilly. One of the weaker albums in this series. Standout track: Tom James's "Track Down Baby" (great lyrics). Includes one by Joe Poovey.

Rock-A-Billy Time. LP: WLP 8827. The best of Lin and Kliff labels of Texas.

Includes lovely Buck Griffin songs ("Let's Elope Baby" and three more) and one by Frank "Andy" Starr.

More Rock-A-Billy Rock. LP: WLP 8828. Has four Bob Luman tracks from 1955 with the band of Mac Curtis.

FIRST-ISSUE ANTHOLOGIES

Flyright: England
The Legendary Jay Miller Sessions, Vol. 17: Boppin' It. LP: FLY 554, 1980. Unissued 1950s songs recorded in Louisiana; some are raw demos. One song each by Al Ferrier and Johnny Jano, as well as others.

Harvest Heritage: England
Four Rock 'n' Roll Legends: Recorded Live in London, April 1977. LP: SHSM 2024, 1978. An important concert with Charlie Feathers, Buddy Knox, Jack Scott, and Warren Smith.

Nervous: England
Boppin' in Canada. NERCD 061, 1991. Twenty-four tracks from the rockabilly and roots rock scene across Canada, with Ray Condo and his Hardrock Goners (two songs), Herald Nix, Craig Morrison and the Momentz, and many others.

RCA
The Great British Rock 'n' Roll-Rockabilly Album, Vol. 2. LP: RCA International INTS 5102, 1981. Two each from six acts, including Matchbox, Crazy Cavan and the Rhythm Rockers, and Shakin' Stevens and the Sunsets.

Rhino: Los Angeles, Calif.
L. A. Rockabilly. LP: RNLP 56, 1983. Solid revival set; includes Dave Alvin, Los Lobos, Billy Zoom, Johnny Meeks ("Say Mama"), and others.

Rock-A-Billy: Walls, Miss.
Johnny Burnette's Rock 'n' Roll Trio and Their Rockin' Friends from Memphis. LP: RB 1001, 1980. Paul Burlison enlisted former bandmates Tony Austin and Johnny Black and invited Eddie Bond, Jim Dickinson, Al Hobson, Glenn Honeycutt, Smoochy Smith, J. M. Van Eaton, Marcus Van Story, Malcolm Yelvington, and two more friends to a reunion session in tribute to Johnny and Dorsey Burnette. Charlie Feathers is represented by two tracks from 1979 albums. A nice set.

Rockhouse: Holland
Best of British Rockabillies. LP: LPM 7901, 1979. Two songs each from seven artists, including Steve Bloomfield, Crazy Cavan, Freddie "Fingers" Lee, Matchbox, Flying Saucers, and two more.
Best of British Rockabillies, Vol. 2. LP: LPM 8212, 1982. Recordings from 1980

to 1982, including Restless, the Blue Cats, Ray Neale, Shotgun, Dave Phillips and the Hot Rod Gang, and Deltas.

Live at the Rockhouse 25. LP: 8604. A 1985 concert with the Dave Travis Band, Janis Martin, and Eddie Bond.

Rollin' Rock

Rollin' the Rock, Vol. 1. LP: 009, 1976. Recordings from the 1970s: one each by Ray Campi, Johnny Carroll, and Sid King, plus others.

Rollin' the Rock, Vol. 2: California Rockabilly. LP: 12, 1977.

Super Beeb/BBC Soundhouse: England

It's Rock 'n' Roll. LP: BEMP 001, 1977. Two songs each from seven acts for the BBC radio show of that name. Includes Shakin' Stevens, Freddie "Fingers" Lee, Matchbox, and Flying Saucers.

Song Title Index

General Index

CRAIG MORRISON studied at the University of Victoria in British Columbia and Berklee College of Music in Boston and received a master's degree in ethnomusicology from York University in Toronto. A resident of Montreal, he gives private music lessons and teaches courses on country, blues, and rock 'n' roll through McGill University's division of continuing education. He plays guitar and keyboards, sings, and leads his band, Craig Morrison and the Momentz, through a wide range of material. He is currently pursuing a Ph.D. in the humanities at Concordia University.

Books in the Series
Music in American Life